THE COMPLETE BOOK OF THE WINTER OLYMPICS

1994 Edition

THE COMPLETE BOOK OF THE WINTER OLYMPICS

DAVID WALLECHINSKY

Little, Brown and Company

Boston   New York   Toronto   London

TO ELIJAH AND AARON

First Edition

Library of Congress Cataloging-in-Publication Data
Wallechinsky, David.
    The complete book of the Winter Olympics / by David Wallechinsky.
—1994 ed.
        p.   cm.
    ISBN 0-316-92081-9 (hc)
    ISBN 0-316-92080-0 (pb)
    ISBN 0-316-92083-5 (Canadian pb)
    1. Winter Olympics—History.   2. Winter Olympics—Records.
I. Title.
GV841.5.W26   1993
796.98 — dc20   93-17631

HC: 10   9   8   7   6   5   4   3   2   1
PB: 10   9   8   7   6   5   4   3   2   1

MV-NY

*Published simultaneously in Canada
by Little, Brown & Company (Canada) Limited*

Printed in the United States of America

CONTENTS

THE WINTER GAMES

THE WINTER OLYMPIC GAMES

				EVENTS	Men	Women	NATIONS REPRESENTED
I	1924	CHAMONIX, FRANCE	January 25–February 4	14	281	13	16
II	1928	ST. MORITZ, SWITZERLAND	February 11–19	13	468	27	25
III	1932	LAKE PLACID, U.S.A.	February 4–15	14	274	32	17
IV	1936	GARMISCH-PARTENKIRCHEN, GERMANY	February 6–16	17	675	80	28
—	1940	SAPPORO, JAPAN; ST. MORITZ, SWITZERLAND; GARMISCH-PARTENKIRCHEN, GERMANY	Cancelled because of war	—	—	—	—
—	1944	CORTINA D'AMPEZZO, ITALY	Cancelled because of war	—	—	—	—
V	1948	ST. MORITZ, SWITZERLAND	January 30–February 8	22	636	77	28
VI	1952	OSLO, NORWAY	February 14–25	22	623	109	30
VII	1956	CORTINA D'AMPEZZO, ITALY	January 26–February 5	24	686	132	32
VIII	1960	SQUAW VALLEY, U.S.A.	February 18–28	27	521	144	30
IX	1964	INNSBRUCK, AUSTRIA	January 29–February 9	34	986	200	36
X	1968	GRENOBLE, FRANCE	February 6–18	35	1081	212	37
XI	1972	SAPPORO, JAPAN	February 3–13	35	1015	217	35
XII	1976	INNSBRUCK, AUSTRIA	February 4–15	37	900	228	37
XIII	1980	LAKE PLACID, U.S.A.	February 14–23	38	837	234	37
XIV	1984	SARAJEVO, YUGOSLAVIA	February 7–19	39	1000	277	49
XV	1988	CALGARY, CANADA	February 13–28	46	1113	315	57
XVI	1992	ALBERTVILLE, FRANCE	February 8–23	57	1318	490	64
XVII	1994	LILLEHAMMER, NORWAY	February 12–27	61			
XVIII	1998	NAGANO, JAPAN	February 7-22				

NATIONAL MEDAL TOTALS IN EACH OLYMPICS

1924 Chamonix

	G	S	B*
NOR	4	7	6
FIN	4	3	3
AUT	2	1	0
USA	1	2	1
SWI	1	0	1
CAN	1	0	0
SWE	1	0	0
GBR	0	1	2
BEL	0	0	1
FRA	0	0	1

1928 St. Moritz

	G	S	B
NOR	6	4	5
USA	2	2	2
SWE	2	2	1
FIN	2	1	1
CAN	1	0	0
FRA	1	0	0
AUT	0	3	1
BEL	0	0	1
CZE	0	0	1
GBR	0	0	1
GER	0	0	1

1932 Lake Placid

	G	S	B
USA	6	4	2
NOR	3	4	3
SWE	1	2	0
CAN	1	1	5
FIN	1	1	1
AUT	1	1	0
FRA	1	0	0
SWI	0	1	0
GER	0	0	2
HUN	0	0	1

1936 Garmisch-Partenkirchen

	G	S	B
NOR	7	5	3
GER	3	3	0
SWE	2	2	3
FIN	1	2	3
SWI	1	2	0
AUT	1	1	2
GBR	1	1	1
USA	1	0	3
CAN	0	1	0
FRA	0	0	1
HUN	0	0	1

1948 St. Moritz

	G	S	B
NOR	4	3	3
SWE	4	3	3
SWI	3	4	3
USA	3	4	2
FRA	2	1	2
CAN	2	0	1
AUT	1	3	4
FIN	1	3	2
BEL	1	1	0
ITA	1	0	0
CZE	0	1	0
HUN	0	1	0
GBR	0	0	2

1952 Oslo

	G	S	B
NOR	7	3	6
USA	4	6	1
FIN	3	4	2
GER	3	2	2
AUT	2	4	2
CAN	1	0	1
ITA	1	0	1
GBR	1	0	0
HOL	0	3	0
SWE	0	0	4
SWI	0	0	2
FRA	0	0	1
HUN	0	0	1

*G = gold, S = silver, B = bronze.

1956 Cortina d'Ampezzo

	G	S	B
SOV	7	3	6
AUT	4	3	4
FIN	3	3	1
SWI	3	2	1
SWE	2	4	4
USA	2	3	2
NOR	2	1	1
ITA	1	2	0
GER	1	0	0
CAN	0	1	2
JPN	0	1	0
GDR	0	0	1
HUN	0	0	1
POL	0	0	1

1960 Squaw Valley

	G	S	B
SOV	7	5	9
USA	3	4	3
NOR	3	3	0
SWE	3	2	2
FIN	2	3	3
GER	2	2	1
CAN	2	1	1
GDR	2	1	0
SWI	2	0	0
AUT	1	2	3
FRA	1	0	2
HOL	0	1	1
POL	0	1	1
CZE	0	1	0

1964 Innsbruck

	G	S	B
SOV	11	8	6
AUT	4	5	3
NOR	3	6	6
FIN	3	4	3
FRA	3	4	0
SWE	3	3	1
GDR	2	2	0
USA	1	2	3
HOL	1	1	0
GER	1	0	3
CAN	1	0	2
GBR	1	0	0
ITA	0	1	3
PRK	0	1	0
CZE	0	0	1

1968 Grenoble

	G	S	B
NOR	6	6	2
SOV	5	5	3
FRA	4	3	2
ITA	4	0	0
AUT	3	4	4
HOL	3	3	3
SWE	3	2	3
GER	2	2	3
USA	1	5	1
FIN	1	2	2
GDR	1	2	2
CZE	1	2	1
CAN	1	1	1
SWI	0	2	4
ROM	0	0	1

1972 Sapporo

	G	S	B
SOV	8	5	3
GDR	4	3	7
SWI	4	3	3
HOL	4	3	2
USA	3	2	3
GER	3	1	1
NOR	2	5	5
ITA	2	2	1
AUT	1	2	2
SWE	1	1	2
JPN	1	1	1
CZE	1	0	2
POL	1	0	0
SPA	1	0	0
FIN	0	4	1
FRA	0	1	2
CAN	0	1	0

1976 Innsbruck

	G	S	B
SOV	13	6	8
GDR	7	5	7
USA	3	3	4
NOR	3	3	1
GER	2	5	3
FIN	2	4	1
AUT	2	2	2
SWI	1	3	1
HOL	1	2	3
ITA	1	2	1
CAN	1	1	1
GBR	1	0	0
CZE	0	1	0
LIE	0	0	2
SWE	0	0	2
FRA	0	0	1

1980 Lake Placid

	G	S	B
SOV	10	6	6
GDR	9	7	7
USA	6	4	2
AUT	3	2	2
SWE	3	0	1
LIE	2	2	0
FIN	1	5	3
NOR	1	3	6
HOL	1	2	1
SWI	1	1	3
GBR	1	0	0
GER	0	2	3
ITA	0	2	0
CAN	0	1	1
HUN	0	1	0
JPN	0	1	0
BUL	0	0	1
CZE	0	0	1
FRA	0	0	1

1984 Sarajevo

	G	S	B
GDR	9	9	6
SOV	6	10	9
USA	4	4	0
FIN	4	3	6
SWE	4	2	2
NOR	3	2	4
SWI	2	2	1
CAN	2	1	1
GER	2	1	1
ITA	2	0	0
GBR	1	0	0
CZE	0	2	4
FRA	0	1	2
JPN	0	1	0
YUG	0	1	0
LIE	0	0	2
AUT	0	0	1

1988 Calgary

	G	S	B
SOV	11	9	9
GDR	9	10	6
SWI	5	5	5
FIN	4	1	2
SWE	4	0	2

AUT	3	5	2
HOL	3	2	2
GER	2	4	2
USA	2	1	3
ITA	2	1	2
FRA	1	0	1
NOR	0	3	2
CAN	0	2	3
YUG	0	2	1
CZE	0	1	2
JPN	0	0	1
LIE	0	0	1

1992 Albertville

	G	S	B
GER	10	10	6
SOV	9	6	8
NOR	9	6	5
AUT	6	7	8
USA	5	4	2
ITA	4	6	4
FRA	3	5	1
FIN	3	1	3
CAN	2	3	2

KOR	2	1	1
JPN	1	2	4
HOL	1	1	2
SWE	1	0	3
SWI	1	0	2
CHN	0	3	0
LUX	0	2	0
NZE	0	1	0
CZE	0	0	3
PRK	0	0	1
SPA	0	0	1

A BRIEF HISTORY OF THE OLYMPIC WINTER GAMES

Figure skating was included in the original program of the 1900 Summer Olympics, but the competitions never took place. In **1908,** however, four figure skating events were held at the Prince's Skating Rink in London. Three years later, I.O.C. member Count Brunetta d'Ussaux of Italy proposed that the Swedish Organizing Committee in charge of the 1912 Games include winter sports in the Stockholm Olympics or else stage a separate Olympic gathering for winter events. The Swedes flatly rejected the suggestion on the grounds that it would threaten their own Nordic Games, which had been held every four years since 1901. The German organizers of the **1916** Games planned a separate Skiing Olympia to be held in February in the Black Forest. The Scandinavians opposed the idea, but discussions became irrelevant when World War I broke out and the Olympics were canceled.

When the Summer Olympics resumed in Antwerp in **1920,** figure skating and ice hockey were included. The following year the proposal for separate Winter Olympics was again discussed by the I.O.C. In 1922, over the objections of Olympics founder Baron Pierre de Coubertin, a motion was passed to stage "International Sports Week **1924**" in Chamonix, France. This event was a complete success and was retroactively named the First Olympic Winter Games. Even the Scandinavians, pleased by the fact that their athletes won 28 of the 43 medals presented, dropped their objections and enthusiastically supported a proposal to continue the Winter Olympics every four years.

The **1928** Winter Games were the first to be held in a different nation than the Summer Games of the same year. They also marked the beginning of the endless battle between the Winter Olympics and the weather. Warm temperatures forced the cancellation of the 10,000-meter speed skating contest. Then, 18 hours of rain led to the postponement of an entire day's events.

The third Winter Olympics, in **1932,** was held in Lake Placid, New York, a town of fewer than 4000 people. Faced with major obstacles raising money in the midst of a depression, the president of the organizing committee, Dr. Godfrey Dewey, donated land owned by his family to be used for construction of a bobsled run. Governor Franklin D. Roosevelt opened the Games, and his wife, future first lady Eleanor Roosevelt, took a run down the bobsled course. Leftover rain on the outrun of the ski jump caused some athletes to end up in a pool of water. The first example of ugliness in the Winter Olympics occurred when European speed skaters discovered that the local organizers had decided to impose a completely different set of rules than those with which they were familiar. Ignoring the outrage of the foreigners, the North Americans cheerfully won 10 of 12 speed skating medals, nine more than they won in either the preceding or following Olympics.

The **1936** Games were held in the twin Bavarian towns of Garmisch and Partenkirchen and were viewed by the Nazis as a tune-up for the Berlin Summer Games. Efficient bus service allowed 500,000 people to attend the final day's events. Alpine skiing events were included for the first time, and this led to a major controversy. The I.O.C., overruling the International Ski Federation (F.I.S.), declared that ski instructors could not take part in the Olympics because they were professionals. Incensed, the Austrian and Swiss skiers boycotted the events.

This dispute carried on after the Games and became so heated that it was decided that skiing would not be included in the **1940** Games, which were scheduled for Sapporo, Japan, on the island of Hokkaido. War with China forced the Japanese to admit, in July 1938, that they would be unable to host the Games. St. Moritz was chosen as an alternative site, but the continuing dispute about ski instructors led the Swiss to withdraw as well. The Germans volunteered Garmisch-Partenkirchen in July 1939, but four months later the reality of World War II forced the cancellation of the Olympics.

The first postwar Games were held in St. Moritz in **1948.** Germany and Japan were barred from competing, but everyone else took part eagerly, and it was clear that the Winter Olympics had successfully survived the 12-year hiatus.

In **1952,** the Olympics were finally held in Norway, the birthplace of modern skiing. The Olympic flame was lit in the hearth of the home of Sondre Nordheim (1825-1897), the first famous skier, and relayed by 94 skiers to Oslo. The **1956** Winter Olympics were most notable for the first appearance by a team from the Soviet Union. The Soviets immediately won more medals than any other nation. The Cortina Games were also the last at which the figure skating competitions were held outdoors.

The year **1960** saw the return of the Games to the United States, which led to another controversy when the organizing committee refused to build a bobsled run because only nine nations had indicated an intention to take part. This was the only time that bobsledding was not included in the Olympic program. On the other hand, in the interest of international friendship, U.S. Secretary of State John Foster Dulles magnanimously announced that the requirement that all foreign visitors be fingerprinted would be waived in the case of Olympic athletes and officials. As the Games were held in California, it seemed fitting that the chairman of the Pageantry Committee in charge of the Opening and Closing Ceremonies was none other than Walt Disney.

The **1964** Winter Olympics were threatened by a terrible lack of snow. In a panic, the organizing committee pleaded for help. The Austrian army rushed to the rescue, carving out 20,000 ice bricks from a mountaintop and transporting them to the bobsled and luge runs. They also carried 40,000 cubic meters of snow to the alpine skiing courses and laid in a reserve supply of another 20,000 cubic meters. When rain caused further havoc 10 days before the Opening Ceremony, the army packed down the slopes by hand and foot. On a sad note, two competitors, a British lugist and an Australian downhill skier, were killed in practice.

In **1968,** sex tests for women were introduced, and the greatest of Winter Olympic controversies took place: the mysterious man in black who appeared out of the fog during Karl Schranz's slalom run (see page 126). Schranz was also involved in the biggest incident of the **1972** Sapporo Games, the first to be held outside Europe or the United States. This time he was banned from the Olympics by I.O.C. President Avery Brundage, who accused him of being a professional.

The **1976** Winter Olympics were awarded to Denver, but the people of Colorado wanted nothing to do with it. In a move without precedent, the state's voters ignored appeals and threats from their government, business leaders, and the media and voted overwhelmingly (59.4 percent to 40.6 percent) to prohibit public funds from being used to support the Games. Innsbruck stepped in and hosted the Games only 12 years after its last Olympics.

The **1980** Winter Olympics *were* held in the United States, but turned out to be an organizational disaster. Poor transportation planning left many spectators stranded for hours in freezing weather, and many tickets were left unsold even though people wanted to buy them. This happened because tickets were available at the venues, but only people who already had tickets could enter the area. The Lake Placid Games also saw the only national boycott in the history of the Winter Olympics. The I.O.C., seeking to lure China into the Olympic movement, ordered the team from Taiwan to use the name Taiwan instead of the name it had previously used—The Republic of China. The Taiwan Chinese chose to boycott instead.

In **1984,** the Winter Games took place in a Socialist country for the first and only time. The people of Sarajevo gained high marks for their hospitality, and there was no indication of the tragic war that would engulf the city only a few years later. By 1992, in fact, the Olympic bobsled run had been transformed into an artillery position for Serbian guerrillas.

The **1988** Calgary Games were equally popular with athletes and spectators, although there was some grumbling about the choice of competition sites and the condition of the venues. The celebration was also marred by the gruesome death on the slopes of the Austrian team doctor.

Only 18 of the 57 official events included in the Albertville Olympics of **1992** were actually held in Albertville. In an attempt to satisfy the various competing resorts of the Savoy Alps, seven other towns hosted medal competitions and still others were used for the main Olympic Village, demonstration events, and the press and broadcasting centers. This may have satisfied the locals, but the athletes complained bitterly about the lack of Olympic atmosphere because they were unable to mingle with athletes from other sports. The day before the Closing Ceremony a Swiss speed skier, Nicolas Bochatay, was killed in a noncompetition-related accident.

In 1986 the I.O.C. voted to change the schedule of the Olympics so that the Summer and Winter Games would be held in different years. In order to adjust to this new schedule, the Lillehammer Olympics were slated for **1994,** the only time that two Games have been staged just two years apart.

ACKNOWLEDGMENTS

In the course of my research I have encountered numerous people who have graciously helped me on my way, starting with C. Robert Paul, who made available to me the archives of the United States Olympic Committee, including the Official Reports of the Organizing Committees of the various Olympic Games, which form the basis of the statistics in this book. In addition to the people acknowledged in previous editions of *The Complete Book of the Olympics,* I would like to thank Dr. Bill Mallon, author of *The Unofficial Summary of the 1920 Games;* Ian Buchanan, author of *British Olympians;* Volker Kluge, author of *Winter Olympia Kompakt;* Dr. Karel Wendl, director of the Olympic Research Department of the International Olympic Committee; Benjamin Wright, chairman of the Hall of Fame and Museum Committee of The United States Figure Skating Association; Dale Mitch, director of the World Figure Skating Museum; Ove Karlsson; Brynjar Selseth; Jeff Matlock; Martin Rix; the staff of the library of the Amateur Athletic Foundation in Los Angeles; the staff of the Public Information and Media Department of the United States Olympic Committee; the Olympic research staff of CBS Sports; the overworked and underappreciated sports journalists who cover the Olympic Games; and, especially, my Olympics research assistant, Cheryl Mick.

THE CHARTS

SOURCES

Although the primary sources for the information included in the charts are the Official Reports of the various Olympics, these reports are often incomplete or incorrect. The man who has done the most to correct these inadequacies is Erich Kamper of Austria, coauthor with Bill Mallon of *The Golden Book of the Olympics*. My search for correct spellings and accent marks also led me to *Die Olympischen Spiele von 1896 bis 1980* by Volker Kluge of East Germany; *Starozytne i Nowozytne Igrazyska Olimpyskie* by Zbigniew Porada of Poland; *Meet the Bulgarian Olympians* by Kostadinov, Georgiev, and Kambourov; *Az Olimpiajátékokon Indult Magyar Versenyzök Névsora 1896–1980; Die Deutschen Sportler der Olympischen Spiele 1896 bis 1968;* and *Sveriges Deltagare i de Olympiska Spelen 1896–1952*. I am particularly indebted to Bill Mallon of the United States, and to Benjamin Wright who provided me with those figure skating protocols that were not included in the Official Reports.

HOW TO READ THEM

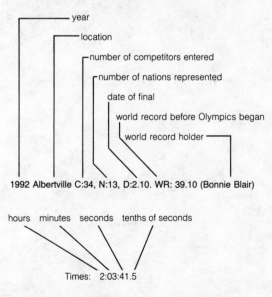

Numbers in the charts indicate times unless otherwise noted. Whenever possible I have included an athlete's first and last names. If the first name was unavailable, I have included the first initial. If that was unavailable I have just included the surname. If a female athlete competed under her maiden name, then married and took part in a second Olympics using her married name, I have included her maiden name in brackets.

In 1956, 1960, and 1964, West Germany (GER) and East Germany (GDR) entered combined teams. Nevertheless, as a matter of historical interest, I have indicated which athletes were actually from each country.

KEY TO ABBREVIATIONS

NATIONS

ARG	Argentina
AUS	Australia
AUT	Austria
BEL	Belgium
BUL	Bulgaria
CAN	Canada
CHN	China
CZE	Czechoslovakia
DEN	Denmark
EST	Estonia
FIN	Finland
FRA	France
GBR	Great Britain and Northern Ireland
GDR	East Germany (German Democratic Republic)
GER	Germany, West Germany (Federal Republic of Germany, 1952–1988)
HOL	Holland (Netherlands)
HUN	Hungary
ITA	Italy
JPN	Japan
KOR	South Korea
LAT	Latvia
LIE	Liechtenstein
LIT	Lithuania
LUX	Luxembourg
NOR	Norway
NZL	New Zealand
POL	Poland
PRK	North Korea (People's Republic of Korea)
ROM	Romania
RUS	Russia
SLO	Slovenia
SOV	Soviet Union (Unified Team, 1992)
SPA	Spain
SWE	Sweden
SWI	Switzerland
USA	United States of America
YUG	Yugoslavia

TERMS

C:	Number of competitors entered
CD	Compulsory dances
CF	Compulsory figures
D:	Date of final
DISQ	Disqualified
EOR	Equaled Olympic record
EWR	Equaled world record
F.I.S.	International Ski Federation
I.O.C.	International Olympic Committee
kg.	Kilograms
KM	Kilometers
L	Lost
lbs.	Pounds
M	Meters
N:	Number of nations entered
OR	Olympic record
PA	Points against
PF	Points for
PTS.	Points
SP	Short program
SPD	Set pattern dance
T:	Number of teams entered
T	Tied
W	Won
WR	World record

THE COMPLETE BOOK OF THE WINTER OLYMPICS

David Wallechinsky was introduced to the joys of
the Olympics by his father, Irving Wallace, who
took him to the Summer Games at Rome in 1960.
Mr. Wallechinsky lives in southern France
with his wife and their two sons.

BOBSLED
The 1932 U.S. four-man bobsled team: (left to right) *Jay O'Brien, Eddie Eagan, Clifford Gray, and Billy Fiske. Eight years later, only Eagan was still alive. (U.S.O.C.)*

During the second run of the 1992 four-man bob, Soviet team member Aleksandr Bortyuk slipped at the start and ended up facing the wrong direction. (Allsport)

ICE HOCKEY
The 1980 U.S. ice hockey team celebrates its final victory over Finland.(Barton Silverman/New York Times)

During the 1992 quarterfinal shootout between Canada and Germany, the German-shot puck stops on the line without going over, thus preserving the victory for Canada.

FIGURE SKATING
Dick Button, men's figure skating champion of 1948 and 1952.

Sonja Henie was only 23 years old when she earned her third consecutive figure skating gold medal. (U.S.O.C.)

Brian Boitano (right) consoles Brian Orser after defeating him in the figure skating competition of 1988. (City of Calgary Archives)

Peggy Fleming won an overwhelming victory in the 1968 women's figure skating competition. (Pressen Bild)

Katarina Witt, who received 35,000 love letters following her victory in the 1984 women's figure skating competition. Four years later she became the event's first repeat champion since Sonja Henie. (Klaus Schlage)

Lyudmila Belousova and Oleg Protopopov, winners of the pairs skating in 1964 and 1968. "These pairs of brother and sister, how can they convey the emotion, the love, that exists between a man and a woman? That is what we try to show." (U.S.O.C.)

SPEED SKATING
Irving Jaffee stumbles across the finish line of the 1932 10,000-meter speed skating race.

Eric Heiden had won only three gold medals when he posed for this photo; he borrowed the other two. Later he won two more of his own.

Lydia Skoblikova won six speed skating gold medals in 1960 and 1964, more than any other athlete in the history of the Winter Olympics. (U.S.O.C.)

ALPINE SKIING
The 1952 giant slalom champion, Stein Eriksen, was the inspiration for the stereotype of the suave and handsome ski instructor.

Alberto Tomba is cheered on by his supporters in 1992 after becoming the first alpine skier to win the same event twice. (Allsport)

In 1976 Rosi Mittermaier came within thirteen one-hundredths of a second of becoming the first woman to win all three alpine skiing events. (AP)

Winner of the 1980 slalom and giant slalom, Hanni Wenzel was the first-ever Olympic gold medalist from the tiny nation of Liechtenstein.

NORDIC SKIING
Right: *Sixten Jernberg won nine medals (four gold, three silver, two bronze) in nordic skiing between 1956 and 1964. (Pressen Bild)* Above: *Torgny Mogren crosses the finish line in the 1988 4 x 10-kilometer nordic ski relay. (Sportverlag Berlin)*

Vegard Ulvang (right) *won the 1992 10-kilometer race after ignoring the advice of his coaches and listening instead to one of his opponents, Ebbe Hartz* (left). *(NTB-Photo)*

(Left to right) *Seiji Aochi (bronze), Yukio Kasaya (gold), and Akitsugu Konno (silver), popular winners of the 1972 normal hill ski jump. (Frederick Fliegner)*

Raisa Smetanina (left) *celebrates with her 1992 4 x 5-kilometer relay teammates after becoming the first athlete to win ten Winter Olympics medals. (AP/Wide World Photos)*

Marja-Liisa Hämäläinen, winner of all three women's individual cross-country races at the 1984 Sarajevo Games, tried to run away from the press after her victories. She was finally cornered and forced to submit to interviews. (ADN)

THE
COMPLETE
BOOK OF THE
WINTER
OLYMPICS

BIATHLON

MEN	WOMEN
10 Kilometers	7.5 Kilometers
20 Kilometers	15 Kilometers
4 × 7.5-Kilometer Relay	3 × 7.5-Kilometer Relay

Biathlon is a combination of cross-country skiing and rifle shooting. The first skiing and shooting competition was held in Norway in 1767. The first modern race was organized by the Norwegian military in 1912, and the first World Biathlon Championships were held at Saalfelden, Austria, in 1958. Competitors may use either the classical or skating method of skiing. They are restricted to .22-caliber small-bore rifles. Automatic or semi-automatic rifles are not allowed. The rifle with all accessories except the magazine and ammunition must weigh at least 7.7 pounds. All targets are set at a distance of 50 meters. The prone target is 4.5 centimeters (1¾ inches) in diameter; the standing target is 11.5 centimeters (4½ inches) in diameter. In individual races, competitors start at one-minute intervals and race against the clock.

MEN

10 KILOMETERS

Each contestant stops twice during the course, once after 3.75 kilometers to shoot five shots prone and once after 7.5 kilometers to shoot five shots standing. Each missed target is penalized by forcing the skier to ski a 150-meter penalty loop.

1924–1976 not held

1980 Lake Placid C: 50, N: 17, D: 2.19.

			MISSED TARGETS	TIME
1.	Frank Ullrich	GDR	2	32:10.69
2.	Vladimir Alikin	SOV	0	32:53.10
3.	Anatoly Alyabyev	SOV	1	33:09.16
4.	Klaus Siebert	GDR	2	33:32.76
5.	Kjell Söbak	NOR	1	33:34.64
6.	Peter Zelinka	CZE	1	33:45.20
7.	Odd Lirhus	NOR	2	34:10.39
8.	Peter Angerer	GER	4	34:13.43

1984 Sarajevo C: 64, N: 25, D: 2.14.

			MISSED TARGETS	TIME
1.	Eirik Kvalfoss	NOR	2	30:53.8
2.	Peter Angerer	GER	1	31:02.4
3.	Matthias Jacob	GDR	0	31:10.5
4.	Kjell Söbak	NOR	1	31:19.7
5.	Šalna Algimantas	SOV	2	31:20.8
6.	Yvon Mougel	FRA	2	31:32.9
7.	Frank-Peter Roetsch	GDR	2	31:49.8
8.	Friedrich Fischer	GER	2	32:04.7

Kvalfoss grew up competing in cross-country skiing. One day when he was 12 years old he showed up for an event and discovered that he wasn't entered. There was an opening in a separate biathlon competition, so he entered that instead. Kvalfoss borrowed a rifle, won the race, and changed sports.

1988 Calgary-Canmore C: 72, N: 22, D: 2.23.

			MISSED TARGETS	TIME
1.	Frank-Peter Roetsch	GDR	1	25:08.1
2.	Valery Medvedtsev	SOV	0	25:23.7
3.	Sergei Chepikov	SOV	0	25:29.4
4.	Birk Anders	GDR	2	25:51.8
5.	André Sehmisch	GDR	2	25:52.3
6.	Frank Luck	GDR	1	25:57.6
7.	Tapio Piipponen	FIN	1	26:02.2
8.	Johann Passler	ITA	2	26:07.7

Roetsch became the first biathlete to win both individual events.

1992 Albertville-Les Saisies C: 94, N: 27, D: 2.12.

			MISSED TARGETS	TIME
1.	Mark Kirchner	GER	0	26:02.3
2.	Ricco Gross	GER	1	26:18.0
3.	Harri Eloranta	FIN	0	26:26.6
4.	Sergei Chepikov	SOV	0	26:27.5
5.	Valery Kirienko	SOV	3	26:31.8
6.	Jens Steinigen	GER	0	26:34.8
7.	Andreas Zingerle	ITA	1	26:38.6
8.	Steve Cyr	CAN	0	26:46.4

Kirchner, the world champion in 1990 and 1991, was only 21 years old, as was silver medalist Gross.

20 KILOMETERS

Each skier stops four times—twice to take five shots prone and twice to take five shots standing. The prone stops are at 5 and 12.5 kilometers; the standing at 8.75 and 17.5. In 1960 and 1964 each missed target incurred a two-minute penalty. In 1968 the penalty was reduced to one minute.

1924–1956 not held

1960 Squaw Valley C: 30, N: 9, D: 2.21.

			TIME	MISSED TARGETS	ADJUSTED TIME
1.	Klas Lestander	SWE	1:33:21.6	0	1:33:21.6
2.	Antti Tyrväinen	FIN	1:29:57.7	2	1:33:57.7
3.	Aleksandr Privalov	SOV	1:28:54.2	3	1:34:54.2
4.	Vladimir Melanin	SOV	1:27:42.4	4	1:35:42.4
5.	Valentin Pshenitsin	SOV	1:30:45.8	3	1:36:45.8
6.	Dmitri Sokolov	SOV	1:28:16.7	5	1:38:16.7
7.	Ola Waerhang	NOR	1:36:35.8	1	1:38:35.8
8.	Martti Meinila	FIN	1:29:17.0	5	1:39:17.0

Lestander was only the 15th fastest skier of 30, but he was also the only one to hit all 20 targets. The fastest man was Victor Arbez of France, who clocked in at

1:25:58.4. However, he missed 18 of 20 targets and placed 25th. In fact, the entire four-man French team seemed ill-prepared for the shooting portion of the event: of 80 shots taken, they missed 68.

1964 Innsbruck-Seefeld C: 50, N: 14, D: 2.4.

			TIME	MISSED TARGETS	ADJUSTED TIME
1.	Vladimir Melanin	SOV	1:20:26.8	0	1:20:26.8
2.	Aleksandr Privalov	SOV	1:23:42.5	0	1:23:42.5
3.	Olav Jordet	NOR	1:22:38.8	1	1:24:38.8
4.	Ragnar Tveiten	NOR	1:19:52.5	3	1:25:52.5
5.	Wilhelm György	ROM	1:22:18.0	2	1:26:18.0
6.	József Rubiś	POL	1:22:31.6	2	1:26:31.6
7.	Valentin Pshenitsin	SOV	1:22:59.0	2	1:26:59.0
8.	Hannu Posti	FIN	1:25:16.5	1	1:27:16.5

1968 Grenoble-Autrans C: 60, N: 18, D: 2.12.

			TIME	MISSED TARGETS	ADJUSTED TIME
1.	Magnar Solberg	NOR	1:13:45.9	0	1:13:45.9
2.	Aleksandr Tikhonov	SOV	1:12:40.4	2	1:14:40.4
3.	Vladimir Goundartsev	SOV	1:16:27.4	2	1:18:27.4
4.	Stanislaw Szczepaniak	POL	1:17:56.8	1	1:18:56.8
5.	Arve Kinnari	FIN	1:17:47.9	2	1:19:47.9
6.	Nikolai Pousanov	SOV	1:17:14.5	3	1:20:14.5
7.	Victor Mamatov	SOV	1:19:20.8	1	1:20:20.8
8.	Stanislaw Lukaszczyk	POL	1:16:28.1	4	1:20:28.1

Magnar Solberg, a 31-year-old policeman, was practically unknown in the world of biathlon. He attained his victory by achieving a perfect shooting score—the first time he had ever accomplished such a feat. As photographers crowded around the surprised champion, he told them, "I am very happy, but too tired to smile."

1972 Sapporo-Makomanai C: 54, N: 14, D: 2.9.

			TIME	MISSED TARGETS	ADJUSTED TIME
1.	Magnar Solberg	NOR	1:13:55.50	2	1:15:55.50
2.	Hansjörg Knauthe	GDR	1:15:07.60	1	1:16:07.60
3.	Lars-Göran Arwidson	SWE	1:14:27.03	2	1:16:27.03
4.	Aleksandr Tikhonov	SOV	1:12:48.65	4	1:16:48.65
5.	Yrjö Salpakari	FIN	1:14:51.43	2	1:16:51.43
6.	Esko Saira	FIN	1:12:34.80	5	1:17:34.80
7.	Victor Mamatov	SOV	1:16:16.26	2	1:18:16.26
8.	Tor Svendsberget	NOR	1:15:26.54	3	1:18:26.54

1976 Innsbruck-Seefeld C: 51, N: 19, D: 2.6.

			TIME	MISSED TARGETS	ADJUSTED TIME
1.	Nikolai Kruglov	SOV	1:12:12.26	2	1:14:12.26
2.	Heikki Ikola	FIN	1:13:54.10	2	1:15:54.10
3.	Aleksandr Elizarov	SOV	1:13:05.57	3	1:16:05.57
4.	Willy Bertin	ITA	1:13:50.36	3	1:16:50.36
5.	Aleksandr Tikhonov	SOV	1:10:18.33	7	1:17:18.33
6.	Esko Saira	FIN	1:15:32.84	2	1:17:32.84
7.	Lino Jordan	ITA	1:15:49.83	2	1:17:49.83
8.	Sune Adolfsson	SWE	1:16:00.50	2	1:18:00.50

1980 Lake Placid C: 49, N: 18, D: 2.16.

		TIME	MISSED TARGETS	ADJUSTED TIME
1. Anatoly Alyabyev	SOV	1:08:16.31	0	1:08:16.31
2. Frank Ullrich	GDR	1:05:27.79	3	1:08:27.79
3. Eberhard Rösch	GDR	1:09:11.73	2	1:11:11.73
4. Svein Engen	NOR	1:08:30.25	3	1:11:30.25
5. Erkki Antila	FIN	1:07:32.32	4	1:11:32.32
6. Yvon Mougel	FRA	1:08:33.60	3	1:11:33.60
7. Vladimir Barnashov	SOV	1:07:49.49	4	1:11:49.49
8. Vladimir Alikin	SOV	1:06:05.30	6	1:12:05.30

1984 Sarajevo C: 63, N: 25, D: 2.11.

		TIME	MISSED TARGETS	ADJUSTED TIME
1. Peter Angerer	GER	1:09:52.7	2	1:11:52.7
2. Frank-Peter Roetsch	GDR	1:10:21.4	3	1:13:21.4
3. Eirik Kvalfoss	NOR	1:09:02.4	5	1:14:02.4
4. Yvon Mougel	FRA	1:10:53.1	4	1:14:53.1
5. Frank Ullrich	GDR	1:11:53.7	3	1:14:53.7
6. Rolf Storsveen	NOR	1:11:23.9	4	1:15:23.9
7. Friedrich Fischer	GER	1:11:49.7	4	1:15:49.7
8. Leif Andersson	SWE	1:13:19.3	3	1:16:19.3

1988 Calgary-Canmore C: 71, N: 21, D: 2.20.

		TIME	MISSED TARGETS	ADJUSTED TIME
1. Frank-Peter Roetsch	GDR	53:33.3	3	56:33.3
2. Valery Medvedtsev	SOV	54:54.6	2	56:54.6
3. Johann Passler	ITA	55:10.1	2	57:10.1
4. Sergei Chepikov	SOV	56:17.5	1	57:17.5
5. Yuri Kashkarov	SOV	55:43.1	2	57:43.1
6. Eirik Kvalfoss	NOR	54:54.6	3	57:54.6
7. André Sehmisch	GDR	55:11.4	3	58:11.4
8. Tapio Piipponen	FIN	55:18.3	3	58:18.3

1992 Albertville-Les Saisies C: 94, N: 27, D: 2.20.

		TIME	MISSED TARGETS	ADJUSTED TIME
1. Yevgeny Redkine	SOV	57:34.4	0	57:34.4
2. Mark Kirchner	GER	54:40.8	3	57:40.8
3. Mikael Löfgren	SWE	55:40.8	2	57:59.4
4. Aleksandr Popov	SOV	56:02.9	2	58:02.9
5. Harri Eloranta	FIN	57:15.7	1	58:15.7
6. Vesa Hietalahti	FIN	57:24.6	1	58:24.6
7. Johann Passler	ITA	54:25.9	4	58:25.9
8. Frode Loberg	NOR	57:32.4	1	58:32.4

Andreas Zingerle of Italy led by over a minute after 17.5 kilometers, but missed four of his last five shots and finished 17th. Kirchner, Löfgren, and Popov each had a shot at the gold, but each missed once in the last shooting sequence. When the snow settled, the victory went to unheralded 21-year-old Yevgeny Redkine of Belarus. Redkine, a former junior champion, was not even listed in the Unified Team teambook, and he learned that he was entered in the race only two days before it took place. Redkine's time was only the 18th fastest, but his shooting was perfect.

4 × 7.5-KILOMETER RELAY

Each skier shoots twice, once prone and once standing, and has eight shots to make five hits. However, only five rounds can be loaded into the magazine. The three extra must be loaded one at a time. For each miss beyond three, the skier has to ski a penalty loop of 150 meters. Unlike the individual events, in which the competitors race against the clock, one after another, in the biathlon relay all teams start at the same time.

1924–1964 not held

1968 Grenoble-Autrans T: 14, N: 14, D: 2.15.

			MISSED TARGETS	TIME
1.	SOV	(Aleksandr Tikhonov, Nikolai Pousanov, Victor Mamatov, Vladimir Goundartsev)	2	2:13:02.4
2.	NOR	(Ola Waerhang, Olav Jordet, Magnar Solberg, Jon Istad)	5	2:14:50.2
3.	SWE	(Lars-Göran Arwidson, Tore Eriksson, Olle Petrusson, Holmfrid Olsson)	0	2:17:26.3
4.	POL	(Józef Rózak, Andrzej Fiedor, Stanislaw Lukaszczyk, Stanislaw Szczepaniak)	4	2:20:19.6
5.	FIN	(Juhani Suutarinen, Heikki Flöjt, Kalevi Vähäkylä, Arve Kinnari)	5	2:20:41.8
6.	GDR	(Heinz Kluge, Hans-Gert Jahn, Horst Koschka, Dieter Speer)	4	2:21:54.5
7.	ROM	(Gheorghe Cimpoia, Constant Carabela, Nicolae Barbarescu, Wilhelm Gyorgy)	4	2:25:39.8
8.	USA	(Ralph Wakely, Edward Williams, William Spencer, John Ehrensbeck)	8	2:28:35.5

1972 Sapporo-Makomanai T: 13, N: 13, D: 2.11.

			MISSED TARGETS	TIME
1.	SOV	(Aleksandr Tikhonov, Rinnat Safine, Ivan Biakov, Victor Mamatov)	3	1:51:44.92
2.	FIN	(Esko Saira, Juhani Suutarinen, Heikki Ikola, Mauri Röppänen)	3	1:54:37.25
3.	GDR	(Hansjörg Knauthe, Joachim Meischner, Dieter Speer, Horst Koschka)	4	1:54:57.67
4.	NOR	(Tor Svendsberget, Kåre Hovda, Ivar Nordkild, Magnar Solberg)	7	1:56:24.41
5.	SWE	(Lars-Göran Arwidson, Olle Petrusson, Torsten Wadman, Holmfrid Olsson)	6	1:56:57.40
6.	USA	(Peter Karns, Dexter Morse, Dennis Donahue, William Bowerman)	1	1:57:24.32
7.	POL	(Józef Rózak, Józef Stopka, Andrzej Rapacz, Aleksander Klima)	4	1:58:09.92
8.	JPN	(Isao Ohno, Shozo Sasaki, Miki Shibuya, Kazuo Sasakubo)	5	1:59:09.48

1976 Innsbruck-Seefeld T: 15, N: 15, D: 2.13.

		MISSED TARGETS	TIME
1. SOV	(Aleksandr Elizarov, Ivan Biakov, Nikolai Kruglov, Aleksandr Tikhonov)	0	1:57:55.64
2. FIN	(Henrik Flöjt, Esko Saira, Juhani Suutarinen, Heikki Ikola)	2	2:01:45.58
3. GDR	(Karl-Heinz Menz, Frank Ullrich, Manfred Beer, Manfred Geyer)	5	2:04:08.61
4. GER	(Heinrich Mehringer, Gerd Winkler, Josef Keck, Claus Gehrke)	4	2:04:11.86
5. NOR	(Kjell Hovda, Terje Hanssen, Svein Engen, Tor Svendsberget)	6	2:05:10.28
6. ITA	(Lino Jordan, Pierantonio Clementi, Luigi Weiss, Willy Bertin)	3	2:06:16.55
7. FRA	(Rene Arpin, Yvon Mougel, Marius Falquy, Jean Claude Viry)	5	2:07:34.42
8. SWE	(Mats-Åke Lantz, Torsten Wadman, Sune Adolfsson, Lars Göran Arwidson)	8	2:08:46.90

1980 Lake Placid T: 15, N: 15, D: 2.22.

		MISSED TARGETS	TIME
1. SOV	(Vladimir Alikin, Aleksandr Tikhonov, Vladimir Barnashov, Anatoly Alyabyev)	0	1:34:03.27
2. GDR	(Mathias Jung, Klaus Siebert, Frank Ullrich, Eberhard Rösch)	3	1:34:56.99
3. GER	(Franz Bernreiter, Hans Estner, Peter Angerer, Gerd Winkler)	2	1:37:30.26
4. NOR	(Svein Engen, Kjell Sobak, Odd Lirhus, Sigleif Johansen)	3	1:38:11.76
5. FRA	(Yvon Mougel, Denis Sandona, André Geourjon, Christian Poirot)	0	1:38:23.36
6. AUT	(Rudolf Horn, Franz-Josef Weber, Josef Koll, Alfred Eder)	4	1:38:32.02
7. FIN	(Keijo Kuntola, Erkki Antila, Kari Saarela, Raimo Seppanen)	6	1:38:50.84
8. USA	(Martin Hagen, Lyle Nelson, Donald Nielsen, Peter Hoag)	0	1:39:24.29

Thirty-three-year-old Aleksandr Tikhonov announced his retirement after winning his fourth straight biathlon relay gold medal.

1984 Sarajevo T: 17, N: 17, D: 2.17.

		MISSED TARGETS	TIME
1. SOV	(Dmitri Vasilyev, Yuri Kachkarov, Šalna Algimantas, Sergei Buligin)	2	1:38:51.7
2. NOR	(Odd Lirhus, Eirik Kvalfoss, Rolf Storsveen, Kjell Söbak)	2	1:39:03.9
3. GER	(Ernst Reiter, Walter Pichler, Peter Angerer, Friedrich Fischer)	1	1:39:05.1
4. GDR	(Holger Wick, Frank-Peter Roetsch, Matthias Jacob, Frank Ullrich)	1	1:40:04.7
5. ITA	(Adriano Darioli, Gottlieb Taschler, Johann Passler, Andreas Zingerle)	0	1:42:32.8
6. CZE	(Jaromir Šimůnek, Zdeněk Hák, Petr Zelinka, Jan Matouš)	4	1:42:40.5
7. FIN	(Keijo Tiitola, Toivo Makikyro, Arto Jaaskelainen, Tapio Piipponen)	2	1:43:16.0
8. AUT	(Rudolf Horn, Walter Hoerl, Franz Schuler, Alfred Eder)	1	1:43:28.1

1988 Calgary-Canmore T: 16, N: 16, D: 2.26.

			MISSED TARGETS	TIME
1.	SOV	(Dmitri Vasilyev, Sergei Chepikov, Aleksandr Popov, Valery Medvedtsev)	0	1:22:30.0
2.	GER	(Ernst Reiter, Stefan Höck, Peter Angerer, Friedrich Fischer)	0	1:23:37.4
3.	ITA	(Werner Kiem, Gottlieb Taschler, Johann Passler, Andreas Zingerle)	0	1:23:51.5
4.	AUT	(Anton Lengauer-Stockner, Bruno Hofstätter, Franz Schuler, Alfred Eder)	0	1:24:17.6
5.	GDR	(Jürgen Wirth, Frank-Peter Roetsch, Matthias Jacob, André Sehmisch)	3	1:24:28.4
6.	NOR	(Geir Einang, Frode Löberg, Gisle Fenne, Eirik Kvalfoss)	0	1:25:57.0
7.	SWE	(Peter Sjödén, Mikael Löfgren, Roger Westling, Leif Andersson)	3	1:29:11.9
8.	BUL	(Vasil Bozhilov, Vladimir Velichkov, Krasimir Videnov, Hristo Vodenicharov)	7	1:29:24.9

The East Germans took four of the top six places in the 10-kilometer individual event and thus were expected to give the Soviet team a stiff challenge. However, leadoff skier Jürgen Wirth, who had test-fired in windy conditions, failed to readjust the sight on his rifle when the wind died down and missed three of his first five shots, leaving East Germany in twelfth place with an insurmountable deficit of almost two minutes.

1992 Albertville-Les Saisies T: 21, N: 21, D: 2.16.

			MISSED TARGETS	TIME
1.	GER	(Ricco Gross, Jens Steinigen, Mark Kirchner, Friedrich Fischer)	0	1:24:43.5
2.	SOV	(Valery Medvedtsev, Aleksandr Popov, Valery Kirienko, Sergei Chepikov)	0	1:25:06.3
3.	SWE	(Ulf Johansson, Leif Andersson, Tord Wiksten, Mikael Löfgren)	0	1:25:38.2
4.	ITA	(Hubert Leitgeb, Johann Passler, Pieralberto Carrara, Andreas Zingerle)	2	1:26:18.1
5.	NOR	(Geir Einang, Frode Loberg, Gisle Fenne, Eirik Kvalfoss)	1	1:26:32.4
6.	FRA	(Xavier Blond, Thierry Gerbier, Christian Dumont, Hervé Flandin)	0	1:27:13.3
7.	CZE	(Martin Rypl, Tomas Kos, Jiří Holubeč, Ivan Masrik)	0	1:27:15.7
8.	FIN	(Vesa Hietalahti, Jaakko Niemi, Harri Eloranta, Kari Kataja)	1	1:27:39.5

The German team got off to a rough start when France's Xavier Blond crashed into Ricco Gross on the first downhill and knocked him down. Gross handed over to Steinigen in only 13th place. As he watched the rest of the race, Gross commented, "If we don't win this I will be the most hated man in Germany." He needn't have worried. Steinigen pulled the Germans up to fifth, and Kirchner put them into the lead. The 35-year-old German anchor, Fritz Fischer, carried a German flag for the last 50 meters as the Soviet win streak in this event was finally broken.

WOMEN

7.5 KILOMETERS

Each contestant stops twice during the course, once after 2.5 kilometers, to shoot five shots prone, and once after 5 kilometers, to shoot five shots standing. Each missed target is penalized by forcing the skier to ski a 150-meter penalty loop.

1924-1988 not held

1992 Albertville-Les Saisies C: 69, N: 20, D: 2.11.

		MISSED TARGETS	TIME
1. Anfisa Reztsova	SOV	3	24:29.2
2. Antje Miserky	GER	2	24:45.1
3. Yelena Belova	SOV	2	24:50.8
4. Nadezda Aleksieva	BUL	0	24:55.8
5. Jirina Adamičková	CZE	0	24:57.6
6. Petra Schaaf	GER	1	25:10.4
7. Anne Briand	FRA	2	25:29.8
8. Silvana Blagoeva	BUL	2	25:33.5

In the 1988 Calgary Olympics, Anfisa Reztsova, of Sverdlovsk, Russia, won a gold medal in the cross-country relay and then earned a silver in the 20-kilometer individual event. After the Games, she took two years off to have a baby. Her husband, who happened to be the men's biathlon coach for the U.S.S.R., encouraged her to return to competition and switch to biathlon. In 1992, at the age of 27, Reztsova became the first woman to win gold medals in two winter sports. For the record, all three medalists in this, the first-ever women's biathlon event, had blue eyes.

15 KILOMETERS

Each skier stops four times during the course, twice to shoot five shots prone and twice to shoot five shots standing. The prone stops are at 3.75 and 10 kilometers, the standing at 6.25 and 12.5 kilometers. One minute is added to a competitor's elapsed time for each missed shot.

1924-1988 not held

1992 Albertville-Les Saisies C: 68, N: 20, D: 2.19.

		TIME	MISSED TARGETS	ADJUSTED TIME
1. Antje Misersky	GER	50:47.2	1	51.47.2
2. Svetlana Pecherskaya	SOV	50:58.5	1	51:58.5
3. Myriam Bédard	CAN	50:15.0	2	52:15.0
4. Véronique Claudel	FRA	50:21.2	2	52:21.2
5. Nadezda Aleksieva	BUL	51:30.2	1	52:30.2
6. Delphine Burlet	FRA	50:00.8	3	53:00.8
7. Corinne Niogret	FRA	51:06.6	2	53:06.6
8. Nathalie Santer	ITA	50:10.3	3	53:10.3

Misersky's father, Henner, was a cross-country coach in East Germany who objected to the training methods of the sports establishment. The East German leaders wanted all their Nordic skiers to concentrate solely on the freestyle "skating" technique. Henner Misersky believed that it was healthier to continue to practice the traditional "diagonal" stride as well. When Henner was ousted from his position in 1985, his daughter Antje, who was the reigning East German national champion at 5 and 10 kilometers, quit in protest. After four years away from sports, she took up biathlon in 1989. At the Albertville Games she won one gold medal and two silvers. A rarity among biathletes, bronze medalist Bédard had competed as a figure skater until the age of 12. Nadezda Aleksieva came painfully close to winning Bulgaria's first Winter Olympics gold medal. After 18 straight hits, she missed her next-to-last shot by 3.5 millimeters. The resultant one-minute penalty dropped her from first to fifth.

3 × 7.5-KILOMETER RELAY

Each skier shoots twice, once prone and once standing, and has eight shots to make five hits. However, only five rounds can be loaded into the magazine. The other three have to be loaded one at a time. For each miss beyond three, the competitor must ski a 150-meter penalty loop. Unlike the individual races, in which the competitors race against the clock, in the relay all teams start at the same time.

1924-1988 not held

1992 Albertville-Les Saisies T: 16, N: 16, D: 2.14.

			MISSED TARGETS	TIME
1.	FRA	(Corinne Niogret, Véronique Claudel, Anne Briand)	0	1:15:55.6
2.	GER	(Uschi Disl, Antje Misersky, Petra Schaaf)	1	1:16:18.4
3.	SOV	(Yelena Belova, Anfisa Reztsova, Yelena Melnikova)	2	1:16:54.6
4.	BUL	(Silvana Blagoeva, Nadezda Aleksieva, Iwa Schkodreva)	0	1:18:54.8
5.	FIN	(Mari Lampinen, Tuija Sikiö, Terhi Markkanen)	0	1:20:17.8
6.	SWE	(Christina Eklund, Inger Björkbom, Mia Stadig)	0	1:20:56.6
7.	NOR	(Signe Trosten, Hildegunn Fossen, Elin Kristiansen)	1	1:21:20.0
8.	CZE	(Gabriela Suvová, Jana Kulhavá, Jirina Adamičková)	3	1:23:12.7

Since world championships were inaugurated in women's biathlon in 1984, the Soviet Union had won every relay—eight in a row. In addition, three days before the Olympic championship, ex-Soviet skiers Reztsova and Belova had finished first and third in the individual 7.5-kilometer race. However, it was Germany that had won the first World Cup relay of the season and France the last on January 26. The French victory in Anterselva, Italy, had been considered an unexpected breakthrough. At Les Saisies, Corinne Niogret gave France a surprise lead after the first leg with Bulgaria 4.2 seconds behind. Belova of the Unified Team and Disl of Germany each had to ski a penalty loop and trailed by 27.2 seconds and 39 seconds, respectively. The second leg saw blazing performances by Misersky and Reztsova. At the final exchange, the Unified Team led Germany by 7.2 seconds and France by 30 seconds. Melnikova, competing in her only race of the Olympics, gradually fell behind, and the contest developed into a duel between Petra Schaaf and Anne Briand, who had finished sixth and seventh in the individual race, 19.4 seconds apart. Briand caught Schaaf as they entered the shooting range for the last time. Although she missed her third and fourth shots, Briand sensed that Schaaf, who was only a few feet away at the next shooting lane, was more nervous than she was. Indeed, the German missed twice as well, and Briand was able to return to the course first and then pull away. There were only nine certified female biathletes in France, but by the end of the day three of them were Olympic champions.

BOBSLED

Two-Man
Four-Man

Bobsleds were invented in the 1880s by lashing together two toboggans. Current rules limit the length and weight of the sleds. Two-man bobs must not exceed 2.70 meters and 390 kilograms (including the riders). The four-man limitations are 3.80 meters and 630 kilos. The driver steers the bobsled by means of nylon cords connected to the front runners. Sleds do have brakes, but braking during a run is grounds for immediate disqualification. Women are not allowed to compete. The reason for this prohibition has nothing to do with lack of ability: in 1938 Katherine Dewey won the U.S. National Championship. In order to avoid chewing up of the course by lesser teams, a seeding system like that used in alpine skiing was instituted in 1992. This allows the top 15 teams to go down first. The final time is the combined total of four separate runs, two on one day, two more on the next.

TWO-MAN

1924–1928 not held

1932 Lake Placid T: 12, N: 8, D: 2.10.

1.	USA	(J. Hubert Stevens, Curtis Stevens)	8:14.74
2.	SWI	(Reto Capadrutt, Oscar Geier)	8:16.28
3.	USA	(John Heaton, Robert Minton)	8:29.15
4.	ROM	(Papana Alexandru, Hubert Dumitru)	8:32.47
5.	GER	(Hanns Kilian, Sebastian Huber)	8:35.36
6.	ITA	(Teofilo Rossi di Montelera, Italo Casini)	8:36.33
7.	GER	(Werner Huth, Max Ludwig)	8:45.05
8.	ITA	(Agostini Lanfranchi, Gaetano Lanfranchi)	8:50.66

J. Hubert Stevens and his brother, Curtis, were local residents of Lake Placid. They trailed Capadrutt and Geier by 6.32 seconds after the first run, but registered the fastest times in each of the other three runs to overtake the Swiss team for the victory. The Stevens brothers, aged 41 and 33, attributed part of their success to the fact that they heated their runners with blowtorches for 25 minutes prior to hitting the snow, a tactic that is now highly illegal, but which was then considered unusual but acceptable.

1936 Garmisch-Partenkirchen T: 23, N: 13, D: 2.15.

1.	USA	(Ivan Brown, Alan Washbond)	5:29.29
2.	SWI	(Fritz Feierabend, Joseph Beerli)	5:30.64
3.	USA	(Gilbert Colgate, Richard Lawrence)	5:33.96
4.	GBR	(Frederick McEvoy, James Cardno)	5:40.25
5.	GER	(Hanns Kilian, Hermann von Valta)	5:42.01
6.	GER	(Fritz Grau, Albert Brehme)	5:44.71
7.	SWI	(Reto Capadrutt, Charles Bouvier)	5:46.23
8.	BEL	(Rene Lunden, Eric de Spoelberch)	5:46.28

Ivan Brown of Keene Valley, New York, was an especially superstitious competitor. One of his quirks was a need to find at least one hairpin on the ground every day. Fortunately he had been able to accomplish this feat for 24 consecutive days prior to the Olympics. Brown was also the only driver to compete without goggles; he claimed they dulled his eyesight and added wind resistance.

1948 St. Moritz T: 16, N: 9, D: 1.31.

1.	SWI	(Felix Endrich, Friedrich Waller)	5:29.2
2.	SWI	(Fritz Feierabend, Paul Hans Eberhard)	5:30.4
3.	USA	(Frederick Fortune, Schuyler Carron)	5:35.3
4.	BEL	(Max Houben, Jacques Mouvet)	5:37.5
5.	GBR	(William Coles, Raymond Collings)	5:37.9
6.	ITA	(Mario Vitali, Dario Poggi)	5:38.0
7.	NOR	(Arne Holst, Ivar Johansen)	5:38.2
8.	ITA	(Nino Bibbia, Ediberto Campadese)	5:38.6

In 1953 Felix Endrich won the two-man bobsled world championship at Garmisch-Partenkirchen. Less than a week later he was leading a four-man bob down the same course when his sled hurtled over the wall at "dead man's curve" and crashed into a tree. The 31-year-old Endrich was killed almost instantly.

1952 Oslo T: 18, N: 9, D: 2.15.

1.	GER	(Andreas Ostler, Lorenz Nieberl)	5:24.54
2.	USA	(Stanley Benham, Patrick Martin)	5:26.89
3.	SWI	(Fritz Feierabend, Stephan Waser)	5:27.71
4.	SWI	(Felix Endrich, Werner Spring)	5:29.15
5.	FRA	(André Robin, Henri Rivière)	5:31.98
6.	BEL	(Marcel Leclef, Albert Casteleyns)	5:32.51
7.	USA	(Frederick Fortune, John Helmer)	5:33.82
8.	SWE	(Olle Axelsson, Jan de Man Lapidoth)	5:35.77

Ostler and Nieberl recorded the best time on each of the four runs despite the fact that they were using a 16-year-old bobsled.

1956 Cortina T: 25, N: 14, D: 1.28.

1.	ITA	(Lamberto Dalla Costa, Giacomo Conti)	5:30.14
2.	ITA	(Eugenio Monti, Renzo Alverà)	5:31.45
3.	SWI	(Max Angst, Harry Warburton)	5:37.46
4.	SPA	(Alfonso de Portago, Vicente Sartorius y Cabeza de Vaca)	5:37.60
5.	USA	(Waightman Washbond, Patrick Biesiadecki)	5:38.16
6.	USA	(Arthur Tyler, Edgar Seymour)	5:40.08
7.	SWI	(Franz Kapus, Heinrich Angst)	5:40.11
8.	GER	(Andreas Ostler, Hans Hohenester)	5:40.13

Dalla Costa and Monti finished first and second respectively on each of the four runs. Dalla Costa was a 35-year-old jet pilot who had never raced anywhere but Cortina.

1960 not held

1964 Innsbruck-Igls T: 19, N: 11, D: 2.1.

1.	GBR	(Anthony Nash, T. Robin Dixon)	4:21.90
2.	ITA	(Sergio Zardini, Romano Bonagura)	4:22.02
3.	ITA	(Eugenio Monti, Sergio Siorpaes)	4:22.63
4.	CAN	(Victor Emery, Peter Kirby)	4:23.49
5.	USA	(Lawrence McKillip, James Ernest Lamy)	4:24.60
6.	GER	(Franz Wörmann, Hubert Braun)	4:24.70
7.	USA	(Charles McDonald, Charles Pandolph)	4:25.00
8.	AUT	(Erwin Thaler, Josef Nairz)	4:25.51

Nash and Dixon came from behind to defeat Zardini and Bonagura on the final run, a remarkable achievement considering they came from a nation without a bobsled run.

1968 Grenoble-Alpe d'Huez T: 22, N: 11, D: 2.6.

1.	ITA	(Eugenio Monti, Luciano De Paolis)	4:41.54
2.	GER	(Horst Floth, Pepi Bader)	4:41.54
3.	ROM	(Ion Panţuru, Nicolae Neagoe)	4:44.46
4.	AUT	(Erwin Thaler, Reinhold Durnthaler)	4:45.13
5.	GBR	(Anthony Nash, T. Robin Dixon)	4:45.16
6.	USA	(Paul Lamey, Robert Huscher)	4:46.03
7.	GER	(Wolfgang Zimmerer, Peter Utzschneider)	4:46.40
8.	AUT	(Max Kaltenberger, Fritz Dinkhauser)	4:46.63

"Now I can retire a happy man," said Eugenio Monti after completing his 12-year quest for an Olympic gold medal. But his victory did not come easily. Trailing by one-tenth of a second after three runs, Monti drove his bob to a course record of 1:10.05, only to watch Floth race down in 1:10.15. This left the Italians and Germans in a tie for first place, and it was announced that both teams would be awarded gold medals. However, the judges later reversed their decision, invoking world bobsled rules. Sole possession of first place was given to the team that recorded the fastest single heat time—and 40-year-old Eugenio Monti had finally won his Olympic gold medal.

1972 Sapporo-Taineyama T: 21, N: 11, D: 2.5.

1.	GER	(Wolfgang Zimmerer, Peter Utzschneider)	4:57.07
2.	GER	(Horst Floth, Pepi Bader)	4:58.84
3.	SWI	(Jean Wicki, Edy Hubacher)	4:59.33
4.	ITA	(Gianfranco Gaspari, Mario Armano)	5:00.45
5.	ROM	(Ion Panţuru, Ion Zangor)	5:00.53
6.	SWE	(Carl-Erik Eriksson, Jan Johansson)	5:01.40
7.	SWI	(Hans Candrian, Heinz Schenker)	5:01.44
8.	AUT	(Herbert Gruber, Josef Oberhauser)	5:01.60

1976 Innsbruck-Igls T: 24, N: 13, D: 2.6.

1.	GDR	(Meinhard Nehmer, Bernhard Germeshausen)	3:44.42
2.	GER	(Wolfgang Zimmerer, Manfred Schumann)	3:44.99
3.	SWI	(Erich Schärer, Josef Benz)	3:45.70
4.	AUT	(Fritz Sperling, Andreas Schwab)	3:45.74
5.	GER	(Georg Heibl, Fritz Ohlwärter)	3:46.13
6.	AUT	(Dieter Delle Karth, Franz Köfel)	3:46.37
7.	GDR	(Horst Schönau, Raimund Bethge)	3:46.97
8.	ITA	(Giorgio Alvera, Franco Perruquet)	3:47.30

Nehmer and Germeshausen earned four Olympic medals each in 1976 and 1980, including three golds. A former javelin thrower, Nehmer was 35 years old when he earned his first medal.

1980 Lake Placid T: 20, N: 11, D: 2.16.

1.	SWI	(Erich Schärer, Josef Benz)	4:09.36
2.	GDR	(Bernhard Germeshausen, Hans Jürgen Gerhardt)	4:10.93
3.	GDR	(Meinhard Nehmer, Bogdan Musiol)	4:11.08
4.	SWI	(Hans Hildebrand, Walter Rahm)	4:11.32
5.	USA	(Howard Silher, Dick Nalley)	4:11.73
6.	USA	(Brent Rushlaw, Joseph Tyler)	4:12.12
7.	AUT	(Fritz Sperling, Kurt Oberhöller)	4:13.58
8.	GER	(Peter Hell, Heinz Busche)	4:13.74

1984 Sarajevo T: 28, N: 16, D: 2.11.

1.	GDR	(Wolfgang Hoppe, Dietmar Schauerhammer)	3:25.56
2.	GDR	(Bernhard Lehmann, Bogdan Musiol)	3:26.04
3.	SOV	(Zintis Ekmanis, Vladimir Alexandrov)	3:26.16
4.	SOV	(Jānis Kipurs, Aiwar Šnepsts)	3:26.42
5.	SWI	(Hans Hiltebrand, Meinrad Müller)	3:26.76
6.	SWI	(Ralph Pichler, Rico Freiermuth)	3:28.23
7.	ITA	(Guerrino Ghedina, Andrea Meneghin)	3:29.09
8.	GER	(Anton Fischer, Hans Metzler)	3:29.18

Fifty-three-year-old Carl-Erik Eriksson of Sweden became the first person to compete in six Winter Olympics. His best performance was a sixth-place finish in the 1972 two-man event. In 1984 he finished 19th in the two-man and 21st in the four-man.

1988 Calgary T: 41, N: 23, D: 2.22.

1.	SOV	(Jānis Kipurs, Vladimir Kozlov)	3:53.48
2.	GDR	(Wolfgang Hoppe, Bogdan Musiol)	3:54.19
3.	GDR	(Bernhard Lehmann, Mario Hoyer)	3:54.64
4.	SWI	(Gustav Weder, Donat Acklin)	3:56.06
5.	AUT	(Ingo Appelt, Harald Winkler)	3:56.49
6.	SWI	(Hans Hiltebrand, André Kiser)	3:56.52
7.	GER	(Anton Fischer, Christoph Langen)	3:56.62
8.	AUT	(Peter Kienast, Christian Mark)	3:56.91

Defending Olympic champion Wolfgang Hoppe registered the fastest time of the first run, but finished only eighth best in the second run. Hoppe complained bitterly about the poor racing conditions, comparing his slide down the dirt- and dust-covered track to "running on sandpaper." Hoppe, who was tied for second place after the first day, was not alone in his criticism. Six nations, including the first-place Soviet Union, filed a protest asking that the results of the first two runs be disallowed. The protest was denied and the next day the competition continued. However, the third run was finally canceled—after 28 sleds had already raced—because of excessive sand on the track due to warm weather and high winds.

The competition was resumed one day later. Hoppe clocked the fastest times in both the third and fourth runs, but the 1.21-second deficit he had incurred in the second run was too much to overcome. The upset victory went to Jānis Kipurs, a 30-year-old Latvian who had taken up bobsledding when he answered a newspaper ad in 1980. In Calgary, Kipurs painted his sled with the Latvian colors as a protest against Soviet occupation of his country. (By 1992, Latvia had regained its independence and entered a separate team in Albertville.)

Meanwhile, Hoppe continued to fume about the racing conditions. Besides the failure to protect the run from poor weather, his main objection was that the field was too large. Because bobsled competitions did not, until 1992, allow the top 15 seeds to race first, the course was often badly chewed up before one or more of the favorites got to it. This was precisely what had happened to Hoppe in the second run.

Hoppe's criticisms were not completely unjustified. The 1988 competition did include some unusual entrants, several of whom came from countries with little or no snow. In fact, the snowless nations organized their own informal "Caribbean Cup." Among the warm-weather sledders were the four Tames Perea brothers, who represented Mexico, although they earned their living as waiters in Dallas, Texas; the popular Jamaican bobsled team, which helped finance its training by selling tee-shirts, sweatshirts, and a reggae record; 52-year-old Harvey Hook of the U.S. Virgin Islands; and John Foster, who had previously represented the Virgin

Islands in yachting and did so again in 1988. The "Caribbean Cup" was won by New Zealand's Alexander Peterson and Peter Henry, who tied for twentieth place over-all. The top finish by a team from a truly snow-free country was the twenty-ninth place earned by Bart Carpentier Alting and Bart Dreschsel of the Netherlands Antilles. Carpentier Alting, attempting a rare double, also finished thirty-sixth of thirty-eight in the one-man luge.

1992 Albertville-La Plagne T: 46, N: 25, D: 2.16.

1.	SWI	(Gustav Weder, Donat Acklin)	4:03.26
2.	GER	(Rudolf Lochner, Markus Zimmermann)	4:03.55
3.	GER	(Christoph Langen, Günther Eger)	4:03.63
4.	AUT	(Ingo Appelt, Thomas Schroll)	4:03.67
5.	ITA	(Günther Huber, Stefano Ticci)	4:03.72
6.	GBR	(Mark Tout, Lenox Paul)	4:03.87
7.	USA	(Brian Shimer, Herschel Walker)	4:03.95
8.	AUT	(Gerhard Rainer, Thomas Bachler)	4:04.00

For the first time in Olympic bobsled history, none of the eventual medal winners were in first, second, or third place after the first day's two runs. The surprise leaders at the halfway point of the competition were Tout and Paul. Close behind them were Huber and Ticci and Appelt and Schroll. On the second day, the favorites, Weder and Acklin, roared back from fifth place to record the fastest times of both runs and earn Switzerland's only victory of the Albertville Games. Lochner and Zimmermann staged an even more dramatic recovery, moving up from tenth to second. Lochner, who didn't take up bobsledding until 1982, when he was 27 years old, was a notorious cigarette smoker whose motto was "Smoke openly, train secretly."

FOUR-MAN

1924 Chamonix T: 9, N: 5, D: 2.3.

1.	SWI	(Eduard Scherrer, Alfred Neveu, Alfred Schläppi, Heinrich Schläppi)	5:45.54
2.	GBR	(Ralph Broome, Thomas Arnold, Alexander Richardson, Rodney Soher)	5:48.83
3.	BEL	(Charles Mulder, René Mortiaux, Paul van den Broeck, Victor Verschueren, Henri Willems)	6:02.29
4.	FRA	(A. Berg, H. Aldebert, G. André, Jean de Suarez D'Aulan)	6:22.95
5.	GBR	(William Horton, Archibald Crabbe, Francis Fairlie, George Cecil Pim)	6:40.71
6.	ITA	(Lodovico Obexer, Massimo Fink, Paolo Herbert, Giuseppe Steiner, Aloise Trenker)	7:15.41

1928 St Moritz T: 23, N: 14, D: 2.18.

1.	USA	(William Fiske, Nion Tucker, Geoffrey Mason, Clifford Gray, Richard Parke)	3:20.5
2.	USA	(Jennison Heaton, David Granger, Lyman Hine, Thomas Doe, Jay O'Brien)	3:21.0
3.	GER	(Hanns Kilian, Valentin Krempel, Hans Hess, Sebastian Huber, Hans Nägle)	3:21.9
4.	ARG	(Arturo Gramajo, Ricardo Gonzales Moreno, Mariano Domari, Rafael Iglesias, J. Nash)	3:22.6
5.	ARG	(Eduardo Hope, Justo de Carril, Hector Milberg, Horacio Iglesias, Horacio Gramajo)	3:22.9
6.	BEL	(Ernest Lambert, Marcel Sedille-Courbon, Léon Tom, Max Houben, Walter Ganshof van der Meersch)	3:24.5
7.	ROM	(G. Socolescu, J. Gavat, T. Nitescu, P. Ghitulescu, M. Socolescu)	3:24.6
8.	SWI	(Ch. Stoffel, H. Höhnes, R. Fonjallez, E. Copetti, L. Koch)	3:25.7

The competition was limited to two runs due to heavy thawing. For the only time in Olympic history, there were five men on each team rather than four. Three members of the winning team—Tucker, Mason, and Parke—were chosen after they answered an ad in the Paris edition of the *New York Herald Tribune*. None of them had ever seen a bobsled before. Mason showed up for practice on February 1, won a gold medal 18 days later, and never rode in a bobsled again.

1932 Lake Placid T: 7, N: 5, D: 2.15.

1.	USA	(William Fiske, Edward Eagan, Clifford Gray, Jay O'Brien)	7:53.68
2.	USA	(Henry Homburger, Percy Bryant, F. Paul Stevens, Edmund Horton)	7:55.70
3.	GER	(Hanns Kilian, Max Ludwig, Hans Melhorn, Sebastian Huber)	8:00.04
4.	SWI	(Reto Capadrutt, Hans Eisenhut, Charles Jenny, Oscar Geier)	8:12.18
5.	ITA	(Teofilo Rossi Di Montelera, Agostino Lanfranchi, Gaetano Lanfranchi, Italo Casini)	8:24.21
6.	ROM	(Papana Alexandru, Ionescu Alexandru, Ulise Petrescu, Hubert Dumitru)	8:24.22
7.	GER	(Walther von Mumm, Hasso von Bismarck, Gerhard Hessert, Georg Gyssling)	8:25.45

Eddie Eagan is the only person to have won a gold medal in both the Summer and Winter Olympics. Eagan came from a poor family in Denver, but made his way through Yale, Harvard Law School, and Oxford, became a successful lawyer, and married an automobile heiress. He lived his life according to the precepts of Frank Merriwell, the fictional hero of dime novels. In 1932 he wrote, "To this day I have never used tobacco, because Frank didn't. My first glass of wine, which I do not care for, was taken under social compulsion in Europe. Frank never drank." Back in 1920, Eddie Eagan won the Light Heavyweight boxing championship at the Antwerp Olympics. Later he won the U.S. amateur Heavyweight title and became the first American to win the amateur championship of Great Britain. In 1932 he showed up as a member of the four-man bob team led by boy wonder Billy Fiske, who had driven a U.S. team to victory at the 1928 Olympics when he was only 16 years old. The other members of the 1932 squad were St. Moritz veterans 48-year-old Jay O'Brien, who happened to be the head of the U.S. Olympic Bobsled Committee, and 40-year-old Clifford "Tippy" Gray, a songwriter who was actually a citizen of Great Britain. Their main rivals were the team driven by civil engineer Henry Homburger, which was known as the Saranac Lake Red Devils.

The weather was so poor during the Olympics that the four-man bob had to be delayed until after the official closing ceremony. The officials in charge of the bobsled competitions ordered that all four heats be run on February 14. But after the second round, Paul Stevens of the Red Devils protested the poor racing conditions and stalked off. Most of the competitors followed him, and the officials were forced to reschedule runs 3 and 4 the next day. Fiske's team recorded the fastest time for each of the first three runs. The Red Devils picked up 2.31 seconds on their final run, but it wasn't enough.

Fiske and his partners never raced together again. In fact, three of them died within a one-year period starting in 1940. Jay O'Brien died of a heart attack at the age of 57. Billy Fiske was the first American to join the British Royal Air Force in 1939 and was wounded over southern England during the Battle of Britain, while flying a Hurricane fighter. He died on August 17, 1940, when he was only 29 years old. Tippy Gray, whose 3000 songs included "Got a Date with an Angel" and "If You Were the Only Girl in the World," died in 1941. Gray was such a modest man that his children never even knew that he had won two Olympic gold medals until after he died.

1936 Garmisch-Partenkirchen T: 18, N: 10, D: 2.12.

1.	SWI	(Pierre Musy, Arnold Gartmann, Charles Bouvier, Joseph Beerli)	5:19.85
2.	SWI	(Reto Capadrutt, Hans Aichele, Fritz Feierabend, Hans Bütikofer)	5:22.73
3.	GBR	(Frederick McEvoy, James Cardno, Guy Dugdale, Charles Green)	5:23.41
4.	USA	(J. Hubert Stevens, Crawford Merkel, Robert Martin, John Shene)	5:24.13
5.	BEL	(Max Houben, Martial van Schelle, Louis de Ridder, Paul Graeffe)	5:28.92
6.	USA	(Francis Tyler, James Bickford, Richard Lawrence, Max Bly)	5:29.00
7.	GER	(Hanns Kilian, Sebastian Huber, Fritz Schwarz, Hermann von Valta)	5:29.07
8.	BEL	(Rene Lunden, Eric de Spoelberch, Philippe de Pret Roose, Gaston Braun)	5:29.82

Again the bobsled competition was disrupted by bad weather—this time heavy rain. The first day's two runs were dangerous and unpredictable, but the next day the course was fast and smooth. Musy, a 25-year-old Swiss Army lieutenant, was the son of a former president of Switzerland.

1948 St. Moritz T: 15, N: 9, D: 2.7.

1.	USA	(Francis Tyler, Patrick Martin, Edward Rimkus, William D'Amico)	5.20.1
2.	BEL	(Max Houben, Freddy Mansveld, Louis-Georges Niels, Jacques Mouvet)	5:21.3
3.	USA	(James Bickford, Thomas Hicks, Donald Dupree, William Dupree)	5:21.5
4.	SWI	(Fritz Feierabend, Friedrich Waller, Felix Endrich, Heinrich Angst)	5:22.1
5.	NOR	(Arne Holst, Ivar Johansen, Reidar Berg, Alf Large)	5:22.5
6.	ITA	(Nino Bibbia, Giancarlo Ronchetti, Edilberto Campadese, Luigi Cavalieri)	5:23.0
7.	GBR	(William Coles, William McLean, R.W. Pennington Collings, George Holliday)	5:23.9
8.	SWI	(Franz Kapus, Rolf Spring, B. Schilter, Paul Eberhard)	5:25.4

The competition was halted in the middle of the second round when a water pipe burst, flooding the bob run. The winning team from Lake Placid, New York, weighed a total of 898 pounds.

1952 Oslo T: 15, N: 9, D: 2.22.

1.	GER	(Andreas Ostler, Friedrich Kuhn, Lorenz Nieberl, Franz Kemser)	5:07.84
2.	USA	(Stanley Benham, Patrick Martin, Howard Crossett, James Atkinson)	5:10.48
3.	SWI	(Fritz Feierabend, Albert Madörin, André Filippini, Stephan Waser)	5:11.70
4.	SWI	(Felix Endrich, Fritz Stöckli, Franz Kapus, Werner Spring)	5:13.98
5.	AUT	(Karl Wagner, Franz Eckhart, Hermann Palka, Paul Aste)	5:14.74
6.	SWE	(Kjell Holmström, Felix Fernström, Nils Landgren, Jan de Man Lapidoth)	5:15.01
7.	SWE	(Gunnar Åhs, Börje Ekedahl, Lennart Sandin, Gunnar Garpö)	5:17.86
8.	ARG	(Carlos Tomasi, Roberto Bordeau, Hector Tomasi, Carlos Sareistian)	5:18.85

The four members of the winning German team weighed in at 1041½ pounds. At a meeting held prior to the Olympics, the International Bobsled and Toboganning Federation passed a rule limiting future teams from weighing more than 880 pounds.

1956 Cortina T: 21, N: 13, D: 2.4.

1.	SWI	(Franz Kapus, Gottfried Diener, Robert Alt, Heinrich Angst)	5:10.44
2.	ITA	(Eugenio Monti, Ulrico Giardi, Renzo Alverà, Renato Mocellini)	5:12.10
3.	USA	(Arthur Tyler, William Dodge, Charles Butler, James Lamy)	5:12.39
4.	SWI	(Max Angst, Albert Gartmann, Harry Warburton, Rolf Gerber)	5:14.27
5.	ITA	(Dino DeMartin, Giovanni DeMartin, Giovanni Tabacchi, Carlo Da Prà)	5:14.66
6.	GER	(Hans Rösch, Martin Pössinger, Lorenz Nieberl, Silvester Wackerle, Sr.)	5:18.02
7.	AUT	(K. Loserth, K. Thurner, W. Schwarzböck, F. Dominik)	5:18.29
8.	GER	(Franz Schelle, Jakob Nirschel, Hans Henn, Edmund Koller)	5:18.50

Franz Kapus was 46 years old when he drove the Swiss team to victory by scoring the fastest times in all but the first run.

1960 not held

1964 Innsbruck-Igls T: 18, N: 11, D: 2.7.

1.	CAN	(Victor Emery, Peter Kirby, Douglas Anakin, John Emery)	4:14.46
2.	AUT	(Erwin Thaler, Adolf Koxeder, Josef Nairz, Reinhold Durnthaler)	4:15.48
3.	ITA	(Eugenio Monti, Sergio Siorpaes, Benito Rigoni, Gildo Siorpaes)	4:15.60
4.	ITA	(Sergio Zardini, Romano Bonagura, Sergio Mocellini, Ferruccio Dalla Torre)	4:15.89
5.	GER	(Franz Schelle, Otto Göbl, Ludwig Siebert, Josef Sterff)	4:16.19
6.	USA	(William Hickey, Charles Pandolph, Reginald Benham, William Dundon)	4:17.23
7.	AUT	(Paul Aste, Hans Stoll, Herbert Gruber, Andreas Arnold)	4:17.73
8.	SWI	(Herbert Kiessel, Oskar Lory, Bernhard Wild, Hansrudi Beuggar)	4:18.12

The winning Canadian team was made up of four bachelors from Montreal. Canada had never before entered an Olympic bobsled competition.

1968 Grenoble-Alpe d'Huez T: 19, N: 11, D: 2.15.

1.	ITA	(Eugenio Monti, Luciano De Paolis, Roberto Zandonella, Mario Armano)	2:17.39
2.	AUT	(Erwin Thaler, Reinhold Durnthaler, Herbert Gruber, Josef Eder)	2:17.48
3.	SWI	(Jean Wicki, Hans Candrian, Willi Hofmann, Walter Graf)	2:18.04
4.	ROM	(Ion Panţuru, Nicolae Neagoe, Petre Hristovici, Gheorghe Maftei)	2:18.14
5.	GER	(Horst Floth, Pepi Bader, Willi Schäfer, Frank Lange)	2:18.33
6.	ITA	(Gianfranco Gaspari, Leonardo Cavallini, Giuseppe Rescigno, Andrea Clemente)	2:18.36
7.	FRA	(Francis Luiggi, Maurice Grether, Andre Patey, Gerard Monrazel)	2:18.84
8.	GBR	(Anthony Nash, Robin Dixon, Guy Renwick, Robin Widdows)	2:18.84

The danger of a sudden thaw forced the officials to limit the contest to only two runs. Eugenio Monti won two silver medals in 1956, two bronze medals in 1964, and two gold medals in 1968.

1972 Sapporo-Teineyama T: 18, N: 10, D: 2.11.

1.	SWI	(Jean Wicki, Edy Hubacher, Hans Leutenegger, Werner Carmichel)	4:43.07
2.	ITA	(Nevio De Zordo, Gianni Bonichon, Adriano Frassinelli, Corrado Dal Fabbro)	4:43.83
3.	GER	(Wolfgang Zimmerer, Peter Utzschneider, Stefan Gaisreiter, Walter Steinbauer)	4:43.92
4.	SWI	(Hans Candrian, Heinz Schenker, Erwin Juon, Gaudenz Beeli)	4:44.56
5.	GER	(Horst Floth, Pepi Bader, Donat Ertel, Walter Gilik)	4:45.09
6.	AUT	(Herbert Gruber, Josef Oberhauser, Utz Chwalla, Josef Eder)	4:45.77
7.	AUT	(Werner Dellekarth, Fritz Sperling, Werner Moser, Walter Dellekarth)	4:46.66
8.	ITA	(Gianfranco Gaspari, Luciano De Paolis, Roberto Zandonella, Mario Armano)	4:46.73

1976 Innsbruck-Igls T: 21, N: 12, D: 2.14.

1.	GDR	(Meinhard Nehmer, Jochen Babock, Bernhard Germeshausen, Bernhard Lehmann)	3:40.43
2.	SWI	(Erich Schärer, Ulrich Bächli, Rudolf Marti, Josef Benz)	3:40.89
3.	GER	(Wolfgang Zimmerer, Peter Utzschneider, Bodo Bittner, Manfred Schumann)	3:41.37
4.	GDR	(Horst Schönau, Horst Bernhard, Harald Seifert, Raimund Bethge)	3:42.44
5.	GER	(Georg Heibl, Hans Morant, Siegfried Radant, Fritz Ohlwärter)	3:42.47
6.	AUT	(Werner Delle Karth, Andreas Schwab, Otto Breg, Franz Köfel, Heinz Krenn)	3:43.21
7.	AUT	(Fritz Sperling, Kurt Oberholler, Gerd Zaunschirm, Dieter Gehmacher)	3:43.79
8.	ROM	(Dragos Panaitescu, Paul Neagu, Costel Ionescu, Gheorghe Lixandru)	3:43.91

1980 Lake Placid T: 17, N: 10, D: 2.24.

1. GDR	(Meinhard Nehmer, Bogdan Musiol, Bernhard Germeshausen, Hans-Jürgen Gerhardt)	3:59.92
2. SWI	(Erich Schärer, Ulrich Bächli, Rudolf Marti, Josef Benz)	4:00.87
3. GDR	(Horst Schönau, Ronald Wetzig, Detlef Richter, Andreas Kirchner)	4:00.97
4. AUT	(Fritz Sperling, Heinrich Bergmüller, Franz Rednak, Bernhard Purkrabek)	4:02.62
5. AUT	(Walter Delle Karth, Franz Paulweber, Gerd Zaunschirm, Kurt Oberhöller)	4:02.95
6. SWI	(Hans Hiltebrand, Ulrich Schindler, Walter Rahm, Armin Baumgartner)	4:03.69
7. GER	(Peter Hell, Hans Wagner, Heinz Busche, Walter Barfuss)	4:04.40
8. ROM	(Dragos Panaitescu, Dorel Critudor, Sandu Mitrofan, Gheorghe Lixandru)	4:04.68

1984 Sarajevo T: 24, N: 15, D: 2.18.

1. GDR	(Wolfgang Hoppe, Roland Wetzig, Dietmar Schauerhammer, Andreas Kirchner)	3:20.22
2. GDR	(Bernhard Lehmann, Bogdan Musiol, Ingo Voge, Eberhard Weise)	3:20.78
3. SWI	(Silvio Giobellina, Heinz Stettler, Urs Salzmann, Rico Freiermuth)	3:21.39
4. SWI	(Ekkehard Fasser, Hans Märchy, Kurt Poletti, Rolf Strittmatter)	3:22.90
5. USA	(Jeff Jost, Joe Briski, Thomas Barnes, Hal Hoye)	3:23.33
6. SOV	(Jānis Kipurs, Maris Poikans, Ivar Berzups, Aiwar Šnepsts)	3:23.51
7. ROM	(Dorin Degan, Cornel Popescu, Georghe Lixandru, Costel Petrariu)	3:23.76
8. ITA	(Guerrino Ghedina, Stefano Ticci, Paolo Scaramuzza, Andrea Meneghin)	3:23.77

The top three teams finished 1, 2, 3 in each of the four runs.

1988 Calgary T: 26, N: 17, D: 2.28.

1. SWI	(Ekkehard Fasser, Kurt Meier, Marcel Fässler, Werner Stocker)	3:47.51
2. GDR	(Wolfgang Hoppe, Dietmar Schauerhammer, Bogdan Musiol, Ingo Voge)	3:47.58
3. SOV	(Jānis Kipurs, Guntis Osis, Juris Tone, Vladimir Kozlov)	3:48.26
4. USA	(Brent Rushlaw, Hal Hoye, Michael Wasko, William White)	3:48.28
5. SOV	(Maris Poikans, Olafs Klyavinch, Ivars Bersups, Juris Judzems)	3:48.35
6. AUT	(Peter Kienast, Franz Siegl, Christian Mark, Kurt Teigl)	3:48.65
7. AUT	(Ingo Appelt, Josef Muigg, Gerhard Redl, Harald Winkler)	3:48.95
8. GDR	(Detlef Richter, Bodo Ferl, Ludwig Jahn, Alexander Szelig)	3:49.06

Third after two runs and second after three, 35-year-old Ekkehard Fasser eked out an upset victory in the final competition of his career. Fasser and his crew gained their advantage over Hoppe and the East Germans in the first 50 meters of the 1475-meter course, picking up a combined time of one sixteen-hundredth of a second over four runs.

1992 Albertville-La Plagne T: 31, N: 20, D: 2.22.

1. AUT	(Ingo Appelt, Harald Winkler, Gerhard Haidacher, Thomas Schroll)	3:53.90
2. GER	(Wolfgang Hoppe, Bogdan Musiol, Axel Kühn, René Hannemann)	3:53.92
3. SWI	(Gustav Weder, Donat Acklin, Lorenz Schindelholz, Curdin Morell)	3:54.13
4. CAN	(Christopher Lori, Kenneth LeBlanc, Cal Langford, David MacEachern)	3:54.24
5. SWI	(Christian Meili, Bruno Gerber, Christian Reich, Gerold Löffler)	3:54.38
6. GER	(Harald Czudaj, Tino Bonk, Axel Jang, Alexander Szelig)	3:54.42
7. GBR	(Mark Tout, George Farrell, Paul Field, Lenox Paul)	3:54.89
8. FRA	(Christophe Flacher, Claude Dasse, Thierry Tribondeau, Gabriel Fourmigue)	3:54.91

Ingo Appelt, a 30-year-old jeweler from Stubaital, overcame a 10th place finish in the second run to win the closest four-man contest in Olympic history. The competition was brightened by unexpected moments of comic relief. During the second run, Soviet team member Aleksandr Bortyuk slipped at the start, dived into his sled, and found himself facing the wrong way. The Soviets completed the course convulsed in laughter with Bortyuk nose-to-nose with one of his teammates. At least they did better than Canada's number two team: Chris Farstad slipped while trying to jump into the sled and ended up in the seat that was supposed to be occupied by Jack Pyc. Pyc hesitated, missed the sled entirely, and slid down the run behind the sled until he was saved by a spectator. The Canadians were disqualified, but gained satisfaction from the fact that they finished first in the *three*-man bob.

ICE HOCKEY

The teams in Olympic ice hockey tournaments are divided into two round-robin pools. According to rules instituted in 1992, the winner of each pool plays the fourth-place team in the opposing pool, and the second-place teams play the other pool's third-place team. The winners advance to the semifinals. Matches are divided into three 20-minute periods. In pool play, ties are allowed to stand, but in the playoff rounds, regulation play is followed by a 10-minute sudden-death overtime and then by a shoot-out.

1920 Antwerp T: 7, N: 7, D: 4.26.

			W	L	PF	PA
1.	CAN	(Robert Benson, Wally Byron, Frank Frederickson, Chris Fridfinnson, Magnus "Mike" Goodman, Haldor Halderson, Konrad Johannesson, Allan "Huck" Woodman)	3	0	29	1
2.	USA	(Raymond Bonney, Anthony Conroy, Herbert Drury, J. Edward Fitzgerald, George Geran, Frank Goheen, Joseph McCormick, Lawrence McCormick, Frank Synott, Leon Tuck, Cyril Weidenborner)	3	1	52	2
3.	CZE	(Karel Hartmann, Karel Kotrbá, Josef Loos, Vilém Loos, Jan Peka, Karel Pešek-Kadā, Josef Šroubek, Otakar Vindyš, Jan Palouš, Karel Wälzer)	1	2	1	31
4.	SWE	(Wilhelm Arwe, Erik Burman, Seth Howander, Albin Jansson, Georg Johansson, Einar Lindqvist, Einar Lundell, Hansjacob Mattsson, Nils Molander, Sven Säfwenberg, Einar Svensson)	3	3	17	20

The 1920 ice hockey tournament was played by seven-man teams rather than six-man ones. Canada scored victories of 15–0 over Czechoslovakia, 2–0 over the United States, and 12–1 over Sweden. According to the rules of the tournament, the three teams that lost to Canada then played off for second place. The United States beat Sweden, 7–0, and Czechoslovakia, 16–0. Then Czechoslovakia defeated Sweden, 1–0, to win the bronze medal, even though the Czechs had been outscored 1 to 31 in their three matches. Canada was represented by the Winnipeg Falcons, who had just defeated the University of Toronto for the Canadian championship. The invitation to the Olympics came at such short notice that the Falcons didn't have time to return home to Winnipeg. Funds had to be raised to buy the players new clothes for the overseas journey.

1924 Chamonix T: 8, N: 8, D: 2.8.

			W	L	PF	PA
1.	CAN	(Jack Cameron, Ernest Collett, Albert McCaffery, Harold McMunn, Duncan Munro, W. Beattie Ramsay, Cyril Slater, Reginald Smith, Harry Watson)	5	0	110	3
2.	USA	(Clarence Abel, Herbert Drury, Alphonse Lacroix, John Langley, John Lyons, Justin McCarthy, Willard Rice, Irving Small, Frank Synott)	4	1	73	6
3.	GBR	(William Anderson, Lorne Carr-Harris, Colin Carruthers, Eric Carruthers, George "Guy" Clarkson, Cuthbert Ross Cuthbert, George Holmes, Hamilton Jukes, Edward Pitblado, Blane Sexton)	3	2	40	38
4.	SWE	(Ruben Allinger, Vilhelm Arwe, Erik Burman, Birger Holmqvist, Gustaf Johansson, Hugo Johansson, Karl Josefson, Ernst Karlberg, Nils Molander, Einar Ohlsson)	2	3	21	49

5.	CZE	(W. Stransky, J. Rezač, Otakar Vindyš, Vilém Loos, Josef Šroubek, J. Jirkovsky, J. Malecek, J. Fleischmann, M. Fleischmann, Jan Palouš, J. Krasl)	1	2	14	41
5.	FRA	(B. Poule, P.E. Bouillon, L. Brasseur, A. Charlet, Pierre Charpentier, J. Chaudron, H. Couttet, R. Couvert, M. Del Valle, A. De Rauch, G.F. De Wilde, A. Hassler, C. Lavaivre, H. Levy-Grunwald, J. Nard, C. Payot, P. Payot, Leonhard Quaglia, G. Simond)	1	2	9	42
7.	BEL	(Victor Verschueren, Paul Van den Broeck, Henri Louette, Frederick Rudolph, Andre Poplimont, Gaston Van Volckxsom, Charles Van den Driessche, Louis de Ridder)	0	3	8	35
7.	SWI	(B. Leuzinger, W. deSiebenthal, D. Unger, E. Mottier, René Savoie, Marius Jaccard, F. Auckenthaler, Ernest Jacquet, P. Muller, A. Verdeil, E. Filiol)	0	3	2	53

The Canadian team, the Toronto Granites, displayed extraordinary superiority. After defeating Czechoslovakia, 30–0, and Sweden, 22–0, they outscored Switzerland, 18–0 in the first period alone and then breezed to a 33–0 victory, before crushing Great Britain, 19–2. Meanwhile the U.S. team had beaten Belgium 19–0, France 22–0, Great Britain 11–0, and Sweden 20–0. The final match between Canada and the United States was a rough battle that saw Canada's Harry Watson knocked cold after only 20 seconds of play. Watson recovered, however, and, with blood in his eyes, scored the first two goals of the game. Canada led 2–1 after the first period and 5–1 after the second. A single third-period goal accounted for the final score of 6–1.

1928 St. Moritz T: 11, N: 11, D: 2.19.

			W	L	T	PF	PA
1.	CAN	(Charles Delahay, Frank Fisher, Louis Hudson, Norbert Mueller, Herbert Plaxton, Hugh Plaxton, Roger Plaxton, John Porter, Frank Sullivan, Joseph Sullivan, Ross Taylor, David Trottier)	3	0	0	38	0
2.	SWE	(Carl Abrahamsson, Emil Bergman, Birger Holmqvist, Gustaf Johansson, Henry Johansson, Nils Johansson, Ernst Karlberg, Erik Larsson, Bertil Linde, Sigurd Öberg, Vilhelm Petersen, Kurt Sucksdorf)	3	1	1	12	14
3.	SWI	(Gianni Andreossi, Murezzan Andreossi, Robert Breiter, Louis Dufour, Charles Fasel, Albert Geromini, Fritz Kraatz, Adolf Martignoni, Heinrich Meng, Anton Morosani, Luzius Rüedi, Richard Torriani)	2	2	1	9	21
4.	GBR	(Blane Sexton, Eric Carruthers, Cuthbert Ross Cuthbert, Frederick Melland, Victor Tait, Charles Wyld, Colin Carruthers, William Speechley, Harold Greenwood, William Brown, G.E.F. Rogers, Bernard Fawcett)	2	4	0	11	27

Canada was represented by the 1926 Toronto University team, which had stayed together and, renamed the Toronto Graduates, had won the Canadian championships. They arrived in Switzerland ten days before the opening of the Games. When Olympic officials saw the Canadians practice they realized that the rest of the teams would be completely outclassed. Consequently, they devised an unusual organization for the tournament. Canada was advanced straight to the final round, while the other ten nations were divided into three pools. The winners of the three pools then joined Canada in the final round. This odd system turned out to be well justified, as Canada obliterated Sweden 11–0, Great Britain 14–0, and Switzerland 13–0.

1932 Lake Placid T: 4, N: 4, D: 2.13.

			W	L	T	PF	PA
1.	CAN	(William Cockburn, Clifford Crowley, Albert Duncanson, George Garbutt, Roy Hinkel, Victor Lundquist, Norman Malloy, Walter Monson, Kenneth Moore, N. Romeo Rivers, Harold Simpson, Hugh Sutherland, W. Stanley Wagner, J. Aliston Wise)	5	0	1	32	4
2.	USA	(Osborn Anderson, John Bent, John Chase, John Cookman, Douglas Everett, Franklin Farrell, Joseph Fitzgerald, Edward Frazier, John Garrison, Gerard Hallock, Robert Livingston, Francis Nelson, Winthrop Palmer, Gordon Smith)	4	1	1	27	5
3.	GER	(Rudi Ball, Alfred Heinrich, Erich Herker, Gustav Jaenecke, Werner Korff, Walter Leinweber, Erich Römer, Marquardt Slevogt, Martin Schröttle, Georg Strobl)	2	4	0	7	26
4.	POL	(Adam Kowalski, Aleksander Kowalski, Wlodzimierz Krygier, Albert Maurer, Roman Sabiński, Kazimierz Sokolowski, Jósef Stogowski, Witalis Ludwiczak, Czeslaw Marchewczyk, Kazimierz Materski)	0	6	0	3	34

Because of the worldwide Depression, only four nations appeared for the Olympic hockey tournament. Consequently, it was decided that each team would play each other team twice. The Canadian team from Winnipeg won their first five matches, including a 2–1 victory over the United States. This meant that a win or a tie in the second match against the United States would assure Canada of first place. If the United States won, then a third match would be required. The United States took a 2–1 lead, but with 50 seconds to play, Rivers shot a bouncing puck into the net to tie the score. Three scoreless overtimes later, Canada was declared the tournament winner.

1936 Garmisch-Partenkirchen T: 15, N: 15, D: 2.16.

			W	L	T	PF	PA
1.	GBR	(Alexander "Sandy" Archer, James Borland, Edgar Brenchley, James Chappell, John Coward, Gordon Dailley, John Davey, Carl Erhardt, James Foster, John Kilpatrick, Archibald Stinchcombe, James Wyman)	5	0	2	17	3
2.	CAN	(Maxwell Deacon, Hugh Farquharson, Kenneth Farmer, James Haggarty, Walter Kitchen, Raymond Milton, Francis Moore, Herman Murray, Arthur Nash, David Neville, Ralph St. Germain, Alexander Sinclair, William Thomson)	7	1	0	54	7
3.	USA	(John Garrison, August Kammer, Philip LaBatte, John Lax, Thomas Moone, Eldrige Ross, Paul Rowe, Francis Shaugnessy, Gordon Smith, Francis Spain, Frank Stubbs)	5	2	1	10	4
4.	CZE	(Josef Boháč, Alois Cetkovsky, Karel Hromádka, Drahos Jirotka, Zdenek Jirotka, Jan Košek, Oldřich Kučera, Josef Maleček, Jan Peka, Jaroslav Pusbauer, Jiři Tožička, Ladislav Troják, Walter Ullrich)	5	3	0	16	16
5.	GER	(Wilhelm Egginger, Joachim Albrecht von Bethmann-Hollweg, Gustav Jaenecke, Phillip Schenk, Rudi Ball, Karl Kögel, Anton Wiedemann, Herbert Schibukat, Alois Kuhn, Werner George, Georg Strohl, Paul Trautmann)	3	2	1	10	9
5.	SWE	(Hermann Carlsson, Sven Bergquist, Bertil Lundell, Holger Engberg, Torsten Jöhncke, Yngve Liljeberg, Bertil Norberg, Vilhelm Petersen, Åke Ericson, Stig Andersson, Lennart Hellman, Vilhelm Larsson, Ruben Carlsson)	2	3	0	5	7

7. AUT (Hermann Weiss, Hans Trauttenberg, Rudolf Vojta, Oskar Nowak,   2   4   0   12   11
Friedrich Demmer, Franz Csöngei, Hans Tatzer, Willibald Stanek,
Lambert Neumaier, Franz Schüssler, Emil Seidler, Josef Göbl)

7. HUN (István Csak, Ferenc Monostori, Miklós Barcza, László Róna,   2   4   0   16   77
Frigyes Helmeczi, Sándor Magyar, András Gergely, László
Gergely, Béla Háray, Zoltán Jeney, Sándor Miklós, Ferenc Sza-
mosi, Mátyás Farkas)

Germany's leading hockey player was Rudi Ball, a Jew who fled the country
when the Nazis began their campaign of anti-Semitism. One month before the
Games began, he returned to lead the German team after being invited back by
the Nazi leadership. He was the only Jewish member of the German Winter
Olympics team.

Canada's Olympic undefeated streak was halted at 20 by Great Britain in the
semifinal round, when Edgar Brenchley scored a goal in the 14th minute of the final
period to give the British a 2–1 victory. Great Britain remained unbeaten by
surviving a 0–0 triple overtime tie with the United States in their final match. Eight
of the 12 members of the British team were born in Great Britain, but moved to
Canada as children and learned to play ice hockey there. A ninth player, Gordon
Dailley, was actually born in Canada and served in the Canadian Army.

1948 St. Moritz T: 9, N: 9, D: 2.8.

		W	L	T	PF	PA
1. CAN	(Murray Dowey, Bernard Dunster, Jean Orval Gravelle, Patrick	7	0	1	69	5
	Guzzo, Walter Halder, Thomas Hibbert, Henri-André Laperrière,					
	John Lecompte, George Mara, Albert Renaud, Reginald					
	Schroeter, Irving Taylor)					
2. CZE	(Vladimir Bouzek, Augustin Bubnik, Jaroslav Drobny, Přemysl	7	0	1	80	18
	Hajny, Zdenek Jarkovský, Stanislav Konopásek, Bohumil Modry,					
	Miloslav Pokorny, Václav Rozinák, Moroslav Sláma, Karel Stibor,					
	Vilibald Štovik, Ladislav Troják, Josef Trousilek, Oldřich Zábrod-					
	sky, Vladimir Zábrodský, Vladimir Kobranov)					
3. SWI	(Hans Bänninger, Alfred Bieler, Heinrich Boller, Ferdinand Cat-	6	2	0	67	21
	tini, Hans Cattini, Hans Dürst, Walter Dürst, Emil Handschin, Heini					
	Lohrer, Werner Lohrer, Reto Perl, Gebhard Poltera, Ulrich Poltera,					
	Beat Rüedi, Otto Schubiger, Richard Torriani, Hans Trepp)					
—USA	(Robert Baker, Ruben Bjorkman, Robert Boeser, Bruce Cunliffe,	5	3	0	86	33
	John Garrity, Donald Geary, Goodwin Harding, Herbert Van					
	Ingen, John Kirrane, Bruce Mather, Allan Opsahl, Fred Pearson,					
	Stanton Priddy, Jack Riley, Ralph Warburton)					
4. SWE	(Stig Andersson, Åke Andersson, Stig Carlsson, Åke Ericson, Rolf	4	4	0	55	28
	Ericson, Svante Granlund, Arne Johansson, Rune Johansson,					
	Gunnar Landelius, Klas Lindström, Lars Ljungman, Holger					
	Nurmela, Bror Pettersson, Rolf Pettersson, Kurt Svanberg, Sven					
	Thunman)					
5. GBR	(Leonard Baker, George Baillie, James Chappell, J. Gerry Davey,	3	5	0	39	47
	Frederick Dunkelman, Arthur Green, Frank Green, Frank Jardine,					
	John Murray, John Oxley, Stanley Simon, William Smith, Archi-					
	bald Stinchcombe, Thomas Syme)					
6. POL	(Henryk Bromer, Mieczyslaw Burda, Stefan Csorich, Tadeusz	2	6	0	20	97
	Dolewski, Alfred Gansiniec, Thomas Jasiński, Mieczslaw					
	Kasprzycki, Boleslaw Kolasa, Adam Kowalski, Eugeniusz					
	Lewacki, Jan Maciejko, Czeslaw Marchewczyk, Mieczyslaw Pa-					
	lus, Henryk Przeździecki, Hilary Skarzyński, Maksymilian Wiecek,					
	Ernest Ziaja)					

		W	L	T	PF	PA
7. AUT	(Albert Böhm, Franz Csöngei, Friedrich Demmer, Egon Engel, Walter Feistritzer, Gustav Gross, Adolf Hafner, Alfred Huber, Julius Juhn, Oskar Nowack, Jörg Reichel, Johann Schneider, Willibald Stanek, Herbert Ulrich, Fritz Walter, Helfried Winger, Rudolf Wurmbrandt)	1	7	0	33	77
8. ITA	(C. Apollonio, G. Bassi, M. Bedogni, L. Bestagini, C. Bulgheroni, I. Dionisi, A. Fabris, V. Fardella, A. Federici, U. Gerli, D. Innocenti, C. Mangini, D. Menardi, O. Rauth, F. Rossi, G. Zopegni)	0	8	0	24	156

The controversy that engulfed the 1948 ice hockey tournament actually began a year earlier, when the International Ice Hockey Federation ruled that the Amateur Athletic Union was being replaced as the governing body for amateur ice hockey in the United States by the American Hockey Association (A.H.A.). Avery Brundage, chairman of the American Olympic Committee (A.O.C.), accused the A.H.A. of being under commercial sponsorship and refused to sanction its team. Consequently, two U.S. teams arrived in Switzerland prepared to play in the Olympic tournament. Two days before the opening ceremony, the executive committee of the International Olympic Committee (I.O.C.) voted to bar both U.S. teams from competition. However, the Swiss Olympic Committee, siding with the International Ice Hockey Federation, defied the International Olympic Committee and announced that the A.H.A. team would be allowed to play. The A.O.C. team got to take part in the opening-day parade, while the A.H.A. team watched from the stands. But after that, the A.O.C. team had nothing to do but enjoy their paid vacation.

Meanwhile, the A.H.A. players raked up a couple of amazing scores, beating Poland 23–4 and Italy 31–1. Their coach justified these thrashings because the rules stated that if two teams were tied at the end of the tournament, the one with the largest cumulative scoring margin would be declared the winner.

' The I.O.C. disowned the ice hockey tournament, but later gave it official approval on the condition that the A.H.A. team not be included in the placings.

With one day left in the competition, three nations—Canada, Czechoslovakia, and Switzerland—all had a chance to finish in first place. In the morning Czechoslovakia defeated the United States, 4–3, which eliminated Switzerland's hopes of placing higher than second. The final match pitted Canada against the Swiss. Two days earlier the Czechs and the Canadians had played a 0–0 tie. Consequently, Canada needed to beat Switzerland by at least two goals to win the gold medal on the basis of the goal differential tie-breaker. About 5000 Swiss perched on mountain cliffs and watched the game, pelting officials with snowballs whenever they disagreed with a call. Their enthusiasm did little good, as the Canadian team tallied a goal in each period and won, 3–0. A final note about the Italian team: in addition to their 31–1 loss to the United States, they lost to Sweden 23–0, Canada 21–1, Czechoslovakia 22–3, and Switzerland 16–0.

1952 Oslo T: 9, N: 9, D: 2.24.

		W	L	T	PF	PA
1. CAN	(George Abel, John Davies, William Dawe, Robert Dickson, Donald Gauf, William Gibson, Ralph Hansch, Robert Meyers, David Miller, Eric Paterson, Thomas Pollock, Allan Purvis, Gordon Robertson, Louis Secco, Francis Sullivan, Robert Watt)	7	0	1	71	14
2. USA	(Ruben Bjorkman, Leonard Ceglarski, Joseph Czarnota, Richard Desmond, Andre Gambucci, Clifford Harrison, Gerald Kilmartin, John Mulhern, John Noah, Arnold Oss, Robert Rompre, James Sedin, Allen Van, Donald Whiston, Kenneth Yackel)	6	1	1	43	21

3. SWE (Göte Almqvist, Hans Andersson, Stig "Tvilling" Andersson, Åke Andersson, Lars Björn, Göte Blomqvist, Thord Flodqvist, Erik Johansson, Gösta Johansson, Rune Johansson, Sven Johansson, Åke Lassas, Holger Nurmela, Hans Öberg, Lars Pettersson, Lars Svensson, Sven Thunman) 7 2 0 53 22

4. CZE (Slavomir Barton, Miloslav Blažek, Václav Bubnik, Vlastimil Bubnik, Miloslav Charouzd, Bronislav Danda, Karel Gut, Vlastimil Hajšman, Jan Lidral, Miroslav Nový, Miloslav Ošmera, Zdenek Pýcha, Miroslav Rejman, Jan Richter, Oldrich Sedlak, Jiri Sekyra, Josef Záhorsky) 6 3 0 50 23

5. SWI (Gian Bazzi, Hans Bänninger, François Blank, Bixio Celio, Reto Delnon, Walter Dürst, Emil Golaz, Emil Handschin, Paul Hofer, Willy Pfister, Gebhard Poltera, Ulrich Poltera, Otto Schläpfer, Otto Schubiger, Alfred Streun, Hans Trepp, Paul Wyss) 4 4 0 40 40

6. POL (Michal Antuszewicz, Henryk Bromowicz, Kazimierz Chodakowski, Stefan Csorich, Rudolf Czech, Alfred Gansiniec, Jan Hampel, Marian Jezak, Eugeniusz Lewacki, Roman Pęczek, Hilary Skarzyński, Konstanty Świcarz, Stanislaw Szlendak, Zdzislaw Trojanowski, Adolf Wróbel, Alfred Wróbel) 2 5 1 21 56

7. FIN (Yrjo Hakala, Aarne Honkavaara, Erkki Hytonen, Pentti Isotalo, Matti Karumaa, Ossi Kauppi, Keijo Kuusela, Kauko Makinen, Pekka Myllyla, Christian Rapp, Esko Rehoma, Matti Rintakoski, Eero Saari, Eero Salisma, Lauri Silvan, Unto Vitala, Jukka Vuolio) 2 6 0 21 60

8. GER (Karl Bierschel, Markus Egen, Karl Enzler, Georg Guggemos, Alfred Hoffmann, Engelbert Holderied, Walter Kremershof, Ludwig Kuhn, Dieter Niess, Hans Georg Pescher, Fritz Poitsch, Herbert Schibukat, Xaver Unsinn, Heinz Wackers, Karl Wild) 1 6 1 21 53

Canada, represented by the Edmonton Mercurys, won their first seven games. A final 3–3 tie with the United States gave them the championship. The Americans were just as thrilled by the outcome, since it meant they would finish second instead of fourth. The U.S. team was not popular with the spectators because of their rough style of play. In fact, three of the U.S. players, Czarnota, Yackel, and Gambucci, spent more time in the penalty box than the team totals of any of the other eight teams in the tournament.

Between 1920 and 1952, Canadian ice hockey teams compiled an extraordinary Olympic record of 37 wins, 1 loss, and 3 ties. In those 41 games they scored 403 goals while allowing only 34.

1956 Cortina T: 10, N: 10, D: 2.4.

		W	L	T	PF	PA
1.	SOV (Yevgeny Babich, Usevolod Bobrov, Nikolai Chlystov, Aleksei Guryshev, Yuri Krylov, Alfred Kuchevsky, Valentin Kusin, Grigory Mkrtchan, Viktor Nikiforov, Yuri Pantyuchov, Nikolai Puchkov, Viktor Shuvalov, Genrich Sidorenkov, Nikolai Sologubov, Ivan Tregubov, Dmitri Ukolov, Aleksandr Uvarov)	7	0	0	40	9
2.	USA (Wendell Anderson, Wellington Burnett, Eugene Campbell, Gordon Christian, William Cleary, Richard Dougherty, Willard Ikola, John Matchefts, John Mayasich, Daniel McKinnon, Richard Meredith, Weldon Olson, John Petroske, Kenneth Purpur, Donald Rigazio, Richard Rodenheiser, Edward Sampson)	5	2	0	33	16
3.	CAN (Denis Brodeur, Charles Brooker, William Colvin, Alfred Horne, Arthur Hurst, Byrle Klinck, Paul Knox, Kenneth Laufman, Howard Lee, James Logan, Floyd Martin, Jack McKenzie, Donald Rope, Georges Scholes, Gérald Théberge, Robert White, Keith Woodall)	6	2	0	53	12

		W	L	T	PF	PA
4. SWE	(Lars Björn, Sigurd Bröms, Stig Carlsson, Yngve Casslind, Sven Johansson, Vilgot Larsson, Åke Lassas, Lars-Erik Lundvall, Ove Malmberg, Nils Nilsson, Holger Nurmela, Hans Öberg, Ronald Pettersson, Lars Svensson, Hans Tvilling [Andersson], Stig "Tvilling" Andersson, Bertz Zetterberg)	2	4	1	17	27
5. CZE	(Stanislav Bacilek, Stavomir Barton, Václav Bubnik, Vlastimil Bubnik, Jaromir Bünter, Otto Čimrman, Bronislav Danda, Karel Gut, Jan Jendek, Jan Kasper, Miroslav Kluc, Ždenek Návrat, Václav Pantuček, Bohumil Prošek, František Vaněk, Jan Vodička, Vladimir Zábrodsky)	3	4	0	32	36
6. GER	(Paul Ambros, Martin Beck, Toni Biersack, Karl Bierschel, Markus Egen, Arthur Endress, Bruno Guttowski, Alfred Hoffmann, Hans Huber, Ulrich Jansen, Günther Jochems, Rainer Kossmann, Rudolf Pittrich, Hans Rampf, Kurt Sepp, Ernst Trautwein, Martin Zach)	1	5	2	15	41
7. ITA	(Carmine Tucci, Carlo Montemurro, Aldo Federici, Mario Bedogni, Bernardo Tomei, Giovanni Furlani, Giampiero Branduardi, Aldo Maniacco, Ernesto Crotti, Giancarlo Agazzi, Gianfranco Darin, Rino Alberton, Giulio Oberhammer, Francesco Macchietto)	3	1	2	26	14
8. POL	(Janusz Zawadzki, Kazimierz Chodakowski, Stanislaw Olczyk, Mieczyslaw Chmura, Henryk Bromowicz, Józef Kurek, Zdzislaw Nowak, Szymon Janiczko, Adolf Wróbel, Kazimierz Bryniarski, Marian Herda, Hilary Skarżyński, Bronislaw Gosztyla, Rudolf Czech, Alfred Wróbel, Edward Koczᶏb, Wladyslaw Pabisz)	2	3	0	15	22

The Soviet team made a great impression, not only with their excellent play, but with their good sportsmanship and clean style as well.

1960 Squaw Valley T: 9, N: 9, D: 2.28.

		W	L	T	PF	PA
1. USA	(Roger Christian, William Christian, Robert Cleary, William Cleary, Eugene Grazia, Paul Johnson, John Kirrane, John Mayasich, Jack McCartan, Robert McVey, Richard Meredith, Weldon Olson, Edwyn Owen, Rodney Paavola, Lawrence Palmer, Richard Rodenheiser, Thomas Williams)	7	0	0	48	17
2. CAN	(Robert Attersley, Maurice "Moe" Benoit, James Connelly, Jack Douglas, Fred Etcher, Robert Forhan, Donald Head, Harold Hurley, Kenneth Laufman, Floyd Martin, Robert McKnight, Clifford-Pennington, Donald Rope, Robert Rousseau, George Samolenko, Harry Sinden, Darryl Sly)	6	1	0	55	15
3. SOV	(Veniamin Aleksandrov, Aleksandr Alyimetov, Yuri Baulin, Mikhail Bychkov, Vladimir Grebennikov, Yevgeny Groshev, Viktor Yakushev, Yevgeny Yerkin, Nikolai Karpov, Alfred Kuchevsky, Konstantin Loktev, Stanislav Petuchov, Viktor Prjazhnikov, Nikolai Puchkov, Genrich Sidorenkov, Nikolai Sologubov, Yuri Tsitsinov)	4	2	1	40	23
4. CZE	(Vlastimil Bubnik, Josef Černy, Bronislav Danda, Vladimir Dvořaček, Josef Golonka, Karel Gut, Jaroslav Jiřik, Jan Kasper, František Maslan, Vladimir Nadrchal, Vaclav Pantuček, Rudolf Potsch, Jan Starsi, František Tikal, František Vanek, Miroslav Vlach, Jaroslav Volf)	3	4	0	44	31

5. SWE	(Anders Andersson, Lars Björn, Gert Blomé, Sigurd Bröms, Einar Granath, Sven Johansson, Bengt Lindqvist, Lars-Erik Lundvall, Nils Nilsson, Bert-Ola Nordlander, Carl-Göran Öberg, Ronald Pettersson, Ulf Sterner, Roland Stoltz, Hans Svedberg, Kjell Svensson, Sune Wretling)	2	4	1	40	24
6. GER	(Paul Ambros, Georg Eberl, Markus Egen, Ernst Eggerbauer, Michael Hobelsberger, Hans Huber, Uli Jansen, Hans Rampf, Josef Reif, Otto Schneitberger, Siegfried Schubert, Horst Schuldes, Kurt Sepp, Ernst Trautwein, Xaver Unsinn, Leonhard Waitl, Horst Metzer)	1	6	0	9	54
7. FIN	(Yrjo Hakala, Raimo Kilpiö, Kolso, Lampainen, Esko Luostarinen, Niemii, Nieminen, Kalevi Numminen, Heino Pulli, Rassa, Rastio, Jouni Seistamo, Sonio, Vainio, Juhani Wahlsten)	3	2	1	63	23
8. JPN	(Akazawa, S. Honma, T. Honma, H. Inatsu, A. Irie, Iwaoka, Kakihara, Miyasaki, Murano, I. Ono, Segawa, S. Shimada, Takagi, Takeshima, M. Tanabu, Tomita, Yamada)	2	3	1	34	68

When they first started playing together, the U.S. squad hardly seemed to be the "Team of Destiny" that they were to become. Before leaving for Squaw Valley, they played an 18-game training tour and compiled an unimpressive record of ten wins, four losses, and four ties. Not only did they lose to Michigan Tech and Denver University, but less than three weeks before the Olympics began, the U.S. team actually lost, 7–5, to the Warroad Lakers of Warroad, Minnesota. However their first Olympic match set the tone for the rest of the tournament. Trailing Czechoslovakia 4–3 after two periods, they scored four straight goals in the final period and won, 7–5. This was followed by three convincing victories over Australia (12–1), Sweden (6–3), and Germany (9–1).

On February 25 they faced the cofavorite Canadian team. Bob Cleary of Westwood, Massachusetts, took a pass from John Mayasich and scored the first goal after 12 minutes and 47 seconds. Paul Johnson, formerly of the University of Minnesota, scored an unassisted goal in the second period, and the United States held on to win, 2–1. The real star of the game was goalie Jack McCartan, who turned back 39 shots, including 20 in the second period alone.

Two days later the United States went up against the defending champions from the U.S.S.R. The Americans drew first blood after 4:04 of the first period, when Bill Cleary scored after taking a pass from his brother Bob. However the Soviets tied the score a minute later on a goal by Aleksandrov. At the 9:37 mark Bychkov struck from 15 feet in front of the cage and the U.S.S.R. led 2–1. Their lead held for the rest of the first period and most of the second until Billy Christian, with an assist from *his* brother, Roger, fired a shot past Puchkov, the Soviet goalie, to make the score 2–2. The two teams fought on even terms for the next 24 minutes. Then, with five minutes to play, the Christian brothers teamed up for another goal. From there on McCartan took over and heroically protected the U.S. goal, while the partisan overflow crowd screamed with joy. It was the first time that the United States had beaten the U.S.S.R. at ice hockey.

All that stood between the U.S. team and the Olympic championship was an eight a.m. game the next day against the same Czechoslovakian team they had beaten to open the tournament. But the Americans were so emotionally spent that they were unable to sleep, and they arrived at the arena exhausted and tense. The Czechs wasted no time, scoring their first goal after only eight seconds. After two periods, Czechoslovakia led 4–3. During the break between periods, Nikolai Sologubov, the captain of the U.S.S.R. team, entered the U.S. dressing room to give the Americans a piece of advice. Since he didn't speak English, Sologubov pantomimed that the U.S. players should take some oxygen. A tank was obtained, and the revived Americans went back on the ice with visions of the gold medals that were almost within their grasp. After almost six scoreless minutes, the U.S. team went on a rampage, as the Clearys and Christians scored six straight goals to win 9–4. The very same team that had lost to the Warroad, Minnesota, Lakers had won the Olympic gold medal.

A few words about the 1960 Australian team: They lost all six of their matches, giving up 88 goals while scoring only ten. Even when things went right for the Australians they went wrong. Trailing in the first period of a consolation match against Finland, Cunningham scored Australia's only goal of the game. In his excited attempt to follow through the shot, Australian center Ivor Vesley went straight into the net, smashed his head on the iron crossbar, and had to be taken to the hospital. Finland won, 14–1.

1964 Innsbruck T: 16, N: 16, D: 2.8.

		W	L	T	PF	PA
1. SOV	(Veniamin Aleksandrov, Aleksandr Alyimetov, Vitaly Davydov, Anatoly Firsov, Eduard Ivanov, Viktor Konovalenko, Viktor Kuzkin, Konstantin Loktev, Boris Mayorov, Yevgeny Mairov, Stanislav Petuchov, Aleksandr Ragulin, Vyacheslav Starshinov, Leonid Volkov, Victor Yakushev, Boris Zaitsev)	7	0	0	54	10
2. SWE	(Anders Andersson, Gert Blomé, Lennart Häggroth, Lennart Johansson, Nils Johansson, Sven "Tumba" Johansson, Lars Lundvall, Eilert Määttä, Hans Mild, Nils Nilsson, Bert Nordlander, Carl Öberg, Uno Öhrlund, Ronald Pettersson, Ulf Sterner, Roland Stoltz, Kjell Svensson)	5	2	0	47	16
3. CZE	(Vlastimil Bubnik, Josef Černý, Jiři Dolana, Vladimir Dzurilla, Josef Golonka, František Gregor, Jiři Holik, Jaroslav Jiřik, Jan Klapáč, Vladimir Nadrchal, Rudolf Potsch, Stanislav Pryl, Ladislav Smid, Stanislav Sventek, František Tikal, Miroslav Vlach, Jaroslav Walter)	5	2	0	38	19
4. CAN	(Henry Akervall, Gary Begg, Roger Bourbonnais, Kenneth Broderick, Raymond Cadieux, Terrence Clancy, Brian Conacher, Paul Conlin, Gary Dineen, Robert Forhan, Larry Johnston, Seth Martin, John McKenzie, Terrence O'Malley, Rodney-Albert Seiling, George-Raymond Swarbrick)	5	2	0	32	17
5. USA	(David Brooks, Herbert Brooks, Roger Christian, William Christian, Paul Coppo, Daniel Dilworth, Dates Fryberger, Paul Johnson, Thomas Martin, James McCoy, Wayne Meredith, William Reichart, Donald Ross, Patrick Rupp, Gary Schmaltzbauer, James Westby, Thomas Yurkovich)	2	5	0	29	33
6. FIN	(Raimo Kilpiö, Juhani Lahtinen, Rauno Lehtiö, Esko Luostarinen, Ilka Mäsikämmen, Seppo Nikkilä, Kalevi Numminen, Lasse Oksanen, Jorma Peltonen, Heino Pulli, Matti Reunamäki, Jouni Seistamo, Jorma Suokko, Juhani Wahlsten, Jarmo Wasama)	2	5	0	10	31
7. GER	(Paul Ambros, Bernd Herzig, Michael Hobelsberger, Ernst Köpf, Albert Loibl, Josef Reif, Otto Schneitberger, Georg Scholz, Siegfried Schubert, Dieter Schwimmbeck, Ernst Trautwein, Leonhard Waitl, Helmut Zanghellini)	2	5	0	13	49
8. SWI	(Franz Berry, Roger Chappot, Rolf Diethelm, Elvin Friedrich, Gaston Furrer, Oskar Jenny, René Kiener, Pio Parolini, Kurt Pfammatter, Gerald Rigolet, Max Ruegg, Walter Salzmann, Herold Truffer, Peter Wespi, Otto Wittwer)	0	7	0	9	57

The tournament was actually much closer than the standings make it appear. If Canada had been able to defeat the U.S.S.R. in their final match, they would have finished first instead of fourth. The Canadians did in fact take a 2–1 lead, but the well-balanced Soviet team tied the score with a goal by Starshinov at the end of the second period. The U.S.S.R. gained a 3–2 victory, thanks to an early third-period goal by Veniamin Aleksandrov. During the Canada-Sweden match (won by Canada 3–1), Sweden's Karl Oberg bashed the Canadian coach, Father David Bauer, on the head with his stick. Bauer ordered his players not to retaliate. They grudgingly obeyed. The referee was suspended for two games for failing to give Oberg a 10-minute misconduct penalty.

1968 Grenoble T: 14, N: 14, D: 2.17.

			W	L	T	PF	PA
1.	SOV	(Viktor Konovalenko, Viktor Zinger, Viktor Blinov, Aleksandr Ragulin, Viktor Kuzkin, Oleg Zaitsev, Igor Romichevsky, Vitaly Davydov, Yevgeny Zymin, Vyacheslav Starshinov, Boris Mayorov, Viktor Polupanov, Anatoly Firsov, Yuri Moiseyev, Anatoly Ionov, Yevgeny Michakov, Veniamin Aleksandrov, Vladimir Vikulov)	6	1	0	48	10
2.	CZE	(Vladimir Dzurilla, Vladimir Nadrchal, Josef Horešovský, Karel Masopust, Jan Suchý, František Pospišil, Jan Hrbatý, Jiři Kochta, Jan Klapáč, Jiři Holik, František Sevčik, Jaroslav Jiřik, Josef Černý, Jan Havel, Petr Hejma, Václav Nedomanský, Jozef Golonka, Oldřich Machač, Petr Hejma)	5	1	1	33	17
3.	CAN	(Wayne Stephenson, Kenneth Broderick, Terrence O'Malley, Paul Conlin, John Barry MacKenzie, Brian Glennie, Marshall Johnstone, Francis Huck, Morris Mott, Raymond Cadieux, Gerry Pinder, Stephen Monteith, Dan O'Shea, Roger Bourbonnais, William McMillan, Ted Hargreaves, Gary Dineen, Herbert Pinder)	5	2	0	28	15
4.	SWE	(Leif Holmqvist, Hans Dahllöf, Lars-Erik Sjöberg, Arne Carlsson, Lennart Svedberg, Roland Stoltz, Nils Johansson, Björn Palmqvist, Folke Bengtsson, Carl-Göran Öberg, Håkan Wickberg, Tord Lundström, Henric Hedlund, Svante Granholm, Roger Olsson, Leif Henriksson, Lars-Göran Nilsson)	4	2	1	23	18
5.	FIN	(Urpo Ylönen, Pentti Koskela, Paavo Tirkonen, Juha Rantasila, Ilpa Koskela, Pekka Kuusisto, Lalli Partinen, Seppo Lindström, Matti Reunamäki, Juhani Wahlsten, Matti Keinonen, Lasse Oksanen, Jorma Peltonen, Esa Peltonen, Karl Johanson, Veli-Pekka Ketola, Matti Harju, Pekka Leimu)	4	3	1	28	25
6.	USA	(Herbert Brooks, John Cunniff, John Dale, Craig Falkman, Robert Paul Hurley, Thomas Hurley, Leonard Lilyholm, James Logue, John Morrison, Louis Nanne, Robert Paradise, Lawrence Pleau, Bruce Riutta, Donald Ross, Patrick Rupp, Larry Stordahl, Douglas Volmar, Patrick Loyne)	2	4	1	23	28
7.	GER	(Ernst Köpf, Bernd Kuhn, Lorenz Funk, Gustav Hanig, Horst Meindl, Heinz Weisenbach, Leonhard Waitl, Heinz Bader, Josef Schramm, Günther Knauss, Hans Schichtl, Josef Völk, Rudolf Thanner, Manfred Gmeiner, Peter Lax, Josef Reif, Alois Schloder)	2	6	0	20	39
8.	GDR	(Ullrich Noack, Bernd Karrenbauer, Hartmut Nickel, Helmut Novy, Wolfgang Plotka, Wilfried Sock, Dieter Pürschel, Klaus Hirche, Dieter Kratzsch, Dieter Voigt, Manfred Buder, Lothar Fuchs, Peter Prusa, Joachim Ziesche, Bernd Poindl, Dietmar Peters, Bernd Hiller, Rüdiger Noack)	1	7	0	16	49

The final outcome of the 1968 competition was still in doubt with only two matches left to be played. The heavily favored Soviet team had received a shocking 5–4 defeat at the hands of Czechoslovakia, their first loss since 1963. This meant that the championship hinged on the games between Czechoslovakia and Sweden and the U.S.S.R. and Canada, all of whom had records of five wins and one loss. A Czech win combined with a Soviet win would give the gold medal to Czechoslovakia. However, the overcautious Czechoslovakian players, physically and emotionally exhausted by their upset victory over the U.S.S.R. in their previous game, fell behind the determined Swedes 2–1 late in the second period. They managed to score one goal to tie in the seventh minute of the final period, but that was all. The game ended in a 2–2 draw, which closed the door on Czechoslovakia's chances for first place. This left the Canada-U.S.S.R. match to decide the winner. Firsov scored first for the Soviets after 14:51. Michakov made it 2–0 after 12:44 of the second period. Three more Soviet goals in the final period settled the issue, 5–0 for the U.S.S.R.

1972 Sapporo T: 11, N: 11, D: 2.13.

			W	L	T	PF	PA
1.	SOV	(Vladislav Tretiak, Aleksandr Pachkov, Vitaly Davydov, Vladimir Lutchenko, Aleksandr Ragulin, Viktor Kuzkin, Gennady Tsygankov, Valery Vasilyev, Valery Kharlamov, Yuri Blinov, Vladimir Petrov, Anatoly Firsov, Aleksandr Maltsev, Vladimir Chadrin, Boris Mikhailov, Vladimir Vikulov, Aleksandr Yakushev)	4	0	1	33	13
2.	USA	(Michael Curran, Peter Sears, James McElmury, Thomas Mellor, Frank Sanders, Charles Brown, Richard McGlynn, Walter Olds, Kevin Ahearn, Stuart Irving, Mark Howe, Henry Boucha, Keith Christiansen, Robbie Ftorek, Ronald Naslund, Craig Sarner, Timothy Sheehy)	4	2	0	23	18
3.	CZE	(Vladimir Dzurilla, Jiři Holeček, František Pospišil, Karel Vohralik, Josef Horešovský, Oldřich Machač, Vladimir Bednář, Rudolf Tajcnár, Josef Černý, Jiři Holik, Bohuslav Štastný, Richard Farda, Ivan Hlinka, Vacláv Nedomanský, Jiři Kochta, Vladimir Martinec, Eduard Novák, Jaroslav Holik)	4	2	0	34	15
4.	SWE	(Leif Holmqvist, Christer Abrahamsson, Thomas Abrahamsson, Lars-Erik Sjöberg, Kjell-Rune Milton, Stig Östling, Bert-Ola Nordlander, Kenneth Ekman, Tord Lundstrom, Lars-Göran Nilsson, Håkan Pettersson, Håkan Wickberg, Mats Åhlberg, Björn Palmqvist, Hans Hansson, Inge Hammarström, Hans Lindberg, Thomas Bergman, Stig-Göran Johansson, Mats Lindh)	3	2	1	25	14
5.	FIN	(Jorma Valtonen, Stig Wetzell, Ilpo Koskela, Seppo Lindström, Heikki Riihiranta, Heikki Järn, Juha Rantasila, Pekka Marjamäki, Jorma Vehmanen, Jorma Peltonen, Veli-Pekka Ketola, Matti Murto, Matti Keinonen, Harri Linnonmaa, Juhani Tamminen, Lasse Oksanen, Esa Peltonen, Jorma Peltonen, Seppo Repo, Lauri Mononen, Timo Turunen)	3	3	0	27	25
6.	POL	(Andrzej Tkacz, Walery Kosyl, Ludwik Czachowski, Stanislaw Fryźlewicz, Jerzy Potz, Marian Feter, Adam Kopczyński, Andrzej Szczepaniec, Feliks Góralczyk, Tadeusz Kacik, Krzysztof Bialynicki, Józef Slowakiewicz, Leszek Tokarz, Wieslaw Tkacz, Józef Batkiewicz, Tadeusz Oblój, Walenty Ziętara, Robert Góralczyck, Stefan Chowaniec)	1	5	0	13	39
7.	GER	(Anton Kehle, Rainer Makatsch, Otto Schneitberger, Josef Völk, Werner Modes, Paul Langner, Rudolf Thanner, Karl Egger, Rainer Phillip, Bernd Kuhn, Reinhold Bauer, Johann Eimannsberger, Lorenz Funk, Erich Kühnhackl, Alois Schloder, Anton Hofherr, Hans Rothkirch)	3	2	0	22	14
8.	NOR	(Kare Ostensen, Tore Walberg, Oyvind Berg, Jan Kinder, Svein Hansen, Terje Steen, Birger Jansen, Thor Martinsen, Tom Roymark, Thom Kristensen, Steinar Bjolbakk, Svein Hagensten, Roy Jansen, Bjorn Johansen, Morten Sethereng, Terje Thoen, Arne Mikkelsen)	3	2	0	17	27

Again the championship was decided by the final match—this time between the U.S.S.R. and Czechoslovakia. The winner-take-all game turned out to be an anticlimax, as the Soviet team took a 4–0 lead in the second period and coasted to a 5–2 victory. The United States was awarded second place because they had beaten Czechoslovakia, 5–1. For the first time since the Winter Olympics began, Canada did not take part in the ice hockey tournament. The Canadians withdrew from international amateur competition in 1969 because they objected to facing the professional amateurs of the U.S.S.R. and other Communist countries.

1976 Innsbruck T: 12, N: 12, D: 2.14.

			W	L	PF	PA
1.	SOV	(Vladislav Tretiak, Aleksandr Sidelnikov, Boris Aleksandrov, Sergei Babinov, Aleksandr Gusiev, Valery Kharlamov, Aleksandr Yakushev, Viktor Zlukov, Sergei Kapustin, Vladimir Lutchenko, Yuri Lyapkin, Aleksandr Maltsev, Boris Mikhailov, Vladimir Petrov, Vladimir Chadrin, Viktor Szalimov, Gennady Tsygankov, Valery Vasilyev)	5	0	40	11
2.	CZE	(Jiři Holeček, Jiři Crha, Oldřich Machač, Milan Chalupa, František Pospišil, Miroslav Dvořák, Milan Kajkl, Jiři Bubla, Milan Nový, Vladimir Martinec, Jiři Novák, Bohuslav Štastný, Jiri Holik, Ivan Hlinka, Eduard Novák, Jaroslav Pouzar, Bohuslav Ebermann, Josef Augusta)	2	2	17	10
3.	GER	(Erich Weishaupt, Anton Kehle, Rudolf Thanner, Josef Völk, Udo Kiessling, Stefan Metz, Klaus Auhuber, Ignaz Berndaner, Rainer Philipp, Lorenz Funk, Wolfgang Boos, Ernst Köpf, Ferenc Vozar, Walter Köberle, Erich Kühnhackl, Alois Schloder, Martin Hinterstorcker, Franz Reindl)	2	3	21	24
4.	FIN	(Matti Hagman, Reijo Laksola, Antti Leppänen, Henry Leppä, Seppo Lindström, Pekka Marjamäki, Matti Murto, Timo Nummelin, Esa Peltonen, Timo Saari, Jorma Vehmanen, Urpo Ylönen, Hannu Haapalainen, Seppo Ahokainen, Tapio Koskinen, Pertti Koivulahti, Hannu Kapanen, Matti Rautiainen)	2	3	19	18
5.	USA	(Steven Alley, Daniel Bolduc, Blane Comstock, Robert Dobek, Robert Harris, Jeffrey Hymanson, Paul Jensen, Steven Jensen, Richard Lamby, Robert Lundeen, Robert Miller, Douglas Ross, Gary Ross, William "Buzz" Schneider, Stephen Sertich, John Taft, Theodore Thorndike, James Warden)	2	3	15	21
6.	POL	(Stefan Chowaniec, Andrzej Tkacz, Andrzej Iskrzycki, Marek Marcińczak, Josef Matiewicz, Tadeusz Obłój, Jerzy Potz, Andrzej Slowakiewicz, Andrzej Zabawa, Walenty Ziętara, Karol Žurek, Walery Kosyl, Robert Góralczyk, Kordian Jajszczok, Wieslaw Jobezyk, Leszek Kokoszka, Henryk Pytel, Mieczyslaw Jaskierski, Marian Kajzerek)	0	4	9	37
7.	ROM	(Valerian Netedu, Vasile Morar, Elöd Antal, Sandor Gall, George Justinian, Ion Ionita, Desideriu Varga, Doru Morosan, Doru Tureanu, Dumitru Axinte, Eduard Pana, Vasile Hutanu, Ion Gheorghiu, Tibri Miclos, Alexandru Halauca, Marian Pisaru, Nicolae Visan)	4	1	23	15
8.	AUT	(Daniel Gritsch, Franz Schilcher, Walter Schneider, Gerhard Hausner, Johann Schuller, Michael Herzog, Günther Oberhuber, Othmar Russ, Max Moser, Rudolf Koenig, Josef Ruschnig, Franz Voves, Josef Schwitzer, Peter Cini, Josef Kriechbaum, Alexander Sadjina, Herbert Poek, Herbert Moertl)	3	2	18	14

The tournament was thrown into confusion when Czechoslovakia's captain, František Pospišil, was chosen for a random drug test after a victory over Poland. The team trainer immediately admitted that Pospišil had been given codeine to combat a virus infection. The I.O.C. expelled Pospišil and ordered the game against Poland declared null and void. The final decision on the case was actually delayed, so as not to spoil the drama of the winner-take-all game between Czechoslovakia and the U.S.S.R. In that match, the Czechs led 3–2 in the final period. But with five minutes to play Aleksandr Yakushev tied the score. Twenty-four seconds later Valery Kharlamov knocked the puck into the net again to give the U.S.S.R. their fourth straight set of gold medals in ice hockey.

1980 Lake Placid T: 12, N: 12, D: 2.24.

			W	L	T	PF	PA
1.	USA	(James Craig, Kenneth Morrow, Michael Ramsey, William Baker, John O'Callahan, Bob Suter, David Silk, Neal Broten, Mark Johnson, Steven Christoff, Mark Wells, Mark Pavelich, Eric Strobel, Michael Eruzione, David Christian, Robert McClanahan, William "Buzz" Schneider, Philip Verchota, John Harrington)	6	0	1	33	15
2.	SOV	(Vladimir Myshkin, Vladislav Tretiak, Vyacheslav Fetisov, Vasily Pervukhin, Valery Vasilyev, Aleksei Kasatonov, Sergei Starikov, Zinetula Bilyaletdinov, Vladimir Krutov, Aleksandr Maltsev, Yuri Lebedev, Boris Mikhailov, Vladimir Petrov, Valery Kharlamov, Helmūts Balderis, Viktor Zlukov, Aleksandr Golikov, Sergei Makarov, Vladimir Golikov, Aleksandr Skvortsov)	6	1	0	63	17
3.	SWE	(Per-Eric "Pelle" Lindbergh, William Löfqvist, Tomas Jonsson, Sture Andersson, Ulf Weinstock, Jan Eriksson, Tommy Samuelsson, Mats Waltin, Thomas Eriksson, Per Lundqvist, Mats Åhlberg, Håkan Eriksson, Mats Näslund, Lennart Norberg, Bengt Lundholm, Leif Holmgren, Dan Söderström, Harald Lückner, Lars Mohlin, Bo Berglund)	4	1	2	31	19
4.	FIN	(Antero Kivelä, Jorma Valtonen, Seppo Suoraniemi, Olli Saarinen, Hannu Haapalainen, Tapio Levo, Kari Eloranta, Lasse Litma, Esa Peltonen, Ismo Villa, Mikko Leinonen, Markku Kiimalainen, Jari Kurri, Jukka Koskilahti, Hannu Koskinen, Reijo Leppänen, Markku Hakulinen, JUkka Porvari, Jarmo Mäkitalo, Timo Susi)	3	3	1	31	25
5.	CZE	(Jiři Kralik, Karel Lang, Jan Neliba, Vitezslav Duras, Milan Chalupa, Arnold Kadleč, Miroslav Dvořak, František Kaberle, Jiři Bubla, Milan Nový, Jiři Novák, Miroslav Frycer, Marian Štastný, Anton Štastný, Vincent Lukač, Karel Holy, Jaroslav Pouzar, Bohuslav Ebermann, Peter Štastný)	4	2	0	40	17
6.	CAN	(Robert Dupuis, Paul Pageau, Warren Anderson, J. Bradley Pirie, Randall Gregg, Timothy Watters, D. Joseph Grant, Donald Spring, Terrence O'Malley, Ronald Davidson, Glenn Anderson, Kevin Maxwell, James Nill, John Devaney, Paul Maclean, Daniel D'Alvise, Ken Berry, David Hindmarch, Kevin Primeau, Stelio Zupancich)	3	3	0	29	18
7.	POL	(Henryk Wojtynek, Pawel Lukaszka, Andrzej Ujwary, Henryk Janiszewski, Henryk Gruth, Andrzej Jańczy, Jerzy Potz, Ludwik Synowiec, Marek Marcińczak, Stefan Chowaniec, Wieslaw Jobczyk, Tadeusz Obłój, Dariusz Sikora, Leszek Kokoszka, Andrzej Zabawa, Henryk Pytel, Stanislaw Klocek, Leszek Jachna, Bogdan Dziubiński, Andrzej Malysiak)	2	3	0	15	23
7.	ROM	(Valerian Netedu, Gheorghe Hutan, Mihail Popescu, Ion Berdila, Sandor Gall, Elöd Antal, Istvan Antal, Doru Morosan, George Justinian, Doru Tureanu, Dumitru Axinte, Marian Costea, Constantin Nistor, Alexandru Halauca, Laszlo Solyom, Bela Nagy, Traian Cazacu, Adrian Olenici, Marian Pisaru, Zoltan Nagy)	1	3	1	13	29

Just as Canada dominated Olympic ice hockey from 1920 through 1952, so the Soviet Union took control after that. Between 1956 and 1992 the U.S.S.R. played 68 games, tallying 60 victories, six defeats, and two ties. In those 68 games they scored 457 goals while giving up only 125. The only nation to break the Soviet monopoly has been the United States, which won the ice hockey tournament the two times during that period that the Winter Olympics were held in the United States—in 1960 and 1980. The 1960 and 1980 U.S. squads were remarkably similar. Both were patchwork teams whose success was completely unexpected. Both teams put together a series of upsets and come-from-behind wins, culminating in a come-from-behind victory over the favored Soviet team followed by one final come-from-behind performance against a lesser opponent, who almost spoiled the whole drama.

But there *were* two important differences. The first was television. In 1960 appreciation of the thrilling victories of the U.S. team was limited mostly to sports fans. In 1980 the excitement of the tournament reached into almost every U.S. household and united the country in a remarkable manner. The other difference was the mood of the country. In 1960 most Americans were feeling prosperous and proud. The victory of the Olympic ice hockey team was basically perceived as a pleasant surprise. In 1980 the United States was in the midst of an identity crisis. It is difficult for most people in the world to understand that Americans, as a nation, could ever feel persecuted and mistreated, but that was the case in 1980. With hostages in Iran, Russians in Afghanistan, and inflation on the rise, it seemed that nothing was going right. When President Jimmy Carter ordered a boycott of the Summer Olympics, Americans were left with the Winter Olympics as their only vehicle for regaining a sense of pride in the world arena. The problem was that speed skater Eric Heiden was the only likely prospect for a gold medal that the U.S. had. Then, with theatrically perfect timing, the 20 young men who comprised the U.S. ice hockey team showed up to offer the ideal tonic to cure the American malaise.

Nine of the U.S. players were from the University of Minnesota, as was the coach, two-time Olympian Herb Brooks. Known as "The Khomeini of Ice Hockey," Brooks was a fanatic disciplinarian who told his young team (average age: 22), "Gentlemen, you don't have enough talent to win on talent alone." Instead they played 63 exhibition games, including a final match, three days before the Olympics opened, against the same U.S.S.R. team that had beaten the National Hockey League All-Stars. The U.S. Olympic team was crushed by the Soviets, 10–3. When the tournament began, the United States was seeded seventh out of 12 teams.

The teams were split into two round-robin divisions. The first- and second-place teams in each division would then advance to a final round-robin of four teams. Favored to advance from the division in which the United States had been placed were Czechoslovakia and Sweden, who happened to be the Americans' first two opponents. In the opening game between the United States and Sweden, the Swedes scored first and led 2–1 as the contest entered its final minute. In desperation, Brooks pulled goalie Jim Craig and put in an extra skater. The gamble paid off as Bill Baker slammed in a shot from 55 feet with 27 seconds left in the game, allowing the United States to escape with a tie. Next came the powerful Czech team. Again the United States gave up the first goal, this time after only 2:23 of the first period. However, the Americans had the game tied up 2–2 by the end of the period. Then, surprisingly, they forged ahead to a shocking 7–3 victory. By this time the U.S. ice hockey team had attracted the nation's attention. In their third game, they spotted Norway a 1–0 lead and then scored five goals in the last two periods to win 5–1. Their next match, against Romania, a 7–2 victory, was notable because it was the only one of seven games in which the Americans scored first. Against West Germany they fell behind 2–0 and then won 4–2.

This put the United States into the medal round along with Sweden, Finland, and the U.S.S.R. The 2–2 tie with Sweden was carried over as part of the final round-robin, as was the Soviets' 4–2 victory over Finland. At five p.m. on Friday, February 22, the U.S. team went out onto the ice to face the best ice hockey team in the world, professional or amateur. That morning Coach Brooks had given his team an uncharacteristic pep talk. "You're born to be a player," he said. "You're meant to be here. This moment is yours. You're meant to be here at this time." Not surprisingly, the U.S.S.R. scored the first goal, as Vladimir Krutov cut off a slap shot by Aleksei Kasatonov and deflected it into the net. Buzz Schneider evened the score five minutes later, but three and a half minutes after that Sergei Makorov put the Soviets ahead again. It looked like the period would end with the score 2–1, but Mark Johnson knocked in a blocked shot with one second left, to bring the United States even once more.

When the second period began, Vladislav Tretiak, considered by many to be the best goalie in the world, had been replaced by Vladimir Myshkin. The U.S.S.R. quickly moved back into the lead on a power-play goal by Aleksandr Maltsev at 2:18, and the period ended with the Soviets ahead 3–2. Amazed to find themselves only one goal behind with 20 minutes to play, the U.S. players sensed their destiny. After 8:39 of the third period Mark Johnson picked up the puck as it slipped away from a Soviet defender and shoveled it past Myshkin from five feet out. The United States was tied again. Less than one and a half minutes later, at the ten-minute mark, team captain Mike Eruzione, using a Soviet defender as a screen, fired off a 30-foot shot that went through Myshkin and into the net. The partisan crowd burst into wild cheering that continued for the rest of the game. For the final 10 minutes goalie Jim Craig (who recorded 39 saves in the game) and the rest of the U.S. team fought off a seemingly endless barrage of attacks by the Soviets. When the last seconds had finally ticked off, the emotional excitement that filled the arena was so great that even many of the Soviet players had to smile as they congratulated their American counterparts. Back in the dressing room, the U.S. team sang "God Bless America," even though they couldn't remember all the words. Meanwhile, Coach Brooks had locked himself in the men's room with his emotions. "Finally I snuck out into the hall," he said, "and the state troopers were all standing there crying."

But there was still one more game to be played. In fact, if the United States lost to Finland on February 24, they would only finish in third place, and the U.S.S.R. would win the tournament anyway. And the Finns were not prepared to roll over and concede defeat. They scored first and led 2–1 after two periods. But the Americans had come too far to lose it all in the final match. Dave Christian, whose father and uncle had been members of the 1960 U.S. squad, sent a pass to Phil Verchota, who sped down the left side of the ice and tied the score with a 15-foot shot at 2:25. At 6:05 Rob McClanahan put the United States in the lead with a stuff shot, and at 16:25 Mark Johnson scored an insurance goal. When the game ended three and a half minutes later, the score was 4–2. American TV viewers were treated to two more emotional moments. While the rest of the team jumped for joy and hugged each other, Jim Craig skated around the rink until he found in the crowd the one person with whom he most wanted to share this moment—his widowed father. Later, at the medal ceremony, Mike Eruzione took the stand as the captain of his team. But after the playing of "The Star-Spangled Banner," he called his teammates onto the platform to join him in accepting the cheers of the crowd. Twelve years later, Jim Craig was still receiving 600 fan letters a year.

1984 Sarajevo T: 12, N: 12, D: 2.19.

			W	L	T	PF	PA
1.	SOV	(Zinatula Bilyaletdinov, Sergei Chepelev, Nikolai Drozdetsky,	7	0	0	48	5
		Vyacheslav Fetisov, Aleksandr Gerasimov, Aleksei Kasatonov, An-					
		drei Komutov, Vladimir Kovin, Aleksandr Kozhernikov, Vladimir					
		Krutov, Igor Larionov, Sergei Makarov, Vladimir Myshkin, Vasily					
		Pervukhin, Aleksandr Skvortsov, Sergei Starikov, Igor Stelnov, Vla-					
		dislav Tretiak, Victor Tumenev, Michail Vasiliev)					

			W	L	T	PF	PA
2.	CZE	(Jaroslav Benák, Vladimir Caldr, František Cernik, Milan Chalupa, Miloslav Horava, Jiří Hrdina, Arnold Kadlec, Jaroslav Korbela, Jiří Králik, Vladimir Kynos, Jiří Lála, Igor Liba, Vincent Lukáč, Dušan Pašek, Pavel Richter, Darius Rusnák, Vladimir Růzička, Jaromir Sindel, Radoslav Svoboda, Eduard Uvíra)	6	1	0	40	9
3.	SWE	(Thomas Ahlen, Per-Erik Eklund, Thomas Eklund, Bo Ericsson, Lars Erikson, Peter Gradin, Mats Hessel, Peter Michael Hjälm, Göran Lindblom, Tommy Mörth, Leif Nordin, Jens Öhling, Rolf-Lennart Riddervall, Thomas Rundquist, Tomas Sandström, Karl Södergren, Mats Thelin, Arne Thelvén, Göte Wälitalo, Mats Waltin)	4	2	1	36	17
4.	CAN	(Warren Anderson, Robin Bartel, Russ Courtnall, Jean Daigneault, Kevin Dineen, Dave Donnelly, Bruce Driver, Darren Eliot, Pat Flatley, Dave Gagner, Mario Gosselin, Vaugh Karpan, Doug Lidster, Darren Lowe, Kirk Muller, James Patrick, Craig Redmond, Dave Tippett, Carey Wilson, Dan Wood)	4	3	0	24	16
5.	GER	(Manfred Ahne, Ignaz Berndaner, Michael Betz, Bernhard Englbrecht, Karl Friesen, Dieter Hegen, Ulrich Hiemer, Ernst Höfner, Udo Kiessling, Harold Kreis, Marcus Kuhl, Erich Kühnhackl, Andreas Niederberger, Joachim Reil Franz Reindl, Roy Roedger, Peter Scharf, Helmut Steiger, Gerhard Truntschka, Manfred Wolf)	4	1	1	34	21
6.	FIN	(Raimo Helminen, Risto Jalo, Arto Javanainen, Timo Jutila, Erkki Laine, Markus Lehto, Mika Lehto, Pertti Lehtonen, Jarmo Mäkitalo, Anssi Melametsä, Hannu Oksanen, Arto Ruotanen, Simo Saarinen, Ville Siren, Arto Sirviö, Perti Skriko, Raimo Summanen, Kari Takko, Juka Tammi, Harri Tuohimaa, Jorma Valtonen)	2	3	1	31	26
7.	USA	(Marc Behrend, Barry Scott Bjugstad, Robert Brooke, Chris Chelios, Richard Costello, Mark Fusco, Scott Fusco, Steven Griffith, Paul Guay, Gary Haight, John Harrington, Tomas Hirsch, Al Iafrate, David A. Jensen, David H. Jensen, Kurt Kleinendorst, Mark Kumpel, Pat Lafontaine, Robert Mason, Corey Millen, Edward Olczyk, Gary Sampson, Tim Thomas, Philip Verchota)	2	2	2	23	21
8.	POL	(Janusz Adamiec, Marek Cholewa, Andrzey Chowaniec, Jerzy Christ, Jozef Chrzastek, Czeslaw Drozd, Bogdan Gebczyk, Henrik Gruth, Andrzej Hachula, Andrezej Hanisz, Leszek Jachna, Wieslaw Jobszyk, Stanislaw Klocek, Andrzey Nowak, Wlodzimierz Olszewski, Bogdan Pawlik, Jan Piecko, Henryk Pytel, Gabriel Samolej, Dariusz Sikora, Krystian Sikorski, Jan Stopczyk, Ludwik Synowiec, Robert Szopinski, Andrzej Ujwary, Andrzey Zabawa)	1	5	0	20	44

With the Winter Olympics once again being held outside the United States, the ice hockey tournament returned to normalcy. As usual, the Soviets overwhelmed every team they played. Even their final 2–0 victory over Czechoslovakia was never really in doubt. The U.S. team, seeded seventh, finished seventh.

1988 Calgary T: 12, N: 12, D: 2.28.

			W	L	T	PF	PA
1.	SOV	(Ilya Byakin, Igor Stelnov, Vyacheslav Fetisov, Aleksei Gusarov, Aleksei Kasatonov, Sergei Starikov, Vyacheslav Bykov, Sergei Yashin, Valery Kamensky, Sergei Svetlov, Aleksandr Chernykh, Andrei Khomutov, Vladimir Krutov, Igor Larionov, Andrei Lomakin, Sergei Makarov, Aleksandr Mogilny, Anatoly Semenov, Aleksandr Kozhevnikov, Igor Kravchuk, Vitaly Samoylov, Sergei Mylnikov)	7	1	0	45	13

			W	L	T	PF	PA
2.	FIN	(Timo Blomqvist, Kari Eloranta, Jyrki Lumme, Jukka Virtanen, Arto Ruotanen, Reijo Ruotsalainen, Simo Saarinen, Kai Suikkanen, Raimo Helminen, Iiro Järvi, Esa Keskinen, Erkki Lehtonen, Reijo Mikkolainen, Janne Ojanen, Timo Susi, Pekka Tuomisto, Teppo Numminen, Jari Torkki, Jukka Tammi, Jarmo Myllys)	5	2	1	34	14
3.	SWE	(Peter Andersson, Anders Eldebrink, Lars Ivarsson, Lars Karlsson, Mats Kihlström, Tommy Samuelsson, Mikael Andersson, Bo Berglund, Jonas Bergqvist, Peter Eriksson, Michael Hjälm, Mikael Johansson, Lars Molin, Lars-Gunnar Pettersson, Thomas Rundqvist, Ulf Sandström, Håkan Södergren, Jens Öhling, Thomas Eriksson, Thom Eklund, Peter Åslin, Anders Bergman, Peter Lindmark)	4	1	3	33	21
4.	CAN	(Chris Felix, Randy Gregg, Timothy Watters, Anthony Stiles, Trent Yawney, Zarley Zalapski, Claude Vilgrain, Kenneth Berry, Serge Boisvert, Brian Bradley, Ken Yaremchuk, Marc Habscheid, Robert Joyce, Vaughn Karpan, Merlin Malinowski, Steven Tambellini, Wallace Schreiber, Gordon Sherven, Serge Roy, Jim Peplinski, Sean Burke, Andrew Moog)	5	2	1	31	21
5.	GER	(Ron Fischer, Udo Kiessling, Horst-Peter Kretschmer, Dieter Medicus, Andreas Niederberger, Harold Kreis, Manfred Schuster, Manfred Wolf, Christian Brittig, Peter Draisaitl, Georg Franz, Dieter Hegen, Georg Holzmann, Peter Obresa, Roy Roedger, Peter Schiller, Helmut Steiger, Gerd Truntschka, Bernd Truntschka, Joachim Reil, Helmut de Raaf, Karl-Heinz Friesen, Josef Schlickenrieder)	5	3	0	25	27
6.	CZE	(Jaroslav Benák, Mojmir Božik, Rudolf Suchánek, Miloslav Hořava, Bedrich Ščerban, Antonin Stavjaña, Jiří Sejba, Jiří Doležal, Oto Haščák, Jiří Hrdina, Rostislav Vlach, Jiří Lála, Igor Liba, Petr Vlk, David Volek, Dušan Pašek, Petr Rosol, Vladimir Růžička, Radim Raděvic, Eduard Uvíra, Dominik Hašek, Jaromir Šindel, Petr Bříza)	4	4	0	33	28
7.	USA	(Greg Brown, Guy Gosselin, Peter Laviolette, Jeffrey Norton, Eric Weinrich, Dave Snuggerud, Allen Bourbeau, Kevin Stevens, John Donatelli, Scott Fusco, Tony Granato, Craig Janney, James Johannson, Scott Young, Stephen Leach, Bradley MacDonald, Cory Millen, Kevin Miller, Brian Leetch, Todd Okerlund, Michael Richter, Chris Terreri, John Blue)	3	3	0	35	31
8.	SWI	(Patrice Brasey, André Künzi, Jakob Kölliker, Fausto Mazzoleni, Andreas Ritsch, Bruno Rogger, Philipp Neuenschwander, Gaëtan Boucher, Manuele Celio, Thomas Vrabec, Jörg Eberle, Felix Hollenstein, Peter Jaks, Roman Wäger, Markus Leuenberger, Fredy Lüthi, Gil Montandon, Peter Schlagenhauf, Urs Burkart, Andreas Zehnder, Thomas Mueller, Pietro Cunti, Olivier Anken, Richard Bucher, Renato Tosio)	3	3	0	23	18

In the weeks leading up to the Calgary Olympics, the international press was filled with articles declaring the end of the Soviet ice hockey dynasty. Perhaps the team from the U.S.S.R. was still favored, but only by a slight margin. But once the tournament began, it was clear that nothing had changed. The Soviets cruised through the preliminary round, then crushed Canada 5–0 and Sweden 7–1. They did lose 2–1 to Finland in their final match, but by that time they had already clinched first place.

1992 Albertville-Méribel T: 12, N: 12, D: 2.23.

		W	L	T	PF	PA
1. SOV	(Sergei Bautin, Igor Boldin, Nikolai Borchevsky, Vyacheslav Butsayev, Vyacheslav Bykov, Mikhail Shtalenkov, Yevgeny Davydov, Aleksei Zhamnov, Aleksei Zhitnik, Darus Kasparaitis, Yuri Khmylev, Andrei Khomutov, Andrei Kovalenko, Aleksei Kovalev, Igor Kravchuk, Vladimir Malakhov, Dmitri Mironov, Sergei Petrenko, Vitaly Prokhorov, Andrei Trefilov, Dmitri Yuchkevich, Sergei Zubov)	7	1	0	46	14
2. CAN	(David Archibald, Todd Brost, Sean Burke, Kevin Dahl, Curt Giles, David Hannan, Gordon Hynes, Fabian Joseph, Joe Juneau, Trevor Kidd, Patrick Lebeau, Chris Lindberg, Eric Lindros, Kent Manderville, Adrian Plavsic, Dan Ratushny, Brad Schlegel, Wallace Schreiber, Randy Smith, David Tippett, Brian Tutt, Jason Wooley)	6	2	0	37	17
3. CZE	(Petr Bríza, Oldrich Svoboda, Leo Gudas, Miloslav Horava, Drahomir Kadlec, Bedrich Scerban, Richard Smehlik, Frantisek Prochazka, Robert Svehla, Petr Rosol, Robert Lang, Kamil Kasták, Richard Zemlicka, Ladislav Lubina, Radek Toupal, Peter Veselovsky, Petr Hrbek, Otakar Janecky, Patrick Augusta, Jirí Slegr, Tomas Jelinek, Igor Liba)	6	2	0	36	21
4. USA	(Greg Brown, Clark Donatelli, Theodore Donato, Thedore Drury, David Emma, Scott Gordon, Guy Gosselin, Bret Hedican, Steve Heinze, Sean Hill, James Johannson, Scott Lachance, Ray LeBlanc, Moe Mantha, Shawn McEachern, Marty McInnis, Joe Sacco, Tim Sweeney, Keith Tkachuk, David Tretowicz, Carl Young, Scott Young)	5	3	0	25	19
5. SWE	(Peter Andersson, Peter Andersson, Charles Berglund, Patrik Carnbäck, Lars Edström, Patrik Erickson, Bengt-Åke Gustavsson, Mikael Johansson, Kenneth Kennholt, Patric Kjellberg, Petri Liimatainen, Håkan Loob, Roger Nordström, Mats Näslund, Peter Ottosson, Thomas Rundqvist, Daniel Rydmark, Börje Salming, Tommy Sjödin, Fredrik Stillman, Tommy Söderström, Jan Viktorsson)	5	3	0	30	19
6. GER	(Richard Amann, Thomas Brandl, Andreas Brockmann, Peter Draisaitl, Ronald Fischer, Karl Friesen, Dieter Hegen, Michael Heidt, Joseph Heiss, Ulrich Hiemer, Raimond Hilger, Georg Holzmann, Axel Kammerer, Udo Kiessling, Ernst Köpf, Jörg Mayr, Andreas Niederberger, Helmut De Raaf, Jürgen Rumrich, Michael Rumrich, Michael Schmidt, Bernd Truntschka, Gerd Truntschka)	3	5	0	22	24
7. FIN	(Pekka Tuomisto, Markus Ketterer, Jukka Tammi, Timo Blomqvist, Kari Eloranta, Timo Jutila, Janne Laukkanen, Harri Laurila, Arto Ruotanen, Simo Saarinen, Ville-Jussi Siren, Raimo Helminen, Hannu Järvenpää, Jari Lindroos, Mikko Mäkelä, Mika Nieminen, Timo Peltomaa, Timo Saarikoski, Teemu Selänne, Petri Skriko, Raimo Summanen, Keijo Säilynoja)	4	3	1	29	21
8. FRA	(Peter Almasy, Michaël Babin, Stéphane Barin, Stépane Botteri, Philippe Bozon, Arnaud Briand, Yves Crettenand, Jean-Marc Djian, Patrick Dunn, Gerald Guennelon, Benoît Laporte, Michel Leblanc, Jean-Philippe Lemoine, Pascal Margerit, Denis Perez, Serge Poudrier, Christian Pouget, Pierre Pousse, Antoine Richer, Bruno Saunier, Christophe Ville, Petri Ylonen)	2	6	0	20	36

Final: SOV 3–1 CAN
3rd Place: CZE 6–1 USA
5th Place: SWE 4–3 GER
7th Place: FIN 4–1 FRA

In 1992, the ex–Soviet Union, now known as the Unified Team, was again considered vulnerable, especially after finishing only third at the 1991 Swedish-won world championship. The warnings seemed justified when Czechoslovakia beat them 4–3 in a preliminary match. It was only the fourth loss by a Soviet team in the last eight Olympics. But then the Czechoslovaks were beaten 5–1 by Canada, and the Unified Team came back to defeat the Canadians 5–4. This left Canada, the Unified Team, and Czechoslovakia in a three-way tie for first place in pool B. The tie-breaking rule—goal differential in games played among the three—put Canada on top of the pool and gave them the right to play Germany, which had placed fourth in pool A with a mediocre record of two wins and three losses, in the quarter-finals.

However, what should have been an easy victory for Canada turned out to be a thrilling and memorable contest. Trailing 2–3, the Germans scored with 2:22 to go in the third period and sent the game into sudden-death overtime. When neither team scored after 10 minutes, a five-man shoot-out was called for. Canada took a 2–0 lead, but the Germans made their last two shots to put the match into a new phase: sudden-death shoot-out. Eric Lindros shot first for Canada and scored. Peter Draisaitl came up for Germany. If he scored, the shoot-out would continue. If he missed, Canada would advance to the semifinals. Draisaitl squeezed the puck through goalie Sean Burke's legs, but Burke managed to slow it down with his pads. The puck rolled toward the goal, wobbled, and landed *on* the goal line. According to the rules of hockey, a point isn't scored unless the puck goes *past* the goal line. Canada escaped a major upset by one inch. One of the other quarter-finals saw the world champion Swedish team defeated 3–1 by Czechoslovakia.

In the first semifinal, the Unified Team broke open a 2–2 tie with the United States midway through the third period by scoring three goals in 6¼ minutes. In the second semi, Canada scored twice in the final period to beat Czechoslovakia 4–2.

The final was scoreless after two periods. Vyacheslav Butsayev struck first at the 1:01 mark of the third period. Igor Boldin made it 2–0 at 15:54. Lindberg of Canada scored at 17:20, but a final goal by Vyacheslav Bykov sealed another Olympic championship for the ex-Soviets. The victors were the youngest team in the tournament as well as the least penalized. Although the team was overwhelmingly Russian, one member, Darus Kasparaitis, was actually from Lithuania even though Lithuania was competing as a separate nation in Albertville.

COMMON ICE HOCKEY PENALTIES

Charging—Applying a body check after taking more than two steps toward the opposing player.

Cross checking—Hitting an opponent while holding the stick in the air with both hands.

Elbowing—Applying a check with the arms or elbows instead of the body.

High sticking—Holding the stick above shoulder level while moving toward an opponent.

Holding—Using the hands to grab an opposing player or his stick.

Hooking—Using the stick to restrain an opponent.

Slashing—Using the stick to try to hit an opponent.

Spearing—Using the stick to stab an opponent.

Tripping—Using an arm, foot, leg, or stick to knock down an opposing player.

LUGE (TOBOGGAN)

MEN	WOMEN
Single	Single
Two-Seater	
Discontinued Event	

Luge sleds are similar to toboggans. A singles sled can weigh no more than 22 kilograms (48.4 lbs.), a doubles sled no more than 25 kg (55.1 lbs.). The runners may be no more than 18 inches apart. It is forbidden to heat the runners before the competition. Participants, known as sliders, careen down the course feet first, guiding the luge with their legs and shoulders. Luge has the reputation of being one of the most dangerous sports in the Olympics. The two-seater event is decided on the basis of two runs, the singles on a total of four. The first organized luge competition was a four-kilometer race held in Davos, Switzerland, in 1883; the first world championships were held in Oslo in 1955. All 72 medals awarded in luge since its permanent inclusion in the Olympic program in 1964 have been won by four nations: Germany, Austria, Italy, and the U.S.S.R. Twenty-three of the 24 gold medals have been won by German-speaking athletes.

MEN

SINGLE

1924–1960 not held

1964 Innsbruck-Igls C: 36, N: 10, D: 2.1.

1.	Thomas Köhler	GDR	3:26.77
2.	Klaus Bonsack	GDR	3:27.04
3.	Hans Plenk	GDR	3:30.15
4.	Rolf Greger Ström	NOR	3:31.21
5.	Josef Feistmantl	AUT	3:31.34
6.	Mieczyslaw Pawelkiewicz	POL	3:33.02
7.	Carlo Prinoth	ITA	3:33.49
8.	Franz Tiefenbacher	AUT	3:33.86

Critics who had contended that luge was too dangerous a sport to be included in the Olympics gained sad support for their arguments when Polish-born British slider Kazimierz Kay-Skrzypeski was killed during a trial run on the Olympic course at Igls two weeks before the Games began. German sliders Josef Fleischmann and Josef Lenz were also severely injured in a separate accident.

1968 Grenoble-Villard de Lans C: 50, N: 15, D: 2.15.

1.	Manfred Schmid	AUT	2:52.48
2.	Thomas Köhler	GDR	2:52.66
3.	Klaus Bonsack	GDR	2:53.33
4.	Zbigniew Gawior	POL	2:53.51
5.	Josef Feistmantl	AUT	2:53.57
6.	Hans Plenk	GDR	2:53.67
7.	Horst Hörnlein	GDR	2:54.10
8.	Jerzy Wojnar	POL	2:54.62

After the East German women were disqualified for heating the runners on their sleds, the coaches of seven of the men's teams signed a petition saying they would all walk out if the East German men were allowed to continue in the contest, which still had one round to go. The International Luge Federation decided against suspending the East German men, but bad weather intervened and the competition was ended after three runs anyway.

1972 Sapporo-Teineyama C: 45, N: 13, D: 2.7.

1.	Wolfgang Scheidel	GDR	3:27.58
2.	Harald Ehrig	GDR	3:28.39
3.	Wolfram Fiedler	GDR	3:28.73
4.	Klaus Bonsack	GDR	3:29.16
5.	Leonhard Nagenrauft	GER	3:29.67
6.	Josef Fendt	GER	3:30.03
7.	Manfred Schmid	AUT	3:30.05
8.	Paul Hildgartner	ITA	3:30.55

1976 Innsbruck-Igls C: 43, N: 15, D: 2.7.

1.	Dettlef Günther	GDR	3:27.688
2.	Josef Fendt	GER	3:28.196
3.	Hans Rinn	GDR	3:28.574
4.	Hans-Heinrich Wickler	GDR	3:29.454
5.	Manfred Schmid	AUT	3:29.511
6.	Anton Winkler	GER	3:29.520
7.	Reinhold Sulzbacher	AUT	3:30.398
8.	Dainis Bremze	SOV	3:30.576

During the 1975 Olympic Test Competition on the same course that would be used for the Olympics, the East Germans set up cameras and timers all along the run to help determine the fastest routes through each of the straightaways and curves.

1980 Lake Placid C: 30, N: 13, D: 2.16.

1.	Bernhard Glass	GDR	2:54.796
2.	Paul Hildgartner	ITA	2:55.372
3.	Anton Winkler	GER	2:56.545
4.	Dettlef Günther	GDR	2:57.163
5.	Gerhard Sandbichler	AUT	2:57.451
6.	Franz Wilhelmer	AUT	2:57.483
7.	Gerd Böhmer	GER	2:57.769
8.	Anton Wembacher	GER	2:58.012

After two runs Dettlef Günther seemed to be well on his way to a repeat victory. However, he crashed near the end of his third run and, although he was able to climb back aboard and finish, the three seconds he had lost effectively removed him from the competition for first place. This left Italy's Ernst Haspinger in the lead, with one run to go. Unfortunately, he fell victim to the same turn as Günther and lost nine seconds, which dropped him to 21st place. Bernhard Glass ended up with the gold medal even though he didn't place first in a single run.

1984 Sarajevo C: 32, N: 16, D: 2.12.

1.	Paul Hildgartner	ITA	3:04.258
2.	Sergei Danilin	SOV	3:04.962
3.	Valery Dudin	SOV	3:05.012
4.	Michael Walter	GDR	3:05.031
5.	Torsten Görlitzer	GDR	3:05.129
6.	Ernst Haspinger	ITA	3:05.327
7.	Yuri Kharchenko	SOV	3:05.548
8.	Markus Prock	AUT	3:05.839

Görlitzer led after the first two runs, but 31-year-old Paul Hildgartner of Kiens (Chienes) in the Südtyrol region of Italy recorded the fastest time in both of the final two runs. Hildgartner had previously won a gold medal in the 1972 two-seater event and a silver in the 1980 single competition.

1988 Calgary C: 38, N: 18, D: 2.15.

1.	Jens Müller	GDR	3:05.548
2.	Georg Hackl	GER	3:05.916
3.	Yuri Kharchenko	SOV	3:06.274
4.	Thomas Jacob	GDR	3:06.358
5.	Michael Walter	GDR	3:06.933
6.	Sergei Danilin	SOV	3:07.098
7.	Johannes Schettel	GER	3:07.371
8.	Hansjörg Raffl	ITA	3:07.525

Müller, second to Hackl at the European championship two weeks prior to the Olympics, won three of the four runs and was three one-thousandths of a second out of first in the other.

1992 Albertville-La Plagne C: 34, N: 18, D: 2.10.

1.	Georg Hackl	GER	3:02.363
2.	Markus Prock	AUT	3:02.669
3.	Markus Schmid	AUT	3:02.942
4.	Norbert Huber	ITA	3:02.973
5.	Jens Müller	GER	3:03.197
6.	Robert Manzenreiter	AUT	3:03.267
7.	Oswald Haselrieder	ITA	3:03.276
8.	René Friedl	GER	3:03.543

Georg Hackl grew up four miles from the Königssee luge course in the Bavarian town of Berchtesgaden. After being pipped for the gold medal in 1988 because of problems with his start, a start range was built for him at Königssee. The increased practice paid off. In 1992, the 25-year-old army sergeant posted the fastest time in three of the four runs to win the closest men's single competition in 24 years.

TWO-SEATER

1924–1960 not held

1964 Innsbruck-Igls T: 14, N: 8, D: 2.1.

1.	AUT	(Josef Feistmantl, Manfred Stengl)	1:41.62
2.	AUT	(Reinhold Senn, Helmut Thaler)	1:41.91
3.	ITA	(Walter Aussendorfer, Sigisfredo Mair)	1:42.87
4.	DEN	(Walter Eggert, Helmut Vollprecht)	1:43.08
5.	ITA	(Giampaolo Ambrosi, Giovanni Graber)	1:43.77
5.	POL	(Lucjan Kudzia, Ryszard Pędrak)	1:43.77
7.	POL	(Edward Fender, Mieczyslaw Pawelkiewicz)	1:45.13
8.	CZE	(Jan Hamrik, Jiři Hujer)	1:45.41

1968 Grenoble-Villard de Lans T: 14, N: 8, D: 2.18.

1.	GDR	(Klaus Bonsack, Thomas Köhler)	1:35.85
2.	AUT	(Manfred Schmid, Ewald Walch)	1:36.34
3.	GER	(Wolfgang Winkler, Fritz Nachmann)	1:37.29
4.	GER	(Hans Plenk, Bernhard Aschauer)	1:37.61
5.	GDR	(Horst Hörnlein, Reinhard Bredow)	1:37.81
6.	POL	(Zbigniew Gawior, Ryszard Gawior)	1:37.85
7.	AUT	(Josef Feistmantl, Wilhelm Biechl)	1:38.11
8.	ITA	(Giovanni Graber, Enrico Graber)	1:38.15

1972 Sapporo-Teineyama T: 20, N: 11, D: 2.10.

1.	GDR	(Horst Hörnlein, Reinhard Bredow)	1:28.35
1.	ITA	(Paul Hildgartner, Walter Plaikner)	1:28.35
3.	GDR	(Klaus Bonsack, Wolfram Fiedler)	1:29.16
4.	JPN	(Satoru Arai, Masatoshi Kobayashi)	1:29.63
5.	GER	(Hans Brandner, Balthasar Schwarm)	1:29.66
5.	POL	(Miroslaw Więckowski, Wojciech Kubik)	1:29.66
7.	AUT	(Manfred Schmid, Ewald Walch)	1:29.75
8.	ITA	(Sigisfredo Mair, Ernst Mair)	1:30.26

The results of the first run, which had been won by Hildgartner and Plaikner, were cancelled due to a malfunctioning starting gate. The Italians argued that the run should be counted, since all contestants had suffered equally. Their protest was denied. The tie which resulted from the two official runs caused a sticky problem. Finally the International Luge Federation, in consultation with I.O.C. president Avery Brundage, decided to award gold medals to both teams.

1976 Innsbruck-Igls T: 25, N: 15, D: 2.10.

1.	GDR	(Hans Rinn, Norbert Hahn)	1:25.604
2.	GER	(Hans Brandner, Balthasar Schwarm)	1:25.889
3.	AUT	(Rudolf Schmid, Franz Schachner)	1:25.919
4.	GER	(Stefan Hölzlwimmer, Rudolf Grösswang)	1:26.238
5.	AUT	(Manfred Schmid, Reinhold Sulzbacher)	1:26.424
6.	CZE	(Jindřich Zeman, Vladimir Resl)	1:26.826
7.	ITA	(Karl Feichter, Ernst Haspinger)	1:27.171
8.	SOV	(Dainis Bremze, Aigars Krikis)	1:27.407

1980 Lake Placid T: 19, N: 12: D: 2.19.

1.	GDR	(Hans Rinn, Norbert Hahn)	1:19.331
2.	ITA	(Peter Gschnitzer, Karl Brunner)	1:19.606
3.	AUT	(Georg Fluckinger, Karl Schrott)	1:19.795
4.	GDR	(Bernd Hahn, Ulrich Hahn)	1:19.914
5.	ITA	(Hansjörg Raffl, Alfred Silginer)	1:19.976
6.	GER	(Anton Winkler, Anton Wembacher)	1:20.012
7.	GER	(Hans Brandner, Balthasar Schwarm)	1:20.063
8.	CZE	(Jindřich Zeman, Vladimir Resl)	1:20.142

Hans Rinn and Norbert Hahn became the first repeat winners of an Olympic luge event. Norbert was no relation to Bernd and Ulrich Hahn, two brothers who finished fourth.

1984 Sarajevo T: 15, N: 9, D: 2.15.

1.	GER	(Hans Stanggassinger, Franz Wembacher)	1:23.620
2.	SOV	(Yevgeny Belousov, Aleksandr Belyakov)	1:23.660
3.	GDR	(Jörg Hoffmann, Jochen Pietzsch)	1:23.887
4.	AUT	(Georg Fluckinger, Franz Wilhelmer)	1:23.902
5.	AUT	(Günther Lemmerer, Franz Lechleitner)	1:24.133
6.	ITA	(Hansjörg Raffl, Norbert Huber)	1:24.353
7.	SOV	(Yuris Eyssak, Eynar Veykcha)	1:24.366
8.	GER	(Thomas Schwab, Wolfgang Staudinger)	1:24.634

Belousov and Belyakov led after the first run and were on their way to the best time of the second run when they faltered just before the end, losing about one-sixth of a second in the last few meters. This gave Stanggassinger and Wembacher the victory by four one-hundredths of a second.

1988 Calgary T: 18, N: 11, D: 2.19.

1.	GDR	(Jörg Hoffmann, Jochen Pietzsch)	1:31.940
2.	GDR	(Stefan Krausse, Jan Behrendt)	1:32.039
3.	GER	(Thomas Schwab, Wolfgang Staudinger)	1:32.274
4.	GER	(Stefan Ilsanker, Georg Hackl)	1:32.298
5.	AUT	(Georg Fluckinger, Robert Manzenreiter)	1:32.364
6.	SOV	(Vitaly Melnik, Dmitri Alexeev)	1:32.459
7.	ITA	(Kurt Brugger, Wilfried Huber)	1:32.553
7.	SOV	(Yevgeny Belousov, Aleksandr Belyakov)	1:32.553

1992 Albertville-La Plagne T: 20, N: 15, D: 2.14.

1.	GER	(Stefan Krausse, Jan Behrendt)	1:32.053
2.	GER	(Yves Mankel, Thomas Rudolph)	1:32.239
3.	ITA	(Hansjörg Raffl, Norbert Huber)	1:32.298
4.	ROM	(Ioan Apostol, Liviu Cepoi)	1:32.649
5.	ITA	(Kurt Brugger, Wilfried Huber)	1:32.810
6.	SWE	(Hans Kohala, Carl-Johan Lindqvist)	1:33.134
7.	AUT	(Gerhard Gleirscher, Markus Schmid)	1:33.257
8.	SOV	(Albert Demchenko, Aleksei Zelensky)	1:33.299

The two Italian teams dominated the pre-Olympic season, finishing one-two in every World Cup event they entered, but both faltered on the course at La Plagne. Krausse and Behrendt were childhood friends who grew up in Ilmenau, the hometown of both 1988 individual gold medalists, Jens Müller and Ute Oberhoffner.

Discontinued Event

SKELETON (CRESTA RUN)

The skeleton is a heavy sled which is ridden head first in a prone position and steered by dragging one's feet and shifting one's weight. The event is held only when the Olympics are in St. Moritz.

1928 St. Moritz C: 10, N: 6, D: 2.17.

1.	Jennison Heaton	USA	3:01.8
2.	John Heaton	USA	3:02.8
3.	David Northesk	GBR	3:05.1
4.	Agostino Lanfranchi	ITA	3:08.7
5.	A. Berner	SWI	3:08.8
6.	Franz Unterlechner	AUT	3:13.5
7.	A. del Torso	ITA	3:14.9
8.	L. Hasenknopf	AUT	3:36.7

The Heaton brothers recorded the two fastest times in each of the three runs.

1932–1936 not held

1948 St. Moritz C: 15, N: 6, D: 2.4.

1.	Nino Bibbia	ITA	5:23.2
2.	John Heaton	USA	5:24.6
3.	John Crammond	GBR	5:25.1
4.	William Martin	USA	5:28.0
5.	Gottfried Kägi	SWI	5:29.9
6.	Richard Bott	GBR	5:30.4
7.	James Coates	GBR	5:31.9
8.	Fairchilds MacCarthy	USA	5:35.5

John Heaton of New Haven, Connecticut, had the rare experience of winning consecutive silver medals in the same event—20 years apart. The first time he was 19, the second time 39.

WOMEN

SINGLE

1924–1960 not held

1964 Innsbruck-Igls C: 16, N: 6, D: 2.4.

1.	Ortrun Enderlein	GDR	3:24.67
2.	Ilse Geisler	GDR	3:27.42
3.	Helene Thurner	AUT	3:29.06
4.	Irena Pawelczyk	POL	3:30.52
5.	Barbara Gorgón-Flont	POL	3:32.73
6.	Oldřiska Tylová	CZE	3:32.76
7.	Friederike Matejka	AUT	3:34.68
8.	Helena Macher	POL	3:35.87

1968 Grenoble-Villard de Lans C: 26, N: 10, D: 2.15.

1.	Erica Lechner	ITA	2:28.66
2.	Christa Schmuck	GER	2:29.37
3.	Angelika Dünhaupt	GER	2:29.56
4.	Helena Macher	POL	2:30.05
5.	Jadwiga Damse	POL	2:30.15
6.	Dana Beldová	CZE	2:30.35
7.	Anna Mąka	POL	2:30.40
8.	Ute Gaehler	GER	2:30.42

DISQ: Ortrun Enderlein (GDR) 2:28.04, Anna-Maria Müller (GDR) 2:28.06, Angela Knösel (GDR) 2:28.93

The weather-shortened competition ended with defending champion Ortrun Enderlein in first place and East German teammates Anna-Maria Müller and Angela Knösel in second and fourth. However the East German women aroused suspicion by consistently showing up at the last minute and then disappearing as soon as they finished a run. Their toboggans were examined, and it was discovered that their runners had been illegally heated. The three East Germans were disqualified by unanimous vote of the Jury of Appeal. The East German Olympic Committee made a pathetic attempt to blame the affair on a "capitalist revanchist plot," but they failed to address the fact that the problem had been discovered by the Polish president of the Jury, Lucian Swiderski.

1972 Sapporo-Teineyama C: 22, N: 8, D: 2.7.

1.	Anna-Maria Müller	GDR	2:59.18
2.	Ute Rührold	GDR	2:59.49
3.	Margit Schumann	GDR	2:59.54
4.	Elisabeth Demleitner	GER	3:00.80
5.	Yuko Otaka	JPN	3:00.98
6.	Halina Kanasz	POL	3:02.33
6.	Wieslawa Martyka	POL	3:02.33
8.	Sarah Felder	ITA	3:02.90

After the 1968 scandal, I.O.C. president Avery Brundage had spoken with the disqualified East German women and encouraged them to win the medals next time around. Anna-Maria Müller took this advice to heart and did exactly that, winning a close battle with her two teenage teammates. Asked why she enjoyed such a dangerous sport, Müller replied, "I love this sport because it provides a harmonious counterbalance to my work as a pharmacist."

1976 Innsbruck-Igls C: 26, N: 12, D: 2.7.

1.	Margit Schumann	GDR	2:50.621
2.	Ute Rührold	GDR	2:50.846
3.	Elisabeth Demleitner	GER	2:51.056
4.	Eva-Maria Wernicke	GDR	2:51.262
5.	Antonia Mayr	AUT	2:51.360
6.	Margit Graf	AUT	2:51.459
7.	Monika Schefftschik	GER	2:51.540
8.	Angelika Schafferer	AUT	2:52.322

Undefeated since the 1972 Olympics, Lieutenant Margit Schumann was only in fifth place after the first two runs, but recorded the best times on each of the last two runs to take the victory. The unusually attractive Ute Rührold won her second straight silver medal, even though she was only 21 years old.

1980 Lake Placid C: 18, N: 8, D: 2.16.

1.	Vera Zozulya	SOV	2:36.537
2.	Melitta Sollmann	GDR	2:37.657
3.	Ingrīda Amantova	SOV	2:37.817
4.	Elisabeth Demleitner	GER	2:37.918
5.	Ilona Brand	GDR	2:38.115
6.	Margit Schumann	GDR	2:38.255
7.	Angelika Schafferer	AUT	2:38.935
8.	Astra Ribena	SOV	2:39.011

Latvian Vera Zozulya recorded the fastest time in each of the four runs to upset two-time world champion Melitta Sollmann. Zozulya is the only non-German-speaking athlete to win a luge medal.

1984 Sarajevo C: 27, N: 15, 2.12.

1.	Steffi Martin	GDR	2:46.570
2.	Bettina Schmidt	GDR	2:46.873
3.	Ute Weiss	GDR	2:47.248
4.	Ingrīda Amantova	SOV	2:48.480
5.	Vera Zozulya	SOV	2:48.641
6.	Marie Luise Rainer	ITA	2:49.138
7.	Annefried Goellner	AUT	2:49.373
8.	Andrea Hatle	GER	2:49.491

World champion Steffi Martin recorded the fastest time in each of the four runs.

1988 Calgary C: 24, N: 14, D: 2.16.

1.	Steffi Walter [Martin]	GDR	3:03.973
2.	Ute Oberhoffner [Weiss]	GDR	3:04.105
3.	Cerstin Schmidt	GDR	3:04.181
4.	Veronika Bilgeri	GER	3:05.670
5.	Yulia Antipova	SOV	3:05.787
6.	Bonny Warner	USA	3:06.056
7.	Marie-Claude Doyon	CAN	3:06.211
8.	Nadezhda Danilina	SOV	3:06.364

Defending champion Steffi Walter trailed teammate Ute Oberhoffner by thirty-eight thousandths of a second after two runs. The final two runs were delayed for one day because of heavy winds. When the competition resumed, Walter picked up one hundred eighty-one thousandths of a second on the third run, giving her the margin of victory. The East German women clocked the three fastest times for each of the four runs.

1992 Albertville-La Plagne C: 24, N: 12, D: 2.12.

1.	Doris Neuner	AUT	3:06.696
2.	Angelika Neuner	AUT	3:06.769
3.	Susi Erdmann	GER	3:07.115
4.	Gerda Weissensteiner	ITA	3:07.673
5.	Cammy Myler	USA	3:07.973
6.	Gabriele Kohlisch	GER	3:07.980
7.	Andrea Tagwerker	AUT	3:08.018
8.	Natalya Yakuchenko	SOV	3:08.383

After the Austrians stood 1-2-3 following the first day's two runs, the U.S. and Italian coaches filed a protest claiming that the Austrians' suits were illegally strapped to the heels of their boots, causing their toes to point inside. This scandalous flouting of the rules could have led to the Austrians' disqualification, but the Jury of Appeal rejected the protest. Doris Neuner, a 20-year-old secretary from Innsbruck, took a huge lead (two-tenths of a second) after the first run and held on for the victory despite not winning another run. Her sister, Angelika, a 22-year-old bank clerk, closed the gap with each of her remaining runs, but fell seventy-three thousandths of a second short.

FIGURE SKATING

MEN
WOMEN
Pairs
Ice Dance
Discontinued Event

The first international figure skating competition was held in Vienna in 1882 and the first world championship in St. Petersburg in 1896. A separate event for women's singles was not created until 1906, and the first world championship for pairs took place in 1908. According to current rules, each skater or pair appears twice, performing a two-minute and forty-second short or original program with eight required moves (33⅓ percent of the total score) and a freestyle long program (66⅔ percent of the score). The men's and pairs' long programs last four and a half minutes, the women's only four. Prior to 1992, singles skaters were also required to perform compulsory (or special) figures.

In singles and pairs competitions, the nine judges assign each entrant two scores from 0 to 6 points, one for technical merit and one for artistic impression. More important, in both the short program and the long program, each judge ranks the skaters according to the points awarded. The numerical equivalents for each place (1 for first, 2 for second, etc.) are called ordinals. At the end of each stage of the competition, the skaters are ranked in consensus order. If one skater receives a majority of first-place votes, that skater is ranked first. If no one receives a majority of first-place votes, then the second-place votes are added to the first-place votes. If there is still no one with a majority of votes, then the person with the lowest ordinal total is ranked first. If a tie still exists, the skater with the most points is awarded first place. The same procedure is used to determine all other places. To determine final scores, a skater's short-program ranking is multiplied by 0.5 and added to the long-program ranking. Until 1984, the ordinals were based on total scores, not on separate programs.

MEN

1908 London C: 9, N: 5, D: 10.29.

				JUDGES' RANKINGS				
			GBR	SWE	SWI	RUS	GER	ORDINALS
1.	Ulrich Salchow	SWE	1	1	2	2	1	7
2.	Richard Johansson	SWE	2	2	3	1	2	10
3.	Per Thorén	SWE	4	3	1	3	3	14
4.	John Keiller Greig	GBR	3	4	4	4	4	19
5.	Albert March	GBR	5	5	7	6	6	29
6.	Irving Brokaw	USA	6	7	5	5	7	30
7.	Henri Torromé	ARG	7	6	6	7	5	31

Early in 1908 Salchow suffered his first defeat in six years, losing to Nicolai Panin (Kolomenkin) of Russia. At the London Olympics, the two met again. Salchow was given three first-place votes for his compulsory figures to Panin's two. Panin withdrew in protest, claiming that the judging was stacked against him. Salchow was the originator of the jump which now bears his name. To perform a Salchow, a skater must take off from the back inside edge of one skate, make a complete turn in the air, and land on the back outside edge of the opposite skate.

1920 Antwerp C: 9, N: 6, D: 4.27.

		SWE	FRA	HUN	NOR	GBR	BEL	FIN	ORDINALS
				JUDGES' RANKINGS					
1. Gillis Grafström	SWE	1	1	1	1	1	1	1	7
2. Andreas Krogh	NOR	3	2	2	2	4	3	2	18
3. Martin Stixrud	NOR	2	3	3.5	3	5	5	3	24.5
4. Ulrich Salchow	SWE	4	4	3.5	5	2	2	5	25.5
5. Sakari Ilmanen	FIN	5	5	5	4	3	4	4	30
6. Nathaniel Niles	USA	6	9	6	6	8	8	6	49
7. Basil Williams	GBR	8	6	7	8	6	7	7.5	49.5
8. Alfred Mégroz	SWI	7	8	8	9	7	6	7.5	52.5

Bronze medalist Stixrud was 44 years old.

1924 Chamonix C: 11, N: 9, D: 1.30.

JUDGES' RANKINGS

		FRA	FRA	CZE	SWI	GBR	AUT	AUT	ORDINALS
1. Gillis Grafström	SWE	1	1	2	1	1	2	2	10
2. Willy Böckl	AUT	2	2	3	2	2	1	1	13
3. Georges Gautschi	SWI	3	4	4	3	3	3	3	23
4. Josef Sliva	CZE	4	3	1	4	5	4	7	28
5. John Page	GBR	5	5	7	6	4	5	4	36
6. Nathaniel Niles	USA	7	6	9	5	7	6	6	46
7. Melville Rogers	CAN	6	7	8	7	6	9	8	51
8. Pierre Brunet	FRA	8	8	5	9	8	7	9	54

The Czech judge ranked Sliva of Czechoslovakia first, the two Austrian judges voted for Böckl of Austria, and the other four judges, none of whom was Swedish, gave first place to Gillis Grafström.

1928 St. Moritz C: 17, N: 10, D: 2.17.

JUDGES' RANKINGS

		GER	AUT	BEL	USA	FIN	GBR	CZE	ORDINALS
1. Gillis Grafström	SWE	1	3	3	2	1	1	1	12
2. Willy Böckl	AUT	2	1	2	1	2	2	3	13
3. Robert von Zeebroeck	BEL	3	4	1	7	3	4	5	27
4. Karl Schäfer	AUT	4	2	4	3	6	7	9	35
5. Josef Sliva	CZE	5	6	8	4	5	6	2	36
6. Marcus Nikkanen	FIN	7	5	7	8	4	10	6	46
7. Pierre Brunet	FRA	10	7	5	9	7	8	4	50
8. Ludwig Wrede	AUT	8	8	7	10	8	5	7	53

The 34-year-old Grafström won his third straight gold medal despite suffering from a badly swollen knee. Grafström's smooth, orthodox, and perfectly executed routines appealed to the judges more than Böckl's more aggressive performance and von Zeebroeck's spectacular leaps and spins.

1932 Lake Placid C: 12, N: 8, D: 2.9.

		JUDGES' RANKINGS							
		NOR	GBR	AUT	FIN	CAN	HUN	USA	ORDINALS
1. Karl Schäfer	AUT	1	2	1	2	1	1	1	9
2. Gillis Grafström	SWE	3	1	2	1	2	2	2	13
3. Montgomery Wilson	CAN	4	3	4	4	3	3	3	24
4. Marcus Nikkanen	FIN	2	4	3	3	5	5	6	28
5. Ernst Baier	GER	5	5	5	5	4	4	7	35
6. Roger Turner	USA	6	6	6	6	6	6	4	40
7. James Madden	USA	7	7	8	8	8	9	5	52
8. Gail Borden II	USA	8	8	7	7	9	7	8	54

This competition marked a changing of the guard, as 38-year-old three-time Olympic champion Gillis Grafström lost to 22-year-old, soon-to-be two-time Olympic champion Karl Schäfer. Grafström suffered a sudden mental lapse at the very beginning of his performance, evidently starting to trace a different figure than the one that was required. He recovered and skated smoothly thereafter, but he was penalized an average of almost eight points by each judge.

1936 Garmisch-Partenkirchen C: 25, N: 12, D: 2.14.

		JUDGES' RANKINGS							
		USA	GBR	FIN	CAN/GER	AUT	HUN	CZE	ORDINALS
1. Karl Schäfer	AUT	1	1	1	1	1	1	1	7
2. Ernst Baier	GER	4	4	4	2	3	5	2	24
3. Felix Kaspar	AUT	3	3	2	4	2	7	3	24
4. Montgomery Wilson	CAN	2	5	3	3	4	8	5	30
5. Henry Graham Sharp	GBR	6	2	6	7	5	4	4	34
6. John Dunn	GBR	5	6	7	6	6	6	6	42
7. Marcus Nikkanen	FIN	7	7	5	5	12	9	9	54
8. Elemer Tardonfalvi	HUN	10	9	9	8	9	3	8	56

An extreme example of national prejudice by a judge was committed by Judge von Orbán of Hungary, who placed the two Hungarian skaters, Dénes Pataky and Elemer Tardonfalvi, second and third, while none of the other judges ranked them higher than seventh and eighth.

1948 St. Moritz C: 16, N: 10, D: 2.5.

		JUDGES' RANKINGS								
		GBR	SWI	USA	CZE	AUT	BEL	CAN	DEN	HUN	ORDINALS
1. Richard Button	USA	1	2	1	1	1	1	1	1	1	10
2. Hans Gerschwiler	SWI	2	1	5	2	3	2	3	2	3	23
3. Edi Rada	AUT	7	3	3	3	2	3	4	6	2	33
4. John Lettengarver	USA	3	4	2	5	6	4	2	3	7	36
5. Ede Király	HUN	5	5	6	4	4	5	5	4	4	42
6. James Grogan	USA	6	7	4	8	10	6	6	5	10	62
7. Henry Graham Sharp	GBR	4	9	10	7	8	10	7	7	5	67
8. Hellmut May	AUT	8	6	9	6	5	9	11	8	6	68

Two days before the free-skating portion of the competition, 18-year-old Dick Button, a Harvard freshman from Englewood, New Jersey, successfully completed a double axel for the first time. He was anxious to include this new move in his program but, as the leader going into the final round, he was hesitant to risk his position by trying a move with which he was not fully confident. In his book *Dick Button on Skates,* he recalled, "I disliked being so unprepared. But the cravenness of backing away from something because of the pressure of the Olympic games repulsed me and, once I had made up my mind, I could not divert the steps that culminated in the double axel." The jump went perfectly and Button was awarded first place by eight of the nine judges. Only the Swiss judge voted a first for Gerschwiler of Switzerland.

1952 Oslo C: 14, N: 11, D: 2.21.

JUDGES' RANKINGS

		USA	GER	ITA	AUT	DEN	CAN	FIN	FRA	HUN	ORDINALS
1.	Richard Button	USA	1	1	1	1	1	1	1	1	1	9
2.	Helmut Seibt	AUT	4	2	2	2	2	3	2	4	2	23
3.	James Grogan	USA	2	3	3	3	3	2	3	2	3	24
4.	Hayes Alan Jenkins	USA	3	5	5	5	5	5	4	3	5	40
5.	Peter Firstbrook	CAN	5	4	6	6	4	4	5	5	4	43
6.	Carlo Fassi	ITA	6	6	4	4	6	6	6	6	6	50
7.	Alain Giletti	FRA	7	7	7	7	7	7	7	7	7	63
8.	Freimut Stein	GER	8	8	8	8	8	8	8	8	8	72

By 1952 Dick Button was a Harvard senior working on a thesis entitled "International Socialism and the Schumann Plan." Once again he had a new move to unveil at the Olympics—the triple loop, which required him to make three complete revolutions in the air and then come down smoothly. No one had ever performed a triple jump of any kind in competition. Button could have played it safe, skipped the triple loop, and probably won anyway, but he felt that this would have been a form of failure. Button was very anxious, and his parents were so nervous that they couldn't sit together. In his autobiography, Button describes the triple loop: "I forgot in momentary panic which shoulder should go forward and which back. I was extraordinarily conscious of the judges, who looked so immobile at rinkside. But this was it. . . . The wind cut my eyes, and the coldness caused tears to stream down my checks. Up! Up! Height was vital. Round and around again in a spin which took only a fraction of a second to complete before it landed on a clean steady back edge. I pulled away breathless, excited and overjoyed, as applause rolled from the faraway stands like the rumbling of a distant pounding sea."

All nine judges placed Button first, far ahead of the other skaters. Dick Button turned professional a few months later and toured with the Ice Capades. Later he became a lawyer, an actor, a TV sports commentator, and an entrepreneur. The seventh-place finisher in 1952, Alain Giletti, was only 12 years old.

1956 Cortina C: 16, N: 11, D: 2.1.

JUDGES' RANKINGS

		AUS	AUT	CAN	CZE	FRA	GER	GBR	USA	SWI	ORDINALS
1.	Hayes Alan Jenkins	USA	3	1	1	1	2	2	1	1	1	13
2.	Ronald Robertson	USA	1	2	2	2	1	1	3	2	2	16
3.	David Jenkins	USA	2	3	4	3	3	4	2	3	3	27
4.	Alain Giletti	FRA	4	5	3	5	4	3	5	4	4	37
5.	Karol Divin	CZE	7	4	5	4	5.5	5	6	8	5	49.5
6.	Michael Booker	GBR	5	6	8	6	5.5	7	4	6	6	53.5
7.	Norbert Felsinger	AUT	9	7	7	7	9	10	8	7	7	71
8.	Charles Snelling	CAN	8	9	6	9	8	6	7	5	9	67

The three Americans finished in the same order as they had in the 1955 world championships. Twenty-two-year-old Hayes Alan Jenkins of Colorado Springs, Colorado, had practiced 40 hours a week, 10 months a year, for nine years.

1960 Squaw Valley C: 19, N: 10, D: 2.26.

		JUDGES' RANKINGS									
		AUT	CAN	CZE	FRA	GER	GBR	JPN	SWI	USA	ORDINALS
1. David Jenkins	USA	1	1	1	1	1	2	1	1	1	10
2. Karol Divin	CZE	2	3	2	4	3	1	2	3	2	22
3. Donald Jackson	CAN	5	2	3	3	4	3	4	4	3	31
4. Alain Giletti	FRA	3	4	4	2	2	4	5	2	5	31
5. Timothy Brown	USA	4	5	5	6	5	6	3	6	4	43
6. Alain Calmat	FRA	6	6	6	5	6	6	7	5	7	54
7. Robert Brewer	USA	7	8	8	8	7	7	6	9	6	66
8. Manfred Schnelldorfer	GER	8	7	7	7	10	9	9	8	10	75

Medical student David Jenkins, the younger brother of 1956 champion Hayes Alan Jenkins, trailed Karol Divin after the compulsory figures. However, his free-skating program won first-place votes from all nine judges, and he won eight of nine first places overall.

1964 Innsbruck C: 24, N: 11, D: 2.6.

		JUDGES' RANKINGS									
		GER	FRA	GBR	ITA	CAN	AUT	CZE	USA	SOV	ORDINALS
1. Manfred Schnelldorfer	GER	1	2	1	3	1	1	1	2	1	13
2. Alain Calmat	FRA	3	1	2	1	3	2	4	3	3	22
3. Scott Allen	USA	2	3	3	2	2	5	3	1	5	26
4. Karol Divin	CZE	4	4	4	4	4	4	2	4	2	32
5. Emmerich Danzer	AUT	5	5	5	5	5	3	5	5	4	42
6. Thomas Litz	USA	10	8	11	6	6	6	6	12	12	77
7. Peter Jonas	AUT	6	6	6	13	14	8	10	9	7	79
8. Nobuo Sato	JPN	8	9	7	9	12	9	9	10	15	88

Manfred Schnelldorfer, a 20-year-old architecture student from Munich, was a former German roller skating champion. Two days shy of his 15th birthday, Scotty Allen of Smoke Rise, New Jersey, became the youngest person to win a medal in the Winter Olympics.

1968 Grenoble C: 28, N: 15, D: 2.16.

		JUDGES' RANKINGS									
		AUT	CAN	CZE	FRA	GER	GBR	ITA	JPN	USA	ORDINALS
1. Wolfgang Schwarz	AUT	1	1	1	2	1	1	2	2	2	13
2. Timothy Wood	USA	3	2	2	1	3	3	1	1	1	17
3. Patrick Pera	FRA	4	3	3	3	4	4	3	4	3	31
4. Emmerich Danzer	AUT	2	4	4	4	2	2	4	3	4	29
5. Gary Visconti	USA	7	6	8	5	5	5	5	5	6	52
6. John "Misha" Petkevich	USA	8	5	5	6	8	6	7	6	5	56
7. Jay Humphry	CAN	5	7	7	9	7	8	6	7	7	63
8. Ondrej Nepela	CZE	6	9	6	7	6	11	9	8	8	70

Wolfgang Schwarz, who was famous for consistently finishing second behind fellow Austrian Emmerich Danzer, won the narrowest of victories over Tim Wood. If either the Canadian judge or the British judge had given one more point to Wood, he would have won. Instead, Schwarz earned five first-place votes, while Wood was awarded only four. World champion Danzer had the best scores of the free-skating portion of the competition, but he was only fourth in the compulsories. He lost out on a bronze medal because of the placement rule, five to four, despite the fact that he had more points and fewer ordinals than Patrick Pera.

1972 Sapporo C: 17, N: 10, D: 2.11.

JUDGES' RANKINGS

		FRA	GDR	CAN	GBR	AUT	CZE	JPN	USA	SOV	ORDINALS
1. Ondrej Nepela	CZE	1	1	1	1	1	1	1	1	1	9
2. Sergei Chetveroukhin	SOV	3	2	3	2	2	2	2	2	2	20
3. Patrick Pera	FRA	2	3	2	3	3	3	3	6	3	28
4. Kenneth Shelley	USA	5	5	4	5	5	5	4	3	7	43
5. John "Misha" Petkevich	USA	4	6	5	8	6	4	5	4	5	47
6. Jan Hoffmann	GDR	9	4	8	7	4	6	6	7	4	55
7. Haig Oundjian	GBR	7	7	7	6	7	7	7	9	8	65
8. Vladimir Kovalev	SOV	10	11	10	9	10	8	8	8	6	80

Ondrej Nepela first competed in the Olympics in 1964, when he was 13 years old. That year he placed 22nd out of 24. In 1968 he moved up to eighth place, and in 1972, a seasoned veteran of 21, he was the unanimous choice of the judges, despite falling during a competition for the first time in four years. He had been attempting a triple-toe loop jump. Nepela died of AIDS at the age of 38.

1976 Innsbruck C: 20, N: 13, D: 2.11.

JUDGES' RANKINGS

		CAN	HUN	GBR	CZE	USA	FRA	JPN	SOV	GDR	ORDINALS
1. John Curry	GBR	2	1	1	1	1	1	1	2	1	11
2. Vladimir Kovalev	SOV	4	2	4	2	4	5	3	1	3	28
3. Toller Cranston	CAN	1	3	2	4	6	2	5	3	4	30
4. Jan Hoffman	GDR	3	5	5	3	3	3	4	6	2	34
5. Sergei Volkov	SOV	6	4	6	5	7	12	2	4	7	53
6. David Santee	USA	5	7	3	7	2	6	6	7	6	49
7. Terry Kubicka	USA	7	6	8	6	5	4	7	8	5	56
8. Yuri Ovchinnikov	SOV	9	8	10	8	10	9	8	5	8	75

Birmingham-born John Curry had two major obstacles to overcome on his way to a gold medal. The first was a lack of proper training facilities in England. This he solved by moving to Colorado in 1973. His second obstacle was the fact that the Soviet and Eastern European judges did not approve of his style of skating, which they considered too feminine. Actually Curry, who believed that figure skating was an art as well as a sport, felt that his style was in the tradition of three-time gold medalist Gillis Grafström. For the Olympics, however, Curry supplemented his natural elegance with enough "masculine" jumps, so that even the Communist judges could find no fault with his performance. The Soviet judge gave first place to Kovalev and the Canadian judge gave first place to Cranston, but even they placed Curry second. During his long program, Terry Kubicka became the only skater to perform a backflip during Olympic competition. The move was banned immediately afterward.

1980 Lake Placid C: 17, N: 10, D: 2.21.

JUDGES' RANKINGS

		CAN	GDR	SOV	USA	FRA	SWE	GBR	GER	JPN	ORDINALS
1. Robin Cousins	GBR	1	2	1	3	1	1	1	2	1	13
2. Jan Hoffman	GDR	2	1	2	1	2	2	2	1	2	15
3. Charles Tickner	USA	4	3	3	2	3	3	4	3	3	28
4. David Santee	USA	3	4	4	4	4	4	3	4	4	34
5. Scott Hamilton	USA	5	5	5	5	5	5	5	5	5	45
6. Igor Bobrin	SOV	6	6	6	6	7	6	6	6	6	55
7. Jean-Christophe Simond	FRA	7	8	7	9	6	7	7	7	6	64
8. Mitsuru Matsumura	JPN	8	7	9	8	9	9	9	8	8	75

There were four favorites in the 1980 competition: world champion Vladimir Kovalev of the U.S.S.R., former world champions Charles Tickner and Jan Hoffman, and European champion Robin Cousins of Bristol, England. Hoffman was taking part in his fourth Olympics, having first competed in 1968 when he was 12 years old. Twenty-sixth in 1968, he moved up to sixth in 1972 and fourth in 1976. Cousins, like John Curry before him, trained in Colorado with Carlo and Christa Fassi, who had also coached Peggy Fleming and Dorothy Hamill. In Denver Cousins lived only a few blocks from Charles Tickner.

Kovalev dropped out after placing fifth in the compulsories. Hoffman was in first place, followed by Tickner, Santee, and Cousins. The next day Cousins skated a brilliant short program to move into second place. He made one slip at the beginning of his long program, but otherwise skated flawlessly. Six judges gave Cousins first place, while three voted for Hoffman. Actually Cousins' worst fall came at the awards ceremony, where, dazzled by the lights and the applause and the emotion, he stumbled while trying to negotiate the one and a half steps to the victory platform. In his book, *Skating for Gold,* Cousins recalls the raising of the British flag to honor his victory: "As it was slowly going up, I lost sight of [my parents] for a while. But when the Union Jack was finally above our heads, we were looking directly at each other. So I was able to know how they were feeling and they could see how I was feeling, but it is difficult to describe that to anyone else."

1984 Sarajevo C: 23, N: 14, D: 2.16.

JUDGES' RANKINGS (FREE SKATING)

		CF	SP	YUG	GER	FRA	USA	GDR	SWE	SOV	CZE	CAN	ORDINALS
1. Scott Hamilton	USA	1	2	3	2	1	2	2	5	5	2	2	3.4
2. Brian Orser	CAN	7	1	1	1	2	1	1	1	1	1	1	5.6
3. Josef Sabovčik	CZE	4	5	2	5	5	3	3	2	2	3	4	7.4
4. Rudi Cerne	GER	3	6	7	4	4	6	4	4	7	4	3	8.2
5. Brian Boitano	USA	8	3	5	5	3	4	6	3	3	5	9	11.0
6. Jean-Christophe Simond	FRA	2	4	9	7	6	11	9	8	10	8	7	11.8
7. Aleksandr Fadeyev	SOV	5	8	10	3	10	10	5	7	4	6	11	13.2
8. Vladimir Kotin	SOV	11	9	6	10	9	5	7	5	5	9	5	16.2

Scott Hamilton, the adopted son of two college professors in Bowling Green, Ohio, was considered a shoo-in to win at Sarajevo. Beginning in September 1980, the 5-foot 2½-inch, 108-pound Hamilton had won 16 straight tournaments including three world championships. But the pressure of great expectations got to him and the quality of his performance was below that of his usual brilliance. He finished second to Brian Orser in both the short and long programs. However, the big lead that Hamilton had built up during the compulsories, in which Orser placed seventh, carried him to the top platform at the medal ceremony. Despite his own disappointment with his performance, Hamilton's good nature and dry wit made him a most popular winner.

1988 Calgary C: 28, N: 21, D: 2.20.

JUDGES' RANKINGS (FREE SKATING)

		CF	SP	GER	USA	DEN	SOV	SWI	JPN	GDR	CAN	CZE	ORDINALS
1. Brian Boitano	USA	2	2	2	1	1	1	1	1	2	2	2	3.0
2. Brian Orser	CAN	3	1	1	2	2	2	2	2	1	1	1	4.2
3. Viktor Petrenko	SOV	6	3	3	3	3	2	4	3	5	3	3	7.8
4. Aleksandr Fadeyev	SOV	1	9	4	4	4	4	3	4	3	4	4	8.2

5. Grzegorz Filipowski	POL	7	4	7	6	5	8	8	6	6	6	6	10.8
6. Vladimir Kotin	SOV	5	6	8	9	7	6	9	5	4	8	5	13.4
7. Christopher Bowman	USA	8	5	5	5	8	7	5	8	8	5	8	13.8
8. Kurt Browning	CAN	11	7	6	7	6	9	7	9	7	7	9	15.4

The North American media promoted this event as "The Battle of the Brians": Brian Orser of Penetanguishene, Ontario, and Brian Boitano of Sunnyvale, California. They had met 10 times in international competition, with Orser leading the series 7–3. However, by 1988 they were so evenly matched that it was impossible to choose a favorite. Over the years, Orser had developed a reputation as a nervous performer who stumbled at major championships. He placed second at the 1984 Olympics, second at the 1984 world championships, second at the 1985 world championships, and second again at the 1986 world championships. In 1987 he finally broke through his invisible barrier and won his first world title. Boitano, meanwhile, had been crowned world champion in 1986 before finishing second to Orser in 1987.

In Calgary, Orser placed first in the short program and trailed Boitano by a negligible margin going into the long program, which was worth 50 percent of the total score. Boitano skated first and gave a stunning performance, with only a barely perceptible bobble in a triple jump landing. In figure skating it is rare for a champion to do his best in a major competition because of the enormous pressure involved, but Boitano broke the rule. "I felt like angels were lifting and spinning me," he would later explain.

Despite Boitano's near-perfection, it was still possible for Orser, a superior artistic skater, to salvage the gold medal. But the pressure on Orser was even greater than that on Boitano. On top of the natural stress brought on by competing for an Olympic title, Orser carried with him the burden of being the host country's only gold medal hope. Ninety seconds into his routine, Orser nearly missed a triple flip jump, landing on two feet instead of one. Still, in the words of Dick Button, it was only "the slightest of slightest glitches," and not enough to settle the contest in Boitano's favor. But late in his routine, a fatigued Orser downgraded a triple axel to a double and his fate was sealed.

As it was, the judging could hardly have been closer. Four judges voted for Orser, three for Boitano, and two scored it a tie. In figure skating, judges are given the option of breaking ties based on the criterion of their choice. In this case, both judges who had scored the Brians evenly chose the score for technical merit as their tiebreaker. As both had awarded Boitano higher marks for technical merit, he ended up winning 5–4.

All of the hype about the "Battle of the Brians" aside, Boitano and Orser were actually good friends. At the medal ceremony, Boitano was plagued by contradictory emotions. "I almost felt guilty feeling great," he would later say. "I tried to hold it back, so me feeling great wouldn't make him feel worse."

The third-place winner, Viktor Petrenko, was the first Ukrainian to win a medal in an individual event at a Winter Olympics.

1992 Albertville C: 31, N: 23, D: 2.15.

		JUDGES' RANKINGS (FREE SKATING)										
		SP	AUS	FIN	SOV	ITA	CAN	CZE	JPN	USA	FRA	ORDINALS
1. Viktor Petrenko	SOV	1	2	1	1	1	3	1	1	1	1	1.5
2. Paul Wylie	USA	3	1	2	4	3	1	5	3	2	2	3.5
3. Petr Barna	CZE	2	3	3	2	2	4	2	2	3	3	4.0
4. Christopher Bowman	USA	7	4	5	4	5	5	6	5	4	7	7.5

		SP	AUS	FIN	SOV	ITA	CAN	CZE	JPN	USA	FRA	ORDINALS
	JUDGES' RANKINGS (FREE SKATING)											
5. Aleksei Urmanov	SOV	5	6	6	3	8	6	3	9	6	5	7.5
6. Kurt Browning	CAN	4	8	4	8	6	2	4	4	9	6	8.0
7. Elvis Stojko	CAN	6	7	7	7	4	7	7	6	7	9	10.0
8. Vyacheslav Zagorodniuk	SOV	10	5	8	6	7	9	9	7	5	4	13.0

At the last two world championships, Viktor Petrenko had ranked first after the short program only to lose to Kurt Browning because he wilted toward the end of his long program. Once again Petrenko led after the short program, and once again he wilted in the second half of his long program, even falling once, but this time Browning, slow to recover from a back injury, was unable to match the performances that had earned him three straight world titles. The star of the competition was Harvard graduate Paul Wylie, at 27 the oldest skater on the ice. Wylie was the only one of the top six men to complete his long program without falling or touching the ice with his hand. However, his program was not as challenging as Petrenko's. Bronze medalist Petr Barna became the first skater to successfully perform a quadruple jump in the Olympics.

WOMEN

1908 London C: 5, N: 3, D: 10.29.

		GBR	SWE	SWI	RUS	GER	ORDINALS
	JUDGES' RANKINGS						
1. Florence "Madge" Syers	GBR	1	1	1	1	1	5
2. Elsa Rendschmidt	GER	3	2	2	2	2	11
3. Dorothy Greenhough-Smith	GBR	2	3	4	3	3	15
4. Elna Montgomery	SWE	4	4	5	4	4	21
5. Gwendolyn Lycett	GBR	5	5	3	5	5	23

In 1902, 20-year-old Madge Syers caused a sensation by becoming the first woman to enter the world championships. Even more shocking was the fact that she placed second behind Ulrich Salchow. Figure skating authorities immediately banned women from international competitions, although Syers did take part in the British national championship, winning in 1903 and again in 1904, when she defeated her husband. In 1906 a separate women's event was introduced at the world championships, and Syers won easily. She won again the following year and then was the unanimous choice of the five judges at the Olympics.

1920 Antwerp C: 6, N: 4, D: 4.25.

		SWE	FRA	BEL	NOR	GBR	ORDINALS
	JUDGES' RANKINGS						
1. Magda Julin-Mauroy	SWE	2	3	2	3	2	12
2. Svea Norén	SWE	1	1.5	3	4	3	12.5
3. Theresa Weld	USA	3	1.5	1	6	4	15.5
4. Phyllis Johnson	GBR	4.5	4	4	5	1	18.5
5. Margot Moe	NOR	4.5	6	6	1	5	22.5
6. Ingrid Gulbrandsen	NOR	6	5	5	2	6	24

Magda Julin won the closest of all Olympic figure skating contests despite the fact that she received no first-place votes. The British judge voted for Johnson, the Swedish judge for Norén, and the Norwegian judge placed Moe and Gulbrandsen first and second, even though the other judges put them last. The Belgian judge voted for Weld and the French judge declared a tie between Norén and Weld. Julin did receive three second-place votes and won according to the placings countback rule. At one point Weld was cautioned by the judges for making jumps "unsuitable for a lady."

1924 Chamonix C: 8, N: 6, D: 1.29.

		JUDGES' RANKINGS							
		AUT	FIN	GBR	AUT	FRA	BEL	FRA	ORDINALS
1. Herma Planck-Szabó	AUT	1	1	1	1	1	1	1	7
2. Beatrix Loughran	USA	2	2	2	2	2	2	2	14
3. Ethel Muckelt	GBR	4	3	3	4	4	5	3	26
4. Theresa Blanchard-Weld	USA	3	4	4	3	5	3	5	27
5. Andrée Joly	FRA	6	6	7	5	3	4	7	38
6. Cecil Smith	CAN	5	7	5	8	6	7	6	44
7. G. Kathleen Shaw	GBR	7	8	6	6	7	8	4	46
8. Sonja Henie	NOR	8	5	8	7	8	6	8	50

In retrospect, the 1924 competition was most notable for the appearance of the last-place finisher, 11-year-old Sonja Henie, who was to become the most famous figure skater of all time.

1928 St. Moritz C: 20, N: 8, D: 2.18.

		JUDGES' RANKINGS							
		NOR	FRA	GBR	BEL	USA	GER	AUT	ORDINALS
1. Sonja Henie	NOR	1	1	1	1	2	1	1	8
2. Fritzi Burger	AUT	3	2	4	5	6	3	2	25
3. Beatrix Loughran	USA	7	3	2	4	1	6	5	28
4. Maribel Vinson	USA	4	5	5	3	3	4	8	32
5. Cecil Smith	CAN	6	4	3	2	5	5	7	32
6. Constance Wilson	CAN	5	6	6	6	4	2	6	35
7. Melitta Brunner	AUT	2	7	8	10	8	9	4	48
8. Ilse Hornung	AUT	8	9	10	8	9	7	3	54

Sonja Henie was born in Oslo on April 8, 1912. Her father was a wealthy furrier, the owner of Norway's largest fur company, as well as the owner of Oslo's first automobile. Sonja gained valuable experience at the 1924 Olympics. Two years later she had improved enough to finish second at the world championships. In 1927 the world championships were held on Henie's home rink in Oslo. Henie won the title, but not without some controversy concerning the judging. There were five judges: one Austrian, one German, and three from Norway. The Austrian and the German both gave their first-place votes to Herma Planck-Szabó. However, all three Norwegian judges voted for Sonja Henie, giving her the championship. The ensuing uproar prompted the International Skating Union to institute a rule, still in effect, allowing only one judge per country in international meets. At the 1928 Olympics there was no such controversy, as Henie was awarded first place by six of the seven judges. Only the American judge voted for Beatrix Loughran, who had the unusual distinction of receiving one vote for each of the first seven places.

1932 Lake Placid C: 15, N: 7, D: 10.9.

			JUDGES' RANKINGS						
			NOR	GBR	AUT	FIN	CAN	FRA	USA	ORDINALS
1.	Sonja Henie	NOR	1	1	1	1	1	1	1	7
2.	Fritzi Burger	AUT	2	4	2	3	2	2	3	18
3.	Maribel Vinson	USA	4	2	3	4	5	3	2	23
4.	Constance Wilson-Samuel	CAN	3	5	4	5	3	4	4	28
5.	Vivi-Anne Hultén	SWE	5	3	5	2	4	5	5	29
6.	Yvonne de Ligne	BEL	6	6	8	6	7	6	6	45
7.	Megan Taylor	GBR	8	10	7	9	6	7	8	55
8.	M. Cecilia Colledge	GBR	14	9	6	7	13	8	7	64

Sonja Henie was the unanimous choice of the seven judges. Already Sonja Henie imitators were springing up wherever figure skating was appreciated. Two 11-year-olds from Great Britain, Megan Taylor and Cecilia Colledge, placed seventh and eighth at Lake Placid. Bronze medalist Maribel Vinson later became the first female sportswriter for the *New York Times.*

1936 Garmisch-Partenkirchen C: 26, N: 13, D: 2.15.

			JUDGES' RANKINGS						
			USA	GBR	GER	BEL	SWE	AUT	CZE	ORDINALS
1.	Sonja Henie	NOR	1	1	1	1	1	1.5	1	7.5
2.	M. Cecilia Colledge	GBR	2	2	2	2	2	1.5	2	13.5
3.	Vivi-Anne Hultén	SWE	4	4	3	4	3	7	3	28
4.	Liselotte Landbeck	BEL	6	5	5	3	6	3	4	32
5.	Maribel Vinson	USA	3	3	9	7	4	8	5	39
6.	Hedy Stenuf	AUT	5	7	8	5	5	4	6	40
7.	Emmy Putzinger	AUT	8	10	6	6	7	5	7	49
8.	Viktoria Lindpaintner	GER	7	6	4	8	8	10	8	51

By 1936 Sonja Henie was so popular that police had to be called out to control the crowds around her in places as far apart as New York City and Prague. She had announced that she would retire from competition following the 1936 world championships, to be held one week after the Olympics. She wanted to close out her amateur career with a third Olympic gold medal, so she felt great tension preceding the competition. When the scoring totals were posted for the compulsory figures, Henie was only 3.6 points ahead of Colledge. When Henie was told the results she tore the offending sheet of paper off the announcements board and ripped it to shreds, stating that it was a misrepresentation. Fifteen-year-old Cecilia Colledge was the second skater to perform her free-skating program. As she glided onto the ice she gave the Nazi salute, which pleased the crowd. Just as she prepared to begin her routine, it was discovered that someone had put on the wrong music, and she was forced to endure a delay while the proper record was found. Not surprisingly, Colledge almost fell during the first minute of her performance. But she recovered sufficiently to earn an average score of 5.7. Sonja Henie, the last of the 26 skaters, appeared nervous, but skated with great vigor and precision. An average score of 5.8 assured her of her third gold medal. A week later she won her tenth straight world championship, a feat surpassed only by Ulrich Salchow, who won 11 consecutive world titles from 1901 through 1911.

During her competitive career, Sonja Henie accumulated 1473 cups, medals, and trophies. After she turned professional her parents convinced Twentieth Century-Fox to put her in the movies. Henie's first film, *One in a Million,* was a big success, and nine more films followed. In 1937 she earned over $200,000. Her father died that year, but Sonja definitely inherited his business acumen. She made enough money to allow her to engage in an occasional indulgence. The only person she trusted to sharpen her skates was Eddie Pec. One time while Sonja was performing in Chicago, she needed her skates sharpened. So she called Eddie Pec in New York. Pec took the next train to Chicago, arriving the following day. He spent a couple minutes sharpening Henie's skates, then turned around and took the next train back to New York.

Sonja Henie became a U.S. citizen in 1941. After divorcing two Americans, the 44-year-old Henie married her childhood sweetheart, Norwegian shipowner Niels Onstad. Sonja Henie died of leukemia at the age of 57, while on an ambulance airplane flying her from Paris to Oslo. She was worth over $47 million at the time of her death.

Another future actress who took part in the 1936 figure skating competition was Vera Hruba of Czechoslovakia, who placed 17th. As Vera Hruba Ralston, she starred in numerous B pictures, including *The Lady and the Monster, Hoodlum Empire,* and *I, Jane Doe.* Her specialties were Westerns and pioneer films. She also married the president of Republic Pictures, Herbert Yates, who was sued by stockholders for using company profits to further his wife's career.

1948 St. Moritz C: 25, N: 10, D: 2.6.

				JUDGES' RANKINGS							
		ITA	USA	SWI	GBR	CAN	AUT	FRA	HUN	CZE	ORDINALS
1.	Barbara Ann Scott	CAN	1	1	1	2	1	2	1	1	1	11
2.	Eva Pawlik	AUT	2	2	3	3	4	1	2	2	5	24
3.	Jeannette Altwegg	GBR	3	4	2	1	2	5	3	4	4	28
4.	Jirina Nekolová	CZE	5	3	4	4	3	4	5	3	3	34
5.	Alena Vrzánová	CZE	6	6	6	6	6	3	4	5	2	44
6.	Yvonne Sherman	USA	9	7	7	8	5	6	6	7	7	62
7.	Bridget Shirley Adams	GBR	7	8	5	5	11	7	11	6	9	69
8.	Gretchen Merrill	USA	4	5	8	7	8	9	8	9	15	73

Barbara Ann Scott, the 19-year-old world champion, had put in 20,000 hours of practice prior to the Olympics. Shortly before the Games, her hometown of Ottawa awarded her a yellow convertible. However, I.O.C. member Avery Brundage contended that such a gift would make her a professional and disqualify her from the Olympics. After weeping in public, she reluctantly returned the car. The day of the free-skating competition, the ice was badly chewed up by two hockey matches. Just before Scott went out to perform, one of the earlier skaters, Eileen Seigh of the United States, gave her a complete description of the location of all the ruts and clean spots all over the rink. Scott won seven of the nine first-place votes, with the Austrian judge voting for Pawlik and the British judge for Altwegg. Immediately after the Olympics, Scott turned professional and collected her convertible.

1952 Oslo C: 25, N: 12, D: 2.20.

				JUDGES' RANKINGS							
		USA	GBR	GER	SWI	NOR	CAN	AUT	FIN	FRA	ORDINALS
1.	Jeannette Altwegg	GBR	4	2	1	1	1	1	1	1	2	14
2.	Tenley Albright	USA	1	1	3	5	2	2	3	2	3	22
3.	Jacqueline du Bief	FRA	3	3	2	2	4	3	2	4	1	24
4.	Sonya Klopfer	USA	2	5	4	4	3	4	4	5	5	36
5.	Virginia Baxter	USA	5	4	7	9	5	6	7	3	4	50
6.	Suzanne Morrow	CAN	6	6	6	8	8	5	5	6	6	56
7.	Barbara Wyatt	GBR	7	7	5	6	6	9	9	7	7	63
8.	Gundi Busch	GER	10	9	8	7	7	8	8	10	8	75

Jeannette Altwegg placed only fourth in free-skating. However she had built up such a large lead during the compulsory figures that she won anyway.

1956 Cortina C: 21, N: 11, D: 2.2.

			AUS	AUT	CAN	CZE	FRA	GER	GBR	ITA	HOL	USA	SWI	ORDINALS
								JUDGES' RANKINGS						
1.	Tenley Albright	USA	1	1	1	1	1	1	1	1	1	2	1	12
2.	Carol Heiss	USA	2	2	2	2	2	2	2	2	2	1	2	21
3.	Ingrid Wendl	AUT	8	3	4	3	3	3	3	3	3	3	3	39
4.	Yvonne de Monfort Sugden	GBR	3	5	8	4	4	7	4	4	4	5	5	53
5.	Hanna Eigel	AUT	4	4	6	5	6	4	5	5	5	4	4	52
6.	Carole Jane Pachl	CAN	5	7	3	6	5	10	8	9	8	6	6	73
7.	Hannerl Walter	AUT	6	6	7	7	10	8.5	6	8	7	9	9	83.5
8.	Catherine Machado	USA	10	8	5	9	8	8.5	7	10	6	7	8	86.5

Tenley Albright, a surgeon's daughter from Newton Center, Massachusetts, had been stricken by nonparalytic polio at the age of 11. Less than two weeks before the Cortina Olympics, Tenley was practicing when she hit a rut. As she fell, her left skate hit her ankle joint, cut through three layers of her right boot, slashed a vein, and severely scraped the bone. Her father arrived two days later and patched her up. In the Olympic competition she skated well enough to earn the first-place votes of ten of the 11 judges. Back in the United States she entered Harvard Medical School and eventually became a surgeon herself.

1960 Squaw Valley C: 26, N: 13, D: 2.23.

			AUT	CAN	CZE	GER	GBR	ITA	JPN	HOL	USA	ORDINALS
						JUDGES' RANKINGS						
1.	Carol Heiss	USA	1	1	1	1	1	1	1	1	1	9
2.	Sjoukje Dijkstra	HOL	2	2	2	2	2	2	3	2	3	20
3.	Barbara Roles	USA	3	4	3	3	3	3	2	3	2	26
4.	Jana Mrázková	CZE	5	7	4	5	4	4	10	5	9	53
5.	Joan Haanappel	HOL	7	5	7	6	6	6	6	4	5	52
6.	Laurence Owen	USA	6	3	6	13	7	5	4	9	4	57
7.	Regine Heitzer	AUT	4	9	5	4	5	7	12	6	6	58
8.	Anna Galmarini	ITA	9	10	9	7	8	8	11	7	10	79

In 1956, 16-year-old Carol Heiss of Ozone Park, Queens, traveled to Cortina with her mother, who was dying of cancer. She gained a silver medal at the Olympics, but two weeks later, she defeated Tenley Albright for the first time to win the world championship in Garmisch-Partenkirchen. In October her mother died, but Carol Heiss took a vow to win an Olympic gold medal in her honor. This she did with extraordinary ease in 1960, earning the first-place votes of all nine judges. After the Olympics, Heiss attempted a Hollywood career, but understandably lost interest after making one film: *Snow White and the Three Stooges*.

1964 Innsbruck C: 30, N: 14, D: 2.2.

			GER	FRA	GBR	JPN	CAN	HOL	AUT	SWE	CZE	ORDINALS
						JUDGES' RANKINGS						
1.	Sjoukje Dijkstra	HOL	1	1	1	1	1	1	1	1	1	9
2.	Regine Heitzer	AUT	2	2	3	2	3	3	2	3	2	22
3.	Petra Burka	CAN	3	4	2	4	2	2	3	2	3	25
4.	Nicole Hassler	FRA	4	3	4	7	4	4	4	4	4	38

5. Miwa Fukuhara	JPN	7	5	7	3	5	5	5	8	5	50
6. Peggy Fleming	USA	5	7	11	5	8	6	6	5	6	59
7. Christine Haigler	USA	15	8	9	8	6	7	7	7	7	74
8. Albertina Noyes	USA	10	6	5	6	10	9	10	9	8	73

Two-time world champion Sjoukje Dijkstra was the third straight silver medalist to win a gold medal four years later.

1968 Grenoble C: 32, N: 15, D: 2.11.

		CAN	CZE	GDR	GER	GBR	HUN	JPN	USA	SOV	ORDINALS
						JUDGES' RANKINGS					
1. Peggy Fleming	USA	1	1	1	1	1	1	1	1	1	9
2. Gabriele Seyfert	GDR	2	2	2	2	2	2	2	2	2	18
3. Hana Mašková	CZE	4	3	3	3	4	3	4	4	3	31
4. Albertina Noyes	USA	3	6	6	5	3	4	5	3	5	40
5. Beatrix Schuba	AUT	5	4	4	4	6	6	10	8	4	51
6. Zsuzsa Almássy	HUN	8	5	5	6	5	5	6	10	7	57
7. Karen Magnussen	CAN	7	8	7	7	7	8	8	5	6	63
8. Kumiko Ohkawa	JPN	6	7	8	8	8	7	3	6	8	61

Like Carol Heiss, Peggy Fleming came from a family which had sacrificed greatly to further her passion for figure skating. Peggy's father, who had moved the family from Cleveland to Pasadena, California, to Colorado Springs (and Carlo Fassi), died in 1966. Her mother designed and sewed all of Peggy's dresses. As a competition, the contest at Grenoble had little to offer. Fleming built up a huge lead after the compulsory figures and easily won all of the first-place votes. Likewise, Gaby Seyfert was awarded all of the second-place votes. Peggy Fleming was the only U.S. gold medal winner of the Grenoble Games.

1972 Sapporo C: 19, N: 14, D: 2.7.

		ITA	SOV	GDR	SWE	AUT	CAN	USA	JPN	HUN	ORDINALS
						JUDGES' RANKINGS					
1. Beatrix Schuba	AUT	1	1	1	1	1	1	1	1	1	9
2. Karen Magnussen	CAN	2	2	2	2	4	2	4	3	2	23
3. Janet Lynn	USA	3	3	3	3	3	3	3	2	4	27
4. Julie Holmes	USA	4	4	5	7	2	4	2	4	7	39
5. Zsuzsa Almássy	HUN	6	5	6	4	6	5	7	5	3	47
6. Sonja Morgenstern	GDR	7	6	4	5	7	7	5	6	6	53
7. Rita Trapanese	ITA	5	7	7	6	5	6	6	8	5	55
8. Christine Errath	GDR	8	9	8	8	9	9	9	9	9	78

World champion Trixi Schuba built up a large lead with her compulsory figures and coasted to victory with a seventh place in free-skating.

1976 Innsbruck C: 21, N: 15, D: 2.13.

		SOV	USA	GDR	JPN	HOL	CZE	CAN	GER	ITA	ORDINALS
						JUDGES' RANKINGS					
1. Dorothy Hamill	USA	1	1	1	1	1	1	1	1	1	9
2. Dianne de Leeuw	HOL	2	2	3	2	2	3	2	2	2	20
3. Christine Errath	GDR	3	3	2	3	3	4	4	3	3	28
4. Anett Pötzsch	GDR	4	4	4	4	4	2	3	4	4	33
5. Isabel de Navarre	GER	7	8	5	10	5	6	8	5	5	59

		SOV	USA	GDR	JPN	HOL	CZE	CAN	GER	ITA	ORDINALS
6. Wendy Burge	USA	5	5	7	7	10	7	6	8	8	63
7. Susanna Driano	ITA	8	7	6	6	8	9	5	7	7	63
8. Linda Fratianne	USA	9	6	9	8	6	8	9	6	6	67

JUDGES' RANKINGS

For the fifth straight time the women's figure skating was decided by unanimous decision. Hamill's victory was particularly exciting for her coach, Carlo Fassi, who achieved a unique double, having also coached the men's winner, John Curry.

1980 Lake Placid C: 22, N: 15, D: 2.23.

		GER	AUT	JPN	USA	YUG	FIN	ITA	GDR	SWI	ORDINALS
1. Anett Pötzsch	GDR	1	1	2	2	1	1	1	1	1	11
2. Linda Fratianne	USA	2	2	1	1	2	2	2	2	2	16
3. Dagmar Lurz	GER	3	3	4	3	3	3	3	3	3	28
4. Denise Biellmann	SWI	4	5	6	6	4	6	4	4	4	43
5. Lisa-Marie Allen	USA	5	4	5	4	6	5	5	5	6	45
6. Emi Watanabe	JPN	6	7	3	5	5	4	6	7	5	48
7. Claudia Kristofics-Binder	AUT	7	6	7	7	7	7	7	5	7	60
8. Susanna Driano	ITA	8	9	10	9	9	8	8	8	8	77

JUDGES' RANKINGS

The closest Olympic women's figure skating competition in 60 years showcased the friendly rivalry between Linda Fratianne of Los Angeles and Anett Pötzsch of Karl-Marx Stadt. In 1977 Fratianne had won the world championship, but in 1978 she was defeated by Pötzsch. The following year, Linda won back the title, but at the Olympics, the pendulum swung Anett's way. Both 19-year-olds tried to increase their chances of victory by altering their appearance. Linda had cosmetic surgery to her nose, while Anett lost ten pounds. Both tried to appear brighter, livelier, sexier. In the end, it turned out that glamour was unimportant, as Pötzsch gained a solid lead in the compulsory figures and Fratianne was unable to close the gap. Denise Biellmann ranked first in free-skating, but her 12th place in the compulsories kept her out of the medals.

1984 Sarajevo C: 23, N: 16, D: 2.18.

		CF	SP	SOV	YUG	GER	ITA	SWI	GDR	USA	CAN	BEL	ORDINALS
1. Katarina Witt	GDR	3	1	1	1	1	2	2	1	2	1	2	3.2
2. Rosalynn Sumners	USA	1	5	2	4	2	1	1	3	1	2	1	4.6
3. Kira Ivanova	SOV	5	3	4	3	5	6	8	5	5	8	5	9.2
4. Tiffany Chin	USA	12	2	3	2	3	3	4	2	3	3	3	11.0
5. Anna Kondrashova	SOV	7	4	6	6	4	5	5	7	6	5	7	11.8
6. Elaine Zayak	USA	13	6	5	5	6	4	3	4	4	4	4	14.2
7. Manuela Ruben	GER	6	11	7	7	8	7	6	8	8	12	10	15.0
8. Yelena Vodorezova	SOV	2	8	11	10	11	13	11	13	12	11	6	15.4

JUDGES' RANKINGS (FREE SKATING)

The 1984 Olympics pitted defending world champion Rosalynn Sumners against 1982 world champion Elaine Zayak and the beautiful up-and-coming East German, Katarina Witt. Zayak removed herself from the competition for the gold medal by placing 13th in the compulsories, which were won by Sumners, with Witt a strong third. Witt took a slight lead following the short program, and turned the free-skating into a head-to-head showdown. Witt, skating before Sumners, achieved high marks, but not high enough to put first place out of reach for Sumners. The Edmonds, Washington, native looked close to victory, but in the closing seconds of her routine, she let up slightly, turning a triple toe loop into a double and a double axel into a single. This lapse probably also turned her gold medal into silver. After her Olympic victory, Katarina Witt received 35,000 love letters.

1988 Calgary C: 31, N: 23, D: 2.27.

					JUDGES' RANKINGS (FREE SKATING)								
			CF	SP	SWI	USA	GBR	JPN	GDR	GER	SOV	CAN	CZE	ORDINALS
1.	Katarina Witt	GDR	3	1	2	2	3	3	1	3	1	2	2	4.2
2.	Elizabeth Manley	CAN	4	3	1	1	1	1	2	1	2	1	1	4.6
3.	Debra Thomas	USA	2	2	5	4	5	4	5	4	4	4	5	6.0
4.	Jill Trenary	USA	5	6	4	5	4	5	4	5	5	5	4	10.4
5.	Midori Ito	JPN	10	4	3	3	2	2	3	2	3	3	3	10.6
6.	Claudia Leistner	GER	6	9	6	6	6	8	6	6	8	6	6	13.2
7.	Kira Ivanova	SOV	1	10	7	15	14	7	8	9	7	11	10	13.6
8.	Anna Kondrashova	SOV	9	7	8	7	8	6	7	7	6	9	9	15.2

The 1988 competition turned out to be a classic matchup between defending Olympic and world champion Katarina Witt and the only person to beat her in five years, the 1986 world champion, Stanford pre-medical student Debi Thomas. After the short program, Thomas held a slight lead over Witt, with local favorite Elizabeth Manley a distant third.

As it happened, both Witt and Thomas chose to perform their long program to Georges Bizet's *Carmen*. Witt, first on the ice, skated cautiously and tentatively. Having immersed herself in the character of Carmen, her artistic presentation was flawless, but because she took few risks, her marks for technical merit were unimpressive and she left the door open for Thomas to seize the gold medal. But Thomas was preceded by Elizabeth Manley. The 5-foot Canadian, who had a reputation for crumbling under pressure, brought down the house with a brilliant performance that would ultimately earn her an unexpected silver medal.

Thomas began her routine with a triple toe loop combination, but she underrotated the second jump and landed badly. Barely 20 seconds into her four-minute program, she gave up. "The whole reason I came here was to be great," she later explained, "and after that I couldn't be great." Thomas missed two more triples, once touching the ice with her hand to keep from falling. Despite her disappointing performance, Thomas made history by becoming the first black athlete to win a medal in the Winter Olympics. Witt, for her part, became the first repeat winner in singles figure skating since Sonja Henie.

1992 Albertville C: 29, N: 21, D: 2.21.

			JUDGES' RANKINGS (FREE SKATING)									
			SP	GER	CAN	CHN	FRA	JPN	DEN	CZE	GBR	SOV	ORDINALS
1.	Kristi Yamaguchi	USA	1	1	1	1	1	2	1	2	1	1	1.5
2.	Midori Ito	JPN	4	2	2	2	2	1	2	1	3	2	4.0
3.	Nancy Kerrigan	USA	2	4	3	3	5	3	3	3	5	3	4.0

		SP	GER	CAN	CHN	FRA	JPN	DEN	CZE	GBR	SOV	ORDINALS
					JUDGES' RANKINGS (FREE SKATING)							
4.	Tonya Harding	USA	6	5	7	4	4	4	8	6	7	4	7.0
5.	Surya Bonaly	FRA	3	3	8	5	3	6	7	4	10	6	7.5
6.	Chen Lu	CHN	11	6	5	6	7	8	4	5	4	5	10.5
7.	Yuka Sato	JPN	7	10	4	7	6	5	6	9	2	8	10.5
8.	Karen Preston	CAN	12	7	6	9	10	7	5	7	9	7	14.0

The two favorites were 22-year-old Midori Ito and 20-year-old Kristi Yamaguchi. As a 12-year-old, Ito had become the first female to land a triple-triple combination. At the Calgary Games she captivated the audience with an exuberant display of breathtaking jumps. Later that year she became the first woman to complete a triple axel in competition, a feat she repeated while winning the 1989 world championship. At the 1991 world championships in Munich, Ito was involved in a memorable incident. During the warm-up period before her short program, she was unintentionally broadsided by French skater Laetitia Hubert. Still dazed when she began her performance a few minutes later, Ito mistimed the takeoff of her double toe loop and went flying out of the rink. In Albertville, she had another unfortunate encounter with a French skater. Just as Ito was about to attempt the first jump in her routine during a practice session, Surya Bonaly cut in front of her and did a backflip—an illegal move. Rattled by this unsportsmanlike conduct, Ito missed seven of ten triple axel attempts. The next day, Ito dropped the triple axel from her short program and replaced it with the easier triple lutz. But she fell during the triple lutz and wound up only fourth going into the free skate. Ito's misfortune smoothed the path for Kristi Yamaguchi.

Yamaguchi, whose mother was born in a World War II internment camp for Japanese-Americans while her grandfather was serving as a lieutenant in the U.S. Army, became obsessed with figure skating as a little girl. Her favorite toy was a Dorothy Hamill doll that she carried with her everywhere. Through 1990, Yamaguchi competed in both singles and pairs (with Rudy Galindo). That year she qualified for the world championships in both events, placing fourth and fifth respectively. Then she dropped out of pairs to concentrate on singles and was rewarded with her first world championship title in 1991.

In Albertville, Yamaguchi led after the original program, with her Olympic roommate, Nancy Kerrigan, in second and Bonaly third. But Yamaguchi had a history of placing first in the original program and then falling behind after the long program. This time she was the first of the leaders to skate. Backstage she was approached, for the first time, by none other than her childhood idol, Dorothy Hamill, who wished her luck and told her to go out and "have fun." Yamaguchi's relatively conservative program was marred by a touchdown at the end of a shaky triple loop. However, all the other contenders fell and Yamaguchi won a clear victory.

PAIRS

1908 London T: 3, N: 2, D: 10.29.

			GER	SWI	GBR	GBR	RUS	ORDINALS
					JUDGES' RANKINGS			
1.	Anna Hübler Heinrich Burger	GER	1	1	1	1	1	5
2.	Phyllis Johnson James Johnson	GBR	2	2	2	2	2	10
3.	Florence "Madge" Syers Edgar Syers	GBR	3	3	3	3	3	13

1920 Antwerp T: 8, N: 6, D: 4.26.

					JUDGES' RANKINGS				
		SWE	FRA	BEL	NOR	FIN	GBR	SWI	ORDINALS
1. Ludovika Jakobsson-Eilers Walter Jakobsson	FIN	1	1	1	1	1	1	1	7
2. Alexia Bryn-Schoien Yngvar Bryn	NOR	2	2	2.5	2	2	2	2	15.5
3. Phyllis Johnson Basil Williams	GBR	3	3	6	3	4	3	3	25
4. Theresa Weld Nathaniel Niles	USA	4	4	2.5	6	3	4	4	28.5
5. Ethel Muckelt Sydney Wallwork	GBR	5	6	4	4	6	5	6	34
6. Georgette Herbos Georges Waegemans	BEL	6.5	5	5	8	5	7	5	41.5
7. Simone Sabouret Charles Sabouret	FRA	6.5	7	7	5	7	6	7	45.5
8. Madelon Beaumont Kenneth Macdonald Beaumont	GBR	8	8	8	7	8	8	8	55

1924 Chamonix T: 9, N: 7, D: 1.31.

					JUDGES' RANKINGS				
		AUT	GBR	SWI	FRA	AUT	FRA	BEL	ORDINALS
1. Helene Engelmann Alfred Berger	AUT	1	2	1	1	1	1	2	9
2. Ludovika Jakobsson-Eilers Walter Jakobsson	FIN	4	3	2	2	3.5	3	1	18.5
3. Andrée Joly Pierre Brunet	FRA	2	6	3	4	2	2	3	22
4. Ethel Muckelt John Page	GBR	6.5	1	7	3	3.5	5.5	4	30.5
5. Georgette Herbos Georges Waegemans	BEL	3	4	6	7	7	4	6	37
6. Theresa Blanchard-Weld Nathaniel Niles	USA	5	5	5	6	5.5	5.5	7	39
7. Cecil Smith Melville Rogers	CAN	6.5	8	4	5	5.5	7	5	41.5
8. F. Mildred Richardson Thomas Richardson	GBR	8	7	8	9	8	8	9	57

Because Canadians Smith and Rogers received the most enthusiastic applause, French newspapers quickly spread the news that they had won the competition. However, when the scores were finally tallied a few hours later, it turned out that they had placed only seventh.

1928 St. Moritz T: 13, N: 10, D: 2.19.

					JUDGES' RANKINGS					
		GER	FIN	SWI	USA	AUT	FRA	GBR	CZE	BEL	ORDINALS
1. Andrée Joly Pierre Brunet	FRA	4	1	1	1	2	1	2	1	1	14
2. Lilly Scholz Otto Kaiser	AUT	3	2	2	2	1	2	1	2	2	17
3. Melitta Brunner Ludwig Wrede	AUT	2	4	3	5	3	3	3	3	3	29

		GER	FIN	SWI	USA	AUT	FRA	GBR	CZE	BEL	ORDINALS
						JUDGES' RANKINGS					
4.	Beatrix Loughran Sherwin Badger	USA	1	9	5	3	5	4	5	7	4	43
5.	Ludovika Jakobsson Walter Jakobsson	FIN	7	3	7	6	7	6	6	4	5	51
6.	Josy van Leberghe Robert van Zeebroeck	BEL	6	7	4	4	6	7	7	5	8	54
7.	Ethel Muckelt John Page	GBR	8.5	6	8	8	8	5	4	8	6	61.5
8.	Ilse Kishauer Ernst Gaste	GER	5	5	6	9	4	9	8	6	11	63

Joly and Brunet dominated pairs figure skating from the time they won their first world championship on Valentine's Day, 1926, until they turned professional in 1936. Joly radicalized the sport by dressing in black like her partner. Previously, female pairs skaters always wore white.

1932 Lake Placid T: 7, N: 4, D: 2.12.

			HUN	NOR	AUT	FIN	FRA	GBR	USA	ORDINALS
					JUDGES' RANKINGS					
1.	Andrée Brunet [Joly] Pierre Brunet	FRA	2.5	1	1.5	3	1	1	2	12
2.	Beatrix Loughran Sherwin Badger	USA	4	2	4	1	2	2	1	16
3.	Emília Rotter László Szollás	HUN	1	3	3	4	3	3	3	20
4.	Olga Orgonista Sándor Szalay	HUN	2.5	5	1.5	5	5	4	5	28
5.	Constance Wilson-Samuel Montgomery Wilson	CAN	5	6	5	6	4	5	4	35
6.	Frances Claudet Chauney Bangs	CAN	6	4	6	2	6	6	6	36
7.	Gertrude Meredith Joseph Savage	USA	7	7	7	7	7	7	7	49

1936 Garmisch-Partenkirchen T: 18, N: 12, D: 2.13.

			USA	GER	SWE	SWI	AUT	BEL	NOR	HUN	FIN	ORDINALS
						JUDGES' RANKINGS						
1.	Maxi Herber Ernst Baier	GER	1	1	1	1	2	1	1	2	1	11
2.	Ilse Pausin Erik Pausin	AUT	3.5	2	2	2	1	2	2	3	2	19.5
3.	Emília Rotter László Szollás	HUN	6	3	3.5	5	4	3	3	1	4	32.5
4.	Piroska Szekrényessy Attila Szekrényessy	HUN	3.5	5	6	4	3	5	5	4	3	38.5
5.	Maribel Vinson George Hill	USA	2	6	5	6	5	4	7	6.5	5	46.5
6.	Louise Bertram Stewert Reburn	CAN	5	14	3.5	7	13	6	4	5	11	68.5
7.	Violet Cliff Leslie Cliff	GBR	9	4	7	3	6	9	6	6.5	6	56.5
8.	Eva Prawitz Otto Weiss	GER	8	7	9.5	10	8	8	8	8	7	74.5

Thirty-year-old Berlin architect Ernst Baier and his 15-year-old protégée, Maxi Herber, were early exponents of "shadow skating," in which both skaters perform the exact same moves without touching. In an unusual reversal of normal procedure, the German government made a film of Baier and Herber's routine and commissioned a composer to create a piece to match their moves. The judges seemed to have trouble with the Canadian pair, Bertram and Reburn, who received a wide variety of scores, ranging from third and fourth place from the Swedish and Norwegian judges to 13th and 14th from the Austrian and German judges.

1948 St. Moritz T: 15, N: 11, D: 2.7.

							JUDGES' RANKINGS						
			NOR	USA	AUT	SWI	CZE	BEL	GBR	CAN	HUN	FRA	ITA	ORDINALS
1.	Micheline Lannoy Pierre Baugniet	BEL	1	2	2.5	1	1.5	1	1	1	4.5	1	1	17.5
2.	Andrea Kékessy Ede Király	HUN	3	4	1	2	1.5	3	3	3	1	2.5	2	26
3.	Suzanne Morrow Wallace Diestelmeyer	CAN	2	1	4	3	3	2	4	2	2.5	2.5	5	31
4.	Yvonne Sherman Robert Swenning	USA	5	3	9	5	4	5	5	4.5	4.5	5	3	53
5.	Winifred Silverthorne Dennis Silverthorne	GBR	6	5	6.5	4	5	4	2	6	2.5	6	6	53
6.	Karol Kennedy Michael Kennedy	USA	4	6	2.5	8.5	6.5	6	6	4.5	7.5	4	4	59.5
7.	Marianna Nagy László Nagy	HUN	7	7	6.5	6	8	10	10	10	6	7.5	11	89
8.	Jennifer Nicks John Nicks	GBR	9	9.5	14	8.5	6.5	7	7	8	9	9.5	10	98

Morrow and Diestelmeyer were the first pair to perform the soon-to-be-ubiquitous death spiral.

1952 Oslo T: 13, N: 9, D: 2.22.

					JUDGES' RANKINGS						
			CAN	USA	NOR	GBR	SWI	GER	SWE	HUN	AUT	ORDINALS
1.	Ria Falk Paul Falk	GER	1	2	2	1	1	1	1.5	1	1	11.5
2.	Karol Kennedy Michael Kennedy	USA	2	1	1	2	2	2	1.5	3	3	17.5
3.	Marianna Nagy László Nagy	HUN	4	4	4	4	5	3	3	2	2	31
4.	Jennifer Nicks John Nicks	GBR	5	5	3	3	4	4	5	4	6	39
5.	Frances Dafoe Norris Bowden	CAN	3	3	5	6	6	7	7	7	4	48
6.	Janet Gerhauser John Nightingale	USA	6	6	6	5	7	6	4	6	8	54
7.	Silvia Grandjean Michel Grandjean	SWI	8	7	7	7	3	5	6	5	5	53
8.	Ingeborg Minor Hermann Braun	GER	7	8	8	8	8	8	8	9	9.5	73.5

1956 Cortina T: 11, N: 7, D: 2.3.

JUDGES' RANKINGS

		AUS	AUT	CAN	CZE	GER	USA	GBR	HUN	SWI	ORDINALS
1. Elisabeth Schwartz Kurt Oppelt	AUT	1	1	2	1	1	2	2	2	2	14
2. Frances Dafoe Norris Bowden	CAN	2	2	1	2	3	1	1	3	1	16
3. Marianna Nagy László Nagy	HUN	5	3	6	3	4	4	3	1	3	32
4. Marika Kilius Franz Ningel	GER	3.5	4.5	4.5	5	2	3	4	5	4	35.5
5. Carole Ormaca Robin Greiner	USA	3.5	7	4.5	8	8	5	5	10	5	56
6. Barbara Wagner Robert Paul	CAN	8	8.5	3	7	5.5	6	6.5	4	6	54.5
7. Lucille Ash Sully Kothmann	USA	7	6	9	5	5.5	7	6.5	6.5	7	59.5
8. Vera Suchanova Zdenek Dolezal	CZE	10	4.5	7	5	7	9	10	8	8	68.5

In this unusually close contest, both Schwarz and Oppelt and Dafoe and Bowden received four first-place votes, with the Hungarian judge voting for the Nagys. The Austrians won because they also received five second-place votes while the Canadians earned three seconds and two thirds. The decisive moment came when a tired Fran Dafoe lost her balance and faltered during a lift. The crowd, which had grumbled all along about the judging, became unruly when the popular German couple of 12-year-old Marika Kilius and 19-year-old Franz Ningel received scores only good enough for fourth place. Members of the audience pelted the judges and referee with oranges, and the ice had to be cleared three times before the competition could go on.

1960 Squaw Valley T: 13, N: 7, D: 2.19.

JUDGES' RANKINGS

		AUS	AUT	CAN	GER	ITA	SWI	USA	ORDINALS
1. Barbara Wagner Robert Paul	CAN	1	1	1	1	1	1	1	7
2. Marika Kilius Hans-Jürgen Bäumler	GER	4	2	3	2	2	2	4	19
3. Nancy Ludington Ronald Ludington	USA	3	3	2	6	6.5	4	3	27.5
4. Maria Jelinek Otto Jelinek	CAN	2	4	4	3	4	7	2	26
5. Margret Göbl Franz Ningel	GER	5	5	8	4	3	3	8	36
6. Nina Zhuk Stanislav Zhuk	SOV	7	6	5	5	5	5	5	38
7. Rita Blumenberg Werner Mensching	GER	9	7.5	7	7	6.5	6	10	53
8. Diana Hinko Heinz Dopfl	AUT	10	7.5	6	8	8	9	6	54.5

Gold medal winner Bob Paul later gained further renown as a choreographer for Peggy Fleming, Dorothy Hamill, and Linda Fratianne, as well as for entertainers Donny and Marie Osmond.

1964 Innsbruck T: 17, N: 7, D: 1.29.

JUDGES' RANKINGS

		GER	FRA	ITA	CAN	AUT	SWI	CZE	USA	SOV	ORDINALS
1. Lyudmila Belousova Oleg Protopopov	SOV	2	2	2	1	2	1	1	1	1	13
2. Marika Kilius Hans-Jürgen Bäumler	GER	1	1	1	3	1	2	2	2	2	15
3. Debbi Wilkes Guy Revell	CAN	4	5	4	2	4.5	3	4	3	6	35.5
4. Vivian Joseph Ronald Joseph	USA	3	3	3	4	4.5	4	5	5	4	35.5
5. Tatyana Zhuk Aleksandr Gavrilov	SOV	6	6	5	9	3	6	3	4	3	45
6. Gerda Johner Rüdi Johner	SWI	5	7.5	7	7.5	7	5	6	6	5	56
7. Judianne Fotheringill Jerry Fotheringill	USA	7	7.5	8	5	12	7	9	7	7	69.5
8. Cynthia Kauffman Ronald Kauffman	USA	8	4	11	6	9	8	11	9	8	74.0

Lyudmila Belousova and her husband, Oleg Protopopov, were awarded five first-place votes to four for Kilius and Bäumler. The Leningrad couple had finished ninth in 1960. In 1966 Kilius and Bäumler returned their silver medals following allegations that they had signed a professional contract before the start of the Innsbruck Games. They were officially rehabilitated by the I.O.C. in 1987.

1968 Grenoble T: 18, N: 8, D: 2.14.

JUDGES' RANKINGS

		AUT	CAN	CZE	FRA	GDR	GER	POL	USA	SOV	ORDINALS
1. Lyudmila Belousova Oleg Protopopov	SOV	1	1	2	1	1	1	1	1	1	10
2. Tatyana Zhuk Aleksandr Gorelik	SOV	2	2	1	2	2	2	2	2	2	17
3. Margot Glockshuber Wolfgang Danne	GER	3	3	3	3	3	3	3	4	5	30
4. Heidemarie Steiner Heinz-Ulrich Walther	GDR	4	5	4	4	4	5	4	3	4	37
5. Tamara Moskvina Aleksei Michine	SOV	5	6	5	5	5	4	5	6	3	44
6. Cynthia Kauffman Ronald Kauffman	USA	8	4	7	6	9	7	6	5	6	58
7. Sandi Sweitzer Roy Wagelein	USA	7	7	6	7	8	8	7	7	7.5	64.5
8. Gudrun Hauss Walter Häfner	GER	6	8	8	8	6	6	8	8	9	67

Belousova and Protopopov, now 32 and 35 years old, respectively, climaxed their spectacular amateur career with an elegant display that earned them a second Olympic championship. Protopopov told the press, "Art cannot be measured by points. We skate from the heart. To us it is spiritual beauty that matters. . . . These pairs of brother and sister, how can they convey the emotion, the love, that exists between a man and a woman? That is what we try to show."

1972 Sapporo T: 16, N: 9, D: 2.6.

			JUDGES' RANKINGS								
		SOV	CAN	GDR	POL	USA	JPN	GBR	GER	FRA	ORDINALS
1. Irina Rodnina Aleksei Ulanov	SOV	1	1	1	1	1	2	1	2	2	12
2. Lyudmila Smirnova Andrei Suraikin	SOV	2	2	2	2	2	1	2	1	1	15
3. Manuela Gross Uwe Kagelmann	GDR	3	3	3	3	4	4	3	3	3	29
4. Alicia "Jojo" Starbuck Kenneth Shelley	USA	5	4	4	4	3	3	4	4	4	35
5. Almut Lehmann Herbert Wiesinger	GER	4	5	5	6	5	6	7	6	8	52
6. Irina Chernieva Vassily Blagov	SOV	6	6	7	5	7	5	6	5	5	52
7. Melissa Militano Mark Militano	USA	9.5	7	8	9	6	8	5	7	6	65.5
8. Annette Kansy Axel Salzmann	GDR	7	9	6	7	8	7	8	9	7	68

At the 1969 European championships, Belousova and Protopopov were dethroned by Irina Rodnina (19) and Aleksei Ulanov (21). The younger couple, knowing they couldn't compete on the same terms with the elegant and sophisticated Olympic champions, had developed a new style, full of dazzling and complex leaps and stunts. Rodnina and Ulanov thrilled the audience and the judges in 1969 and continued undefeated for the next three years. However, as the Sapporo Olympics approached, the Soviet team was in great turmoil. Ulanov, tired of being spurned and mocked by Rodnina, had become romantically involved with Lyudmila Smirnova of the number-two U.S.S.R. team. The harmonious interaction between the partners of the two pairs was severely disrupted. Nevertheless, they finished first and second, with Rodnina leaving the ice in tears.

1976 Innsbruck T: 14, N: 9, D: 2.7.

			JUDGES' RANKINGS								
		SOV	AUT	CZE	CAN	SWI	GBR	GER	USA	GDR	ORDINALS
1. Irina Rodnina Aleksandr Zaitsev	SOV	1	1	1	1	1	1	1	1	1	9
2. Romy Kermer Rolf Österreich	GDR	2	2	2	3	2	3	2	3	2	21
3. Manuela Gross Uwe Kagelmann	GDR	5	4	3	5	3	4	3	4	3	34
4. Irina Vorobieva Aleksandr Vlasov	SOV	3	3	4	2	4	5	4	5	5	35
5. Tai Babilonia Randy Gardner	USA	4	5	5	4	5	2	5	2	4	36
6. Kerstin Stolfig Veit Kempe	GDR	8	6	6	7	7	7	6	6	6	59
7. Karin Künzle Christian Künzle	SWI	6	7	7	9	6	6	9	7	7	64
8. Corinna Halke Eberhard Rausch	GER	9	9	8	6	8	9	7	8	8	72

Following the 1972 season, Aleksei Ulanov married Lyudmila Smirnova and a nationwide search was begun to find a new partner for Irina Rodnina. The winner was Aleksandr Zaitsev of Leningrad. Before long, the new pair had not only clicked as skaters, but they had also become wife and husband. Rodnina, still under the direction of the controversial Soviet trainer Stanislav Zhuk, continued her winning ways as if nothing had happened. American skater Tai Babilonia was the first black athlete to compete in the Winter Olympics.

1980 Lake Placid T: 11, N: 7, D: 2.17.

		GDR	USA	FRA	CAN	AUS	CZE	GER	JPN	SOV	ORDINALS
						JUDGES' RANKINGS					
1.	Irina Rodnina Aleksandr Zaitsev	SOV	1	1	1	1	1	1	1	1	1	9
2.	Marina Cherkosova Sergei Shakrai	SOV	2	3	2	2	2	2	2	2	2	19
3.	Manuela Mager Uwe Bewersdorff	GDR	3	5	3	4	3	4	3	3	5	33
4.	Marina Pestova Stanislav Lednovich	SOV	4	2	4	3	4	3	4	4	3	31
5.	Caitlin "Kitty" Carruthers Peter Carruthers	USA	5	4	5	5	5	6	5	5	6	46
6.	Sabine Baess Tassilo Thierbach	GDR	6	6	7	6	7	5	6	6	4	53
7.	Sheryl Franks Michael Botticelli	USA	7	7	6	7	6	8	8	7	8	64
8.	Christina Riegel Andreas Nischwitz	GER	8	8	8	9	9	7	7	8	7	71

In 1978 Irina Rodnina won her tenth straight world championship. She took off the following year to have a baby and, in her absence, the world title was won by two young people from Los Angeles, Tai Babilonia and Randy Gardner. Tai and Randy had been skating together for over eight years, since they were 10 and 12. The stage was set for a dramatic confrontation as Rodnina and Zaitsev attempted a comeback, while Tai and Randy tried to end the Soviet domination of pairs skating. Unfortunately, Randy Gardner suffered a groin injury prior to his arrival in Lake Placid. With a shot of lidocaine to kill the pain, Randy went out on the ice to warm up before the Olympic short program. But he fell four times, and the disappointed pair were forced to withdraw. Rodnina and Zaitsev skated flawlessly and, for the second straight time, won the first-place votes of all nine judges. Thus Rodnina matched the accomplishments of Sonja Henie by winning ten world championships and three Olympic gold medals.

1984 Sarajevo T: 15, N: 7, D: 2.12.

		SP	GBR	FRA	CZE	USA	GDR	CAN	SOV	GER	JPN	ORDINALS
					JUDGES' RANKINGS (FREE SKATING)							
1.	Yelena Valova Oleg Vasilyev	SOV	1	1	1	1	1	1	1	1	1	1	1.4
2.	Caitlin "Kitty" Carruthers Peter Carruthers	USA	2	2	3	2	2	4	2	3	3	4	2.8
3.	Larissa Selezneva Oleg Makarov	SOV	2	3	2	3	4	3	3	4	3	3.8
4.	Sabine Baess Tassilo Thierbach	GDR	4	3	4	4	3	2	4	4	2	2	5.6
5.	Birgit Lorenz Knut Schubert	GDR	5	5	6	5	5	5	5	6	5	5	7.0
6.	Jill Watson Burt Lancon	USA	8	5	5	7	6	6	7	7	7	6	9.2

				JUDGES' RANKINGS (FREE SKATING)								
		SP	GBR	FRA	CZE	USA	GDR	CAN	SOV	GER	JPN	ORDINALS
7. Barbara Underhill Paul Martini	CAN	6	7	7	6	8	7	6	5	6	7	9.4
8. Katerina Matousek Lloyd Eisler	CAN	9	8	9	8	9	8	8	8	9	8	11.6

Valova and Vasilyev were the unanimous choice of the nine judges. Peter and Kitty Carruthers were brother and sister, separately adopted by Charles and Maureen Carruthers of Burlington, Massachusetts.

1988 Calgary T: 15, N: 8, D: 2.16.

				JUDGES' RANKINGS (FREE SKATING)								
		SP	SOV	GER	USA	GBR	CAN	AUS	CZE	GDR	POL	ORDINALS
1. Yekaterina Gordeyeva Sergei Grinkov	SOV	1	1	1	1	1	1	1	1	1	1	1.4
2. Yelena Valova Oleg Vasilyev	SOV	2	2	2	2	2	2	2	2	2	2	2.8
3. Jill Watson Peter Oppegard	USA	3	4	3	3	4	5	3	3	3	3	4.2
4. Larissa Selezneva Oleg Makarov	SOV	6	3	5	6	6	3	4	4	4	4	6.4
5. Gillian Wachsman Todd Waggoner	USA	4	5	7	4	8	6	5	5	8	8	6.6
6. Denise Benning Lyndon Johnston	CAN	5	7	4	7	3	4	7	8	5	7	9.0
7. Peggy Schwarz Alexander König	GDR	11	6	6	9	7	7	6	7	6	5	10.4
8. Christine Hough Doug Ladret	CAN	8	9	8	10	4	8	9	6	7	9	11.2

The popular Katya Gordeyeva and her partner Sergei Grinkov were the only pair to complete their long program without a major error.

1992 Albertville T: 18, N: 11, D: 2.11.

				JUDGES' RANKINGS (FREE SKATING)								
		SP	FRA	CZE	AUS	USA	GER	CAN	ITA	SOV	GBR	ORDINALS
1. Natalya Mishkutenok Artur Dmitriev	SOV	1	1	1	1	1	1	1	1	1	1	1.5
2. Yelena Betchke Denis Petrov	SOV	2	2	3	2	2	2	2	2	2	2	3.0
3. Isabelle Brasseur Lloyd Eisler	CAN	3	5	4	3	3	5	3	3	3	6	4.5
4. Radka Kovariková René Novotny	CZE	4	3	2	4	4	3	4	5	4	3	6.0
5. Yevgenya Shishkova Vadim Naumov	SOV	5	6	5	5	5	4	5	4	6	4	7.5
6. Natasha Kuchiki Todd Sand	USA	6	4	6	7	6	8	6	9	11	7	9.0
7. Peggy Schwarz Alexander König	GER	8	10	7	8	12	6	7	8	5	5	11.0
8. Mandy Wötzel Axel Rauschenbach	GER	10	8	8	9	8	7	9	7	9	8	13.0

There was so much stumbling and falling in the long program that it almost seemed that something was wrong with the ice. However, when Mishkutenok and Dmitriev performed, it became clear that the problem rested with the other skaters, not with the condition of the ice. Mishkutenok, from Belarus, and Dmitriev, from Siberia, earned a standing ovation from the audience with their interpretation of Franz Liszt's "Liebesträume," the same music the Protopopovs had used in winning the 1964 gold medal. Both of the top two teams were trained in St. Petersburg by Tamara Moskvina.

ICE DANCE

Ice dance competitions consist of two compulsory dances that represent 10 percent of the final score each, a two-minute original set-pattern dance (30 percent), and a four-minute free dance, which accounts for 50 percent of the total. Judging is slightly different than for other figure skating events in that only a single mark is given for each compulsory dance. For the original dance, separate marks are given for composition and presentation, while the free dance is graded like singles and pairs: one mark for technical merit and one for artistic impression.

Following the 1992 Olympics, the Technical Committee on Dance of the International Skating Union issued new restrictions to control dangerous tendencies that were threatening to poison their beloved sport. Among the moves and behavior that are now prohibited are:
1. lying on the ice
2. holding of the partner's skates
3. sitting or lying over the partner's leg without having at least one foot on the ice
4. jumping for more than one revolution
5. spinning or pirouetting for more than three revolutions
6. sitting or lying on the partner's shoulder or back (because it is considered "a feat of prowess")
7. the gentleman wearing tights instead of trousers
8. the lady not wearing a skirt
9. using music originally arranged for use on the stage or in the theater which in its original form is not suitable for use on the dance floor.

Had these rules been in effect in 1992, both the gold and silver medal winners would have been disqualified.

1924–1972 not held

1976 Innsbruck T: 18, N: 9, D: 2.9.

		JUDGES' RANKINGS								
		USA	ITA	SOV	GBR	POL	HUN	AUT	CZE	CAN	ORDINALS
1. Lyudmila Pakhomova Aleksandr Gorshkov	SOV	1	1	1	1	1	1	1	1	1	9
2. Irina Moiseyeva Andrei Minenkov	SOV	3	2	2	3	2	2	2	2	2	20
3. Colleen O'Conner James Millns	USA	2	3	4	2	4	3	3	3	3	27
4. Natalya Linichuk Gennady Karponosov	SOV	5	4	3	4	3	4	4	4	4	35
5. Krisztina Regöczy András Sallay	HUN	4	6	5	6.5	5	5	5	5	7	48.5
6. Matilde Ciccia Lamberto Ceserani	ITA	8	5	6	6.5	6	7	6	6	8	58.5
7. Hilary Green Glyn Watts	GBR	6	7	7	5	7	6	7	7	5	57
8. Janet Thompson Warren Maxwell	GBR	9	9	9	8	9	8	8	8	10	78

Five-time world champions Lyudmila Pakhomova and Aleksandr Gorshkov sat out the 1975 world championships while Gorshkov underwent an operation. He was completely recovered for the Olympics, and the husband-wife team from Moscow had little trouble captivating the judges and garnering all nine first-place votes.

1980 Lake Placid T: 12, N: 8, D: 2.19.

		JUDGES' RANKINGS									
		GER	USA	SOV	CZE	HUN	AUT	CAN	GBR	FRA	ORDINALS
1. Natalya Linichuk Gennady Karponosov	SOV	2	2	1	1	2	1	1	1	2	13
2. Krisztina Regöczy András Sallay	HUN	1	1	3	2	1	2	2	1	1	14
3. Irina Moiseyeva Andrei Minenkov	SOV	3	3	2	3	3	3	3	4	3	27
4. Liliana Rehakova Stanislav Drastich	CZE	4	5	4	4	4	4	4	5	5	39
5. Jayne Torvill Christopher Dean	GBR	5	4	5	5	5	5	6	3	4	42
6. Lorna Wighton John Dowding	CAN	7	6	6	6	6	6	5	6	6	54
7. Judy Blumberg Michael Seibert	USA	6	8	8	7	8	7	8	7	7	66
8. Natalya Bestemianova Andrei Bukin	SOV	9	9	7	8	9	10	7	8	8	75

Four judges voted for the Soviet pair and four for the Hungarians. British judge Brenda Long awarded the same number of points to both couples. Given the option of breaking the tie, she refused. This meant that the gold and silver medals would be decided by total ordinals. Because Soviet judge Igor Kabanov placed Regöczy and Sallay third behind Moiseyeva and Minenkov, the victory went to Linichuk and Karponosov. The announcement of the results was greeted by catcalls and boos from the American audience, which preferred the lively, upbeat style of Regöczy and Sallay to the staid, traditional image of Linichuk and Karponosov.

1984 Sarajevo T: 19, N: 12, D: 2.14.

		JUDGES' RANKINGS (FREE DANCE)											
		CD	SPD	HUN	SOV	GER	GBR	JPN	CZE	ITA	CAN	USA	ORDINALS
1. Jayne Torvill Christopher Dean	GBR	1	1	1	1	1	1	1	1	1	1	1	2.0
2. Natalya Bestemianova Andrei Bukin	SOV	2	2	2	2	2	3	2	2	2	2	3	4.0
3. Marina Klimova Sergei Ponomarenko	SOV	4	4	3	3	3	4	4	3	3	4	4	7.0
4. Judy Blumberg Michael Seibert	USA	3	3	4	4	4	2	3	4	4	3	2	7.0
5. Carol Fox Richard Dalley	USA	6	5	6	9	5	6	6	5	6	6	5	10.6
6. Karen Barber Nicholas Slater	GBR	5	6	5	5	6	5	6	7	5	7	6	11.4
7. Olga Volozhinskaya Aleksandr Svinin	SOV	8	7	8	6	8	10	5	7	9	8	7	14.6
8. Tracy Wilson Robert McCall	CAN	7	8	7	8	9	8	8	6	8	5	9	15.4

The first time that the Nottingham City Council voted to grant £14,000 to Jayne Torvill and Christopher Dean to help them while they trained to become world champions, there were protests that the expenditure was a frivolous waste. Three world championships later, no one was complaining anymore as "T&D" had brought the town more glory than D.H. Lawrence, though not quite as much as Robin Hood.

Dean, a former police trainee, and Torvill, a former insurance clerk, brought to the discipline of ice-dancing a new level of greatness, which earned them the first perfect scores of 6.0 in the event's history. At Sarajevo they mesmerized the audience with their interpretation of Ravel's *Bolero,* receiving from the judges 12 6.0s out of 18 marks including across-the-board perfect scores for artistic impression.

1988 Calgary T: 20, N: 14, D: 2.23.

				JUDGES' RANKINGS (FREE DANCE)									
			CD	SPD	SOV	CAN	USA	GER	ITA	AUT	GBR	HUN	FRA	ORDINALS
1. Natalya Bestemianova Andrei Bukin	SOV		1	1	1	1	1	1	1	1	1	1	1	2.0
2. Marina Klimova Sergei Ponomarenko	SOV		2	2	2	3	2	2	2	2	2	2	2	4.0
3. Tracy Wilson Robert McCall	CAN		3	3	3	2	3	3	3	3	3	3	3	6.0
4. Natalya Annenko Genrich Sretensky	SOV		4	4	4	4	6	4	4	4	4	4	4	8.0
5. Kathrin Beck Christoff Beck	AUT		5	5	5	5	5	5	5	5	6	5	5	10.0
6. Suzanne Semanick Scott Gregory	USA		6	6	6	8	7	6	6	6	7	6	7	12.0
7. Klára Engi Attila Tóth	HUN		7	7	7	7	8	7	7	7	8	7	8	14.0
8. Isabelle Duchesnay Paul Duchesnay	FRA		8	8	10	6	4	9	8	10	5	10	5	16.0

As an athletic competition, the ice dancing tournament left much to be desired. The twenty teams were ranked in the same order in all three sections of the meet, except for the fifteenth- and fourteenth-placed pairs, who switched places after the compulsory dances. Bronze medalist Rob McCall died of AIDS-related brain cancer on November 15, 1991. He was 33 years old.

1992 Albertville T: 19, N: 12, D: 2.17.

				JUDGES' RANKINGS (FREE DANCE)									
			CD	SPD	SOV	GBR	FIN	CAN	HUN	FRA	USA	CZE	ITA	ORDINALS
1. Marina Klimova Sergei Ponomarenko	SOV		1	1	1	2	2	1	2	3	1	1	1	2.0
2. Isabelle Duchesnay-Dean Paul Duchesnay	FRA		3	2	3	1	1	2	1	1	2	2	2	4.4
3. Maya Usova Aleksandr Zhulin	SOV		2	3	2	3	3	3	3	2	3	3	3	5.6
4. Oksana Gritschuk Yvgeny Platov	SOV		4	4	4	4	4	4	4	4	4	4	5	8.0
5. Stefania Calegari Pasquale Camerlengo	ITA		5	5	5	5	5	5	5	5	5	5	4	10.0
6. Susanna Rahkamo Petri Kokko	FIN		7	6	7	6	6	7	7	7	6	6	6	12.4

		CD	SPD	SOV	GBR	FIN	CAN	HUN	FRA	USA	CZE	ITA	ORDINALS
		JUDGES' RANKINGS (FREE DANCE)											
7.	Klára Engi	HUN	6	7	6	7	7	9	6	6	8	7	7	13.6
	Attila Tóth												
8.	Dominique Yvon	FRA	8	9	11	9	8	8	8	8	9	8	8	16.6
	Frédéric Palluel												

The normally calcified world of ice dancing was treated to a showdown between the 1989 and 1990 world champions, Klimova and Ponomarenko, and their 1991 usurpers, Paul and Isabelle Duchesnay. The Duchesnays were brother and sister who were raised in Quebec, trained in Germany, coached by a Slovak, and choreographed by an Englishman, Christopher Dean, who also happened to be Isabelle's husband. They gained fame by challenging the rigid rules of ice dancing with innovative and entertaining programs. For years the judges punished them for their rebelliousness, but at the 1991 Munich World Championships their great popularity finally intimidated the jury into awarding them top honors. Klimova and Ponomarenko, having patiently waited their turn to earn Olympic gold, were furious at this turn of events and lashed out at the Duchesnays, publicly accusing them of manipulating the judges. In February 1991, just before the Munich championships, they also had to fend off charges that Klimova had tested positive for steroids at the European championships. The positive result had been obtained at an unaccredited laboratory in Bulgaria. Klimova's "B" sample was sent to an accredited lab in Germany and she was cleared, raising the specter of sabotage.

In Albertville the Duchesnays appeared tense and flat while Klimova and Ponomarenko were smooth and polished. The competition was decided on the second day when Klimova and Ponomarenko, rather than the Duchesnays, pushed the rules in the original dance by wearing non-polka costumes while performing a polka. In addition, while the Duchesnays stuck to a traditional Bavarian polka, Klimova and Ponomarenko danced to Shostakovich's more waltzlike "Polka for 3 Ballet Suite." Going into the free dance, the Duchesnays needed to place first to win, and even then they would gain the victory only if Klimova and Ponomarenko placed third or worse. Instead, Klimova and Ponomarenko, a married couple, beat the Duchesnays at their own game by presenting a nontraditional, steamy interpretation of Bach that won over the French audience as well as five of the nine judges.

A political footnote: the breakup of the Soviet Union also threatened to break up the ice dancing partnership of Lithuanian Povilas Vanagas and his Ukrainian-born Russian wife, Margarita Drobiavko. Because Lithuania was competing as a separate nation, Olympic rules prevented them from entering as a pair. However, six days before the Opening Ceremony the I.O.C. granted Drobiavko a waiver to compete for Lithuania. The couple finished seventeenth, but happy.

Discontinued Event

SPECIAL FIGURES

1908 London C: 3, N: 2, D: 10.29.

			GBR	SWE	SWI	GER	RUS	ORDINALS
			JUDGES' RANKINGS					
1.	Nikolai Panin (Kolomenkin)	RUS	1	1	1	1	1	5
2.	Arthur Cumming	GBR	2	2	2	2	2	10
3.	Geoffrey Hall-Say	GBR	3	3	3	3	3	15

The first Russian Olympic gold medal winner, 35-year-old Nikolai Kolomenkin, competed under a pseudonym, Nikolai Panin, a common practice among wealthy Russians for whom participation in sports was considered undignified. Four years later in Stockholm, Kolomenkin was a member of the Russian military revolver team, which finished in fourth place.

GLOSSARY OF FIGURE SKATING TERMS

Axel Jump—One of the most difficult jumps, which takes off from the forward outside edge and is landed on the back outside edge of the opposite foot. A single axel consists of 1½ revolutions, a double is 2½ revolutions, and a triple is 3½ revolutions. Named for its inventor Axel Paulsen, it is easily recognizable as it is the only jump that takes off from the forward position.

Crossovers—A method of gaining speed and turning corners in which skaters cross one foot over the other. There are both forward and backward crossovers.

Death Spiral—A pair move in which the man spins in a pivot position while holding one hand of the woman, who is spinning in a horizontal position with her body parallel to the ice.

Edges—The two sides of the skate blade on either side of the grooved center. There is an inside edge—the edge on the inner side of the leg—and an outside edge—that on the outer side of the leg. There is a forward and backward for each edge, equaling a total of four different edges.

Flip Jump—A toe pick–assisted jump, taken off from the back inside edge of one foot, and landed on the back outside edge of the opposite foot.

Hand-to-Hand Loop Lift—A lift in which the man raises his partner, who is in front of him and facing the same direction, above his head. She remains facing the same direction, in the sitting position with her hands behind her, while her partner supports her by the hands.

Hydrant Lift—A lift in which the man throws his partner over his head while skating backwards, rotates one-half turn, and catches his partner facing him.

Jump Combination—The combining of several jumps such that the landing edge of one jump serves as the takeoff edge of the next jump.

Lateral Twist—A move in which the man throws his partner overhead. She rotates once, while in a lateral position to the ice, and is caught.

Layback Spin—Generally performed by women, the layback spin involves an upright spin position where the head and shoulders are dropped backward and the back arches.

Lifts—Pair moves in which the man lifts his partner above his head with arm(s) fully extended. Lifts consist of precise ascending, rotational, and descending movements.

Loop Jump—An edge jump, taken off from a back outside edge and landed on the same back outside edge.

Lutz Jump—A toe pick–assisted jump, taken off from a back outside edge and landed on the back outside edge of the opposite foot. The skater approaches on a wide curve, taps his toe pick into the ice, and rotates in the opposite direction of the curve.

Platter Lift—A lift in which the man raises his partner overhead, with his hands resting on her hips. She is horizontal to the ice, facing the back of the man. In a platter position.

Salchow—Another edge jump, taken off from the back inside edge of one foot and landed on the back outside edge of the opposite foot. Created by Ulrich Salchow.

Shadow Skating—Any movement in pair skating performed by both partners simultaneously while skating in close proximity.

Sit Spin—A spin which is done in a "sitting" position. The body is low to the ice with the skating (spinning) knee bent and the non-skating or "free" leg extended beside it.

Star Lift—A lift in which the man raises his partner by her hip, from his side into the air. She is in the scissor position, with either one hand touching his shoulder, or in a hands-free position.

Throw Jump—A pair move in which the male partner assists the woman into the air.

Toe Loop—A toe pick–assisted jump that takes off and lands on the same back outside edge.

Toe Overhead Lift—A lift in which the man swings his partner from one side of his body, around behind his head, and into a raised position. She is facing the same direction as the man, in a split position.

Toe Picks—The teeth at the front of the blade, used primarily for jumping and spinning.

Source: United States Figure Skating Association

SPEED SKATING

MEN
500 Meters
1000 Meters
1500 Meters
5000 Meters
10,000 Meters
Short Track: 500 Meters
Short Track: 1000 Meters
Short Track: 5000-Meter Relay
Discontinued Event

In speed skating, the competitors skate against the clock, although they race in pairs. They are required to change lanes in the back straightaway of each lap. The skater on the outside is considered to have the right of way. The skater leaving the inside lane is held responsible for a collision except in cases of obvious obstruction. The first world championships were held in Amsterdam in 1889, although racing records date back to the 18th century. All Olympic races are held on a 400-meter oval.

MEN

500 METERS

1924 Chamonix C: 27, N: 10, D: 1.26. WR: 43.4 (Oscar Mathisen)

1. Charles Jewtraw	USA	44.0
2. Oskar Olsen	NOR	44.2
3. Roald Larsen	NOR	44.8
3. A. Clas Thunberg	FIN	44.8
5. Asser Vallenius	FIN	45.0
6. Axel Blomqvist	SWE	45.2
7. Charles Gorman	CAN	45.4
8. Joseph Moore	USA	45.6
8. Harald Ström	NOR	45.6

This was the first event to be decided in the first Olympic Winter Games. Figure skating and ice hockey competitions held prior to 1924 were incorporated in the regular Summer Games. Jewtraw came from a poor family in Lake Placid, New York, where his father was the caretaker of the speed skating rink on Mirror Lake. In the 1930s Jewtraw found himself unemployed at the height of the Depression. He returned to Lake Placid and asked for a job teaching skating. Instead, the first-ever Winter Olympics champion was given the task of sweeping floors. His gold medal is now in a drawer at the Smithsonian Institution in Washington, D.C.

1928 St. Moritz C: 33, N: 14, D: 2.13. WR: 43.1 (Roald Larsen)

1.	Bernt Evensen	NOR	43.4	OR
1.	A. Clas Thunberg	FIN	43.4	OR
3.	John O'Neil Farrell	USA	43.6	
3.	Jaako Friman	FIN	43.6	
3.	Roald Larsen	NOR	43.6	
6.	Håkon Pedersen	NOR	43.8	
7.	Charles Gorman	CAN	43.9	
8.	Bertel Backmann	FIN	44.4	

1932 Lake Placid C: 16, N: 4, D: 2.4. WR: 42.6 (A. Clas Thunberg)

1.	John Shea	USA	43.4	EOR
2.	Bernt Evensen	NOR	—	
3.	Alexander Hurd	CAN	—	
4.	Frank Stack	CAN	—	
5.	William Logan	CAN	—	
6.	John O'Neil Farrell	USA	—	

In 1932 the speed skating competitions were held as actual races, with five or six men in a heat, rather than the usual way of two skaters at a time racing against the clock. This new method, known as the North American Rules, so outraged world record holder and five-time Olympic champion Clas Thunberg that he refused to participate. New York Governor Franklin D. Roosevelt officially opened the Third Olympic Winter Games on the morning of February 4. A local speed skater, 21-year-old Jack Shea, recited the Olympic oath on behalf of the 306 assembled athletes. A short time later the three qualifying heats were held for the 500 meters speed skating. Not surprisingly, five of six qualifiers were North Americans. Following the heats, the first period of the Canada–U.S.A. ice hockey game was played. Then came the 500 meters final. Shea tore into the lead and finished five yards ahead of co-defending champion Bernt Evensen. Shea's victory was very popular, since he was a hometown boy from Lake Placid, as was 1924 winner Charles Jewtraw.

1936 Garmisch-Partenkirchen C: 36, N: 14, D: 2.11. WR: 42.4 (Allan Potts)

1.	Ivar Ballangrud	NOR	43.4	EOR
2.	George Krog	NOR	43.5	
3.	Leo Freisinger	USA	44.0	
4.	Shozo Ishihara	JPN	44.1	
5.	Delbert Lamb	USA	44.2	
6.	Karl Leban	AUT	44.8	
6.	Allan Potts	USA	44.8	
8.	Antero Ojala	FIN	44.9	
8.	Jorma Ruissalo	FIN	44.9	
8.	Birger Vasenius	FIN	44.9	

1948 St. Moritz C: 42, N: 15, D: 1.31. WR: 41.8 (Hans Engnestangen)

1.	Finn Helgesen	NOR	43.1	OR
2.	Kenneth Bartholomew	USA	43.2	
2.	Thomas Byberg	NOR	43.2	
2.	Robert Fitzgerald	USA	43.2	
5.	Kenneth Henry	USA	43.3	
6.	Sverre Farstad	NOR	43.6	
6.	Torodd Hauer	NOR	43.6	
6.	Delbert Lamb	USA	43.6	
6.	Frank Stack	CAN	43.6	

1952 Oslo C: 41, N: 14, D: 2.16. WR: 41.2 (Yuri Sergeev)

1.	Kenneth Henry	USA	43.2
2.	Donald McDermott	USA	43.9
3.	Gordon Audley	CAN	44.0
3.	Arne Johansen	NOR	44.0
5.	Finn Helgesen	NOR	44.0
6.	Hroar Elvenes	NOR	44.1
6.	Kiyotaka Takabayashi	JPN	44.1
8.	Gerardus Maarse	HOL	44.2
8.	Toivo Salonen	FIN	44.2

The Norwegian Skating Union chose as one of their four entrants in this race Finn Hodt, who had served a sentence for collaborating with the Nazis, and who had gone so far as to fight for the Germans on the Eastern Front. One month before the Oslo Games, the Norwegian Olympic committee overruled the Skating Union, voting 25–2 to ban Hodt and all other collaborators from representing Norway in the Oslo Olympics. Helgesen was placed fifth despite his time because he was paired with Audley and finished behind him.

1956 Cortina C: 47, N: 17, D: 1.28. WR: 40.2 (Yevgeny Grishin)

1.	Yevgeny Grishin	SOV	40.2	EWR
2.	Rafael Gratch	SOV	40.8	
3.	Alv Gjestvang	NOR	41.0	
4.	Yuri Sergeev	SOV	41.1	
5.	Toivo Salonen	FIN	41.7	
6.	William Carow	USA	41.8	
7.	Colin Hickey	AUS	41.9	
7.	Bengt Malmsten	SWE	41.9	

1960 Squaw Valley C: 46, N: 15, D: 2.24. WR: 40.2 (Yevgeny Grishin)

1.	Yevgeny Grishin	SOV	40.2	EWR
2.	William Disney	USA	40.3	
3.	Rafael Gratch	SOV	40.4	
4.	Hans Wilhelmsson	SWE	40.5	
5.	Gennady Voronin	SOV	40.7	
6.	Alv Gjestvang	NOR	40.8	
7.	Richard "Terry" McDermott	USA	40.9	
7.	Toivo Salonen	FIN	40.9	

Grishin's time was remarkable, considering that he stumbled and skidded in the homestretch, losing at least a second.

1964 Innsbruck C: 44, N: 19, D: 2.4. WR: 39.5 (Yevgeny Grishin)

1.	Richard "Terry" McDermott	USA	40.1	OR
2.	Alv Gjestvang	NOR	40.6	
2.	Yevgeny Grishin	SOV	40.6	
2.	Vladimir Orlov	SOV	40.6	
5.	Keiichi Suzuki	JPN	40.7	
6.	Edward Rudolph	USA	40.9	
7.	Heike Hedlund	FIN	41.0	
8.	William Disney	USA	41.1	
8.	Villy Haugen	NOR	41.1	

Terry McDermott, a 23-year-old barber from Essexville, Michigan, stunned the skating world with his surprise victory, the only U.S. gold medal of the 1964 Winter Games. McDermott used skates that he had borrowed from the U.S. coach, Leo Freisinger. He also got some help from Mrs. Freisinger. When Lydia Skoblikova won four speed skating gold medals in 1964, she wore a good-luck pin that had been given to her by Mrs. Freisinger. McDermott heard about this story and asked the coach's wife if he too could have such a pin. Freisinger gave McDermott her last pin, and he put it to good use. In 1968 Dianne Holum also received a Freisinger pin, although she didn't win her gold medal until 1972.

1968 Grenoble C: 48, N: 17, D: 2.14. WR: 39.2 (Erhard Keller)

1.	Erhard Keller	GER	40.3
2.	Richard "Terry" McDermott	USA	40.5
2.	Magne Thomassen	NOR	40.5
4.	Yevgeny Grishin	SOV	40.6
5.	Neil Blatchford	USA	40.7
5.	Arne Herjuaunet	NOR	40.7
5.	John Wurster	USA	40.7
8.	Seppo Hänninen	FIN	40.8
8.	Haakan Holmgren	SWE	40.8
8.	Keiichi Suzuki	JPN	40.8

In 1968 McDermott had the misfortune of being drawn in the last of 24 pairs on ice that had been badly melted by the sun. Keller, a dental student from Munich, was a gracious winner. He said of McDermott, "What he did today was just sheer guts. If he had started in the earlier heats while the ice was still good, I'd have lost. It's as simple as that."

1972 Sapporo C: 37, N: 16, D: 2.5. WR: 38.0 (Leo Linkovesi)

1.	Erhard Keller	GER	39.44	OR
2.	Hasse Börjes	SWE	39.69	
3.	Valery Muratov	SOV	39.80	
4.	Per Björang	NOR	39.91	
5.	Seppo Hänninen	FIN	40.12	
6.	Leo Linkovesi	FIN	40.14	
7.	Ove König	SWE	40.25	
8.	Masaki Suzuki	JPN	40.35	

This was the only one of the 1972 men's skating races that wasn't won by Ard Schenk, who fell after four steps and finished 34th.

1976 Innsbruck C: 29, N: 15, D: 2.10. WR: 37.00 (Yevgeny Kulikov)

1.	Yevgeny Kulikov	SOV	39.17	OR
2.	Valery Muratov	SOV	39.25	
3.	Daniel Immerfall	USA	39.54	
4.	Mats Wallberg	SWE	39.56	
5.	Peter Mueller	USA	39.57	
6.	Jan Bazen	HOL	39.78	
6.	Arnulf Sunde	NOR	39.78	
8.	Andrei Malikov	SOV	39.85	

1980 Lake Placid C: 37, N: 18, D: 2.15. WR: 37.00 (Yevgeny Kulikov)

1.	Eric Heiden	USA	38.03	OR
2.	Yevgeny Kulikov	SOV	38.37	
3.	Lieuwe de Boer	HOL	38.48	
4.	Frode Rönning	NOR	38.66	
5.	Daniel Immerfall	USA	38.69	
6.	Jarle Pedersen	NOR	38.83	
7.	Anatoly Medennikov	SOV	38.88	
8.	Gaétan Boucher	CAN	38.90	

As a 17-year-old, Eric Heiden had competed in the 1976 Olympics in Innsbruck, finishing seventh in the 1500 and 19th in the 5000. Thus it came as quite a shock the following year when he seemingly appeared from nowhere to win the overall title at the 1977 world championships. His victory was so unexpected that even Heiden wondered if his performance might have been a fluke. It wasn't. He successfully defended his world title in 1978 and 1979, and became a national hero—not in his native country, the United States, but in Norway and the Netherlands, where speed skating is taken more seriously.

The 1980 Olympics began with Heiden the favorite in all five men's speed skating events. If there was one distance at which he was thought to be shaky, it was the 500. A week earlier Heiden had lost at 500 meters to teammate Tom Plant at the world speed skating sprint championship. At Lake Placid Heiden was paired against world record holder Yevgeny Kulikov. The two favorites were the first pair to skate. Kulikov was slightly ahead at 100 meters, but they raced neck and neck most of the way. Coming out of the last curve, Kulikov slipped slightly and Heiden, who had a 32-inch waist but 27-inch thighs, pulled ahead and won.

1984 Sarajevo C: 42, N: 20, D: 2.10. WR: 36.57 (Pavel Pegov)

1.	Sergei Fokichev	SOV	38.19
2.	Yoshihiro Kitazawa	JPN	38.30
3.	Gaétan Boucher	CAN	38.39
4.	Dan Jansen	USA	38.55
5.	K. Nick Thometz	USA	38.56
6.	Vladimir Kozlov	SOV	38.57
7.	Frode Rönning	NOR	38.58
8.	Uwe-Jens Mey	GDR	38.65

Fokichev's victory was a total surprise. He had not previously competed in a major international meet and was not even considered by pre-meet prognosticators.

1988 Calgary C: 37, N: 15, D: 2.14. WR: 36.55 (K. Nick Thometz)

1.	Uwe-Jens Mey	GDR	36.45	WR
2.	Jan Ykema	HOL	36.76	
3.	Akira Kuroiwa	JPN	36.77	
4.	Sergei Fokichev	SOV	36.82	
5.	Bae Ki-tae	KOR	36.90	
6.	Igor Zhelezovsky	SOV	36.94	
7.	Guy Thibault	CAN	36.96	
8.	K. Nick Thometz	USA	37.16	

One of the favorites was Dan Jansen of West Allis, Wisconsin, who won the World Sprint Championship held in his hometown one week before the Olympics. At 6:00 a.m. on the day of the 500-meter event, Jansen received a phone call informing him that his sister, Jane Beres, was about to succumb to the leukemia she had been fighting for over a year. Dan spoke to her and although she could not respond, she indicated to him through another brother who was with her that she wanted Dan to remain in Calgary and compete. At noon, Dan Jansen learned that his sister had died less than three hours after he had spoken to her. At 5:00 p.m. he was on the ice, preparing for his race. After false starting, he took off quickly, but at the first turn he slipped and fell, just as he had at the World Cup meet on the same track two months earlier. Four days later, Jansen took part in the 1000-meter race but fell again.

1992 Albertville C: 43, N: 17, D: 2.15. WR: 36.41 (Dan Jansen)

1.	Uwe-Jens Mey	GER	37.14
2.	Toshiyuki Kuroiwa	JPN	37.18
3.	Junichi Inoue	JPN	37.26
4.	Dan Jansen	USA	37.46
5.	Yasunori Miyabe	JPN	37.49
5.	Gerard van Velde	HOL	37.49
7.	Aleksandr Golubev	SOV	37.51
8.	Igor Zhelezovsky	SOV	37.57

The men's 500 meters looked to be the most hotly contested duel of the Albertville Olympics. Uwe-Jens Mey and Dan Jansen had met six times during the pre-Olympic season. Mey won three times, Jansen twice, and once they tied. In addition, they had taken turns breaking the world record. On January 19, in Davos, Switzerland, Mey clocked a 36.43 to beat his own 1988 record by two hundredths of a second. Six days later, on the same Davos oval, Jansen took the record down to 36.41. The stage was set in Albertville, but the tight contest was not to be. Skating in the second pair, Jansen, apparently haunted at a deep level by his falls four years earlier, hesitated entering the final turn and lost precious tenths of a second. Two pairs later, Mey skated a solid race and earned his second straight gold medal. Jansen ended up in fourth place, just as he had eight years earlier as an 18-year-old in Sarajevo.

1000 METERS

1924–1972 not held

1976 Innsbruck C: 31, N: 16, 2.12. WR: 1:16.92 (Valery Muratov)

1.	Peter Mueller	USA	1:19.32
2.	Jörn Didriksen	NOR	1:20.45
3.	Valery Muratov	SOV	1:20.57
4.	Aleksandr Safronov	SOV	1:20.84
5.	Hans van Helden	HOL	1:20.85
6.	Gaétan Boucher	CAN	1:21.23
7.	Mats Wallberg	SWE	1:21.27
8.	Pertti Niittylä	FIN	1:21.43

1980 Lake Placid C: 41, N: 19, D: 2.19. WR: 1:13.60 (Eric Heiden)

1.	Eric Heiden	USA	1:15.18	OR
2.	Gaétan Boucher	CAN	1:16.68	
3.	Vladimir Lobanov	SOV	1:16.91	
3.	Frode Rönning	NOR	1:16.91	
5.	Peter Mueller	USA	1:17.11	
6.	Bert de Jong	HOL	1:17.29	
7.	Andreas Dietel	GDR	1:17.71	
8.	Oloph Granath	SWE	1:17.74	

Boucher had the good fortune to be skating first, paired against Eric Heiden. The silver medals in the three shortest races in 1980 were won by whoever was paired with Heiden.

1984 Sarajevo C: 43, N: 20, D: 2.14. WR: 1:12.58 (Pavel Pegov)

1.	Gaétan Boucher	CAN	1:15.80
2.	Sergei Khlebnikov	SOV	1:16.63

 3. Kai Arne Engelstad   NOR   1:16.75
 4. K. Nick Thometz   USA   1:16.85
 5. André Hoffmann   GDR   1:17.33
 6. Viktor Chacherin   SOV   1:17.42
 7. Andreas Dietel   GDR   1:17.46
 7. Hilbert van der Duim   HOL   1:17.46

1988 Calgary C: 40, N: 16, D: 2.18. WR: 1:12.58 (Pavel Pegov)
 1. Nikolai Gulyaev   SOV   1:13.03   OR
 2. Uwe-Jens Mey   GDR   1:13.11
 3. Igor Zhelezovsky   SOV   1:13.19
 4. Eric Flaim   USA   1:13.53
 5. Gaétan Boucher   CAN   1:13.77
 6. Michael Hadschieff   AUT   1:13.84
 7. Guy Thibault   CAN   1:14.16
 8. Peter Adeberg   GDR   1:14.19

Two months before the Olympics, Gulyaev was caught passing a packet of anabolic steroids to a Norwegian skater. Gulyaev claimed that the packet had been given to him by a Soviet trainer and that he was unaware of its contents. The I.O.C. and the International Skating Union, although skeptical of his account, were unable to uncover evidence to disprove it. Two days before the Opening Ceremony, Gulyaev was cleared to compete.

1992 Albertville C: 46, N: 21, D: 2.18. WR: 1:12.58 (Pavel Pegov, Igor Zhelezovsky)
 1. Olaf Zinke   GER   1:14.85
 2. Kim Yoon-man   KOR   1:14.86
 3. Yukinori Miyabe   JPN   1:14.92
 4. Gerard van Velde   HOL   1:14.93
 5. Peter Adeberg   GER   1:15.04
 6. Igor Zhelezovsky   SOV   1:15.05
 7. Guy Thibault   CAN   1:15.36
 8. Nikolai Gulyaev   SOV   1:15.46

The upset victory went to 25-year-old Olaf Zinke, an auto mechanic who was given a job by the city of Berlin so that he could train. Even more of an outsider than Zinke was silver medalist Kim, a Seoul University student whose goal had been to finish in the top ten. Actually, Kim's superb performance wasn't totally unexpected. On the morning of the race he spoke on the phone to his mother back in Euijungbu City, and she told him she had dreamed about a dragon. "That was a good omen for me," explained Kim.

1500 METERS

1924 Chamonix C: 22, N: 9, D: 1.27. WR: 2:17.4 (Oscar Mathisen)
 1. A. Clas Thunberg   FIN   2:20.8
 2. Roald Larsen   NOR   2:22.0
 3. Sigurd Moen   NOR   2:25.6
 4. Julius Skutnabb   FIN   2:26.6
 5. Harald Ström   NOR   2:29.0
 6. Oskar Olsen   NOR   2:29.2
 7. Harry Kaskey   USA   2:29.8
 8. Charles Jewtraw   USA   2:31.6
 8. Joseph Moore   USA   2:31.6

In 1924 30-year-old A. Clas Thunberg won three gold medals, one silver, and one bronze. Four years later he followed up with two more gold medals.

1928 St. Moritz C: 30, N: 14, D: 2.14. WR: 2:17.4 (Oscar Mathisen)

1.	A. Clas Thunberg	FIN	2:21.1
2.	Bernt Evensen	NOR	2:21.9
3.	Ivar Ballangrud	NOR	2:22.6
4.	Roald Larsen	NOR	2:25.3
5.	Edward Murphy	USA	2:25.9
6.	Valentine Bialas	USA	2:26.3
7.	Irving Jaffee	USA	2:26.7
8.	John Farrell	USA	2:26.8

1932 Lake Placid C: 18, N: 6, D: 2.5. WR: 2:17.4 (Oscar Mathisen)

1.	John Shea	USA	2:57.5
2.	Alexander Hurd	CAN	—
3.	William Logan	CAN	—
4.	Frank Stack	CAN	—
5.	Raymond Murray	USA	—
6.	Herbert Taylor	USA	—

American officials, having already irritated the foreign teams with their strange mass starts, left them completely exasperated with a ruling in the second heat. In the middle of the race the judges suddenly stopped the contest, accused the skaters of "loafing," and ordered the race rerun. In the final Taylor was leading, but he lost his balance coming out of the last turn and tumbled across the track into a snowbank. Shea found himself in first place and crossed the finish line eight yards ahead of Hurd.

1936 Garmisch-Partenkirchen C: 37, N: 15, D: 2.13. WR: 2:17.4 (Oscar Mathisen)

1.	Charles Mathisen	NOR	2:19.2	OR
2.	Ivar Ballangrud	NOR	2:20.2	
3.	Birger Wasenius	FIN	2:20.9	
4.	Leo Freisinger	USA	2:21.3	
5.	Max Stiepl	AUT	2:21.6	
6.	Karl Wazulek	AUT	2:22.2	
7.	Harry Haraldsen	NOR	2:22.4	
8.	Hans Engnestangen	NOR	2:23.0	

A brief note about the world record: Oscar Mathisen of Norway first broke the world record for the 1500 meters in 1908. By January 11, 1914, he had lowered his time to 2:19.4. One week later, in Davos, Switzerland, he skated a 2:17.4. This time remained a world record for 23 years, until Michael Staksrud, also skating at Davos, recorded a 2:14.9. Mathisen's performance was bettered only twice in the 38 years between 1914 and 1952.

1948 St. Moritz C: 45, N: 14, D: 2.2. WR: 2:13.8 (Hans Engnestangen)

1.	Sverre Farstad	NOR	2:17.6	OR
2.	Åke Seyffarth	SWE	2:18.1	
3.	Odd Lundberg	NOR	2:18.9	
4.	Lauri Parkkinen	FIN	2:19.6	
5.	Gustav Harry Jansson	SWE	2:20.0	
6.	John Werket	USA	2:20.2	
7.	Kalevi Laitinen	FIN	2:20.3	
8.	Göthe Hedlund	SWE	2:20.7	

Farstad was a 27-year-old cartoonist.

1952 Oslo C: 39, N: 13, D: 2.18. WR: 2:12.9 (Valentin Chaikin)

1. Hjalmar Andersen	NOR	2:20.4	
2. Willem van der Voort	HOL	2:20.6	
3. Roald Aas	NOR	2:21.6	
4. Carl-Erik Asplund	SWE	2:22.6	
5. Cornelis "Kees" Broekman	HOL	2:22.8	
6. Lauri Parkkinen	FIN	2:23.0	
7. Kauko Salomaa	FIN	2:23.3	
8. Sigvard Ericsson	SWE	2:23.4	

1956 Cortina C: 54, N: 18, D: 1.30. WR: 2:09.1 (Yuri Mikhailov)

1. Yevgeny Grishin	SOV	2:08.6	WR
1. Yuri Mikhailov	SOV	2:08.6	WR
3. Toivo Salonen	FIN	2:09.4	
4. Juhani Järvinen	FIN	2:09.7	
5. Robert Merkulov	SOV	2:10.3	
6. Sigvard Ericsson	SWE	2:11.0	
7. Colin Hickey	AUS	2:11.8	
8. Boris Shilkov	SOV	2:11.9	

1960 Squaw Valley C: 48, N: 16, D: 2.26. WR: 2:06.3 (Juhani Järvinen)

1. Roald Aas	NOR	2:10.4
1. Yevgeny Grishin	SOV	2:10.4
3. Boris Stenin	SOV	2:11.5
4. Jouko Jokinen	FIN	2:12.0
5. Per Olov Brogren	SWE	2:13.1
5. Juhani Järvinen	FIN	2:13.1
7. Toivo Salonen	FIN	2:13.2
8. André Kouprianoff	FRA	2:13.3

Grishin registered his second straight tie for first place at 1500 meters and collected his fourth Olympic gold medal. In 1952 he had also competed as a cyclist.

1964 Innsbruck C: 54, N: 21, D: 2.6. WR: 2:06.3 (Juhani Järvinen)

1. Ants Antson	SOV	2:10.3
2. Cornelis "Kees" Verkerk	HOL	2:10.6
3. Villy Haugen	NOR	2:11.2
4. Jouko Launonen	FIN	2:11.9
5. Lev Zaitsev	SOV	2:12.1
6. Ivar Eriksen	NOR	2:12.2
6. Edouard Matoussevich	SOV	2:12.2
8. Juhani Järvinen	FIN	2:12.4

1968 Grenoble C: 53, N: 18, D: 2.16. WR: 2:02.5 (Magne Thomassen)

1. Cornelis "Kees" Verkerk	HOL	2:03.4	OR
2. Ivar Eriksen	NOR	2:05.0	
2. Adrianus "Ard" Schenk	HOL	2:05.0	
4. Magne Thomassen	NOR	2:05.1	
5. Johnny Höglin	SWE	2:05.2	
5. Björn Tveter	NOR	2:05.2	
7. Svein-Erik Stiansen	NOR	2:05.5	
8. Edouard Matoussevich	SOV	2:06.1	

Kees Verkerk was a 25-year-old bartender from the village of Puttershoek who also played the trumpet on a Dutch television show.

1972 Sapporo C: 39, N: 16, D: 2.6. WR: 1:58.7 (Adrianus "Ard" Schenk)

1.	Adrianus "Ard" Schenk	HOL	2:02.96	OR
2.	Roar Grönvold	NOR	2:04.26	
3.	Göran Claesson	SWE	2:05.89	
4.	Björn Tveter	NOR	2:05.94	
5.	Jan Bols	HOL	2:06.58	
6.	Valery Lavrouchkin	SOV	2:07.16	
7.	Daniel Carroll	USA	2:07.24	
8.	Cornelis "Kees" Verkerk	HOL	2:07.43	

1976 Innsbruck C: 30, N: 19, D: 2.13. WR: 1:58.7 (Adrianus "Ard" Schenk)

1.	Jan Egil Storholt	NOR	1:59.38	OR
2.	Yuri Kondakov	SOV	1:59.97	
3.	Hans van Helden	HOL	2:00.87	
4.	Sergei Riabev	SOV	2:02.15	
5.	Daniel Carroll	USA	2:02.26	
6.	Piet Kleine	HOL	2:02.28	
7.	Eric Heiden	USA	2:02.40	
8.	Colin Coates	AUS	2:03.34	

Storholt, an electrician from Trondheim, celebrated his 27th birthday the day he won the gold medal.

1980 Lake Placid C: 36, N: 16, D: 2.21. WR: 1:54.79 (Eric Heiden)

1.	Eric Heiden	USA	1:55.44	OR
2.	Kai Arne Stenshjemmet	NOR	1:56.81	
3.	Terje Andersen	NOR	1:56.92	
4.	Andreas Dietel	GDR	1:57.14	
5.	Yuri Kondakov	SOV	1:57.36	
6.	Jan Egil Storholt	NOR	1:57.95	
7.	S. Tomas Gustafson	SWE	1:58.18	
8.	Vladimir Lobanov	SOV	1:59.38	

Midway through his race against Stenshjemmet, Heiden almost fell when he hit a rut in the ice. But he was able to steady himself before he had lost more than a few hundredths of a second, and he went on to win his fourth gold medal.

1984 Sarajevo C: 40, N: 20, D: 2.16. WR: 1:54.26 (Igor Zhelezovsky)

1.	Gaétan Boucher	CAN	1:58.36	
2.	Sergei Khlebnikov	SOV	1:58.83	
3.	Oleg Bozhyev	SOV	1:58.89	
4.	Hans van Helden	FRA	1:59.39	
5.	Andreas Ehrig	GDR	1:59.41	
6.	Andreas Dietel	GDR	1:59.73	
7.	Hilbert van der Duim	HOL	1:59.77	
8.	Viktor Chacherin	SOV	1:59.81	

Boucher, a 25-year-old marketing student from St. Hubert, Quebec, left Sarajevo with two gold medals and one bronze. He had already won a silver in the 1000 meters in 1980.

1988 Calgary C: 40, N: 20, D: 2.20. WR: 1:52.50 (Igor Zhelezovsky)

1.	André Hoffmann	GDR	1:52.06 WR
2.	Eric Flaim	USA	1:52.12
3.	Michael Hadschieff	AUT	1:52.31
4.	Igor Zhelezovsky	SOV	1:52.63
5.	Toru Aoyanagi	JPN	1:52.85
6.	Aleksandr Klimov	SOV	1:52.97
7.	Nikolai Gulyaev	SOV	1:53.04
8.	Peter Adeberg	GDR	1:53.57

1992 Albertville C: 46, N: 21, D: 2.16. WR: 1:52.06 (André Hoffman)

1.	Johann Olav Koss	NOR	1:54.81
2.	Ådne Sonderål	NOR	1:54.85
3.	Leo Visser	HOL	1:54.90
4.	Rintje Ritsma	HOL	1:55.70
5.	Bart Veldkamp	HOL	1:56.33
6.	Olaf Zinke	GER	1:56.74
7.	Falko Zandstra	HOL	1:56.96
8.	Geir Karlstad	NOR	1:56.98

On February 8, the day of the Opening Ceremony of the Albertville Games, Johann Olav Koss, the son of two doctors, and a medical student himself, was lying in a hospital bed in Bavaria suffering from an inflamed pancreas. After passing a gallstone, he was released the next day and resumed training immediately. On Thursday the thirteenth he placed seventh in the 5000 meters, an event in which he held the world record, and promptly vomited. By Sunday the sixteenth he was back in perfect shape and earned a gold medal in the 1500.

5000 METERS

1924 Chamonix C: 22, N: 10, D: 1.26. WR: 8:26.5 (Harald Ström)

1.	A. Clas Thunberg	FIN	8:39.0
2.	Julius Skutnabb	FIN	8:48.4
3.	Roald Larsen	NOR	8:50.2
4.	Sigurd Moen	NOR	8:51.0
5.	Harald Ström	NOR	8:54.6
6.	Valentine Bialas	USA	8:55.0
7.	Edvin Paulsen	NOR	8:59.0
8.	Richard Donovan	USA	9:05.3

Thunberg won the first of his five Olympic gold medals.

1928 St. Moritz C: 33, N: 14, D: 2.13. WR: 8:26.5 (Harald Ström)

1.	Ivar Ballangrud	NOR	8:50.5
2.	Julius Skutnabb	FIN	8:59.1
3.	Bernt Evensen	NOR	9:01.1
4.	Irving Jaffee	USA	9:01.3
5.	Armand Carlsen	NOR	9:01.5
6.	Valentine Bialas	USA	9:06.3
7.	Michael Staksrud	NOR	9:07.3
8.	Otto Polacsek	AUT	9:08.9

This was the first of Ballangrud's seven Olympic medals.

1932 Lake Placid C: 18, N: 6, D: 2.4. WR: 8:21.6 (Ivar Ballangrud)

1.	Irving Jaffee	USA	9:40.8
2.	Edward Murphy	USA	—
3.	William Logan	CAN	—
4.	Herbert Taylor	USA	—
5.	Ivar Ballangrud	NOR	—
6.	Bernt Evensen	NOR	—
7.	Frank Stack	CAN	—
8.	C. Harry Smyth	CAN	—

1936 Garmisch-Partenkirchen C: 37, N: 16, D: 2.12. WR: 8:17.2 (Ivar Ballangrud)

1.	Ivar Ballangrud	NOR	8:19.6	OR
2.	Birger Vasenius	FIN	8:23.3	
3.	Antero Ojala	FIN	8:30.1	
4.	Jan Langedijk	HOL	8:32.0	
5.	Max Stiepl	AUT	8:35.0	
6.	Ossi Blomqvist	FIN	8:36.6	
7.	Charles Mathisen	NOR	8:36.9	
8.	Karl Wazulek	AUT	8:38.4	

1948 St. Moritz C: 40, N: 14, D: 2.1. WR: 8:13.7 (Åke Seyffarth)

1.	Reidar Liaklev	NOR	8:29.4
2.	Odd Lundberg	NOR	8:32.7
3.	Göthe Hedlund	SWE	8:34.8
4.	Gustav Jansson	SWE	8:34.9
5.	Jan Langedijk	HOL	8:36.2
6.	Cornelis "Kees" Broekman	HOL	8:37.3
7.	Åke Seyffarth	SWE	8:37.9
8.	Pentti Lammio	FIN	8:40.7

Åke Seyffarth, who had set the world record seven years earlier, lost precious seconds on the final lap when he brushed against a photographer who had jumped onto the ice to take a picture. Liaklev and Lundberg were both born and raised in the small village of Brandbu.

1952 Oslo C: 35, N: 13, D: 2.17. WR: 8:03.7 (Nikolai Mamonov)

1.	Hjalmar Andersen	NOR	8:10.6	OR
2.	Cornelis "Kees" Broekman	HOL	8:21.6	
3.	Sverre Haugli	NOR	8:22.4	
4.	Anton Huiskes	HOL	8:28.5	
5.	Willem van der Voort	HOL	8:30.6	
6.	Carl-Erik Asplund	SWE	8:30.7	
7.	Pentti Lammio	FIN	8:31.9	
8.	Arthur Mannsbarth	AUT	8:36.2	

Spurred on by a standing ovation from the crowd of 24,000, 28-year-old truck driver Hjalmar Andersen achieved the largest winning margin in the history of the 5000 meters.

1956 Cortina C: 46, N: 17, D: 1.29. WR: 7:45.6 (Boris Shilkov)

1.	Boris Shilkov	SOV	7:48.7	OR
2.	Sigvard Ericsson	SWE	7:56.7	
3.	Oleg Goncharenko	SOV	7:57.5	
4.	Willem de Graaf	HOL	8:00.2	
4.	Cornelis "Kees" Broekman	HOL	8:00.2	

6. Roald Aas	NOR	8:01.6
7. Olof Dahlberg	SWE	8:01.8
8. Knut Johannesen	NOR	8:02.3

1960 Squaw Valley C: 37, N: 15, D: 2.25. WR: 7:45.6 (Boris Shilkov)

1. Viktor Kosichkin	SOV	7:51.3
2. Knut Johannesen	NOR	8:00.8
3. Jan Pesman	HOL	8:05.1
4. Torstein Seiersten	NOR	8:05.3
5. Valery Kotov	SOV	8:05.4
6. Oleg Goncharenko	SOV	8:06.6
7. Ivar Nilsson	SWE	8:09.1
7. Keijo Tapiovaara	FIN	8:09.1

1964 Innsbruck C: 44, N: 19, D: 2.5. WR: 7:34.3 (Jonny Nilsson)

1. Knut Johannesen	NOR	7:38.4	OR
2. Per Ivar Moe	NOR	7:38.6	
3. Fred Anton Maier	NOR	7:42.0	
4. Victor Kosichkin	SOV	7:45.8	
5. Herman Strutz	AUT	7:48.3	
6. Jonny Nilsson	SWE	7:48.4	
7. Ivar Nilsson	SWE	7:49.0	
8. Rutgerus Liebrechts	HOL	7:50.9	

Skating in the fifth pair, 19-year-old Per Ivar Moe recorded the second-fastest 5000 meters ever. Then he watched as Olympic veteran Knut Johannesen assaulted his time as part of the 14th pair. With five of 12½ laps to go, Johannesen was three seconds behind Moe's pace. But he caught up with two laps left and pushed for the finish with the crowd on its feet, rooting him on. Unfortunately, as he crossed the finish line, the clock stopped at 7:38.7—one-tenth of a second slower than Moe. But then the scoreboard was revised to match the official time—7:38.4—and Johannesen had won his second gold medal. Between 1956 and 1964 he won two gold, two silver, and one bronze.

1968 Grenoble C: 38, N: 17, D: 2.15. WR: 7:26.2. (Fred Anton Maier)

1. Fred Anton Maier	NOR	7:22.4	WR
2. Cornelis "Kees" Verkerk	HOL	7:23.2	
3. Petrus Nottet	HOL	7:25.5	
4. Per-Willy Guttormsen	NOR	7:27.8	
5. Johnny Höglin	SWE	7:32.7	
6. Örjan Sandler	SWE	7:32.8	
7. Jonny Nilsson	SWE	7:32.9	
8. Jan Bols	HOL	7:33.1	

Verkerk broke Maier's world record by three seconds and then watched as the 29-year-old clerk won it back 20 minutes later.

1972 Sapporo C: 28, N: 14, D: 2.4. WR: 7:12.0 (Adrianus "Ard" Schenk)

1. Adrianus "Ard" Schenk	HOL	7:23.61
2. Roar Grönvold	NOR	7:28.18
3. Sten Stensen	NOR	7:33.39
4. Göran Claeson	SWE	7:36.17
5. Willy Olsen	NOR	7:36.47
6. Cornelis "Kees" Verkerk	HOL	7:39.17
7. Valery Lavrouchkin	SOV	7:39.26
8. Jan Bols	HOL	7:39.40

Schenk skated first, while it was snowing, but he still managed to outstrip the field.

1976 Innsbruck C: 31, N: 17, D: 2.11. WR: 7:07.82 (Hans van Helden)

1. Sten Stensen	NOR	7:24.48
2. Piet Kleine	HOL	7:26.47
3. Hans van Helden	HOL	7:26.54
4. Victor Varlamov	SOV	7:30.97
5. Klaus Wunderlich	GDR	7:33.82
6. Daniel Carroll	USA	7:36.46
7. Vladimir Ivanov	SOV	7:37.73
8. Örjan Sandler	SWE	7:39.69

1980 Lake Placid C: 29, N: 15, D: 2.16. WR: 6:56.9 (Kai Arne Stenshjemmet)

1. Eric Heiden	USA	7:02.29	OR
2. Kai Arne Stenshjemmet	NOR	7:03.28	
3. Tom-Erik Oxholm	NOR	7:05.59	
4. Hilbert van der Duim	HOL	7:07.97	
5. Öyvind Tveter	NOR	7:08.36	
6. Piet Kleine	HOL	7:08.96	
7. Michael Woods	USA	7:10.39	
8. Ulf Ekstrand	SWE	7:13.13	

Stenshjemmet, skating two pairs after Eric Heiden, stayed ahead of his pace for ten and a half laps, but began his arm swinging too early and couldn't keep it up. It was Heiden's second gold medal.

1984 Sarajevo C: 42, N: 20, D: 2.12. WR: 6:54.66 (Aleksandr Baranov)

1. S. Tomas Gustafson	SWE	7:12.28
2. Igor Malkov	SOV	7:12.30
3. René Schöfisch	GDR	7:17.49
4. Andreas Ehrig	GDR	7:17.63
5. Oleg Bogzhyev	SOV	7:17.96
6. Pertti Niittylä	FIN	7:17.97
7. Björn Nyland	NOR	7:18.27
8. Werner Jaeger	AUT	7:18.61

Skating in the first pair, Gustafson, who had trained in Wisconsin with Diane Holum and Eric Heiden, came off the ice thinking his time would be good enough for fifth or sixth place. Three pairs later, Malkov, not realizing how close he was to Gustafson's time, faded in the last 400 meters and lost by one-fiftieth of a second.

1988 Calgary C: 38, N: 18, D: 2.17. WR: 6:43.59 (Geir Karlstad)

1. S. Tomas Gustafson	SWE	6:44.63	OR
2. Leo Visser	HOL	6:44.98	
3. Gerard Kemkers	HOL	6:45.92	
4. Eric Flaim	USA	6:47.09	
5. Michael Hadschieff	AUT	6:48.72	
6. David Silk	USA	6:49.95	
7. Geir Karlstad	NOR	6:50.88	
8. Roland Freier	GDR	6:51.42	

Defending champion Tomas Gustafson, skating seven pairs after Leo Visser, was eight tenths of a second behind Visser's pace with 400 meters to go. The public-address announcer informed the audience that Gustafson was going for the silver or bronze medal. But the 28-year-old Swede, who had struggled through knee surgery, meningitis, and the death of his father since his last Olympic victory, had set his sights higher. His final lap was an amazing 31.86. "How do you describe happiness?" he said afterward. "I'd have to write a poem."

1992 Albertville C: 36, N: 20, D: 2.13. WR: 6:41.73 (Johann Olav Koss)

1.	Geir Karlstad	NOR	6:59.97
2.	Falko Zandstra	HOL	7:02.28
3.	Leo Visser	HOL	7:04.96
4.	Frank Dittrich	GER	7:06.33
5.	Bart Veldkamp	HOL	7:08.00
6.	Eric Flaim	USA	7:11.15
7.	Johann Olav Koss	NOR	7:11.32
8.	Yevgeny Sanarov	SOV	7:11.38

In 1988 Geir Karlstad was one of the big disappointments of the Calgary Games. After he set world records in the 5000 and 10,000, he was overwhelmed by media attention in speed skating-crazed Norway. In addition to this distraction, he was implicated in a steroids scandal after he served as a go-between, passing a mysterious package from Nikolai Gulyaev to fellow Norwegian skater Stein Krosly. Although he had been favored in both distance events, Karlstad placed only seventh in the 5000 and fell in the 10,000 and failed to finish. Another controversy involving Karlstad came up before the Albertville Games. Norway's chief medical officer, Inggard Lereim, who was also a member of the I.O.C.'s medical committee, told the press that Karlstad had an abnormally high testosterone level and that he had been issued a "Doping Certificate" proving that his high test levels were a result of natural causes. Prince Alexandre de Merode, the I.O.C. medical commission chairman, denied that such a certificate existed. One good thing that happened to Karlstad between Olympics was the emergence of Johann Olav Koss, who drew away most of the media attention and allowed Karlstad to train in peace. The 5000-meter race in Albertville was run in a steady rain. After his victory, Karlstad told the press, "I didn't like soft ice up to now, but now I do."

10,000 METERS

1924 Chamonix C: 16, N: 6, D: 1.27. WR: 17:22.6 (Oscar Mathisen)

1.	Julius Skutnabb	FIN	18:04.8
2.	A. Clas Thunberg	FIN	18:07.8
3.	Roald Larsen	NOR	18:12.2
4.	Fritjof Paulsen	NOR	18:13.0
5.	Harald Ström	NOR	18:18.6
6.	Sigurd Moen	NOR	18:19.0
7.	Léon Quaglia	FRA	18:25.0
8.	Valentine Bialas	USA	18:34.0

Skutnabb defeated Thunberg head-on, since they were paired together. This reversed the order of finish of the 5000, which had been held the previous day.

1928 St. Moritz C: 10, N: 6, D: 2.14. WR: 17:17.4 (Armand Carlsen)

1.	Irving Jaffee	USA	18:36.5
2.	Bernt Evensen	NOR	18:36.6
3.	Otto Polacsek	AUT	20:00.9
4.	Rudolf Riedl	AUT	20:21.5
5.	Keistutis Bulota	LIT	20:22.2
6.	Armand Carlsen	NOR	20:56.1
7.	Valentine Bialas	USA	21:05.4

Officially, this race never took place. After seven of the ten entrants had completed their heats, the temperature rose suddenly, and the officials in charge ordered the day's times cancelled and the races rerun. By the time a final decision had been reached, the Norwegians, who had already made it clear that they considered Jaffee the champion, had gone home, so the contest was cancelled. As far as the skaters were concerned, the matter had been settled after the first heat, when Jaffee came from behind to nip Evensen just before the finish line. However sports historians generally consider the 1928 10,000 meters to have been a non-event.

1932 Lake Placid C: 18, N: 6, D: 2.8. WR: 17:17.4 (Armand Carlsen)

1.	Irving Jaffee	USA	19:13.6
2.	Ivar Ballangrud	NOR	—
3.	Frank Stack	CAN	—
4.	Edwin Wedge	USA	—
5.	Valentine Bialas	USA	—
6.	Bernt Evensen	NOR	—
7.	Alexander Hurd	CAN	—
8.	Edward Schroeder	USA	—

The turmoil that marred the 1932 speed skating competitions culminated in disputes that broke out during the heats of the 10,000 meters. For this contest the North Americans tacked on a rule that required each skater to do his share in setting the pace. After the first heat, Alex Hurd, who won the race, as well as Edwin Wedge of the United States and Shozo Ishihara of Japan, were disqualified for not doing their share. In the second heat Frank Stack was disqualified for interference after a protest by Bernt Evensen. After much haggling and many threats it was decided to rerun the two races the following day. The same eight men who had originally qualified for the final qualified again. The final race was slow and tactical, as all eight stayed in a bunch until the last lap. Jaffee won by five yards, but the finish was so close that only two yards separated Ballangrud in second place from Evensen in sixth. During the Depression, Jaffee was forced to pawn his two gold medals. Unfortunately, times were so tough that even the pawnshop went out of business and Jaffee never saw his medals again. Bronze medalist Frank Stack was still competing in the Olympics in 1952 when, at the age of 46, he finished 12th in the 500 meters.

1936 Garmisch-Partenkirchen C: 30, N: 14, D: 2.14. WR: 17:17.4 (Armand Carlsen)

1.	Ivar Ballangrud	NOR	17:24.3 OR
2.	Birger Vasenius	FIN	17:28.2
3.	Max Stiepl	AUT	17:30.0
4.	Charles Mathisen	NOR	17:41.2
5.	Ossi Blomqvist	FIN	17:42.4
6.	Jan Langedijk	HOL	17:43.7
7.	Antero Ojala	FIN	17:46.6
8.	Edward Schroeder	USA	17:52.0

Ballangrud and Vasenius, paired together, raced neck and neck for 4000 meters before the Norwegian began to pull away. Ballangrud completed his Olympic career with four gold medals, two silver, and one bronze.

1948 St. Moritz C: 27, N: 11, D: 2.3. WR: 17:05.5 (Charles Mathisen)

1.	Åke Seyffarth	SWE	17:26.3
2.	Lauri Parkkinen	FIN	17:36.0
3.	Pentti Lammio	FIN	17:42.7
4.	Kornel Pajor	HUN	17:45.6

5.	Cornelis "Kees" Broekman	HOL	17:54.7
6.	Jan Langedijk	HOL	17:55.3
7.	Odd Lundberg	NOR	18:05.8
8.	Harry Jansson	SWE	18:08.0

1952 Oslo C: 30, N: 12, D: 2.19. WR: 16:32.6 (Hjalmar Andersen)

1.	Hjalmar Andersen	NOR	16:45.8	OR
2.	Cornelis "Kees" Broekman	HOL	17:10.6	
3.	Carl-Erik Asplund	SWE	17:16.6	
4.	Pentti Lammio	FIN	17:20.5	
5.	Anton Huiskes	HOL	17:25.5	
6.	Sverre Haugli	NOR	17:30.2	
7.	Kazuhiko Sugawara	JPN	17:34.0	
8.	Lauri Parkkinen	FIN	17:36.8	

Hjalmar "Hjallis" Andersen's unusually large margin of victory, the most decisive in Olympic history, earned him his third gold medal in three days.

1956 Cortina C: 32, N: 15, D: 1.31. WR: 16:32.6 (Hjalmar Andersen)

1.	Sigvard Ericsson	SWE	16:35.9	OR
2.	Knut Johannesen	NOR	16:36.9	
3.	Oleg Goncharenko	SOV	16:42.3	
4.	Sverre Haugli	NOR	16:48.7	
5.	Cornelius "Kees" Broekman	HOL	16:51.2	
6.	Hjalmar Andersen	NOR	16:52.6	
7.	Boris Yakimov	SOV	16:59.7	
8.	Olof Dahlberg	SWE	17:01.3	

Skating three pairs after Johannesen, 25-year-old woodchopper Sigge Ericsson kept a steady pace and held on for the victory despite losing two seconds to the fast-finishing Norwegian on the final lap.

1960 Squaw Valley C: 30, N: 15, D: 2.27. WR: 16:32.6 (Hjalmar Andersen)

1.	Knut Johannesen	NOR	15:46.6	WR
2.	Viktor Kosichkin	SOV	15:49.2	
3.	Kjell Bäckman	SWE	16:14.2	
4.	Ivar Nilsson	SWE	16:26.0	
5.	Terence Monaghan	GBR	16:31.6	
6.	Torstein Seiersten	NOR	16:33.4	
7.	Olof Dahlberg	SWE	16:34.6	
8.	Juhani Järvinen	FIN	16:35.4	

Since February 10, 1952, the world record for 10,000 meters had been Hjallis Andersen's 16:32.6. But with the ice perfect and the weather sunny and calm, five different skaters bettered Andersen's mark. Skating in the second pair, Kjell Bäckman chopped over 18 seconds off the record with a 16:14.2. Two pairs later, Knut Johannesen, a 26-year-old carpenter, became the first person to break the 16-minute barrier with a phenomenal 15:46.6. Johannesen's world record lasted for three years, but it almost didn't survive the rest of the day. Two pairs after Johannesen came Viktor Kosichkin, who stayed ahead of Johannesen's pace for 6400 meters and was still even after 7600 meters. After that, though, Kosichkin began to tire and crossed the finish line 2.6 seconds too late. He did, however, have the rare experience of breaking the world record by more than 43 seconds and earning only a silver medal.

1964 Innsbruck C: 33, N: 19, D: 2.7. WR: 15:33.0 (Jonny Nilsson)

1. Jonny Nilsson	SWE	15:50.1	
2. Fred Anton Maier	NOR	16:06.0	
3. Knut Johannesen	NOR	16:06.3	
4. Rutgerus Liebrechts	HOL	16:08.6	
5. Ants Antson	SOV	16:08.7	
6. Victor Kosichkin	SOV	16:19.3	
7. Gerhard Zimmermann	GER	16:22.5	
8. Alfred Malkin	GBR	16:35.2	

1968 Grenoble C: 28, N: 13, D: 2.17. WR: 15:20.3 (Fred Anton Maier)

1. Johnny Höglin	SWE	15:23.6	OR
2. Fred Anton Maier	NOR	15:23.9	
3. Örjan Sandler	SWE	15:31.8	
4. Per-Willy Guttormsen	NOR	15:32.6	
5. Cornelis "Kees" Verkerk	HOL	15:33.9	
6. Jonny Nilsson	SWE	15:39.6	
7. Magne Thomassen	NOR	15:44.9	
8. Petrus Nottet	HOL	15:54.7	

Höglin, who had never before gone faster than 15:40, was one of the surprise winners of the 1968 Winter Games. Maier had the advantage of skating first, but Höglin, in the seventh pair, moved ahead of Maier's pace with three of 25 laps to go.

1972 Sapporo C: 24, N: 14, D: 2.7. WR: 14:55.9 (Adrianus "Ard" Schenk)

1. Adrianus "Ard" Schenk	HOL	15:01.35	OR
2. Cornelis "Kees" Verkerk	HOL	15:04.70	
3. Sten Stensen	NOR	15:07.08	
4. Jan Bols	HOL	15:17.99	
5. Valery Lavrouchkin	SOV	15:20.08	
6. Göran Claesson	SWE	15:30.19	
7. Kimmo Koskinen	FIN	15:38.87	
8. Gerhard Zimmermann	GER	15:43.92	

Handsome Ard Schenk won his third gold medal to match the single Olympics record of Ivar Ballangrud and Hjalmar "Hjallis" Andersen. Two weeks later in Norway, Schenk became the first person in 60 years to sweep all four events at the world championships. The last person to achieve the feat had been Oscar Mathisen in 1912. Schenk was considered such a hero in Holland that a tulip was named after him.

1976 Innsbruck C: 20, N: 13, D: 2.14. WR: 14:50.31 (Sten Stensen)

1. Piet Kleine	HOL	14:50.59	OR
2. Sten Stensen	NOR	14:53.30	
3. Hans van Helden	HOL	15:02.02	
4. Victor Varlamov	SOV	15:06.06	
5. Örjan Sandler	SWE	15:16.21	
6. Colin Coates	AUS	15:16.80	
7. Daniel Carroll	USA	15:19.29	
8. Franz Krienbuhl	SWI	15:36.43	

Stensen had set a world record of 14:50.31 three weeks earlier. In Innsbruck, skating sixth, he was able to do only 14:53.30. Two pairs later, Piet Kleine, a 6-foot 5-inch 24-year-old unemployed carpenter, attacked Stenson's pace in steady fashion. He moved ahead at the halfway mark and stayed at least two seconds faster for the last eight laps.

1980 Lake Placid C: 25, N: 12, D: 2.23. WR: 14:34.33 (Viktor Leskin)

1. Eric Heiden	USA	14:28.13	WR
2. Piet Kleine	HOL	14:36.03	
3. Tom-Erik Oxholm	NOR	14:36.60	
4. Michael Woods	USA	14:39.53	
5. Öyvind Tveter	NOR	14:43.53	
6. Hilbert van der Duim	HOL	14:47.58	
7. Viktor Leskin	SOV	14:51.72	
8. Andreas Ehrig	GDR	14:51.94	

Having already become the first male speed skater to win four gold medals in one Olympics, Eric Heiden took the night off before his final race to attend the United States-U.S.S.R. ice hockey match. The U.S. team included two friends of Heiden's from Madison, Wisconsin, Mark Johnson and Bobby Suter. Heiden was so excited by the U.S. victory—more excited than by his own accomplishments—that he had trouble falling asleep and ended up oversleeping in the morning. Snatching a few pieces of bread for breakfast, he rushed to the track and, skating in the second pair, calmly broke the world record by over six seconds. He had become the first person in Olympic history to win five individual gold medals at one games (three of Mark Spitz's seven gold medals had been in relay events). Repelled by the instant celebrity that followed his feats, Eric Heiden announced that he would retire at the end of the season. "Maybe if things had stayed the way they were," he told the press, "and I could still be obscure in an obscure sport, I might want to keep skating. I really liked it best when I was a nobody."

1984 Sarajevo C: 32, N: 17, D: 2.18. WR: 14:23.59 (S. Tomas Gustafson)

1. Igor Malkov	SOV	14:39.90
2. S. Tomas Gustafson	SWE	14:39.95
3. René Schöfisch	GDR	14:46.91
4. Geir Karlstad	NOR	14:52.40
5. Michael Hadschieff	AUT	14:53.78
6. Dmitri Bochkarov	SOV	14:55.65
7. Michael Woods	USA	14:57.30
8. Henry Nilsen	NOR	14:57.81

Six days after 19-year-old Igor Malkov narrowly missed beating Tomas Gustafson for the 5000-meter gold medal, he again found himself skating after the Swede. This time he paced himself well and finished strongly to win by one-twentieth of a second.

1988 Calgary C: 32, N: 19, D: 2.21. WR: 13:48.51 (Geir Karlstad)

1. S. Tomas Gustafson	SWE	13:48.20	WR
2. Michael Hadschieff	AUT	13:56.11	
3. Leo Visser	HOL	14:00.55	
4. Eric Flaim	USA	14:05.57	
5. Gerard Kemkers	HOL	14:08.34	
6. Yuri Klyuyev	SOV	14:09.68	
7. Roberto Sighel	ITA	14:13.60	
8. Roland Freier	GDR	14:19.60	

Tomas Gustafson brought his career Olympic medal total to three golds and one silver. Gerard Kemkers finished fifth despite falling in the fifth lap. Colin Coates of

Australia, competing in his sixth Olympics, placed twenty-sixth, twenty years after his first appearance.

1992 Albertville C: 30, N: 15, D: 2.20. WR: 13:43.54 (Johann Olav Koss)

1.	Bart Veldkamp	HOL	14:12.12
2.	Johann Olav Koss	NOR	14:14.58
3.	Geir Karlstad	NOR	14:18.13
4.	Robert Vunderink	HOL	14:22.92
5.	Kazuhiro Sato	JPN	14:28.30
6.	Michael Hadschieff	AUT	14:28.80
7.	Per Bengtsson	SWE	14:35.58
8.	Steinar Johansen	NOR	14:36.09

Veldkamp's victory, the first by a Dutch male skater in 16 years, set off wild celebrations among the many Dutch fans in the stands. Veldkamp himself was so excited that he danced on the podium at the medal ceremony and sprayed champagne on the reporters and photographers at his press conference.

Short Track

Short track is the exciting younger cousin of staid long-track speed skating. Instead of racing in pairs against the clock, the skaters race in a pack, usually four at a time. The first person across the finish line is the winner. Elimination heats lead to semifinals and finals. In individual races, semifinal losers take part in a "B" final to decide places 5 through 8. In relays, fifth through eighth places are determined by semifinal placings and times. The track is only 111.12 meters around. The course is marked by four rubber blocks in the corners. Skaters may cross into the infield, but they must come back outside to go around the blocks. They are allowed to touch the ice inside the blocks with their hands. Although the sport is often compared to roller derby, pushing, colliding, and obstructing are grounds for immediate disqualification. Passing must be done without body contact.

Pack-style speed skating first appeared in the 1932 Olympics, although it was held on a normal 400-meter oval with a different set of rules. The first short-track world championship was held at Meudon-la-Forêt, France, in 1981, and the sport was included as a demonstration at the 1988 Olympics.

SHORT TRACK: 500 METERS

This event will be held for the first time in 1994.

SHORT TRACK: 1000 METERS

1924-1988 not held

1992 Albertville C: 28, N: 16, D: 2.20. WR: 1:31.80 (Tsutomu Kawasaki)

1.	Kim Ki-hoon	KOR	1:30.76 WR
2.	Frédéric Blackburn	CAN	1:31.11
3.	Lee Joon-ho	KOR	1:31.16

4.	Michael McMillen	NZL	1:31.32
5.	Wilfred O'Reilly	GBR	1:36.24
6.	Geert Blanchart	BEL	1:36.28
7.	Mark Lackie	CAN	1:36.28
8.	Michel Daignault	CAN	1:37.10

World record holder Tsutomu Kawasaki was eliminated in the quarterfinals. Wilf O'Reilly, winner of the 1988 Olympic demonstration event and the defending world champion, fell in his semifinal heat and was also eliminated. That race was won by Lee Joon-ho in a world record time of 1:31.27. The other semi was won by Lee's countryman, Kim Ki-hoon. Kim, the 1989 world champion, had spent four months in the hospital that same year after being spiked in an artery during a race. In the final, the two Koreans went out fast. Blackburn caught Lee, but Kim eluded him, as all four skaters broke the pre-Olympic world record.

SHORT TRACK: 5000-METER RELAY

Short-track relay racing is probably the most exciting spectator event at the Winter Olympics. Each team includes four skaters. There are no rules regulating who skates when and for how long, except that no changeover may be made in the final two laps. Changeovers are performed by touch, although in actual practice the retiring skater vigorously pushes the new skater. If a racer falls, a new skater may take over by touching his or her fallen comrade. An alternate is allowed to mill around in the infield to replace an injured skater.

1924-1988 not held

1992 Albertville T: 9, N: 9, D: 2.22. WR: 7:22.12 (HOL—Mos, Sagten, Van de Velde, Veldhoven)

1.	KOR	(Kim Ki-hoon, Lee Joon-ho, Song Jae-kun, Mo Ji-su)	7:14.02 WR
2.	CAN	(Frédéric Blackburn, Mark Lackie, Michel Daignault, Sylvain Gagnon)	7:14.06
3.	JPN	(Tatsuyoshi Ishihara, Tsutomu Kawasaki, Toshinobu Kawai, Yuichi Akasaka)	7:18.18
4.	NZL	(Michael McMillen, Christopher Nicholson, Andrew Nicholson, Tony Smith)	7:18.91
5.	FRA	(Marc Bella, Arnaud Drouet, Rémi Ingres, Claude Nicouleau)	7:26.09
6.	GBR	(Nicky Gooch, Stuart Horsepool, Jasper Matthew, Wilf O'Reilly)	7:29.40
7.	AUS	(Kieran Hansen, John Kah, Andrew Murtha, Richard Nizielski)	7:32.57
8.	ITA	(Orazio Fagone, Hugo Herrnhof, Roberto Peretti, Mirko Vuillermin)	7:32.80

The South Korean team set a world record of 7:14.07 in the first preliminary heat. The final was a spectacular dual between the Koreans and the Canadians. The lead changed hands five times during the first 30 laps. Then Canada took over while the Koreans tucked in behind them for the next 1500 meters. Michel Daignault slipped slightly midway through the final lap, then went a bit wide on the final turn. Kim Ki-hoon took advantage of the opening to slither by on the inside. He edged ahead of Daignault in the final stride to win in a photo finish and set another world record.

Discontinued Event

FOUR RACES COMBINED EVENT

1924 Chamonix C: 22, N: 9, D: 1.27.

			PTS.
1.	A. Clas Thunberg	FIN	5.5
2.	Roald Larsen	NOR	9.5
3.	Julius Skutnabb	FIN	11
4.	Sigurd Moen	NOR	17
4.	Harald Ström	NOR	17
6.	León Quaglia	FRA	25
7.	Alberts Rumba	LAT	27
8.	Leon Jucewicz	POL	32

The concept of an all-around champion has continued to be a matter of major importance in world championships, but was never included again in the Olympics.

SPEED SKATING

WOMEN
500 Meters
1000 Meters
1500 Meters
3000 Meters
5000 Meters
Short Track: 500 Meters
Short Track: 1000 Meters
Short Track: 3000-Meter Relay

WOMEN

500 METERS

Twenty-six of the 28 medals awarded in this event have been won by skaters from only three nations: the U.S.S.R. (10), the U.S.A. (9), and Germany (7).

1924–1956 not held

1960 Squaw Valley C: 23, N: 10, D: 2.20. WR: 45.6 (Tamara Rylova)

1. Helga Haase	GDR	45.9	
2. Natalya Donchenko	SOV	46.0	
3. Jeanne Ashworth	USA	46.1	
4. Tamara Rylova	SOV	46.2	
5. Hatsue Takamizawa	JPN	46.6	
6. Klara Guseva	SOV	46.8	
6. Elwira Seroczyńska	POL	46.8	
8. Fumie Hama	JPN	47.4	

1964 Innsbruck C: 28, N: 14, D: 1.30. WR: 44.9 (Inga Voronina)

1. Lydia Skoblikova	SOV	45.0	OR
2. Irina Yegorova	SOV	45.4	
3. Tatyana Sidorova	SOV	45.5	
4. Jeanne Ashworth	USA	46.2	
4. Janice Smith	USA	46.2	
6. Gunilla Jacobsson	SWE	46.5	
7. Janice Lawler	USA	46.6	
8. Helga Haase	GDR	47.2	

On January 27, 1962, Inga Voronina of the U.S.S.R. set world records for the 500 meters and 1500 meters. The next day she broke the world record at 3000 meters. However, the following year it was another Soviet skater, Lydia Skoblikova, a teacher from Chelyabinsk, who won the gold medal for all four distances at the world championships in Karuizawa, Japan. Voronina, not fully recovered from a bad stomach ailment, failed to make the Soviet Olympic team in 1964. Skoblikova, on the other hand, entered the competition as the favorite in three of the four events. Only in the 500 meters, the first distance to be contested, was she expected to have a tough time. Yegorova opened the day with a 45.4. This held up as the best time until Skoblikova, skating in the 13th of 14 pairs, zipped past the finish line in 45.0. Before the week was out she had duplicated her world championship feat by sweeping all four women's events.

1968 Grenoble C: 28, N: 11, D: 2.9. WR: 44.7 (Tatyana Sidorova)

1.	Lyudmila Titova	SOV	46.1
2.	Jennifer Fish	USA	46.3
2.	Dianne Holum	USA	46.3
2.	Mary Meyers	USA	46.3
5.	Elisabeth van den Brom	HOL	46.6
6.	Kaija Mustonen	FIN	46.7
6.	Sigrid Sundby	NOR	46.7
8.	Kirsti Biermann	NOR	46.8

On February 3, Tatyana Sidorova set a world record of 44.7, but six days later in Grenoble she could do no better than 46.9 and finished in a tie for ninth place. The unusual triple American tie for second place was accomplished by Mary Meyers of St. Paul, Minnesota (the day before her 22nd birthday), 16-year-old Dianne Holum of Northbrook, Illinois, and 18-year-old Jennifer Fish of Strongville, Ohio.

1972 Sapporo C: 29, N: 12, D: 2.10. WR: 42.5 (Anne Henning)

1.	Anne Henning	USA	43.33	OR
2.	Vera Krasnova	SOV	44.01	
3.	Lyudmila Titova	SOV	44.45	
4.	Sheila Young	USA	44.53	
5.	Monika Pflug	GER	44.75	
6.	Atje Keulen-Deelstra	HOL	44.89	
7.	Kay Lunda	USA	44.95	
8.	Alla Boutova	SOV	45.17	

Sixteen-year-old Anne Henning of Northbrook, Illinois, the world record holder and heavy favorite, was paired against Canada's Sylvia Burka, who had impaired vision in one eye. At the crossover Burka didn't see Henning and headed toward a collision. Rather than push her way past Burka, Henning stood up, let her pass, and then dug in faster than ever. Despite losing a full second because of the mishap (which caused Burka's disqualification), Henning still won the gold medal with a time of 43.70. The officials allowed her another run at the end of the competition and she improved to 43.33. Henning was undoubtedly aided by her superstitious mother, who watched the race while holding a clutch of good-luck charms, including a four-leaf clover, Japanese beads, a Christmas ornament, and two U.S. flags. Afterward Henning told reporters, "I just can't wait to be normal again. But, you know, I suppose people will never really let me be normal again, will they?"

1976 Innsbruck C: 27, N: 13, D: 2.6. WR: 40.91 (Sheila Young)

1.	Sheila Young	USA	42.76	OR
2.	Cathy Priestner	CAN	43.12	
3.	Tatyana Averina	SOV	43.17	
4.	Leah Poulos	USA	43.21	
5.	Vera Krasnova	SOV	43.23	
6.	Lyubov Sachikova	SOV	43.80	
7.	Makiko Nagaya	JPN	43.88	
8.	Paula Halonen	FIN	43.99	

Sheila Young, who began skating when she was two years old, won a complete set of medals at the 1976 Games. She was the first U.S. athlete to win three medals at a single Winter Olympics.

1980 Lake Placid C: 31, N: 15, D: 2.15. WR: 40.68 (Sheila Young)

1. Karin Enke	GDR	41.78	OR
2. Leah Mueller [Poulos]	USA	42.26	
3. Natalya Petruseva	SOV	42.42	
4. Ann-Sofie Järnström	SWE	42.47	
5. Makiko Nagaya	JPN	42.70	
6. Cornelia Jacob	GDR	42.98	
7. Beth Heiden	USA	43.18	
8. Tatiana Tarasova	SOV	43.26	

Eighteen-year-old Karin Enke was practically unknown in speed skating circles until a week before the Olympics, when she won the world sprint championship in West Allis, Wisconsin, after qualifying for the East German team as an alternate. She showed that her victory was no fluke when she took the Olympic gold medal at Lake Placid.

1984 Sarajevo C: 33, N: 16, D: 2.10. WR: 39.67 (Christa Rothenburger)

1. Christa Rothenburger	GDR	41.02	OR
2. Karin Enke	GDR	41.28	
3. Natalya Chive	SOV	41.50	
4. Irina Kuleshova	SOV	41.70	
5. Skadi Walter	GDR	42.16	
6. Natalya Petruseva	SOV	42.19	
7. Monika Holzner [Pflug]	GER	42.40	
8. Bonnie Blair	USA	42.53	

Two years after earning her Olympic gold medal, Christa Rothenburger of Dresden won the women's match sprint title at the 1986 world cycling championships.

1988 Calgary C: 30, N: 15, D: 2.22. WR: 39.39 (Christa Rothenburger)

1. Bonnie Blair	USA	39.10	WR
2. Christa Rothenburger	GDR	39.12	
3. Karin Kania [Enke]	GDR	39.24	
4. Angela Stahnke	GDR	39.68	
5. Seiko Hashimoto	JPN	39.74	
6. Shelley Rhead	CAN	40.36	
7. Monika Holzner-Gawenus [Pflug]	GER	40.53	
8. Shoko Fusano	JPN	40.61	

Defending champion Christa Rothenburger, skating in the second pair, blasted her own world record by a quarter of a second. Two pairs later, Bonnie Blair of Champaign, Illinois, who began skating at the age of two, and competing at the age of four, got off to the best start of her life, clocking 10.55 seconds for the first 100 meters to Rothenburger's 10.57. That difference of two one-hundredths of a second turned out to be Blair's final margin of victory.

1992 Albertville C: 34, N: 13, D: 2.10. WR: 39.10 (Bonnie Blair)

1. Bonnie Blair	USA	40.33
2. Ye Qiaobo	CHN	40.51
3. Christa Luding [Rothenburger]	GER	40.57
4. Monique Garbrecht	GER	40.63
5. Christine Aaftink	HOL	40.66
6. Susan Auch	CAN	40.83
7. Kyoko Shimazaki	JPN	40.98
8. Angela Hauck [Stahnke]	GER	41.10

The first person to tell Bonnie Blair that she would someday win a gold medal was her father, Charlie. After Charlie Blair died on Christmas Day, 1989, Bonnie's skating began to lose its intensity. In 1990 she lost the world sprint championship to Angela Hauck, and in 1991 she slipped to fifth. But then she decided to dedicate her Olympic performance to her father. She swept through the 1991-92 season undefeated at both 500 meters and 1000 meters and went to Albertville as the favorite in both events. Almost fifty family members and friends traveled to France to watch Blair compete. Once there, they lined the side of the track with pro-Blair posters.

The start of the competition was delayed one hour in order to let the outdoor oval harden. Blair's leading challenger, Ye Qiaobo, skated in the second pair against Yelena Tiushniakova of Russia. At the crossover, Tiushniakova, on the inside, failed to make way for Ye as she moved to the outside and Ye was forced to rise out of her crouch to avoid a collision. Three pairs later, Blair quickly pulled away from Angela Hauck and beat Ye's time by eighteen hundredths of a second. Chinese officials asked that Ye be given a rerun, but surprisingly, their protest was rejected.

At the postrace press conference, Ye told her "long, sad story," as she put it. In 1987, her team doctor began giving all the female speed skaters medicine that made her put on 14 kilograms (31.5 lbs.). In 1988, just before the start of the Calgary Olympics, Ye was informed that she and a teammate had tested positive for anabolic steriods. Ye, who had no idea that she had been taking a banned substance, was sent home in disgrace. She served a 15-month suspension. She considered quitting, but a friend told her she was "a little flower that didn't open. And if I quit skating, as I thought of quitting everything, I would never open." So Ye, who had switched from running to skating at age ten because she wanted "to capture the joy" she saw in the eyes of skaters, decided to keep competing. In Albertville she became the first Asian woman and the first Chinese athlete of either sex to win a Winter Olympic medal.

Bonnie Blair, for her part, became the first U.S. woman to win a gold medal in two different Olympics, while Christa Luding, at age 32, matched Karen Kania's feat of winning a complete set of medals at 500 meters.

1000 METERS

1924–1956 not held

1960 Squaw Valley C: 22, N: 10, D: 2.22. WR: 1:33.4 (Tamara Rylova)

1.	Klara Guseva	SOV	1:34.1
2.	Helga Haase	GDR	1:34.3
3.	Tamara Rylova	SOV	1:34.8
4.	Lydia Skoblikova	SOV	1:35.3
5.	Helena Pilejczyk	POL	1:35.8
5.	Hatsue Takamizawa	JPN	1:35.8
7.	Fumie Hama	JPN	1:36.1
8.	Jeanne Ashworth	USA	1:36.5

Elwira Seroczyńska of Poland had the fastest time going into the final curve, but with 100 meters to go, one of her skates hit the dividing line, and she fell.

1964 Innsbruck C: 28, N: 13, D: 2.1. WR: 1:31.8 (Lydia Skoblikova)

1.	Lydia Skoblikova	SOV	1:33.2 OR
2.	Irina Yegorova	SOV	1:34.3
3.	Kaija Mustonen	FIN	1:34.8
4.	Helga Haase	GDR	1:35.7

5. Valentina Stenina	SOV	1:36.0	
6. Gunilla Jacobsson	SWE	1:36.5	
7. Janice Smith	USA	1:36.7	
8. Kaija-Liisa Keskivitikka	FIN	1:37.6	

With this race Skoblikova became the first woman to win three gold medals at one Winter Olympics and the first person of either sex to win five Winter gold medals.

1968 Grenoble C: 29, N: 12, D: 2.11. WR: 1:31.8 (Lydia Skoblikova)

1. Carolina Geijssen	HOL	1:32.6	OR
2. Lyudmila Titova	SOV	1:32.9	
3. Dianne Holum	USA	1:33.4	
4. Kaija Mustonen	FIN	1:33.6	
5. Irina Yegorova	SOV	1:34.4	
6. Sigrid Sundby	NOR	1:34.5	
7. Jeanne Ashworth	USA	1:34.7	
8. Kaija-Liisa Keskivitikka	FIN	1:34.8	

Geijssen was a 21-year-old Amsterdam secretary who skated to work each day. She was the first Dutch skater to win an Olympic gold medal.

1972 Sapporo C: 33, N: 12, D: 2.11. WR: 1:27.3 (Anne Henning)

1. Monika Pflug	GER	1:31.40	OR
2. Atje Keulen-Deelstra	HOL	1:31.61	
3. Anne Henning	USA	1:31.62	
4. Lyudmila Titova	SOV	1:31.85	
5. Nina Statkevitch	SOV	1:32.21	
6. Dianne Holum	USA	1:32.41	
7. Elly van den Brom	HOL	1:32.60	
8. Sylvia Burka	CAN	1:32.95	

Seventeen-year-old Monika Pflug was a surprise winner. A bookbinding apprentice from Munich, she false-started twice. Threatened with disqualification if she jumped the gun again, she started slowly, but was able to make up lost time after the first 200 meters.

1976 Innsbruck C: 27, N: 10, D: 2.7. WR: 1:23.46 (Tatyana Averina)

1. Tatyana Averina	SOV	1:28.43	OR
2. Leah Poulos	USA	1:28.57	
3. Sheila Young	USA	1:29.14	
4. Sylvia Burka	CAN	1:29.47	
5. Monika Holzner [Pflug]	GER	1:29.54	
6. Cathy Priestner	CAN	1:29.66	
7. Lyudmila Titova	SOV	1:30.06	
8. Heike Lange	GDR	1:30.55	

1980 Lake Placid C: 37, N: 16, D: 2.17. WR: 1:23.46 (Tatyana Averina)

1. Natalya Petruseva	SOV	1:24.10	OR
2. Leah Mueller [Poulos]	USA	1:25.41	
3. Silvia Albrecht	GDR	1:26.46	
4. Karin Enke	GDR	1:26.66	
5. Beth Heiden	USA	1:27.01	
6. Annie Borckink	HOL	1:27.24	
7. Sylvia Burka	CAN	1:27.50	
8. Ann-Sofie Järnström	SWE	1:28.10	

Petruseva and Mueller were the second pair to skate. Mueller was ahead at 200 meters, but Petruseva took the lead and eventually pulled away to win by 40 feet. For Mueller, it was her third Olympic silver medal. A couple of weeks earlier, Petruseva had won the world sprint championship in Norway, but then had taken seven hours to produce a urine sample, leading to rumors that she had taken illegal drugs. Suspicions seemed confirmed when she finished only eighth in the 1500 meters, the opening Olympic event. But after taking the bronze medal in the 500 meters, she won the 1000 meters and passed the urine test for drugs without any problems. Part of the Soviet success in speed skating had to be due to the fact that, by 1980, there were 1202 Olympic-size speed skating rinks in the U.S.S.R., whereas in the United States, a nation of comparable population, there were only two.

1984 Sarajevo C: 38, N: 17, D: 2.13. WR: 1:19.31 (Natalya Petruseva)

1. Karin Enke	GDR	1:21.61	OR
2. Andrea Schöne [Mitscherlich]	GDR	1:22.83	
3. Natalya Petruseva	SOV	1:23.21	
4. Valentina Lalenkova	SOV	1:23.68	
5. Christa Rothenburger	GDR	1:23.98	
6. Yvonne van Gennip	HOL	1:25.36	
7. Erwina Rys-Ferens	POL	1:25.81	
8. Monika Holzner [Pflug]	GER	1:25.87	

Enke, skating one pair after Schöne, won her second gold medal of the Sarajevo Games and her third overall.

1988 Calgary C: 27, N: 12, D: 2.22. WR: 1:18.11 (Karin Kania [Enke])

1. Christa Rothenburger	GDR	1:17.65	WR
2. Karin Kania [Enke]	GDR	1:17.70	
3. Bonnie Blair	USA	1:18.31	
4. Andrea Ehrig [Mitscherlich, Schöne]	GDR	1:19.32	
5. Seiko Hashimoto	JPN	1:19.75	
6. Angela Stahnke	GDR	1:20.05	
7. Leslie Bader	USA	1:21.09	
8. Katie Class	USA	1:21.10	

Seven months after earning the gold medal at 1000 meters, Christa Rothenburger took a silver in the cycling sprint race in Seoul to become the only athlete in Olympic history to win medals in winter and summer in the same year.

1992 Albertville C:36, N: 14, D: 2.14. WR: 1:17.65 (Christa Luding [Rothenburger])

1. Bonnie Blair	USA	1:21.90
2. Ye Qiaobo	CHN	1:21.92
3. Monique Garbrecht	GER	1:22.10
4. Christine Aaftink	HOL	1:22.60
5. Seiko Hashimoto	JPN	1:22.63
6. Mihaela Dascalu	ROM	1:22.85
7. Yelena Tiushniakova	SOV	1:22.97
8. Christa Luding [Rothenburger]	GER	1:23.06

Bonnie Blair took advantage of a strong start to become the first U.S. woman to win three gold medals in the Winter Olympics. Her total margin of victory for all three wins was twenty-two one-hundredths of a second. Ye and Garbrecht skated head-to-head three pairs after Blair.

1500 METERS

1924–1956 not held

1960 Squaw Valley C: 23, N: 10, D: 2.21. WR: 2:25.5 (Khalida Schegoleeva)

1. Lydia Skoblikova	SOV	2:25.2	WR
2. Elwira Seroczyńska	POL	2:25.7	
3. Helena Pilejczyk	POL	2:27.1	
4. Klara Guseva	SOV	2:28.7	
5. Valentina Stenina	SOV	2:29.2	
6. Iris Sihvonen	FIN	2:29.7	
7. Christina Scherling	SWE	2:31.5	
8. Helga Haase	GDR	2:31.7	

This was the first of Skoblikova's six career gold medals.

1964 Innsbruck C: 30, N: 14, D: 1.31. WR: 2:19.0 (Inga Voronina)

1. Lydia Skoblikova	SOV	2:22.6	OR
2. Kaija Mustonen	FIN	2:25.5	
3. Berta Kolokoltseva	SOV	2:27.1	
4. Kim Song-soon	PRK	2:27.7	
5. Helga Haase	GDR	2:28.6	
6. Christina Scherling	SWE	2:29.4	
7. Valentina Stenina	SOV	2:29.9	
8. Kaija-Liisa Keskivitikka	FIN	2:30.0	

1968 Grenoble C: 30, N: 13, D: 2.10. WR: 2:19.0 (Inga Artamonova [Voronina])

1. Kaija Mustonen	FIN	2:22.4	OR
2. Carolina Geijssen	HOL	2:22.7	
3. Christina Kaiser	HOL	2:24.5	
4. Sigrid Sundby	NOR	2:25.2	
5. Lasma Kaouniste	SOV	2:25.4	
6. Kaija-Liisa Keskivitikka	FIN	2:25.8	
7. Lyudmila Titova	SOV	2:26.8	
8. Ruth Schleiermacher	GDR	2:27.1	

Defending champion Lydia Skoblikova finished 11th, while future champion Dianne Holum was 13th.

1972 Sapporo C: 31, N: 12, D: 2.9. WR: 2:15.8 (Christina Baas-Kaiser)

1. Dianne Holum	USA	2:20.85	OR
2. Christina Baas-Kaiser	HOL	2:21.05	
3. Atje Keulen-Deelstra	HOL	2:22.05	
4. Elisabeth van den Brom	HOL	2:22.27	
5. Rosemarie Taupadel	GDR	2:22.35	
6. Nina Statkevitch	SOV	2:23.19	
7. Connie Carpenter	USA	2:23.93	
8. Sigrid Sundby	NOR	2:24.07	

As a 16-year-old in 1968, Dianne Holum had won a silver medal in the 500 meters and a bronze in the 1000. In 1972 she added a gold in the 1500 meters and a silver in the 3000. The success of the Dutch system of training was shown not only by the fact that Dutch skaters finished second, third, and fourth, but by the fact that Dianne Holum used a Dutch coach as well. The following year she took on a young pupil of her own—14-year-old Eric Heiden—and coached him all the way to the 1976 and 1980 Olympics.

1976 Innsbruck C: 26, N: 12, D: 2.5. WR: 2:09.90 (Tatyana Averina)

1. Galina Stepanskaya	SOV	2:16.58	OR
2. Sheila Young	USA	2:17.06	
3. Tatyana Averina	SOV	2:17.96	
4. Lisbeth Korsmo	NOR	2:18.99	
5. Karin Kessow	GDR	2:19.05	
6. Leah Poulos	USA	2:19.11	
7. Ines Bautzmann	GDR	2:19.63	
8. Erwina Ryś	POL	2:19.69	

1980 Lake Placid C: 31, N: 14, D: 2.14. WR: 2:07.18 (Halida Vorobieva)

1. Annie Borckink	HOL	2:10.95	OR
2. Ria Visser	HOL	2:12.35	
3. Sabine Becker	GDR	2:12.38	
4. Björg Eva Jensen	NOR	2:12.59	
5. Sylvia Filipsson	SWE	2:12.84	
6. Andrea Mitscherlich	GDR	2:13.05	
7. Beth Heiden	USA	2:13.10	
8. Natalya Petruseva	SOV	2:14.15	

Borckink, a 28-year-old nursing student, had never before finished in the top three in an international meet.

1984 Sarajevo C: 32, N: 15, D: 2.9. WR: 2:04.04 (Natalya Petruseva)

1. Karin Enke	GDR	2:03.42	WR
2. Andrea Schöne [Mitscherlich]	GDR	2:05.29	
3. Natalya Petruseva	SOV	2:05.78	
4. Gabi Schönbrunn	GDR	2:07.69	
5. Erwina Ryś-Ferens	POL	2:08.08	
6. Valentina Lalenkova	SOV	2:08.17	
7. Natalya Kurova	SOV	2:08.41	
8. Björg Eva Jensen	NOR	2:09.53	

A converted figure skater from Dresden, Karin Enke, the 1980 Olympic champion at 500 meters, had set a world record of 2:03.40 on December 8. However the International Skating Union refused to recognize her record because they had received insufficient advance notice of the meet in which she was competing. Determined to prove herself at the Olympics, Enke again broke Petruseva's world record, which had been set at high-altitude.

1988 Calgary C: 28, N: 13, D: 2.27. WR: 1:59.30 (Karin Kania [Enke])

1. Yvonne van Gennip	HOL	2:00.68	OR
2. Karin Kania [Enke]	GDR	2:00.82	
3. Andrea Ehrig [Mitscherlich, Schöne]	GDR	2:01.49	
4. Bonnie Blair	USA	2:04.02	
5. Yelena Lapuga	SOV	2:04.24	
6. Seiko Hashimoto	JPN	2:04.38	
7. Gunda Kleemann	GDR	2:04.68	
7. Erwina Ryś-Ferens	POL	2:04.68	

Van Gennip bettered her personal best by almost four seconds to earn the second of her three gold medals. At her post-race press conference van Gennip inadvertently caused a sensation. Asked to describe her feelings, she replied, "I am not emotional here, but in my bed, I am emotional." When reporters began to laugh, she made it clear that they had misinterpreted her words. Karin Kania's second-place finish gave her a career total of three gold medals, four silvers, and one bronze.

1992 Albertville C: 33, N: 14, D: 2.12. WR: 1:59.30 (Karin Kania [Enke])

1.	Jacqueline Börner	GER	2:05.87
2.	Gunda Niemann [Kleemann]	GER	2:05.92
3.	Seiko Hashimoto	JPN	2:06.88
4.	Natalya Polozkova	SOV	2:07.12
5.	Monique Garbrecht	GER	2:07.24
6.	Svetlana Bazhanova	SOV	2:07.81
7.	Emese Hunyady	AUT	2:08.29
8.	Heike Warnicke	GER	2:08.52

On August 15, 1990, Jacqueline Börner, the reigning all-around speed skating champion, was cycling with nine teammates on the streets of Wandlitz, an East Berlin suburb known as the home of many Communist Party officials. A car drove by and grazed two of Börner's male companions. Words were exchanged with the driver, who continued down the road, then turned around and drove straight at Börner. She woke up in a hospital with a broken foot, torn knee ligaments, and head injuries. Fortunately, the hit-and-run driver was driving a Trabant, the notoriously weak East German automobile. Otherwise Börner might have died. As it was, she spent four months in the hospital and four more months in a rehabilitation center. Under the old East German system, Börner would have been discarded as an athlete, but while she was recuperating, the two Germanys reunited and her new club continued to support her. Börner returned to competition on November 24, 1991, but placed no higher than third during the pre-Olympic World Cup series. In Albertville, Börner skated in the first pair after a one-hour warm weather delay. Her time of 2:05.87 withstood the challenge, five pairs later, of the favorite, Gunda Niemann.

Fourth-place finisher Natalya Polozkova was the daughter-in-law of Lydia Skoblikova, the only woman to win the 1500-meter event twice.

3000 METERS

1924–1956 not held

1960 Squaw Valley C: 20, N: 10, D: 2.23. WR: 5:13.8 (Rimma Zukova)

1.	Lydia Skoblikova	SOV	5:14.3
2.	Valentina Stenina	SOV	5:16.9
3.	Eevi Huttunen	FIN	5:21.0
4.	Hatsue Takamizawa	JPN	5:21.4
5.	Christina Scherling	SWE	5:25.5
6.	Helena Pilejczyk	POL	5:26.2
7.	Elwira Seroczyńska	POL	5:27.3
8.	Jeanne Ashworth	USA	5:28.5

1964 Innsbruck C: 28, N: 13, D: 2.2. WR: 5:06.0 (Inga Voronina)

1.	Lydia Skoblikova	SOV	5:14.9
2.	Han Pil-hwa	PRK	5:18.5
2.	Valentina Stenina	SOV	5:18.5
4.	Klara Nesterova [Guseva]	SOV	5:22.5
5.	Kaija Mustonen	FIN	5:24.3
6.	Hatsue Nagakubo	JPN	5:25.4
7.	Kim Song-soon	KOR	5:25.9
8.	Doreen McCannel	CAN	5:26.4

With this race Lydia Skoblikova became the first person to win four gold medals in a single Winter Olympics and the first to win six gold medals all together. Further excitement was caused by the last skater, tiny Han Pil-hwa, a previously unknown North Korean who kept up Skoblikova's pace for four of the seven laps before falling back to a tie for second place.

1968 Grenoble C: 26, N: 12, D: 2.12. WR: 4:54.6 (Christina Kaiser)

1. Johanna Schut	HOL	4:56.2	OR
2. Kaija Mustonen	FIN	5:01.0	
3. Christina Kaiser	HOL	5:01.3	
4. Kaija-Liisa Keskivitikka	FIN	5:03.9	
5. Wilhelmina Burgmeijer	HOL	5:05.1	
6. Lydia Skoblikova	SOV	5:08.0	
7. Christina Lindblom	SWE	5:09.8	
8. Anna Sablina	SOV	5:12.5	

1972 Sapporo C: 22, N: 10, D: 2.12. WR: 4:46.5 (Christina Baas-Kaiser)

1. Christina Baas-Kaiser	HOL	4:52.14	OR
2. Dianne Holum	USA	4:58.67	
3. Atje Keulen-Deelstra	HOL	4:59.91	
4. Sippie Tigelaar	HOL	5:01.67	
5. Nina Statkevitch	SOV	5:01.79	
6. Kapitolina Sereguina	SOV	5:01.88	
7. Tuula Vilkas	FIN	5:05.92	
8. Lyudmila Savroulina	SOV	5:06.61	

Baas-Kaiser's margin of victory was the largest ever by a woman skater. After the race, the two Dutch medalists, both of whom were 33 years old, were asked by a reporter if they were planning to retire. Baas-Kaiser replied, "What's the matter, don't we skate fast enough?"

1976 Innsbruck C: 26, N: 12, D: 2.8. WR: 4:44.69 (Tamara Kuznyetsova)

1. Tatyana Averina	SOV	4:45.19	OR
2. Andrea Mitscherlich	GDR	4:45.23	
3. Lisbeth Korsmo	NOR	4:45.24	
4. Karin Kessow	GDR	4:45.60	
5. Ines Bautzmann	GDR	4:46.67	
6. Sylvia Filipsson	SWE	4:48.15	
7. Nancy Swider	USA	4:48.46	
8. Sylvia Burka	CAN	4:49.04	

If the top three skaters had actually been on the ice at the same time, only 16 inches would have separated them at the finish.

1980 Lake Placid C: 29, N: 14, D: 2.20. WR: 4:31.00 (Galina Stepanskaya)

1. Björg Eva Jensen	NOR	4:32.13	OR
2. Sabine Becker	GDR	4:32.79	
3. Beth Heiden	USA	4:33.77	
4. Andrea Mitscherlich	GDR	4:37.69	
5. Erwina Ryś-Ferens	POL	4:37.89	
6. Mary Docter	USA	4:39.29	
7. Sylvia Filipsson	SWE	4:40.22	
8. Natalya Petruseva	SOV	4:42.59	

1984 Sarajevo C: 26, N: 14, D: 2.15. WR: 4:21.70 (Gabi Schönbrunn)

1. Andrea Schöne [Mitscherlich]	GDR	4:24.79	OR
2. Karin Enke	GDR	4:26.33	
3. Gabi Schönbrunn	GDR	4:33.13	
4. Olga Pleshkova	SOV	4:34.42	
5. Yvonne van Gennip	HOL	4:34.80	
6. Mary Docter	USA	4:36.25	
7. Björg Eva Jensen	NOR	4:36.28	
8. Valentina Lalenkova	SOV	4:37.36	

Twenty-three-year-old Andrea Schöne of Dresden skated first and recorded a time that no one else could match.

1988 Calgary C: 29, N: 16, D: 2.23. WR: 4:16.76 (Gabi Zange [Schönbrunn])

1. Yvonne van Gennip	HOL	4:11.94	WR
2. Andrea Ehrig [Mitscherlich, Schöne]	GDR	4:12.09	
3. Gabi Zange [Schönbrunn]	GDR	4:16.92	
4. Karin Kania [Enke]	GDR	4:18.80	
5. Erwina Ryś-Ferens	POL	4:22.59	
6. Svetlana Boyko	SOV	4:22.90	
7. Seiko Hashimoto	JPN	4:23.29	
7. Yelena Lapuga	SOV	4:23.29	

The first pair on the ice were East German veterans Karin Kania and defending champion Andrea Ehrig. Kania, overanxious to win a gold medal, went out too fast, suffered a muscle cramp, and became so exhausted that she barely finished the race. Ehrig, on the other hand, kept to a steady pace and ripped over 4½ seconds off teammate Gabi Zange's world record. But three pairs later, 23-year-old Yvonne van Gennip, trailing Ehrig's pace for 2600 meters, made up eight tenths of a second on the final lap to score an upset victory.

1992 Albertville C: 26, N: 12, D: 2.09. WR: 4:10.80 (Gunda Niemann [Kleemann])

1. Gunda Niemann [Kleemann]	GER	4:19.90
2. Heike Warnicke	GER	4:22.88
3. Emese Hunyady	AUT	4:24.64
4. Carla Zijlstra	HOL	4:27.18
5. Svetlana Boyko	SOV	4:28.00
6. Yvonne van Gennip	HOL	4:28.10
7. Svetlana Bazhanova	SOV	4:28.19
8. Jacqueline Börner	GER	4:28.52

Niemann and Warnicke were training partners from Erfurt. The top four skaters took the same places as they had at the pre-Olympic test competition on the Albertville oval two months earlier.

5000 METERS

1924–1984 not held

1988 Calgary C: 25, N: 14, D: 2.28. WR: 7:20.36 (Yvonne van Gennip)

1. Yvonne van Gennip	HOL	7:14.13	WR
2. Andrea Ehrig [Mitscherlich, Schöne]	GDR	7:17.12	
3. Gabi Zange [Schönbrunn]	GDR	7:21.61	
4. Svetlana Boyko	SOV	7:28.39	
5. Yelena Lapuga	SOV	7:28.65	
6. Seiko Hashimoto	JPN	7:34.43	
7. Gunda Kleeman	GDR	7:34.59	
8. Jasmin Krohn	SWE	7:36.56	

Two months before the Olympics, Yvonne van Gennip was lying in a hospital bed recovering from surgery to her right foot, which had become infected after she cut it by tying her skate lace too tightly. After two weeks in the hospital, van Gennip's Olympic expectations had been reduced to a bronze medal or two. But when she arrived in Calgary, she discovered that she was well rested and in the best condition of her life. Inspired by Bonnie Blair's defeat of the supposedly unbeatable East Germans in the 500-meter race, van Gennip scored upset victories in both the 3000 and the 1500.

Andrea Ehrig, skating in the first pair of the 5000 meters, bettered van Gennip's world record by 3.24 seconds. Four pairs later, van Gennip fell behind Ehrig's pace but finished strongly to earn her third gold medal of the Calgary games. Ehrig, competing in her fourth Olympics and using her third name, brought her combined medal total to one gold, five silvers, and one bronze. After van Gennip's Olympic triumph, 60,000 fans turned out to welcome her back to her hometown of Haarlem.

1992 Albertville C:24, N: 11, D: 2.17. WR: 7:14.13 (Yvonne van Gennip)

1. Gunda Niemann [Kleemann]	GER	7:31.57
2. Heike Warnicke	GER	7:37.59
3. Claudi Pechstein	GER	7:39.80
4. Carla Zijlstra	HOL	7:41.10
5. Lyudmila Prokacheva	SOV	7:41.65
6. Svetlana Boyko	SOV	7:44.19
7. Svetlana Bazhanova	SOV	7:45.55
8. Lia van Schie	HOL	7:46.94

As expected, Gunda Niemann used her 23½-inch (60-cm) thighs and her 17-inch (43-cm) calves to power her to her second gold medal of the Albertville Games.

Short Track

SHORT TRACK: 500 METERS

1924-1988 not held

1992 Albertville C: 27, N: 14, D: 2.22. WR: 46.72 (Sylvie Daigle)

1.	Cathy Turner	USA	47.04
2.	Li Yan	CHN	47.08
3.	Hwang Ok-sil	PRK	47.23
4.	Monique Velzeboer	HOL	47.28
5.	Marina Pylayeva	SOV	48.42
6.	Nathalie Lambert	CAN	48.50
7.	Yulia Vlasova	SOV	48.70
8.	Wang Xiulan	CHN	1:34.12

This volatile event saw some early surprises in the opening-round heats. In the first heat, former world record holder Zhang Yammei fell and was disqualified. In the second heat, the current world record holder, Sylvie Daigle of Quebec, was eliminated after a clash with Cathy Turner entering the first turn. The seventh heat was won by Italy's Marinella Canclini in 47.00. In the first semifinal, Li Yan, winner of the 1000-meter demonstration race at the 1988 Olympics, was beaten by Hwang Ok-sil. In the second semi, Cathy Turner edged Monique Velzeboer, the winner of the 500-meter race in 1988. Turner let Hwang take the lead in the final, then took over after two laps. In the final straightaway, Li came up on the inside and clipped Turner's skate, causing the American to totter. Li inched ahead as they approached the finish line. Turner threw her skate forward at the end, but thought she had lost. When she realized she had won, she rushed over to her mother, who draped her in a gold-trimmed American flag. Turner's path to the Olympic victory podium was an unusual one. She gave up speed skating in 1980 and pursued a career as a songwriter and a lounge singer. In 1988, after an eight-year absence from the sport, the 25-year-old Turner traded in her microphone for skates. Turner's kamikaze style of racing was legendary in short-track circles. At the 1991 world championships, her preliminary heat had to be restarted six times because of crashes in which she was involved as the skaters entered the first turn.

SHORT TRACK: 1000 METERS

This event will be held for the first time in 1994.

SHORT TRACK: 3000-METER RELAY

1924-1988 not held

1992 Albertville T: 8, N: 8, D: 2.20. WR: 4:33.49 (CHN—Li C., Wang, Li Y., Zhang)

1.	CAN	(Angela Cutrone, Sylvie Daigle, Nathalie Lambert, Annie Perreault)	4:36.62
2.	USA	(Darcie Dohnal, Amy Peterson, Cathy Turner, Nikki Ziegelmeyer)	4:37.85
3.	SOV	(Yulia Allagulova, Natalya Ishahova, Viktoria Taranina, Yulia Vlasova)	4:42.69
4.	JPN	(Mie Naito, Rie Sato, Hiromi Takeuchi, Nobuko Yamada)	4:44.50
5.	FRA	(Valerie Barizza, Sandrine Daudet, Morielle Leyssieux, Karine Rubini)	
6.	HOL	(Priscilla Ernst, Van Ankere Van Koetsveld, Monique Velzeboer, Simone Velzeboer)	
7.	ITA	(Marinella Canelini, Maria Candidu, Concetta LaTorre, Cristina Sciolla)	
8.	CHN	(Li Changxiang, Li Yan, Wang Xiulan, Zhang Yanmei)	

This event had the makings of a classic Olympic duel between the Canadians, who had won six straight world championships and ten of the last eleven, and the Chinese, who had set a world record in beating the Canadians at the Olympic test event in Albertville on November 16, 1991. Because there were only eight teams entered at the Olympics, the competition consisted of two semifinal heats with the top two teams in each heat advancing to the final. Canada won the first semi. In the second semi, China pulled out to a huge lead. When Zhang Yanmei began the 27th and final lap, she was on world record pace. The other teams were far behind, and all she had to do to qualify China for the final was to stay on her feet. But midway through the final turn Zhang suddenly lost her footing and crashed into the sideboards. The audience was shocked into a stunned silence. Zhang, who had also fallen in a preliminary heat in the individual event, cried for two hours straight. In the final, the four skaters from Quebec easily beat back every challenge from the U.S. team.

ALPINE SKIING

MEN
Downhill
Slalom
Giant Slalom
Super Giant Slalom
Alpine Combined

MEN

DOWNHILL

The first crude downhill race was held in Kitzbühel, Austria, in 1905. A more formal contest was held in Crans-Montana, Switzerland, in 1911. It was organized by an Englishman, Arnold Lunn, who also invented the modern slalom in 1922 and was the main force in obtaining Olympic recognition for alpine skiing in 1936. Downhill races are decided on the basis of a single run.

Of the 37 medals that have been awarded in the men's downhill race, 35 have gone to Western Europeans; of these, thirteen went to Austria, ten to Switzerland and eight to France.

1924–1936 not held

1948 St. Moritz C: 112, N: 25, D: 2.2.

1. Henri Oreiller	FRA	2:55.0
2. Franz Gabl	AUT	2:59.1
3. Karl Molitor	SWI	3:00.3
3. Rolf Olinger	SWI	3:00.3
5. Egon Schöpf	AUT	3:01.2
6. Silvio Alverà	ITA	3:02.4
6. Carlo Gartner	ITA	3:02.4
8. Fernand Grosjean	SWI	3:03.1

A member of the French underground during World War II, Henri Oreiller was a cocky, clowning fellow who warned the other skiers he was so confident of victory that they needn't bother racing against him. He careened down the two-mile course like an acrobat, flying over bumps without caution and then regaining his balance in midair.

1952 Oslo-Norefjell C: 81, N: 27, D: 2.16.

1. Zeno Colò	ITA	2:30.8
2. Othmar Schneider	AUT	2:32.0
3. Christian Pravda	AUT	2:32.4
4. Fredy Rubi	SWI	2:32.5
5. William Beck	USA	2:33.3
6. Stein Eriksen	NOR	2:33.8
7. Gunnar Hjeltnes	NOR	2:35.9
8. Carlo Gartner	ITA	2:36.5

Zeno Colò was a colorful 31-year-old restaurant owner from Tuscany, whose form on the slopes was almost as unorthodox as that of Oreiller.

1956 Cortina C: 75, N: 27, D: 2.3.

1.	Anton Sailer	AUT	2:52.2
2.	Raymond Fellay	SWI	2:55.7
3.	Andreas Molterer	AUT	2:56.2
4.	Roger Staub	SWI	2:57.1
5.	Hans-Peter Lanig	GER	2:59.8
6.	Gino Burrini	ITA	3:00.2
7.	Kurt Hennrich	CZE	3:01.5
8.	Charles Bozon	FRA	3:01.9

Toni Sailer had already won the giant slalom and the slalom and was confident of completing his alpine sweep, since he held the course record of 2:46.2 for the downhill. However, as he tightened the straps that tied his boots to his skis, one of the straps broke. "That had never happened to me before," he later wrote. "I had not even thought it possible that such straps could break and had therefore not taken along a spare." It was almost his turn to race. If he couldn't find a strap, he would have to withdraw. Unfortunately, the problem was so rare that none of the other skiers had brought along spare straps either. Then Hansl Senger, the trainer of the Italian team, walked by and noticed the Austrians in panic. Senger immediately took the straps from his own bindings and handed them to Sailer. Sailer later claimed that he himself was never worried. After all, "I had at least ten minutes to find another strap." Strong winds and a glassy course prevented 28 of the 75 starters from reaching the finish line, and sent eight men to the hospital. But Sailer was able to survive one near spill and complete the course three and a half seconds faster than anyone else.

After the victory ceremony, Sailer joined his parents and, holding his three gold medals in his hand, said, "It's a good thing there are three medals. One for you, Father, one for you, Mother. Then there is a third one for me." Sailer later became an actor and singer, and then went into business as a hotel owner and an investor in a textile company, before settling in as the operator of a children's ski school. He also coached the Austrian national team during the 1970s.

1960 Squaw Valley C: 63, N: 21, D: 2.22.

1.	Jean Vuarnet	FRA	2:06.0
2.	Hans-Peter Lanig	GER	2:06.5
3.	Guy Périllat	FRA	2:06.9
4.	Willy Forrer	SWI	2:07.8
5.	Roger Staub	SWI	2:08.9
6.	Bruno Alberti	ITA	2:09.1
7.	Karl Schranz	AUT	2:09.2
8.	Charles Bozon	FRA	2:09.6

In 1960 the downhill race was postponed for three days because of heavy snow. Vuarnet was the first Olympic gold medalist to use metal skis and no wax. He is also credited by Europeans with inventing the aerodynamically efficient "egg position" for skiing. At his press conference after the race, Vuarnet, who was clocked at speeds as high as 80 miles per hour, apologized in English for breaking the California speed limit of 65 miles per hour.

1964 Innsbruck C: 84, N: 27, D: 1.30.

1.	Egon Zimmermann	AUT	2:18.16
2.	Léo Lacroix	FRA	2:18.90
3.	Wolfgang Bartels	GER	2:19.48
4.	Joos Minsch	SWI	2:19.54
5.	Ludwig Leitner	GER	2:19.67
6.	Guy Périllat	FRA	2:19.79
7.	Gerhard Nenning	AUT	2:19.98
8.	Willi Favre	SWI	2:20.23

The downhill competition was held under a cloud of gloom following the death of 19-year-old Ross Milne of Australia, who was killed during a practice run on January 25 when he flew off the course and smashed into a tree. Twenty-four-year-old Egon Zimmermann was the third alpine gold medalist to come from Lech, a hamlet of less than 200 people that had been converted to a ski resort following World War II. Also from Lech were Orthmar Schneider, the 1952 slalom winner, and Trude Beiser, who won the women's downhill the same year.

1968 Grenoble-Chamrousse C: 86, N: 29, D: 2.9.

1.	Jean-Claude Killy	FRA	1:59.85
2.	Guy Périllat	FRA	1:59.93
3.	John-Daniel Dätwyler	SWI	2:00.32
4.	Heinrich Messner	AUT	2:01.03
5.	Karl Schranz	AUT	2:01.89
6.	Ivo Mahlknecht	ITA	2:02.00
7.	Gerhard Prinzing	GER	2:02.10
8.	Bernard Orcel	FRA	2:02.22

Jean-Claude Killy grew up in the resort village of Val d'Isère in the French Savoy Alps, hometown of 1948 Olympic champion Henri Oreiller. Killy's mother abandoned her family, and his father was forced to send Jean-Claude to boarding school at age 11. Killy dropped out of school at the age of 15 in order to join the French ski team, and soon became known for his fun-loving attitude. Once he entered a ski-jump competition in Wengen, Switzerland, and caused a sensation by dropping his pants after takeoff and finishing his jump in longjohns. Apparently he dropped his pants in other places as well, since he also contracted VD in Sun Valley and was named in a paternity suit in Austria. He was declared innocent. While serving with the French Army in Algeria, Killy contracted amoebic parasitosis, but he regained his health sufficiently to qualify for the 1964 French Olympic team in all three alpine events. At Innsbruck he placed fifth in the giant slalom, but failed to finish the downhill and slalom. Killy started to pick up speed after the 1964 Olympics, however, and by 1967 he was on top of the world. During the 1966–67 season he won 12 of 16 World Cup meets, and the following summer he won a sports car race in Sicily. Despite some troubles at the start of the 1967–68 season, Killy went to the 1968 Olympics confident of victory.

There was certainly a lot of pressure on Killy to win in Grenoble. French fans were anxious for him to duplicate the 1952 triple-gold performance of Austria's Toni Sailer. In addition, a huge Jean-Claude Killy industry was waiting to spring into production if Killy won three gold medals. Ski-makers, boot-makers, binding-makers, glove-makers, and others were ready with fat contracts for Killy's product endorsements, which he had already been giving out as readily as he could within the restrictions set up by the International Ski Federation. But these restrictions weren't good enough for I.O.C. President Avery Brundage. Shortly before the games, Killy signed a contract with an Italian ski pole manufacturer. The International Ski Federation informed Killy that the contract violated the rules of amateurism, so Killy backed off, whereupon the ski pole manufacturer threatened to sue him. The French Ski Federation and the French Sports Ministry undertook hasty negotiations with the Italian ski pole manufacturer in an attempt to settle the issue before the Olympics. "Payments for damages"—sums never revealed—satisfied the Italians.

Brundage demanded that all trade names and trademarks be removed from the skis used by competitors in the 1968 Olympics. The International Ski Federation, the team managers, and the skiers themselves rejected the ban, claiming that the entire sport of alpine skiing was dependent on the financial support of ski-makers. On the eve of the Games an awkward compromise was reached whereby the skiers would be allowed to keep the trade names and trademarks on their skis, but their skis would be taken away from them before they could be photographed. The policemen in charge of this unpleasant task were particularly on edge when Jean-Claude Killy, the favorite, shot down the slopes as the 14th contestant in the opening alpine race—the downhill. Killy slashed across the finish line eight one-hundredths of a second faster than his teammate, yoga practitioner Guy Périllat. Immediately, Michel Arpin, Killy's friend and adviser, rushed out and embraced Killy, making sure that the photographers got a good view of the pouch on his back, which was emblazoned with the word "Dynamic," the brand of skis that Killy used, and his gloves, which bore the Dynamic trademark—two yellow bars. When a policeman, surrounded by a horde of photographers, confiscated Killy's skis, Michel Arpin took one of his own skis and planted it in the snow so that the two yellow bars on the tip were right next to Killy's head.

Eventually Killy gave up competitive skiing and traveled to the United States, where he signed commercial contracts with Chevrolet, United Air Lines, Bristol-Myers, *Ladies' Home Journal,* Head Skis, Lange boots, Mighty Mac sportswear, Wolverine gloves and after-ski boots, and over 100 other companies. Killy later served as copresident of the organizing committee of the 1992 Albertville Olympics.

1972 Sapporo-Eniwadake C: 55, N: 20, D: 2.7.

1.	Bernhard Russi	SWI	1:51.43
2.	Roland Collombin	SWI	1:52.07
3.	Heinrich Messner	AUT	1:52.40
4.	Andreas Sprecher	SWI	1:53.11
5.	Erik Håker	NOR	1:53.16
6.	Walter Tresch	SWI	1:53.19
7.	Karl Cordin	AUT	1:53.32
8.	Robert Cochran	USA	1:53.39

Most people in the sports world breathed a sigh of relief when Avery Brundage announced that he would retire after the completion of the 1972 Olympics. But the 84-year-old Brundage decided to go out with a bang by staging one final attack against commercialism in alpine skiing. Although he considered at least 30 or 40 skiers to be in violation of the rules of amateurism, Brundage chose to concentrate his attack on Austrian hero Karl Schranz, who was reputedly earning at least $40,000 to $50,000 a year as a "tester and designer" for various ski product manufacturers. Schranz was not alone in receiving such income, but he had also committed the crime of being outspoken in his criticism of Brundage.

Karl Schranz was the son of a poor railway worker in St. Anton in the Arlberg Mountains. His father died of work-related tuberculosis at an early age. In 1962 Schranz won the world downhill and combined championships and in 1964 he earned a silver medal in the Olympic giant slalom. In 1968 he appeared to have won the Olympic slalom until his disqualification for missing a gate was announced. By 1972 he had won every honor that is offered in international alpine skiing—except an Olympic gold medal. The 33-year-old Schranz delayed his retirement in the hope of achieving that final goal. But three days before the opening of the Sapporo Games, Avery Brundage got his way, and the I.O.C. voted 28–14 to ban Schranz from participating in the Olympics. Austrian Olympic officials announced that their ski team would withdraw from the games, but the Austrian skiers decided to compete anyway. While Brundage accused the alpine skiers of being "trained seals of the merchandisers," Schranz told the press, "If Mr. Brundage had been poor, as I was, and as were many other athletes, I wonder if he wouldn't have a different attitude. . . . If we followed Mr. Brundage's recommendations to their true end, then the Olympics would be a competition only for the very rich. No man of ordinary means could ever afford to excel in his sport."

When Schranz returned to Vienna he was met by 100,000 Austrian supporters and treated to a tickertape parade. It was the largest demonstration in Austria since World War II. Because Brundage was an American (he was known in Austria as "the senile millionaire from Chicago"), the U.S. embassy in Vienna was subjected to bomb threats and protests. The hypocrisy of the I.O.C's decision against Schranz was shown by the fact that the eventual downhill gold medalist, Bernhard Russi, had allowed his photo and name to be used on matchboxes, car stickers, and newspaper advertisements as part of a large-scale pre-Olympic publicity campaign for a Swiss insurance company. Karl Schranz announced his retirement from competitive skiing as soon as the 1972 Olympics ended. In 1988, the I.O.C. awarded Schranz a symbolic medal as a participant in the Sapporo Games.

1976 Innsbruck C: 74, N: 27, D: 2.5.

1.	Franz Klammer	AUT	1:45.73
2.	Bernhard Russi	SWI	1:46.06
3.	Herbert Plank	ITA	1:46.59
4.	Philippe Roux	SWI	1:46.69
5.	Ken Read	CAN	1:46.83
6.	Andy Mill	USA	1:47.06
7.	Walter Tresch	SWI	1:47.29
8.	David Irwin	CAN	1:47.41

In 1975 Franz Klammer of Mooswald in Carinthia won eight of nine World Cup downhill races. When the Olympics came to Innsbruck the following year there was great pressure on the 22-year-old Klammer as an Austrian favorite competing in Austria. Further pressure was exerted by defending champion Bernhard Russi, who sped down the 3145-meter (1.95-mile) Olympic hill in 1:46.06. The 15th starter of the day, Klammer fell one-fifth of a second off Russi's pace, but fought back wildly in the last 1000 meters to nip Russi by one-third of a second. Flushed with excitement, Klammer told reporters that at one point he skied so close to the fence lining the course that "I heard a shout or scream from a lady. I thought I was hitting her with a pole. . . . I thought I was going to crash all the way. . . . Now I've got everything. I don't need anything else."

1980 Lake Placid C: 47, N: 22, D: 2.14.

1.	Leonhard Stock	AUT	1:45.50
2.	Peter Wirnsberger	AUT	1:46.12
3.	Steve Podborski	CAN	1:46.62
4.	Peter Müller	SWI	1:46.75
5.	Pete Patterson	USA	1:47.04
6.	Herbert Plank	ITA	1:47.13
7.	Werner Grissmann	AUT	1:47.21
8.	Valery Tsyganov	SOV	1:47.34

The Austrian alpine team was so strong that they had seven men ranked in the top 20 in the world. When it was decided to leave Franz Klammer behind, team manager Karl "Downhill Charlie" Kahr had to explain the decision on national television. Leonhard Stock, who had broken a collarbone in December, was chosen to go to Lake Placid as an alternate. But when he recorded the fastest time in two of the three pre-Olympic trial runs, Austrian alpine officials changed their minds and declared that Stock was now a starter, along with Harti Weirather, but that the other three Austrians—Wirnsberger, Grissmann, and Sepp Walcher—would have to have a race-off for the final two spots. Walcher lost out. The four remaining Austrians all placed in the top nine, as Leonhard Stock went from being an alternate who had never won a World Cup race to being an Olympic champion in less than 30 hours. After the 1980 Olympics, he didn't win another downhill race until 1989.

1984 Sarajevo C: 61, N: 25, D: 2.16.

1.	William Johnson	USA	1:45.59
2.	Peter Müller	SWI	1:45.86
3.	Anton Steiner	AUT	1:45.95
4.	Pirmin Zurbriggen	SWI	1:46.05
5.	Helmut Höflehner	AUT	1:46.32
5.	Urs Räber	SWI	1:46.32
7.	Sepp Wildgruber	GER	1:46.53
8.	Steve Podborski	CAN	1:46.59

When Bill Johnson was seventeen years old, he was caught red-handed trying to steal a car. The judge in charge of his case, upon learning that Johnson was an excellent skier, sent him not to prison, but to a ski academy. The judge's decision turned out to be a fine advertisement for creative sentencing. Not only did Johnson never steal another car, but his skiing led him all the way to the Olympics. Still, two months before the Sarajevo Games, Bill Johnson seemed an unlikely candidate to win a gold medal. No U.S. male skier had ever won an Olympic downhill medal. And there was nothing in the least bit impressive about Johnson's record on the World Cup circuit. But then, in mid-January, he won the prestigious Lauberhorn downhill at Wengen, Switzerland. A couple of undistinguished performances were followed by a fourth at Cortina and Johnson suddenly looked like a serious contender, particularly considering that the Olympic course on Mt. Bjelašnica was relatively free of turns—perfect for a "glider" like Bill Johnson, who was able to keep his tuck longer than other skiers. When he scored the best series of places during the five practice runs, Johnson actually found himself the betting favorite.

Not the modest type, Johnson agreed with the emerging consensus. "I don't even know why everyone else is here," he announced to reporters. "They should hand [the gold medal] to me. Everyone else can fight for second place."

Heavy snow and powerful winds caused the downhill to be postponed three times, but Johnson seemed unperturbed by the delays. "Everyone knows it's my kind of course," he said.

When the weather finally cleared on the mountain, Johnson made good on his boasts. When told afterwards that the beaten skiers of the "downhill mafia," Austria and Switzerland, had grumbled that he had won because the course was an easy one, Johnson snapped, "If it's so easy, why didn't *they* win it?"

1988 Calgary-Nakiska C: 51, N: 18, D: 2.15.

1.	Pirmin Zurbriggen	SWI	1:59.63
2.	Peter Müller	SWI	2:00.14
3.	Franck Piccard	FRA	2:01.24
4.	Leonhard Stock	AUT	2:01.56
5.	Gerhard Pfaffenbichler	AUT	2:02.02
6.	Markus Wasmeier	GER	2:02.03
7.	Anton Steiner	AUT	2:02.19
8.	Martin Bell	GBR	2:02.49

The two favorites in the 1988 downhill, Peter Müller and Pirmin Zurbriggen, were both Swiss and they had both won a world championship in the event (Müller in 1987, Zurbriggen in 1985). But there the similarities ended. Müller was a "flatlander" from the Zurich suburb of Adliswil; Zurbriggen was from the tiny village of Saas Almagell (population 300) in the Valais Alps. Müller, age 30, fit the stereotype of the wild, high-living alpine ski champion; Zurbriggen, age 25, was every Swiss parent's dream son, a homebody who helped his mother do the dishes, prayed three times a day, and made pilgrimages to Lourdes. Müller was a downhill specialist; Zurbriggen was an all-arounder entered in all five alpine events in Calgary. Zurbriggen was also the overall World Cup champion in 1984 and 1987 and runner-up to Marc Girardelli in 1985 and 1986.

Müller, who had a history of skiing well in North America, was the first skier down the course. The next six skiers failed to come within three seconds of Müller's time and it became clear that he had had a great run. By the time Zurbriggen, skiing 14th, started, Müller still led by 1.42 seconds. Zurbriggen had watched the first two turns of Müller's run and knew immediately that he would need the race of his life to beat him. He tried to avoid hearing Müller's final time, but heard it anyway, which increased his nervousness. Nevertheless, Zurbriggen exploded down the course with an aggressiveness that belied his gentle exterior and Müller was forced to settle for his second straight silver medal.

1992 Albertville-Val d'Isère C: 55, N: 24, D: 2.9.

1.	Patrick Ortlieb	AUT	1:50.37
2.	Franck Piccard	FRA	1:50.42
3.	Günther Mader	AUT	1:50.47
4.	Markus Wasmeier	GER	1:50.62
5.	Jan Einar Thorsen	NOR	1:50.79
6.	Franz Heinzer	SWI	1:51.39
7.	Hansjörg Tauscher	GER	1:51.49
8.	Lasse Arnesen	NOR	1:51.63

The big story of the 1992 downhill was the course itself. Designed by 1972 Olympic champion Bernhard Russi, it was unusually steep and filled with curves and turns. Classical downhillers criticized the course as being more like a Super G than a downhill and hinted that it had been designed especially for local favorite Franck Piccard, the defending Super G champion. Technical specialists defended the course by saying that the race would be won "by skiers not by skis." The big loser in the controversy was popular Franz Heinzer, one of the classicists. Known in Switzerland as "Franz the Fourth" because he finished fourth in seven different World Cup downhills, Heinzer fianlly came into his own in 1991, winning the world championship and the World Cup. He also took four of six World Cup downhills in the 1991-1992 pre-Olympic season. In Val d'Isère, Heinzer could do no better than sixth, his worst placing in his last 13 downhill races.

Surprisingly, the Olympic championship was won by one of the course's critics, 6-

foot 2½-inch Patrick Ortlieb. In the words of *Ski Racing* magazine, the 216-pound Ortlieb hurtled down the slope "like a cement truck with power steering," to register his first-ever World Cup victory. Like 1964 winner Egon Zimmermann, Ortlieb came from the village of Lech. Because his father was French, Ortlieb grew up with dual citizenship and turned down an offer to join the French team in 1989.

Despite the loss of Ortlieb, the French had cause for celebration when Franck Piccard, skiing in the 23rd position, took second place in the closest-ever alpine race in Olympic history. If Ortlieb, Piccard, and bronze medalist Günther Mader had been on the course at the same time, they would have finished only 9 feet (2.76 meters) apart.

SLALOM

Whereas the downhill requires pure speed, the slalom (or "special slalom") is more a test of control. Each skier is required to weave in and out of blue- and red-flagged double poles, or "gates." Missing a gate results in immediate disqualification. There are two runs on different courses. Times for the two runs are added to determine final places.

1924–1936 not held

1948 St. Moritz C: 76, N: 22, D: 2.5.

1.	Edi Reinalter	SWI	2:10.3
2.	James Couttet	FRA	2:10.8
3.	Henri Oreiller	FRA	2:12.8
4.	Silvio Alverà	ITA	2:13.2
5.	Olle Dahlman	SWE	2:13.6
6.	Egon Schöpf	AUT	2:14.2
7.	Jack Reddish	USA	2:15.5
8.	Karl Molitor	SWI	2:16.2

Alverà led after the first run, followed by Couttet, Reinalter, and Oreiller. Reinalter's second run of 1:02.6 was a half second faster than the next best skier, Egon Schöpf.

1952 Oslo C: 86, N: 27, D: 2.19.

1.	Othmar Schneider	AUT	2:00.0
2.	Stein Eriksen	NOR	2:01.2
3.	Guttorm Berge	NOR	2:01.7
4.	Zeno Colò	ITA	2:01.8
5.	Stig Sollander	SWE	2:02.6
6.	James Couttet	FRA	2:02.8
7.	Fredy Rubi	SWI	2:03.3
8.	Per Rollum	NOR	2:04.5

The fastest time of the first run, 59.2, was first posted by Stein Eriksen, who had won the giant slalom four days earlier, and then equaled by Hans Senger of Austria. Downhill silver medalist Othmar Schneider was third in 59.5. The second run saw Senger fall, while Schneider's 1:00.5 was beaten only by Fredy Rubi's 59.7. Antoin Miliordos of Greece, disgusted by the fact that he fell 18 times, sat down and crossed the finish line backward. His time for one run was 26.9 seconds slower than Schneider's time for two runs.

1956 Cortina C: 89, N: 29, D: 1.31.

1.	Anton Sailer	AUT	3:14.7
2.	Chiharu Igaya	JPN	3:18.7
3.	Stig Sollander	SWE	3:20.2
4.	Joseph Brooks Dodge	USA	3:21.8
5.	Georges Schneider	SWI	3:22.6
6.	Gérard Pasquier	FRA	3:24.6
7.	Charles Bozon	FRA	3:26.2
8.	Bernard Perret	FRA	3:26.3

Sailer recorded the fastest times in both runs and won his second gold medal.

1960 Squaw Valley C: 63, N: 21, D: 2.24.

1.	Ernst Hinterseer	AUT	2:08.9
2.	Matthias Leitner	AUT	2:10.3
3.	Charles Bozon	FRA	2:10.4
4.	Ludwig Leitner	GER	2:10.5
5.	Josef "Pepi" Stiegler	AUT	2:11.1
6.	Guy Périllat	FRA	2:11.8
7.	Hans-Peter Lanig	GER	2:14.3
8.	Paride Milianti	ITA	2:14.4

Eighteen-year-old Willi Bogner of Germany, whose father was the first designer of stretch pants, had the fastest time of the first run, 1:08.8. Hinterseer and Leitner, fifth and ninth after the first run, led the way on the second course in 58.2 and 59.2. Bogner, meanwhile, had fallen and was disqualified. In last place was Kyung Soon-yim of South Korea, whose time of 2:35.2 for the second run was slower than the combined run times of 22 of the 39 other skiers who completed both runs. Kyung had a good excuse: he had never skied on snow before arriving in Squaw Valley, He had learned to ski by reading books and practicing on grass. The other skiers gave him equipment and lessons. When he crossed the finish line in the slalom competition, the final alpine race of the Olympics, Kyung was met by the other racers, who threw a celebration for him.

A historical footnote to the 1960 men's slalom: at one point, race officials asked CBS-TV if they could review a tape of the race because of a controversy about one skier who was alleged to have missed a gate. It was this incident that gave CBS producers the idea to invent the instant replay.

1964 Innsbruck C: 96, N: 28, D: 2.8.

1.	Josef "Pepi" Stiegler	AUT	2:11.13
2.	William Kidd	USA	2:11.27
3.	James Heuga	USA	2:11.52
4.	Michel Arpin	FRA	2:12.91
5.	Ludwig Leitner	GER	2:12.94
6.	Adolf Mathis	SWI	2:12.99
7.	Gerhard Nenning	AUT	2:13.20
8.	Wallace "Bud" Werner	USA	2:13.46

Pepi Stiegler, a 26-year-old photographer, had twice been removed from the Austrian team and replaced by Egon Zimmermann. Both times he was reinstated after public pressure. After the first run, Stiegler led by a second over Karl Schranz, who was followed by Heuga, Nenning, Mathis, and Kidd. Stiegler skied cautiously the second time around, registering the 8th best time, but his first-round performance turned out to be good enough to edge the Americans. Eighth-place finisher Buddy Werner was killed two months after the Olympics while trying to out-ski a sudden avalanche at St. Moritz.

1968 Grenoble-Chamrousse C: 100, N: 33, D: 2.17.

1.	Jean-Claude Killy	FRA	1:39.73
2.	Herbert Huber	AUT	1:39.82
3.	Alfred Matt	AUT	1:40.09
4.	Dumeng Giovanoli	SWE	1:40.22
5.	Vladimir Sabich	USA	1:40.49
6.	Andrzej Bachleda	POL	1:40.61
7.	James Heuga	USA	1:40.97
8.	Alain Penz	FRA	1:41.14

With two gold medals down and one to go for Jean-Claude Killy, the slalom was held in bad weather, with fog, mist, and shadows prevailing. The skiers pleaded that the contest be postponed, but the officials in charge refused. Appropriately, the sun shone through only once—during Killy's first run, which was good enough to put him in first place. Killy was the first skier of the second round, so he was forced to wait anxiously as the others came down the hill. Häkon Mjön of Norway bettered Killy's time, but was disqualified for missing two gates. Then came the turn of Karl Schranz, the biggest threat to Killy's goal of a triple crown. But something curious happened as Schranz sped through the fog, something that has never been fully explained. As Schranz approached the 22nd gate, a mysterious figure in black crossed the course. Schranz skidded to a halt and, with three witnesses in tow, walked back to the starting point to ask for a rerun. Colonel Robert Readhead, the British referee, granted Schranz's request. This time Schranz achieved an almost perfect run, beat Killy's time, and was declared the unofficial winner. Schranz was allowed to enjoy the postrace press conference, while Killy sulked in the corner. But two hours later it was announced that Schranz had been disqualified for missing two gates just prior to his encounter with the mysterious interloper.

The Austrians were outraged. Schranz claimed that if he did miss a gate or two it was because he had already been distracted by the sight of someone on the course. His supporters contended that the mystery man had been a French policeman or soldier who had purposely interfered with Schranz in order to insure Killy's victory. The French, on the other hand, hinted that Schranz had made up the whole story after he had missed a gate. A final five-hour meeting of the Jury of Appeal ended with a 3–2 vote against Schranz, with two Frenchmen and a Swiss voting to give the gold medal to Killy, while Colonel Readhead and a Norwegian supported Schranz. Because of this incident, the 1968 Winter Olympics ended in a rather ugly mood, but back home in Val d'Isère Killy had no trouble putting it out of his mind. "The party went on for two and a half days," he later recalled, "and the whole time I never saw the sun once."

1972 Sapporo-Teineyama C: 72, N: 31, D: 2.13.

1.	Francisco Fernández Ochoa	SPA	1:49.27
2.	Gustav Thöni	ITA	1:50.28
3.	Roland Thöni	ITA	1:50.30
4.	Henri Duvillard	FRA	1:50.45
5.	Jean-Noël Augert	FRA	1:50.51
6.	Eberhard Schmalzl	ITA	1:50.83
7.	David Zwilling	AUT	1:51.97
8.	Edmund Bruggmann	SWI	1:52.03

The biggest surprise of the 1972 Winter Games was the sensational victory of 21-year-old Paquito Ochoa of Spain, who had never before finished higher than sixth in an international meet. Not only was Ochoa's gold medal the first ever won by Spain in the Winter Olympics, but it was the first Spanish victory of any kind since the equestrian team jumping competition of 1928. From Japan, Ochoa had written to his mother saying, "Mama, pray not for me, but for you. I will win and for you it is very emotional. So pray for your own strength." In fact, Ochoa was so overcome by emotion that he was unable to speak to reporters except to say, "I can't believe it. It can't be true." An hour later, referring to Spain's leading matador, he said, "El Cordobés is a little man compared with me. I am the champion."

1976 Innsbruck C: 94, N: 31, D: 2.14.

1.	Piero Gros	ITA	2:03.29
2.	Gustav Thöni	ITA	2:03.73
3.	Willy Frommelt	LIE	2:04.28
4.	Walter Tresch	SWI	2:05.26
5.	Christian Neureuther	GER	2:06.56
6.	Wolfgang Junginger	GER	2:07.08
7.	Alois Morgenstern	AUT	2:07.18
8.	Peter Luscher	SWI	2:08.10

Fifth after the first run, Gros was "as sure as I could be that I could never beat Thöni. In my opinion at that time Gustavo had the gold medal in his pocket." But Gros gained the victory with a superb second run, over a second faster than that of Thöni, his teammate and mentor.

1980 Lake Placid C: 79, N: 28, D: 2.22.

1.	Ingemar Stenmark	SWE	1:44.26
2.	Phillip Mahre	USA	1:44.76
3.	Jacques Lüthy	SWI	1:45.06
4.	Hans Enn	AUT	1:45.12
5.	Christian Neureuther	GER	1:45.14
6.	Petar Popangelov	BUL	1:45.40
7.	Anton Steiner	AUT	1:45.41
8.	Gustav Thöni	ITA	1:45.99

Skiing with a three-inch metal plate and four screws in his left ankle joint, the result of a bad fall 11 months earlier, Phil Mahre of White Pass, Washington, whizzed down the first run in 53.31. Because he was the first skier to compete, there was no way to judge if this was a good time or a bad time. But by the time the 13th skier, favorite Ingemar Stenmark, had completed the course over a half second slower than Mahre, it was clear that the 22-year-old American would enter the second round in first place. However Stenmark, in fourth place, had come from behind three days earlier to win the giant slalom, and he was known for his lightning second runs. Sure enough, he tore down the course in 50.37, a time that no one could beat. Three skiers later, Phil Mahre, needing a 50.94 to win the gold medal, never gained his rhythm and could only manage 51.45. Ingemar Stenmark, the Silent Swede, had completed his slalom double, but was not impressed by his accomplishment. "History is not important," he said. "The important thing is that I am satisfied with myself." As for Phil Mahre, he was back on the slopes the next day—filming an American Express commercial.

1984 Sarajevo C: 101, N: 37, D: 2.19.

1.	Phillip Mahre	USA	1:39.41
2.	Steven Mahre	USA	1:39.62
3.	Didier Bouvet	FRA	1:40.20
4.	Jonas Nilsson	SWE	1:40.25
5.	Oswald Tötsch	ITA	1:40.48
6.	Petar Popangelov	BUL	1:40.68
7.	Bojan Križaj	YUG	1:41.51
8.	Lars-Göran Halvarsson	SWE	1:41.70

Of the seven World Cup slalom events held prior to the Olympics, six had been won by either Ingemar Stenmark or Marc Girardelli, neither of whom was allowed to take part in the Sarajevo Games. Stenmark's punishment was a result of his being a professional, a rather ludicrous charge considering the huge amounts of money being earned by numerous other skiers. Girardelli's problem was that he competed for Luxembourg even though he was an Austrian citizen.

With Stenmark and Girardelli gone, the natural favorites seemed to be three-time defending World Cup champion Phil Mahre and his twin brother Steve. But after a decade on the circuit, the Mahres seemed to have lost their competitive edge. They were already thinking ahead to their post-Olympic retirement. Phil was also concerned about his pregnant wife, Dolly, who was back in the United States with a due date of February 27. The 1983–84 season had been a disaster for the Mahres. Steve stood 45th in the World Cup standings, Phil 62nd. Even when things went right, they went wrong. On January 16, Steve had won the slalom at Parpan, Switzerland, with Phil placing sixth. Then it was discovered that the twins had inadvertantly switched their number bibs and both were disqualified. Girardelli was awarded the victory. The situation did not improve for the Mahres in Sarajevo. In the giant slalom, held five days before the slalom, Phil finished eighth and Steve seventeenth.

At a press conference, Phil tried to put things in perspective. "I'm pretty mellow about Sarajevo," he said. "I have nothing to prove, nothing to escape. I've enjoyed myself, and that's the essence of sport." Then he added, "I think it is unfortunate that all the emphasis is on coming here and winning medals. The problem with gold medals is that it sets you for life or it doesn't. Well, I'm set for life, so I don't care."

The U.S. press did not take kindly to Phil Mahre's relativist attitude. Referring to his eighth place giant slalom finish, Dan Barreiro of the *Dallas Morning News* ranted, "That's the good news. The bad news is Mahre gets another chance Sunday in the slalom. I hope he chokes again. Or that he doesn't even show up. Phil Mahre is America's best skier, but he could do us all a favor by getting out of town. Right now." Not to be outdone by his crosstown rival, Skip Bayless of the *Dallas Times Herald* referred to Phil as the "ugly American skier." "Perhaps Mahre never sat in front of a free-enterprise TV and got caught up in some Yank beating some communist at some foreign game."

The slalom course on Mt. Bjelašnica turned out to be a difficult one, as only 47 of the 101 starters managed to complete both runs. But while other skiers were literally falling by the wayside and Texas sportswriters were sniffing the odor of crow in their kitchens, the Mahre twins were back to their old form. At the end of the first run, Steve was in first place with a big lead of almost seven-tenths of a second, and Phil was in third. In second place was Jonas Nilsson, who was not considered a threat, due to his inexperience.

Phil Mahre executed an excellent second run and then immediately grabbed a walkie-talkie radio to pass on some final advice to the only person who stood between him and a gold medal—his brother Steve. Steve could have skied a safe race and still won. Instead he attacked the course, made too many mistakes, and had to settle for the silver medal.

For two brothers to win the gold and silver in the same event certainly makes for a fine day, but there was more good news for the Mahres. As they left the Olympic Village to attend the medal ceremony, Phil was informed that his wife had just given birth to their second child and first son. At a press conference after the ceremony, Phil was asked what part his wife had played in his career. He tried to answer, but was stopped by tears. Steve put his arm around his brother, who then recovered enough to say, "Heck, there she was, doing all the work while I was out there playing."

1988 Calgary-Nakiska C: 109, N: 37, D: 2.27.

1.	Alberto Tomba	ITA	1:39.47
2.	Frank Wörndl	GER	1:39.53
3.	Paul Frommelt	LIE	1:39.84
4.	Bernhard Gstrein	AUT	1:40.08
5.	Ingemar Stenmark	SWE	1:40.22
6.	Jonas Nilsson	SWE	1:40.23
7.	Pirmin Zurbriggen	SWI	1:40.48
8.	Oswald Tötsch	ITA	1:40.55

World champion Frank Wörndl recorded the fastest time of the first run, with Jonas Nilsson second and Alberto Tomba, who had won the giant slalom two days earlier, third. The winner of the second run was the legend: Ingemar Stenmark, but his eleventh place earlier in the day kept him out of the medals. Tomba, who had skied with relative caution in the first run, went all out to register the second fastest time of the second run. Then he watched as Wörndl suffered a momentary lapse of concentration in the middle of the course, allowing Tomba to gain the victory.

1992 Albertville-Les Ménuires C: 119, N: 44, D: 2.22.

1.	Finn Christian Jagge	NOR	1:44.39
2.	Alberto Tomba	ITA	1:44.67
3.	Michael Tritscher	AUT	1:44.85
4.	Patrick Staub	SWI	1:45.44
5.	Thomas Fogdö	SWE	1:45.48
6.	Paul Accola	SWI	1:45.62
7.	Michael von Grünigen	SWI	1:46.42
8.	Jonas Nilsson	SWE	1:46.57

An estimated 15,000 Italians made the long trip north to Les Ménuires to cheer on their hero, Alberto Tomba, in his attempt to become the first alpine skier to win four gold medals. Included in the army of fans was a 400-car convoy from Tomba's hometown of Bologna. They avoided the prohibition against private vehicles by arriving 12 hours early and sleeping in their cars (if they slept at all). In eight pre-Olympic slaloms, Tomba had registered five firsts, two seconds, and a third. In addition, he was the defending Olympic champion and had already won his second giant slalom title four days earlier. But it was 25-year-old Finn Christian Jagge, whose mother, Evi, had placed seventh in the 1964 slalom, who recorded the best time of the first run. Tomba could do no better than sixth, 1.58 seconds behind.

Still, there was no reason for Tomba's fans to give up hope. Not only was their idol known for his strong second runs, but the gates on the second course had been set by none other than Tomba's personal coach, Gustavo Thöni. Tomba did have a sensational run, but was able to make up only 1.30 seconds on Jagge.

The good sport award in the slalom went to Robert Scott Detlof, a Brazilian-born American representing Brazil. Detlof sprained his knee while training and was prepared to withdraw until he learned that the Brazilian Ski Federation would have to pay $2500 to cover his expenses if he didn't compete. Knowing that Brazil was strapped for cash, Detlof put on his skis and hit the piste. Although his time was slow—3:18.58—he did complete both runs, which was more than could be said for 54 of the 119 entrants.

But even Detlof was a whiz kid compared to Costa Rica's Julian Munoz Aia, whose combined time was 3:44.11. And then there was Munoz Aia's teammate, Alejandro Preinfalk Lavagni, who seemed to walk down the mountain, testing each step like a bather putting his bare foot into freezing water. His two runs were so slow, 2:09.83 and 2:19.93, that he would have lost to a runner going uphill. When

Preinfalk Lavagni finally reached the finish line, he was met by Jagge and Tomba, who hoisted him onto their shoulders.

GIANT SLALOM

The giant slalom is similar to the slalom except the course is longer, the gates are farther apart, and the corners are not so sharp.

1924–1948 not held

1952 Oslo-Norefjell C: 83, N: 26, D: 2.15.

1.	Stein Eriksen	NOR	2:25.0
2.	Christian Pravda	AUT	2:26.9
3.	Toni Spiss	AUT	2:28.8
4.	Zeno Colò	ITA	2:29.1
5.	Georges Schneider	SWI	2:31.2
6.	Joseph Brooks Dodge	USA	2:32.6
6.	Stig Sollander	SWE	2:32.6
8.	Bernhard Perren	SWI	2:33.1

Stein Eriksen was the first of only five skiers from outside of the Alps to win an Olympic men's alpine gold medal. He was also the first skiing superstar. He was handsome, stylish, and glamorous. At the Oslo Games he proved to be a modest winner, declaring, "I had a great advantage over most of the others because I knew the course by heart." In 1954 Eriksen won the world combined alpine championship. Immediately afterward, he became a ski school director at Boyne Mt., Michigan. He moved on to Heavenly Valley, California, in 1957, Aspen Highlands, Colorado, in 1959, Sugarbush, Vermont, in 1965, Snowmass, Colorado, in 1969, and Park City, Utah, in 1973. Everywhere he went Stein Eriksen became the inspiration for the stereotypical ski instructor of the 1950s and 1960s—rich, good-looking, an outdoorsman who made women melt, and, above all, an Olympic champion.

1956 Cortina C: 95, N: 29, D: 1.29.

1.	Anton Sailer	AUT	3:00.1
2.	Andreas Molterer	AUT	3:06.3
3.	Walter Schuster	AUT	3:07.2
4.	Adrien Duvillard	FRA	3:07.2
5.	Charles Bozon	FRA	3:08.4
6.	Ernst Hinterseer	AUT	3:08.5
7.	Hans-Peter Lanig	GER	3:08.6
8.	Sepp Behr	GER	3:11.4

The 1956 giant slalom was held on the "Ilio Colli" course at Cortina. Ilio Colli was a local skier who had crashed into a tree at 50 m.p.h. during a race. He broke his skull and died instantly. Each participant in the giant slalom was handed a souvenir picture of Colli. In his book *My Way to the Triple Olympic Victory,* Toni Sailer wrote, "It is a beautiful thought to name such a famous course . . . after a dead racer, even if it is not exactly encouraging for those starting to be handed such a death notice." When the sixth skier, Andreas "Anderl" Molterer, came down in 3:06.3, he was mobbed and congratulated. But Molterer waved everyone away, telling them, "Toni hasn't come yet." When Toni did come, he came really fast—in 3:00.1, over six seconds better than any of the other 94 skiers. In the next five days Sailer also won the slalom and the downhill.

1960 Squaw Valley C: 65, N: 21, D: 2.21.

1.	Roger Staub	SWI	1:48.3
2.	Josef "Pepi" Stiegler	AUT	1:48.7
3.	Ernst Hinterseer	AUT	1:49.1
4.	Thomas Corcoran	USA	1:49.7
5.	Bruno Alberti	ITA	1:50.1
6.	Guy Périllat	FRA	1:50.7
7.	Karl Schranz	AUT	1:50.8
8.	Paride Milianti	ITA	1:50.9

1964 Innsbruck C: 96, N: 29, D: 2.2.

1.	François Bonlieu	FRA	1:46.71
2.	Karl Schranz	AUT	1:47.09
3.	Josef "Pepi" Stiegler	AUT	1:48.05
4.	Willy Favre	SWI	1:48.69
5.	Jean-Claude Killy	FRA	1:48.92
6.	Gerhard Nenning	AUT	1:49.68
7.	William Kidd	USA	1:49.97
8.	Ludwig Leitner	GER	1:50.04

François Bonlieu engaged in a running battle with the French coaches and officials and refused to listen to their advice. His rebelliousness turned out to be wisdom, as he upset the Austrians on their own course. However, it later proved his undoing. After working as a mountain guide, he dropped out of conventional society and was eventually murdered on the boardwalk in Cannes.

1968 Grenoble-Chamrousse C: 99, N: 36, D: 2.12.

1.	Jean-Claude Killy	FRA	3:29.28
2.	Willy Favre	SWI	3:31.50
3.	Heinrich Messner	AUT	3:31.83
4.	Guy Périllat	FRA	3:32.06
5.	William Kidd	USA	3:32.37
6.	Karl Schranz	AUT	3:33.08
7.	Dumeng Giovanoli	SWI	3:33.55
8.	Gerhard Nenning	AUT	3:33.61

For the first time the giant slalom was decided by a combination of two runs on separate days, rather than by a single run. This was the second of Killy's three gold medals. He had the fastest time of the first run and extended his winning margin over the second run.

1972 Sapporo-Teineyama C: 73, N: 27, D: 2.10.

1.	Gustavo Thöni	ITA	3:09.62
2.	Edmund Bruggmann	SWI	3:10.75
3.	Werner Mattle	SWE	3:10.99
4.	Alfred Hagn	GER	3:11.16
5.	Jean-Noël Augert	FRA	3:11.84
6.	Max Rieger	GER	3:11.96
7.	David Zwilling	AUT	3:12.32
8.	Reinhard Tritscher	AUT	3:12.42

Erik Håker of Norway had the fastest time of the first run, followed by Alfred Hagn and Gustavo Thöni. When Håker opened the second run by falling and Hagn skied too cautiously, the way was open for the 20-year-old Thöni to become the first Italian to win an alpine gold medal since Zeno Colò won the downhill in 1952.

1976 Innsbruck C: 97, N: 32, N: 2.9.

1.	Heini Hemmi	SWI	3:26.97
2.	Ernst Good	SWI	3:27.17
3.	Ingemar Stenmark	SWE	3:27.41
4.	Gustavo Thöni	ITA	3:27.67
5.	Phillip Mahre	USA	3:28.20
6.	Engelhard Pargätzi	SWI	3:28.76
7.	Fausto Radici	ITA	3:30.09
8.	Franco Bieler	ITA	3:30.24

Neither Hemmi nor Good had ever won a World Cup race. They had been placed third and second after the first run, behind Gustavo Thöni. However, Thöni's second run was only the eighth best of the day, while Hemmi's and Good's were second and third best. Ingemar Stenmark, ninth after the first run, stormed back with the fastest second-round time to take the bronze medal and establish a pattern that was to make him extremely famous in the years to come.

1980 Lake Placid C: 78, N: 28, D: 2.19.

1.	Ingemar Stenmark	SWE	2:40.74
2.	Andreas Wenzel	LIE	2:41.49
3.	Hans Enn	AUT	2:42.51
4.	Bojan Križaj	YUG	2:42.53
5.	Jacques Lüthy	SWI	2:42.75
6.	Bruno Nöckler	ITA	2:42.95
7.	Joel Gaspoz	SWI	2:43.05
8.	Boris Strel	YUG	2:43.24

Born in the small village of Tärnaby in Swedish Lapland, about 100 miles south of the Arctic Circle, Ingemar Stenmark learned to ski at an early age because, "It was a thing I could do alone." When he was 10 years old he wrote a school essay on "How I See My Future." Stenmark wrote that he wanted to be a ski racer. When the teacher returned his paper she told him that his dream was "unrealistic . . . impossible to achieve." She was wrong. Ingemar Stenmark grew up to become the most successful ski racer in history. He was the overall World Cup leader three times and he won the slalom and giant slalom titles eight times each. When he retired in 1989, he had won a record 86 World Cup races. Only Marc Girardelli has won half that many.

On September 14, 1979, Stenmark, then 23 years old, was practicing his downhill technique in the Italian Alps when he lost control and tumbled violently down the hill for 200 meters. Lying unconscious on the snow, he began foaming at the mouth and experiencing spasms. He had suffered a major concussion. But five months later he was in top shape again for the Olympics, although he did skip the downhill race. As usual, Stenmark skied somewhat cautiously on his first run of the giant slalom, placing third behind Andreas Wenzel and Bojan Križaj. But on the second day Stenmark roared down the course almost a full second faster than anyone else. "I'm not disappointed," said silver medalist Wenzel. "I had an idea this would happen."

1984 Sarajevo C: 108, N: 38, D: 2.14.

1.	Max Julen	SWI	2:41.18
2.	Jure Franko	YUG	2:41.41
3.	Andreas Wenzel	LIE	2:41.75
4.	Franz Gruber	AUT	2:42.08
5.	Boris Strel	YUG	2:42.36
6.	Hubert Strolz	AUT	2:42.71
7.	Alex Giorgi	ITA	2:43.00
8.	Phillip Mahre	USA	2:43.25

Twenty-two-year-old Max Julen of Zermatt led after the first run and clocked the second fastest time of the second run to hold off the powerful finish of hometown favorite Jure Franko. Franko, the first Yugoslav to win a Winter Olympics medal, became a national hero, his performance touching off boisterous celebrations in Sarajevo.

1988 Calgary-Nakiska C: 117, N: 39, D: 2.25.

1.	Alberto Tomba	ITA	2:06.37
2.	Hubert Strolz	AUT	2:07.41
3.	Pirmin Zurbriggen	SWI	2:08.39
4.	Ivano Camozzi	ITA	2:08.77
5.	Rudolf Nierlich	AUT	2:08.92
6.	Andreas Wenzel	LIE	2:09.03
7.	Helmut Mayer	AUT	2:09.09
8.	Frank Wörndl	AUT	2:09.22

Alberto Tomba, the son of a wealthy textile merchant, didn't win his first World Cup race until November 27, 1987, but in the two and a half months before the Olympics he won seven slalom and giant slalom races. His sudden success catapulted the raucous Italian from being an unknown into the role of favorite.

Just before taking off on his first run, Tomba turned to his rivals and said, "Okay boys, keep calm. And good luck to all." Then he obliterated the field, registering a time 1.14 seconds faster than Hubert Strolz in second place. While waiting for the second run, Tomba impulsively walked up to a pay phone and placed a collect call to his startled family in Lazzaro di Savenna, a suburb of Bologna. Perhaps he just wanted to remind his father of the elder Tomba's promise to buy his son a Ferrari if he won a gold medal in Calgary.

Two other incidents occurred during the break between runs. Race officials disqualified the entire Canadian team for wearing ski suits that had not been submitted for safety inspection. Having punished the Canadians, they went down the line and eliminated the Bolivians, the Moroccans, the Lebanese, and the Taiwanese, as well. On a darker note, Austria's leading orthopedic surgeon, Jörg Oberhammer, collided with another skier, fell beneath a snow-grooming machine, and was killed instantly. This horrible incident was witnessed by Swiss skiers Pirmin Zurbriggen and Martin Hangl, who happened to be passing overhead in a chairlift. A shaken Zurbriggen still managed to capture the bronze medal, but Hangl collapsed near the starting gate and had to withdraw.

When the competition resumed, Strolz picked up one tenth of a second over Tomba, but it wasn't nearly enough to prevent the latter from qualifying for his Ferrari. "I want it red," he told reporters.

1992 Albertville-Val d'Isère C: 131, N: 47, D: 2.18.

1.	Alberto Tomba	ITA	2:06.98
2.	Marc Girardelli	LUX	2:07.30
3.	Kjetil André Aamodt	NOR	2:07.82
4.	Paul Accola	SWI	2:08.02
5.	Ole Kristian Furuseth	NOR	2:08.16
6.	Günther Mader	AUT	2:08.80
7.	Rainer Salzgeber	AUT	2:08.83
8.	Fredrik Nyberg	SWE	2:09.00

The 1992 men's giant slalom attracted more entrants from more nations than any other event in the history of the Winter Olympics. But for all the color and variety, in the end it was the four favorites who battled for the medals. The man to beat was the defending champion, Alberto Tomba. Following his 1988 triumphs, he put on weight, became distracted by his celebrity, and lost his competitive focus. In the next two years he won only four races, fell often, and broke his collarbone. Finally the Italian Ski Federation stepped in and assigned 1972 gold medalist Gustavo Thöni to be Tomba's personal coach. They also added a full-time fitness coach, a masseur, a psychologist, and an equipment technician. By 1991 Tomba was back on track, winning giant slalom after giant slalom. He continued to dominate the 1991-92 pre-Olympic season. When asked if he was altering his training for the Olympics, Tomba replied, "I used to have a wild time with three women until 5 a.m. In the Olympic Village, I will live it up with five women until 3 a.m."

Tomba's only serious challengers in the giant slalom were thought to be World Cup leader Paul Accola, Super G gold medal winner Kjetil Aamodt, and, most especially, Super G silver medalist Marc Girardelli. Girardelli was known as the skier without a country because he was born in Austria, lived in Switzerland, and acquired citizenship in Luxembourg after his father had a dispute with Austrian ski authorities. Girardelli was one of only three male skiers to win the overall World Cup four times (the others were Gustavo Thöni and Pirmin Zurbriggen), and he ranked third in total World Cup victories, with 36, behind Ingemar Stenmark and Zurbriggen. Until the Albertville Games, Girardelli's best Olympic performance was a ninth in the Calgary downhill.

Aamodt was first down the hill in the 1992 giant slalom. He laid down the challenge with a fine 1:04.81. Tomba, racing sixth, topped him at 1:04.57. Accola followed with a 1:04.88 and Girardelli with 1:04.70. Because the leaders raced the second run in reverse order of their times in the first run, Tomba started immediately after Girardelli and knew that he needed a near-perfect performance to overcome his rival. He got off to a sloppy start and quickly fell behind Girardelli's pace. As his fans watched his intermediate splits in horror, Tomba gradually found his rhythm and ripped through the final third of the course. When he crossed the finish line he didn't know if he had succeeded until he saw the crowd cheering and waving their arms. Only then did he realize that he had made Olympic history by becoming the first alpine skier to win the same event twice. In 1993 Girardelli claimed a bit of history himself, by winning a fifth World Cup title.

Olympic history of a stranger sort was made earlier in the competition at the end of the first run. The skiers took off at 40-second intervals, but the 129th starter, Raymond Kayrouz of Lebanon, was so slow that he was actually passed by the next starter, El Hassan Matha of Morocco. Unfortunately, both Matha and Kayrouz missed a gate and were disqualified.

SUPER GIANT SLALOM

The Super G, first held in 1981 and first included in the World Cup in 1983, is an attempt to combine the speed of the downhill with the technical skills of the giant slalom.

1924–1984 not held

1988 Calgary-Nakiska C: 94, N: 34, D: 2.21.

1.	Franck Piccard	FRA	1:39.66
2.	Helmut Mayer	AUT	1:40.96
3.	Lars-Börje Eriksson	SWE	1:41.08
4.	Hubert Strolz	AUT	1:41.11
5.	Günther Mader	AUT	1:41.96
5.	Pirmin Zurbriggen	SWI	1:41.96
7.	Luc Alphand	FRA	1:42.27
8.	Leonhard Stock	AUT	1:42.36

Franck Piccard, a 23-year-old from Albertville, the hub of the 1992 Winter Games, had never won a World Cup race. He had, however, picked up a bronze medal in the downhill six days before the Super G. When he reached the end of the latter race, he felt he had blown it. "I was really angry with myself," he said. But one by one he watched the favorites fall or at least commit worse mistakes than he had, and before he knew it, he had earned France's first alpine gold in twenty years. Piccard was named after Frank Sinatra, who sent him a congratulatory telegram after he won the gold medal.

1992 Albertville-Val d'Isère C: 118, N: 43, D: 2.16.

1.	Kjetil André Aamodt	NOR	1:13.04
2.	Marc Girardelli	LUX	1:13.77
3.	Jan Einar Thorsen	NOR	1:13.83
4.	Ole Kristian Furuseth	NOR	1:13.87
5.	Josef Polig	ITA	1:13.88
6.	Marco Hangl	SWI	1:13.90
7.	Günther Mader	AUT	1:14.08
8.	Tom Stiansen	NOR	1:14.51

In 1990, Kjetil André Aamodt finished first or second in all five events at the junior world championships. In 1991 he moved up to the senior division and earned a Super G silver medal at the world championships. But on November 4, 1991, Aamodt was hospitalized with mononucleosis. He was so ill that he lost 11 kilograms (24 lbs.) and had to be drip-fed. Despite being told that he wouldn't be able to ski again for six months, the 20-year-old Aamodt recovered quickly and returned to training on January 4. Six weeks later he became Norway's first Olympic alpine medalist since Stein Eriksen in 1952. It was also a happy day for Marc Girardelli, who until then was the greatest skier never to have won an Olympic medal.

ALPINE COMBINED

This event combines one downhill run and, the next day, two slalom runs. Points for each half of the competition are determined by computing the percentage difference between the racer and the leader and then multiplying by a fixed number. In the 1992 combined slalom, for example, that number was 570. Thus, if skier A won the downhill and skier B's time was one percent slower, skier A's score for the downhill would be 0 and skier B's would be 5.70. The scores for the downhill and slalom are added to create the final score.

1924–1932 not held

1936 Garmisch-Partenkirchen C: 66, N: 21, D: 2.9.

			DOWNHILL	SLALOM	PTS.
1.	Franz Pfnür	GER	4:51.8 (2)	2:26.6 (1)	99.25
2.	Gustav Lantschner	GER	4:58.2 (3)	2:32.5 (2)	96.26
3.	Emile Allais	FRA	4:58.8 (4)	2:37.3 (3)	94.69
4.	Birger Ruud	NOR	4:47.4 (1)	2:49.0 (6)	93.38
5.	Roman Wörndle	GER	5:01.2 (6)	2:47.7 (5)	91.16
6.	Rudolf Cranz	GER	5:04.0 (8)	2:47.5 (4)	91.03
7.	Giacinto Sertorelli	ITA	5:05.0 (9)	2:49.4 (7)	90.39
8.	Alf Konningen	NOR	5:00.4 (5)	2:53.6 (9)	90.06

Franz Pfnür, a 27-year-old woodcarver and cabinetmaker from Bavaria, was second to Birger Ruud in the downhill and first in both runs of the slalom. Silver medalist Gustav "Guzzi" Lantschner was described by Albion Ross of the *New York Times* as "a violent Nazi." Born and raised in Innsbruck, Austria, Lantschner moved to Germany and became a cameraman for the Nazi party. Resat Erçes of Turkey showed great patience when he completed the downhill course in 22:44.4—18 minutes slower than Birger Ruud. But, then again, Ruud, a versatile athlete who won the ski jump gold in both 1932 and 1936, had an advantage over Erçes, as well as all the other athletes. Although there was no telephone communication between the start and finish, Ruud knew that the local tram company had its own line connected to the top station a quarter mile from the starting gate. While all the other skiers were waxing their skis for the cold weather appropriate to the gloomy conditions at the top of the two-mile run, Ruud went down to the phone and learned from a friend that the sun had broken through at the bottom of the course and that the snow was turning soft. He changed his wax and outraced the field by 4.4 seconds.

In 1936, skiers were penalized six seconds for each gate missed during the slalom competition rather than being disqualified. Ruud and Wörndle each lost six seconds, while Cranz lost 12.

1948 St. Moritz C: 78, N: 24, D: 2.4.

			DOWNHILL		SLALOM		PTS.
1.	Henri Oreiller	FRA	2:55.0	(1)	2:22.3	(5)	3.27
2.	Karl Molitor	SWI	3:00.3	(2)	2:22.5	(6)	6.44
3.	James Couttet	FRA	3:07.3	(8)	2:14.9	(1)	6.95
4.	Edi Mall	AUT	3:09.3	(13)	2:16.0	(2)	8.54
5.	Silvio Alverà	ITA	3:02.4	(3)	2:24.9	(11)	8.71
6.	Hans Hansson	SWE	3:05.0	(6)	2:23.5	(9)	9.31
7.	Vittorio Chierroni	ITA	3:10.0	(15)	2:18.1	(3)	9.69
8.	Hans Nogler	AUT	3:03.2	(5)	2:27.0	(14)	9.96

1952–1984 not held

1988 Calgary-Nakiska C: 56, N: 20, D: 2.17.

			DOWNHILL		SLALOM		PTS.
1.	Hubert Strolz	AUT	1:48.51	(5)	1:27.31	(7)	36.55
2.	Bernhard Gstrein	AUT	1:50.20	(15)	1:25.82	(3)	43.45
3.	Paul Accola	SWI	1:51.27	(24)	1:24.93	(1)	48.24
4.	Luc Alphand	FRA	1:49.60	(13)	1:28.47	(10)	57.73
5.	Peter Jurko	CZE	1:50.29	(19)	1:27.61	(8)	58.56
6.	Jean-Luc Cretier	FRA	1:50.04	(14)	1:28.52	(11)	62.98
7.	Markus Wasmeier	GER	1:49.32	(8)	1:29.84	(13)	65.44
8.	Adrian Bíreš	CZE	1:50.24	(16)	1:28.94	(12)	68.50

Pirmin Zurbriggen recorded the fastest time in the downhill and led by over two seconds after the first run of the slalom. He seemed well on his way to his second gold of the Calgary Games when he hooked a tip on the 39th of 57 gates on the second slalom run, ran right into the 40th gate, spun around, and landed on his back. Hubert Strolz, a 25-year-old policeman and a good friend of Zurbriggen's, was the immediate beneficiary of the Swiss star's mistake.

Paul Accola took the bronze despite placing only twenty-fourth in the downhill. He did record the best combined time in the slalom. Only 26 of the 56 starters completed all three runs.

1992 Albertville-Val d'Isère C: 66, N: 27, D: 2.11.

			DOWNHILL		SLALOM		PTS.
1.	Josef Polig	ITA	1:45.78	(6)	1:42.16	(5)	14.58
2.	Gianfranco Martin	ITA	1:45.48	(2)	1:42.76	(7)	14.90
3.	Steve Locher	SWI	1:46.53	(12)	1:41.44	(2)	18.16
4.	Jean-Luc Cretier	FRA	1:46.25	(9)	1:42.09	(4)	18.97
5.	Markus Wasmeier	GER	1:45.91	(7)	1:45.15	(13)	32.77
6.	Kristian Ghedina	ITA	1:46.65	(15)	1:44.91	(11)	38.96
7.	Ole Kristian Furuseth	NOR	1:48.94	(33)	1:41.04	(1)	40.47
8.	Xavier Gigandet	SWI	1:45.61	(4)	1:47.19	(15)	41.21

The favorites were Paul Accola, who had won all three pre-Olympic alpine combined competitions, and Marc Girardelli, the 1991 World Cup leader. The downhill portion of the event was delayed 2¼ hours to allow course workers to prepare the piste after a night of heavy snowfall. The first competitor, Girardelli, fell spectacularly. After the twelfth skier, there was another delay while race officials considered canceling the run. After they decided to go ahead, Accola got in a cautious but solid run that left him in fifth place by day's end. Because the four skiers ahead of him were considered weak at the slalom, it looked like the gold medal was Accola's for the taking. But the next day he missed a gate almost immediately. He climbed back and completed the run, but the precious seconds that he lost put him out of contention. Accola was so disgusted that he finished the second run facing backward.

Meanwhile, defending champion Hubert Strolz, after placing thirteenth in the downhill, crushed the field on the first slalom run and found himself poised to make history by becoming the first repeat winner of an alpine event. But barely 100 feet from victory in the final run, he lost his balance, missed a gate, and was disqualified. "I was already at the finish in my thoughts," he explained sheepishly. Suddenly the gold medal was up for grabs. When the computer spit out the results, the winner turned out to be unheralded 23-year-old Josef Polig, who had never before placed higher than fifth in a World Cup event. The silver medal went to his even-less-heralded Italian teammate Gianfranco Martin.

ALPINE SKIING

WOMEN
Downhill
Slalom
Giant Slalom
Super Giant Slalom
Alpine Combined

WOMEN

DOWNHILL

1924–1936 not held

1948 St. Moritz C: 37, N: 11, D: 2.2.
1.	Hedy Schlunegger	SWI	2:28.3
2.	Trude Beiser	AUT	2:29.1
3.	Resi Hammer	AUT	2:30.2
4.	Celina Seghi	ITA	2:31.1
5.	Lina Mittner	SWI	2:31.2
6.	Suzanne Thiollière	FRA	2:31.4
7.	Françoise Gignoux	FRA	2:32.4
7.	Laila Schou Nilsen	NOR	2:32.4

1952 Oslo-Norefjell C: 42, N: 13, D: 2.17.
1.	Trude Jochum-Beiser	AUT	1:47.1
2.	Annemarie Buchner	GER	1:48.0
3.	Giuliana Minuzzo	ITA	1:49.0
4.	Erika Mahringer	AUT	1:49.5
5.	Dagmar Rom	AUT	1:49.8
6.	Madeleine Berthod	SWI	1:50.7
7.	Margit Hvammen	NOR	1:50.9
8.	Joanne Hewson	CAN	1:51.3

1956 Cortina C: 47, N: 16, D: 2.1.
1.	Madeleine Berthod	SWI	1:40.7
2.	Frieda Dänzer	SWI	1:45.4
3.	Lucile Wheeler	CAN	1:45.9
4.	Giuliana Chenal-Minuzzo	ITA	1:47.3
4.	Hilde Hofherr	AUT	1:47.3
6.	Carla Marchelli	ITA	1:47.7
7.	Dorothea Hochleitner	AUT	1:47.9
8.	Josette Neviere	FRA	1:49.2

Madeleine Berthod, the favorite in the event, celebrated her 25th birthday the day she won the downhill gold medal. Her margin of victory was four times larger than any other winner's in this event.

1960 Squaw Valley C: 42, N: 14, D: 2.20.

1.	Heidi Biebl	GER	1:37.6
2.	Penelope Pitou	USA	1:38.6
3.	Traudl Hecher	AUT	1:38.9
4.	Pia Riva	ITA	1:39.9
5.	Jerta Schir	ITA	1:40.5
6.	Anneliese Meggl	GER	1:40.8
7.	Sonja Peril	GER	1:41.0
8.	Erika Netzer	AUT	1:41.1

As a first-year student in high school, Penny Pitou made the boys' varsity ski team and finished fifth in the New Hampshire state slalom championship before being banned from further competition by the local school board. At the age of 15 she qualified for the U.S. Olympic team, finishing 31st, 34th, and 34th. Four years later she was the favorite at Squaw Valley, but the pressure on her was great. "The predictions that I'm going to win make me nervous," she said. "America is putting its hopes on me and it's a terrible feeling. . . . I'd be much happier being a normal girl, sitting at home or going to school." A near-fall three gates from the finish cost her about two seconds and the gold medal. Later she was married for a few years to Austrian downhill gold medalist Egon Zimmermann. And later still she became New Hampshire's first female bank director.

1964 Innsbruck C: 43, N: 15, D: 2.6.

1.	Christl Haas	AUT	1:55.39
2.	Edith Zimmermann	AUT	1:56.42
3.	Traudl Hecher	AUT	1:56.66
4.	Heidi Biebl	GER	1:57.87
5.	Barbara Henneberger	GER	1:58.03
6.	Madeleine Bochatay	FRA	1:59.11
7.	Nancy Greene	CAN	1:59.23
8.	Christine Terraillon	FRA	1:59.66

When she was three years old, Christl Haas told her parents that she wanted to become a ski racer. Seventeen years later the 5-foot 10-inch Haas, skiing in the 13th position, had no trouble living up to her role of an Austrian favorite competing in Austria.

1968 Grenoble-Chamrousse C: 39, N: 14, D: 2.10.

1.	Olga Pall	AUT	1:40.87
2.	Isabelle Mir	FRA	1:41.33
3.	Christl Haas	AUT	1:41.41
4.	Brigitte Seiwald	AUT	1:41.82
5.	Annie Famose	FRA	1:42.15
6.	Felicity Field	GBR	1:42.79
7.	Fernande Bochatay	SWI	1:42.87
8.	Marielle Goitschel	FRA	1:42.95

The Austrians went 1, 3, 4 despite the absence of one of their leading performers: 1966 world champion Erica Schinegger. During routine medical testing prior to the Grenoble Games, doctors were surprised to discover that the saliva of the 20-year-old ski star contained only male hormones. Further examination revealed that Schinegger, who was raised as a girl, actually had male sex organs which had grown inside instead of outside. Schinegger eventually underwent corrective surgery, changed his name to Eric, married, became a father and, in 1988, handed over his world championship gold medal to second-place finisher Marielle Goitschel.

1972 Sapporo-Eniwadake C: 41, N: 13, D: 2.5.

1.	Marie-Theres Nadig	SWI	1:36.68
2.	Annemarie Pröll	AUT	1:37.00
3.	Susan Corrock	USA	1:37.68
4.	Isabelle Mir	FRA	1:38.62
5.	Rosi Speiser	GER	1:39.10
6.	Rosi Mittermaier	GER	1:39.32
7.	Bernadette Zurbriggen	SWI	1:39.49
8.	Annie Famose	FRA	1:39.70

The first noteworthy time was 1:38.62, registered by the eighth skier, Isabelle Mir. Next on the course was French heroine Annie Famose, who was having an exhausting time defending her eligibility from accusations of "commercialism" by the International Ski Federation. Famose finished in eighth place. The tenth skier, unheralded Susan Corrock of Ketchum, Idaho, surprised the experts by taking the lead in 1:37.68. Three skiers later came an even bigger surprise. Seventeen-year-old Marie-Theres Nadig of Flums, Switzerland, who had never won a World Cup race, beat Corrock's time by exactly one second. The 15th skier was the pre-Olympic favorite, 18-year-old Annemarie Pröll. The previous year she had become the youngest-ever overall winner of the World Cup. Pröll skied an excellent race, but finished one third of a second slower than Nadig. Disappointed and angry, she refused to attend the postrace press conference.

According to *Ski* magazine, after her victory Marie-Theres Nadig told the following story to her coach: "I was on the last flat stretch that leads into the steep wall before the finish, when I thought suddenly of a film [*The Love Bug*] I had seen last summer. It was about a funny little car that dreamed of racing in the Grand Prix. The little car was called Herbie. In each race it would start ahead of the other champions who would chase it. Suddenly I saw myself in the role of Herbie. I was being chased by hordes of other racers. A voice inside me said, 'Go, Herbie, go, go, go.' At each 'go,' I would lower my body still further to cut the wind resistance. In my whole life I never skied in such a low crouch. I could easily have fallen. But inside me, I always heard the voice crying out, 'Go, Herbie, go.' "

1976 Innsbruck C: 38, N: 15, D: 2.8.

1.	Rosi Mittermaier	GER	1:46.16
2.	Brigitte Totschnigg	AUT	1:46.68
3.	Cynthia Nelson	USA	1:47.50
4.	Nicola-Andrea Spiess	AUT	1:47.71
5.	Danielle Debernard	FRA	1:48.48
6.	Jacqueline Rouvier	FRA	1:48.58
7.	Bernadette Zurbriggen	SWI	1:48.62
8.	Marlies Oberholzer	SWI	1:48.68

Rosi Mittermaier had never before won a major downhill race, even though she was competing in her tenth World Cup season and her third Olympics.

1980 Lake Placid C: 28, N: 13, D: 2.17.

1.	Annemarie Moser-Pröll	AUT	1:37.52
2.	Hanni Wenzel	LIE	1:38.22
3.	Marie-Theres Nadig	SWI	1:38.36
4.	Heidi Preuss	USA	1:39.51
5.	Kathy Kreiner	CAN	1:39.53
6.	Ingrid Eberle	AUT	1:39.63
7.	Torill Fjeldstad	NOR	1:39.69
7.	Cynthia Nelson	USA	1:39.69

Winning two Olympic silver medals would probably be a dream come true for most skiers, but when Annemarie Pröll won two silvers at Sapporo in 1972, losing both times to Marie-Theres Nadig, she considered it a failure and a humiliation. She was back to her winning ways before long, but in March 1975, after marrying ski salesman Herbert Moser, she retired from competitive skiing and bypassed the 1976 Olympics. After her father died later that year, Annemarie Pröll returned to the circuit. By 1979 she had won six of the last nine annual World Cups and finished second twice. However, the 1980 season had seen her win only one downhill race to Nadig's six. Motivated by the only achievement that had eluded her, Moser-Pröll, the sixth skier, sped down the course on Whiteface Mountain in 1:37.52. Her time withstood the onslaughts of Nadig and Wenzel and earned her the final jewel in her champion's crown. Moser-Pröll holds the record for most World Cup victories by a woman: 62, including 36 downhills.

1984 Sarajevo C: 32, N: 13, D: 2.16.

1.	Michela Figini	SWI	1:13.36
2.	Maria Walliser	SWI	1:13.41
3.	Olga Charvátová	CZE	1:13.53
4.	Ariane Ehrat	SWI	1:13.95
5.	Jana Gantnerová	CZE	1:14.14
6.	Marina Kiehl	GER	1:14.30
6.	Gerry Sorensen	CAN	1:14.30
8.	Lea Sölkner	AUT	1:14.39

Michela Figini scored her first World Cup victory only two weeks before the Olympics. At Sarajevo she recorded the fastest time in three of the five practice runs and was leading the real race on February 15th when it was cancelled because of fog. The next day she confirmed her new consistency by becoming, at age 17, the youngest skier ever to win an Olympic gold medal.

1988 Calgary-Nakiska C: 35, N: 14, D: 2.19.

1.	Marina Kiehl	GER	1:25.86
2.	Brigitte Oertli	SWI	1:26.61
3.	Karen Percy	CAN	1:26.62
4.	Maria Walliser	SWI	1:26.89
5.	Laurie Graham	CAN	1:26.99
6.	Petra Kronberger	AUT	1:27.03
7.	Regine Mösenlechner	GER	1:27.16
8.	Elisabeth Kirchler	AUT	1:27.19

Marina Kiehl, a 23-year-old millionaire's daughter from Munich, had a reputation for having a lofty and generally unpleasant personality. Her manager and her sponsors finally convinced her to control her sharp tongue and to make an effort to be friendly to those around her. Kiehl succeeded in making herself more likable, but her race results declined dramatically. Things got so bad that a popular German sports writer urged her, in print, to "go ahead and be rude again, because when you are bad you are better." When German Olympic officials threatened to drop her from the roster for the Super G, her best event, Kiehl exploded at them, much to the relief of her fans. A deal was worked out: if Kiehl finished in the top six of the downhill, she could also take part in the Super G. If she failed, she would be bumped from the starting lineup.

In seven years on the World Cup circuit, Kiehl had never won a downhill race. In Calgary she had a wild run, almost falling twice. "I was out of control up there," she explained afterward, "so I just let the skis go faster and faster." Because she had twice lost races to unheralded, late-starting skiers, Kiehl refused to celebrate her victory until the final Argentinian had skied off the course. Three days later Kiehl competed in the Super G—and finished in a tie for twelfth place.

1992 Albertville-Méribel C: 30, N: 12, D: 2.15.

1.	Kerrin Lee-Gartner	CAN	1:52.55
2.	Hilary Lindh	USA	1:52.61
3.	Veronika Wallinger	AUT	1:52.64
4.	Katja Seizinger	GER	1:52.67
5.	Petra Kronberger	AUT	1:52.73
6.	Katharina Gutensohn	GER	1:53.71
7.	Barbara Sadleder	AUT	1:53.81
8.	Svetlana Gladicheva	SOV	1:53.85

The course, designed by Bernhard Russi, was universally acknowledged to be the most difficult women's course ever. At 2770 meters (1⅔ miles) it was also the longest and, with a vertical drop of 828 meters, the steepest. In addition, an impending snowstorm prompted race officials to move up the start of the contest and to send the racers down the slope at shorter-than-usual intervals. Intermittent fog made the course more challenging for some than for others.

Kerrin Lee-Gartner grew up in Rossland, British Columbia, five doors down from the parents of 1968 giant slalom medalist Nancy Greene. In 1990 Lee-Gartner had a dream in which she heard an announcer say, "*Médaille d'or,* Kerrin Lee-Gartner, Canada." She didn't speak French, but she knew enough of the language to know that "*médaille d'or*" meant "gold medal." It seemed as much a fantasy as a dream since ten years of World Cup races had earned her only a single third-place finish. Although she had placed eighth in the Calgary combined, she had finished only fifteenth in the downhill.

But some dreams do come true. In Méribel, Lee-Gartner had the race of her life and really did get to hear an announcer say, "*Médaille d'or,* Kerrin Lee-Gartner, Canada." She was the first winner of the women's downhill to come from a non-German-speaking country. The silver medalist was also an outsider: Hilary Lindh of Juneau, Alaska, whose best placing in a World Cup event had been a sixth in 1989.

The 1992 women's downhill was by far the tightest-ever alpine race in Olympic history. Only eighteen one-hundredths of a second separated Lee-Gartner in first from Petra Kronberger in fifth.

SLALOM

1924–1936 not held

1948 St. Moritz C: 28, N: 10, D: 2.5.

1.	Gretchen Fraser	USA	1:57.2
2.	Antoinette Meyer	SWI	1:57.7
3.	Erika Mahringer	AUT	1:58.0
4.	Georgette Miller-Thiollière	FRA	1:58.8
5.	Renée Clerc	SWI	2:05.8
6.	Anneliese Schuh-Proxauf	AUT	2:06.7
7.	Rese Hammerer	AUT	2:08.6
8.	Andrea Mead	USA	2:08.8

Gretchen Fraser of Vancouver, Washington, had qualified for the U.S. team for the 1940 Olympics that were never held. Eight years later she was considered an unknown quantity. Skiing in the first position she clocked the fastest time of the first run—59.7. Erika Mahringer was one-tenth of a second behind her. As Fraser prepared to lead off the second round, a problem suddenly developed in the telephone timing system between the top and the bottom of the hill. Despite a 17-minute delay at such a critical time, Fraser finished the second run in 57.5, a time beaten only by Antoinette Meyer (57.0.)

1952 Oslo C: 40, N: 14, D: 2.20.

1.	Andrea Mead Lawrence	USA	2:10.6
2.	Ossi Reichert	GER	2:11.4
3.	Annemarie Buchner	GER	2:13.3
4.	Celina Seghi	ITA	2:13.8
5.	Imogene Anna Opton	USA	2:14.1
6.	Madeleine Berthod	SWI	2:14.9
7.	Agnel Marysette	FRA	2:15.6
8.	Trude Jochum-Beiser	AUT	2:15.9
8.	Giuliana Minuzzo	ITA	2:15.9

Nineteen-year-old Andrea Mead Lawrence of Rutland, Vermont, fell early in her first run, but got up, and showed her superiority by finishing the course with the fourth best time. She overhauled the leaders with a second run that was two seconds faster than anyone else's. Lawrence became the first American skier to win two gold medals. By the time of the opening of the 1956 Games, she had given birth to three children.

1956 Cortina C: 48, N: 16, D: 1.30.

1.	Renée Colliard	SWI	1:52.3
2.	Regina Schöpf	AUT	1:55.4
3.	Yevgenya Sidorova	SOV	1:56.7
4.	Giuliana Chenal-Minuzzo	ITA	1:56.8
5.	Josefine Frandl	AUT	1:57.9
6.	Inger Björnbakken	NOR	1:58.0
6.	Astrid Sandvik	NOR	1:58.0
8.	Josette Neviere	FRA	1:58.3

Renée Colliard, a pharmacy student from Geneva, was making her first appearance as a member of the Swiss team. Racing in the number-one position, she registered the fastest time in each run.

1960 Squaw Valley C: 43, N: 14, D: 2.26.

1.	Anne Heggtveit	CAN	1:49.6
2.	Betsy Snite	USA	1:52.9
3.	Barbara Henneberger	GER	1:56.6
4.	Thérèse Leduc	FRA	1:57.4
5.	Hilde Hofherr	AUT	1:58.0
5.	Liselotte Michel	SWI	1:58.0
7.	Stalian Korzukhina	SOV	1:58.4
8.	Sonja Sperl	GER	1:58.8

1964 Innsbruck C: 48, N: 16, D: 2.1.

1.	Christine Goitschel	FRA	1:29.86
2.	Marielle Goitschel	FRA	1:30.77
3.	Jean Saubert	USA	1:31.36
4.	Heidi Biebl	GER	1:34.04
5.	Edith Zimmermann	AUT	1:34.27
6.	Christl Haas	AUT	1:35.11
7.	Liv Jagge	NOR	1:36.38
8.	Patricia du Roy de Blicquy	BEL	1:37.01

Christine and Marielle Goitschel, teenaged sisters from Val d'Isère, the home of Jean-Claude Killy, were the stars of the 1964 ski contests. Marielle, the favorite, had the fastest time of the first run, 43.09, with her older sister, Christine, in second place at 43.85. Christine prevailed in the second round, giving the Goitschels a one-two finish. That same day, back in France, their younger sister, Patricia, won a National Junior title.

1968 Grenoble-Chamrousse C: 49, N: 18, D: 2.13.

1.	Marielle Goitschel	FRA	1:25.86
2.	Nancy Greene	CAN	1:26.15
3.	Annie Famose	FRA	1:27.89
4.	Georgina Hathorn	GBR	1:27.92
5.	Isabelle Mir	FRA	1:28.22
6.	Burgl Färbinger	GER	1:28.90
7.	Glorianda Cipolla	ITA	1:29.74
8.	Bernadette Rauter	AUT	1:30.44

Sixteen-year-old Judy Nagel of Enumclaw, Washington, was the surprise leader of the first run, but she fell at the beginning of her second run. Although she finished the course, she was disqualified for missing a gate.

1972 Sapporo-Teineyama C: 42, N: 13, D: 2.11.

1.	Barbara Cochran	USA	1:31.24
2.	Danièlle Debernard	FRA	1:31.26
3.	Florence Steurer	FRA	1:32.69
4.	Judy Crawford	CAN	1:33.95
5.	Annemarie Pröll	AUT	1:34.03
6.	Pamela Behr	GER	1:34.27
7.	Monika Kaserer	AUT	1:34.36
8.	Patricia Boydstun	USA	1:35.59

Back home in Richmond, Vermont, Barbara Cochran's father had taught his talented children how to save a tenth of a second by setting their bodies in motion before pushing open the starting wand that sets off the timing mechanism. That one-tenth second turned out to be the difference between gold and silver for Barbara Cochran. Her time for the first run was three one-hundredths of a second faster than Danièlle Debernard. In the final run Debernard was able to pick up only one of the three-hundredths of a second. Only 19 of 42 starters made it through both runs without falling or missing a gate. Cochran's brother, Robert, and her sister, Marilyn, also competed at the 1972 Olympics. Her youngest sister, Linda, placed sixth in the 1976 slalom.

1976 Innsbruck C: 42, N: 14, D: 2.11.

1.	Rosi Mittermaier	GER	1:30.54
2.	Claudia Giordani	ITA	1:30.87
3.	Hanni Wenzel	LIE	1:32.20
4.	Danièlle Debernard	FRA	1:32.24
5.	Pamela Behr	GER	1:32.31
6.	Linda Cochran	USA	1:33.24
7.	Christa Zechmeister	GER	1:33.72
8.	Wanda Bieter	ITA	1:35.66

For the second straight time, 42 women started the Olympic slalom, but only 19 finished both courses without missing a gate. Rosi Mittermaier recorded the fastest time of the second run after trailing teammate Pamela Behr by nine-hundredths of a second after the first run. Mittermaier had already won the downhill race three days earlier.

1980 Lake Placid C: 47, N: 21, D: 2.23.

1. Hanni Wenzel	LIE	1:25.09
2. Christa Kinshofer	GER	1:26.50
3. Erika Hess	SWI	1:27.89
4. Mariarosa Quario	ITA	1:27.92
5. Claudia Giordani	ITA	1:29.12
6. Nadezhda Patrakeeva	SOV	1:29.20
7. Daniela Zini	ITA	1:29.22
8. Christin Cooper	USA	1:29.28

German-born Hanni Wenzel moved to tiny Liechtenstein (population 25,000) when she was one year old. She was granted Liechtenstein citizenship after winning the slalom at the 1974 world championships in St. Moritz. Having already finished second in the downhill and first in the giant slalom at the 1980 Olympics, Wenzel breezed through the slalom, registering the best time in both the first and second runs. By earning two gold medals and one silver in one Olympics, she matched the 1976 feat of Rosi Mittermaier. Hanni's brother, Andreas, won the silver medal in the downhill, to give Liechtenstein four medals at the Lake Placid Games, one for every 6250 people. If the U.S. had won the same number of medals per capita it would have won 36,000 medals. Actually there were only 114 medals awarded.

1984 Sarajevo C: 45, N: 19, D: 2.17.

1. Paoletta Magoni	ITA	1:36.47
2. Perrine Pelen	FRA	1:37.38
3. Ursula Konzett	LIE	1:37.50
4. Roswitha Steiner	AUT	1:37.84
5. Erika Hess	SWI	1:37.91
6. Malgorzata Tlalka	POL	1:37.95
7. Maria Rosa Quario	ITA	1:37.99
8. Anni Kronbichler	AUT	1:38.05

The first run leader was unheralded Christelle Guignard of France; however, she missed a turn on the top half of the second run and failed to finish. In fact, only 21 of the 45 starters completed both runs without missing a gate. The winner was 19-year-old Paoletta Magoni, a bricklayer's daughter from Selvino who had never before finished better than sixth in a World Cup race.

1988 Calgary-Nakiska C: 57, N: 25, D: 2.26.

1. Vreni Schneider	SWI	1:36.69
2. Mateja Svet	YUG	1:38.37
3. Christa Kinshofer-Güthlein	GER	1:38.40
4. Roswitha Steiner	AUT	1:38.77
5. Blanca Fernández Ochoa	SPA	1:39.44
6. Ida Ladstätter	AUT	1:39.59
7. Paoletta Magoni Sforza	ITA	1:39.76
8. Dorota Tlalka-Mogore	FRA	1:39.86

Schneider, who had already won the giant slalom two days earlier, recorded the fastest time in both runs. Camilla Nilsson of Sweden trailed Schneider by only one one-hundredth of a second after the first run, but fell early in the second run and was eliminated. In 1988-89, Schneider won 14 World Cup events, breaking Ingemar Stenmark's 10-year-old season record of 13.

1992 Albertville-Méribel C: 63, N: 31, D: 2.20.

1.	Petra Kronberger	AUT	1:32.68
2.	Annelise Coberger	NZL	1:33.10
3.	Blanca Fernández Ochoa	SPA	1:33.35
4.	Julie Parisien	USA	1:33.40
5.	Karin Buder	AUT	1:33.68
6.	Patricia Chauvet	FRA	1:33.72
7.	Vreni Schneider	SWI	1:33.96
8.	Anne Berge	NOR	1:34.22

Julie Parisien, who had lost three teeth and fractured her wrist in separate accidents less than a month before the start of the Olympics, led the first run with a time of 48.22. Close behind were Blanca Fernández Ochoa at 48.25 and Petra Kronberger at 48.28. But Parisien faltered after the three-hour break between runs and recorded only the eighth-fastest time of the second run. Kronberger, who had won the combined event seven days earlier, did not falter. Coberger was the first athlete from the Southern Hemisphere to win a Winter Olympic medal. Competing in her fourth Olympics, Fernández Ochoa, whose brother Paco won the 1972 slalom, was the first Spanish woman to win an Olympic medal in either winter or summer.

GIANT SLALOM

1924–1948 not held

1952 Oslo-Norefjell C: 45, N: 15, D: 2.14.

1.	Andrea Mead Lawrence	USA	2:06.8
2.	Dagmar Rom	AUT	2:09.0
3.	Annemarie Buchner	GER	2:10.0
4.	Trude Klecker	AUT	2:11.4
5.	Katy Rodolph	USA	2:11.7
6.	Borghild Niskin	NOR	2:11.9
7.	Celina Seghi	ITA	2:12.5
8.	Ossi Reichert	GER	2:13.2

Silver medalist Dagmar Rom was a well-known Austrian film actress.

1956 Cortina C: 49, N: 16, D: 1.27.

1.	Ossi Reichert	GER	1:56.5
2.	Josefine Frandl	AUT	1:57.8
3.	Dorothea Hochleitner	AUT	1:58.2
4.	Madeleine Berthod	SWI	1:58.3
4.	Andrea Mead Lawrence	USA	1:58.3
6.	Lucile Wheeler	CAN	1:58.6
7.	Borghild Niskin	NOR	1:59.0
8.	Marysette Agnel	FRA	1:59.4

1960 Squaw Valley C: 44, N: 14, D: 2.23.

1.	Yvonne Rügg	SWI	1:39.9
2.	Penelope Pitou	USA	1:40.0
3.	Giuliana Chenal-Minuzzo	ITA	1:40.2
4.	Betsy Snite	USA	1:40.4
5.	Carla Marchelli	ITA	1:40.7
5.	Anneliese Meggl	GER	1:40.7
7.	Thérèse Leduc	FRA	1:40.8
8.	Anne-Marie Leduc	FRA	1:41.5

1964 Innsbruck C: 46, N: 15, D: 2.3.

1.	Marielle Goitschel	FRA	1:52.24
2.	Christine Goitschel	FRA	1:53.11
2.	Jean Saubert	USA	1:53.11
4.	Christl Haas	AUT	1:53.86
5.	Annie Famose	FRA	1:53.89
6.	Edith Zimmermann	AUT	1:54.21
7.	Barbara Henneberger	GER	1:54.26
8.	Traudl Hecher	AUT	1:54.55

On February 1, Christine Goitschel had won the slalom with her younger sister, Marielle, second and Jean Saubert third. Christine was the first of the three to go down the course of the giant slalom two days later. Her time of 1:53.11 looked good. Three skiers later Jean Saubert clocked the exact same time despite the introduction of timing to the hundredth of a second. When Marielle Goitschel, the 14th skier, heard that Saubert had equaled her sister's time, she attacked the course with extra determination and earned herself the gold medal.

After her victory, 18-year old Marielle announced to the press that she had just become engaged to a 20-year-old French skier by the name of Jean-Claude Killy, who had finished fifth in the giant slalom the day before. "I am happy and I am in love," she enthused. While the more gullible reporters scurried away to spread the exciting news around the world, Marielle and Christine sat back and enjoyed their little hoax. When the press caught up with Killy, he smiled and spilled out the truth. "The joke of a tomboy," he said. "Marielle talks too much." It says a lot about the fully justified self-confidence of the Goitschel sisters that they had actually planned their practical joke the night before the race, on the assumption that one of them would win the gold medal.

1968 Grenoble-Chamrousse C: 47, N: 18, D: 2.15.

1.	Nancy Greene	CAN	1:51.97
2.	Annie Famose	FRA	1:54.61
3.	Fernande Bochatay	SWI	1:54.74
4.	Florence Steurer	FRA	1:54.75
5.	Olga Pall	AUT	1:55.61
6.	Isabelle Mir	FRA	1:56.07
7.	Marielle Goitschel	FRA	1:56.09
8.	Divina Galica	GBR	1:56.58

In 1967 Nancy Greene of Rossland, British Columbia, won the inaugural World Cup despite missing three of the nine meets. The following year she participated in her third Olympics. After finishing tenth in the downhill and second in the slalom, she realized that the giant slalom was her last chance to win a gold medal. The Canadian coaches brought her to the top of the slope 45 minutes early and suggested that they fill the time by eating a snack at a nearby restaurant. Over tea and rolls they became involved in a spirited discussion about ski politics. Suddenly one of the coaches realized that the race had already started. When they reached the start hut, the fifth skier, Annie Famose, was already in the gate. Green was number nine. In fact, the coaches had planned the whole thing so that Greene would be distracted from her nervousness. When it came her turn to start in the gate, she told herself, "Anne Heggtveit won a slalom gold when I was on the team in 1960, and she washes her clothes the same way I do." Green skied a perfect race, but when she turned around to look at the electronic clock, the numbers were still moving. "My heart almost stopped," she later recalled. "I thought, I've just skied the race of my life and they missed my time." After two or three seconds the clock malfunction was corrected and her time appeared. "But that's all it took for my blood pressure to shoot out of sight. I had a headache for the next two days."

1972 Sapporo-Teineyama C: 42, N: 13, D: 2.8.

1.	Marie-Theres Nadig	SWI	1:29.90
2.	Annemarie Pröll	AUT	1:30.75
3.	Wiltrud Drexel	AUT	1:32.35
4.	Laurie Kreiner	CAN	1:32.48
5.	Rosi Speiser	GER	1:32.56
6.	Florence Steurer	FRA	1:32.59
7.	Divina Galica	GBR	1:32.72
8.	Brit Lafforgue	FRA	1:32.80

Hoping to avenge her upset defeat at the hands of Marie-Theres Nadig in the downhill, Annemarie Pröll, the second skier, slammed down the course in 1:30.75. Her time held up until Nadig, in the tenth spot, clocked 1:29.90. Pröll, bearing the burden of being the favorite, was bitterly disappointed. "Two silver medals don't equal one gold medal," she said. Nadig attributed her victory to the fact that she was relaxed while Pröll had been under enormous pressure. After the Olympics, however, Nadig learned firsthand what her rival had had to endure. "After Sapporo," Nadig later said, "people expected everything from me. They expected me to win all the time, and after a while I didn't know where I was."

1976 Innsbruck C: 45, N: 17, D: 2.13.

1.	Kathy Kreiner	CAN	1:29.13
2.	Rosi Mittermaier	GER	1:29.25
3.	Danièlle Debernard	FRA	1:29.95
4.	Lise-Marie Morerod	SWI	1:30.40
5.	Marie-Theres Nadig	SWI	1:30.44
6.	Monika Kaserer	AUT	1:30.49
7.	Wilma Gatta	ITA	1:30.51
8.	Evi Mittermaier	GER	1:30.64

There was great excitement before the running of the giant slalom because everyone wanted to know if Rosi Mittermaier would become the first woman to sweep the three alpine races. They didn't have to wait long to find out. The first skier on the course, 18-year-old Kathy Kreiner of Timmins, Ontario, had an excellent run and flashed across the finish line in 1:29.13. Three skiers later it was Rosi Mittermaier's turn. A half-second ahead of Kreiner's pace at the halfway mark, Mittermaier lost precious fractions of a second when she approached one of the lower gates too directly. Her final time was one-eighth of a second slower than Kreiner's.

1980 Lake Placid C: 46, N: 21, D: 2.21.

1.	Hanni Wenzel	LIE	2:41.66
2.	Irene Epple	GER	2:42.12
3.	Perrine Pelen	FRA	2:42.41
4.	Fabienne Serrat	FRA	2:42.42
5.	Christa Kinshofer	GER	2:42.63
6.	Annemarie Moser-Pröll	AUT	2:43.19
7.	Christin Cooper	USA	2:44.71
8.	Maria Epple	GER	2:45.56

For the first time, the women's giant slalom was held as a two-run competition. Wenzel had the fastest time of the first run and the third fastest of the second. She was Liechtenstein's first Olympic gold medal winner.

1984 Sarajevo C: 54, N: 21, D: 2.13.

1.	Debbie Armstrong	USA	2:20.98
2.	Christin Cooper	USA	2:21.38
3.	Perrine Pelen	FRA	2:21.40
4.	Tamara McKinney	USA	2:21.83
5.	Marina Kiehl	GER	2:22.03
6.	Blanca Fernández Ochoa	SPA	2:22.14
7.	Erika Hess	SWI	2:22.51
8.	Olga Charvátová	CZE	2:22.57

With hundreds of sports journalists crowding around and pestering the world's leading skiers from the moment they arrived in Sarajevo, 20-year-old Debbie Armstrong of Seattle, Wash., was blessed with anonymity. The night before the giant slalom, she watched Peter and Kitty Carruthers win silver medals for pairs figure skating and then stayed up late indulging her addiction to peanut butter. The next day, relaxed and "having fun," she recorded the second fastest time of the first run, only one-tenth of a second behind teammate Christin Cooper. During the 2½ hour break before the final run, Armstrong, who had never won a World Cup race, was more than a little excited.

"I felt so good at the top," she would say afterwards. "I was so happy waiting for that second run. It was so much fun. I knew it was a good hill for me. I knew if I stayed relaxed the skiing would take care of itself. I didn't feel the pressure."

According to Cooper, who would hit the course immediately after Armstrong, "She was so hyped up, it was really funny. She kept coming up to me and bouncing all over me and telling me to have a good time. She would say, 'I'm just going to have fun out there, just have fun, have fun!' And when she was in the gate, I could hear her talking to herself. She was saying, 'Okay, De . . . have a good run, have a good run. Just have a good time.' And then she turned to me and said, 'You too, Coop. Have the run of your life.' " With that, Armstrong was out of the starting gate and down the slope. Her time was the fourth best of the second run, but when Cooper slipped at the fifth gate, losing valuable moments, the gold medal went to the ebullient Armstrong.

At the post-race press conference she was asked what she had sacrificed to become a champion skier. She replied, "Nothing. Skiing is my life. That's what I love to do." Then she added characteristically, "It's fun."

Armstrong, who finished 13th in the 1988 giant slalom, never won another international race.

1988 Calgary-Nakiska C: 64, N: 26, D: 2.24.

1.	Vreni Schneider	SWI	2:06.49
2.	Christa Kinshofer-Güthlein	GER	2:07.42
3.	Maria Walliser	SWI	2:07.72
4.	Mateja Svet	YUG	2:07.80
5.	Christine Meier	GER	2:07.88
6.	Ulrike Maier	AUT	2:08.10
7.	Anita Wachter	AUT	2:08.38
8.	Catherine Quittet	FRA	2:08.84

The first-round leader was Spain's Blanca Fernández Ochoa. She was followed by 1980 silver medalist Christa Kinshofer-Güthlein, Anita Wachter, Christine Meier, and, in fifth place, the favorite, world champion and World Cup champion Vreni Schneider. Fernández Ochoa fell early in her second run. Schneider, on the other hand, registered the fastest time of the round to score one of her patented come-from-behind victories.

Only 29 of the 64 starters completed both runs. In 28th place was Seba Johnson of the U.S. Virgin Islands, the first black skier to take part in the Olympics and, at age 14, the youngest competitor at the Calgary Games.

1992 Albertville-Méribel C: 69, N: 32, D: 2.19.

1.	Pernilla Wiberg	SWE	2:12.74
2.	Diann Roffe	USA	2:13.71
2.	Anita Wachter	AUT	2:13.71
4.	Ulrike Maier	AUT	2:13.77
5.	Julie Parisien	USA	2:14.10
6.	Carole Merle	FRA	2:14.24
7.	Eva Twardokens	USA	2:14.47
8.	Katja Seizinger	GER	2:14.96

Wiberg, the defending world champion, finished second in the first run. The second run was set by the Swedish alpine coach, Jarl Svanberg. Wiberg took advantage of this psychological boost to record the fastest time of the run. Co-silver medalist Diann Roffe had won the 1985 world championship at age 17 but hadn't won an international race since. The first-run leader was Uli Maier, the only mother on the World Cup circuit. However, like Julie Parisien in the slalom the following day, she faltered in the second run and missed a medal by less than one-tenth of a second.

SUPER GIANT SLALOM

1924–1984 not held

1988 Calgary-Nakiska C: 46, N: 20, D: 2.22.

1.	Sigrid Wolf	AUT	1:19.03
2.	Michela Figini	SWI	1:20.03
3.	Karen Percy	CAN	1:20.29
4.	Regine Mösenlechner	GER	1:20.33
5.	Anita Wachter	AUT	1:20.36
6.	Maria Walliser	SWI	1:20.48
7.	Zoë Haas	SWI	1:20.91
7.	Micaela Marzola	ITA	1:20.91

Five weeks before the Olympics, Sigrid Wolf won a Super G race in Lech, Austria, but was disqualified for wearing a safety pin on her number bib to keep it from flapping in the wind. In Calgary, Wolf again raced with a safety pin—but this time it was attached to a necklace for good luck.

1992 Albertville-Méribel C: 59, N: 26, D: 2.18.

1.	Deborah Compagnoni	ITA	1:21.22
2.	Carole Merle	FRA	1:22.63
3.	Katja Seizinger	GER	1:23.19
4.	Petra Kronberger	AUT	1:23.20
5.	Ulrike Maier	AUT	1:23.35
6.	Kerrin Lee-Gartner	CAN	1:23.76
7.	Michaela Gerg-Leitner	GER	1:23.77
8.	Eva Twardokens	USA	1:24.19

The three pre-Olympic World Cup Super G races had been won by Seizinger, Merle, and Compagnoni. The other major contender was Maier, who had won two world championships, one in 1989 while she was pregnant and the other in 1991 after she was a mother. Racing in the fourth position, Merle, under intense pressure as France's leading medal hope, skied beautifully and took a big lead. The French crowd watched with glee as Seizinger, Maier, and nine others fell far short of Merle's time. But then came Italy's heroine, 21-year-old Deborah Compagnoni. In addition to the usual severe knee injuries common to alpine skiers, Compagnoni survived emergency surgery in October 1990, during which a 20-inch length of her intestines was removed. Doctors told her father that had they waited twenty minutes longer, Compagnoni might have died. In Méribel, she didn't believe she could win a gold medal, even during the race, which she won handily. The very next day, during the first run of the giant slalom, she leaned too heavily on her inner ski, fell, tore ligaments in her left knee, and ended up back in the hospital.

ALPINE COMBINED

1924–1932 not held

1936 Garmisch-Partenkirchen C: 37, N: 13, D: 2.8.

		DOWNHILL		SLALOM		PTS.
1. Christl Cranz	GER	5:23.4	(6)	2:22.1	(1)	97.06
2. Käthe Grasegger	GER	5:11.0	(3)	2:33.4	(2)	95.26
3. Laila Schou Nilsen	NOR	5:04.4	(1)	2:43.4	(5)	93.48
4. Erna Steuri	SWI	5:20.4	(4)	2:38.4	(3)	92.36
5. Hadi Pfeiffer	GER	5:21.6	(5)	2:39.6	(4)	91.85
6. Lisa Resch	GER	5:08.4	(2)	3:00.4	(8)	88.74
7. Johanne Dybwad	NOR	5:32.0	(8)	2:57.4	(7)	85.90
8. Jeannette Kessler	GBR	6:05.4	(12)	2:47.9	(6)	83.97

Christl Cranz was only sixth in the downhill, but her times in the two slalom runs were so superior that she won anyway. Her first run was 4 seconds faster than her closest competitor and her second run was 7.2 seconds better than any of her rivals. The times of Schou Nilsen and Dybwad include 6-second penalties for missing a gate in the slalom. Resch's time includes a 12-second penalty for missing two gates. Diana Gordon-Lennox, representing Canada, received an ovation because she skied both the downhill and slalom with one arm in a cast and using only one pole. She also wore a monocle while competing. Gordon-Lennox finished 29th.

1948 St. Moritz C: 28, N: 10, D: 2.4.

		DOWNHILL		SLALOM		PTS.
1. Trude Beiser	AUT	2:29.1	(2)	2:10.5	(8)	6.58
2. Gretchen Fraser	USA	2:37.1	(11)	2:11.0	(2)	6.95
3. Erika Mahringer	AUT	2:39.3	(15)	1:58.1	(1)	7.04
4. Celina Seghi	ITA	2:31.1	(4)	2:09.7	(7)	7.46
5. Françoise Gignoux	FRA	2:32.4	(7)	2:09.0	(5)	8.14
6. Rosmarie Bleuer	SWI	2:33.3	(9)	2:09.3	(6)	8.80
7. Anneliese Schuh-Proxauf	AUT	2:39.0	(13)	2:04.3	(3)	9.76
8. Hedy Schlunegger	SWI	2:28.3	(1)	2:18.5	(15)	10.20

1952–1984 not held

1988 Calgary-Nakiska C: 39, N: 14, D: 2.21.

			DOWNHILL		SLALOM		PTS.
1.	Anita Wachter	AUT	1:17.14	(3)	1:22.97	(2)	29.25
2.	Brigitte Oertli	SWI	1:18.37	(11)	1:20.71	(1)	29.48
3.	Maria Walliser	SWI	1:16.98	(2)	1:25.92	(11)	51.28
4.	Karen Percy	CAN	1:18.22	(9)	1:24.00	(3)	54.47
5.	Lenka Kebrlová	CZE	1:18.43	(13)	1:24.38	(5)	60.87
6.	Lucia Medzihradská	CZE	1:18.62	(15)	1:24.35	(4)	63.56
7.	Michelle McKendry	CAN	1:17.58	(4)	1:26.44	(13)	64.85
8.	Kerrin Lee	CAN	1:18.15	(8)	1:25.43	(9)	65.26

Wachter's surprising third-place finish in the downhill run set her up as the overnight favorite. Oertli, the pre-Olympic favorite, picked up 2.26 seconds in the two slalom runs, but it wasn't enough to overcome her eleventh-place finish in the downhill.

1992 Albertville-Méribel C: 40, N: 18, D: 2.13.

			DOWNHILL		SLALOM		PTS.
1.	Petra Kronberger	AUT	1:25.84	(1)	1:09.60	(3)	2.55
2.	Anita Wachter	AUT	1:27.25	(12)	1:09.51	(2)	19.39
3.	Florence Masnada	FRA	1:27.08	(10)	1:10.01	(5)	21.38
4.	Chantal Bournissen	SWI	1:26.92	(7)	1:10.69	(6)	24.98
5.	Anne Berge	NOR	1:28.67	(22)	1:09.29	(1)	35.28
6.	Michelle McKendry	CAN	1:27.32	(14)	1:11.79	(7)	39.02
7.	Natasa Bokal	SLO	1:29.02	(25)	1:09.65	(4)	42.60
8.	Lucia Medzihradská	CZE	1:27.89	(17)	1:11.95	(9)	47.43

Petra Kronberger was the overwhelming favorite in this event, especially after her most serious challenger, teammate Sabine Ginther, fell on the downhill course the day before the competition and fractured a disk. Kronberger was such a well-rounded skier that in December 1990 she won a World Cup event in each of the four alpine disciplines and then added a combined victory the following month. She easily won the downhill run at the Olympics, but the next day she skied conservatively on the first slalom run and placed only sixth. Two months earlier, the Austrian women's slalom coach, Aloïs Kahr, had been killed in a car crash. Just before her second run, Kronberger sensed Kahr talking to her and giving her advice. This time she attacked the course and recorded a faster time than any of the other skiers.

FREESTYLE SKIING

MEN
Aerials
Moguls
WOMEN
Aerials
Moguls

The first freestyle skiing competition was held in Attitash, New Hampshire, in 1966. The International Ski Federation (F.I.S.) recognized the sport in 1979, and the following year a World Cup series was organized. In 1986 the first world championship was held in Tignes, France, site of the 1992 Olympic competition. There are three freestyle disciplines: moguls, aerials, and ballet, all of which were included as demonstration events at the 1988 Calgary Olympics. Moguls was awarded medal status in 1992, and aerials will be added in 1994.

MEN

AERIALS

Competitors perform two acrobatic jumps in the qualifying round. Finalists perform two more jumps. Qualifying scores are not carried over to the final round. Jumps range from the relatively simple front tuck, a front somersault performed in the tuck position, to the doublefull full full, a backward triple somersault, the first somersault with two twists, and the second and third with single full twists. A panel of judges score the skiers for three elements: height and distance, known as "air," account for 20 percent of the score; execution and precision, known as "form," for 50 percent; and landing for 30 percent.

This event will be held for the first time in 1994.

MOGULS

Moguls are snow bumps. Competitors ski on a run filled with high-speed turns on a heavily moguled course. Finalists perform a second run. Qualifying scores are not carried over to the final round. Turns account for 50 percent of a competitor's score and are judged according to the skier's ability to keep a clean, controlled line down the course. Two aerial maneuvers performed during the run are judged on the basis of height, distance, landing, execution, and degree of difficulty. They account for 25 percent of the score and are blessed with such poetic names as the back scratcher, the mule kick, the daffy, and the zadnik. The remaining 25 percent is based on time from start to finish. Moguls competitions are accompanied by loud rock and roll music.

1924-1988 not held

1992 Albertville-Tignes C: 47, N: 17, D: 2.13.

		PTS.
1. Edgar Grospiron	FRA	25.81
2. Olivier Allamand	FRA	24.87
3. Nelson Carmichael	USA	24.82
4. Eric Berthon	FRA	24.79
5. John Smart	CAN	24.15
6. Jörgen Pääjärvi	SWE	24.14
7. Jean-Luc Brassard	CAN	23.71
8. Leif Persson	SWE	22.99

Grospiron recorded the fastest time of the final and the second best scores for turns and air to earn a popular hometown victory. His fans broke down the security fence lining the course to embrace the gregarious champion and hoist him on their shoulders. When asked if he followed a special diet while training, the 22-year-old Grospiron replied, "Yes. One week red wine and the next week white wine."

WOMEN

AERIALS

This event will be held for the first time in 1994.

MOGULS

1924-1988 not held

1992 Albertville-Tignes C: 24, N: 11, D: 2.13.

		PTS.
1. Donna Weinbrecht	USA	23.69
2. Yelizaveta Kozhevnikova	SOV	23.50
3. Stine Lise Hattestad	NOR	23.04
4. Tatjana Mittermayer	GER	22.33
5. Birgit Stein	GER	21.44
6. Liz McIntyre	USA	21.24
7. Silvia Marciandi	ITA	19.66
8. Raphaelle Monod	FRA	15.57

Skiing in a snowstorm to the accompaniment of "Rock 'n' Roll High School" by the Ramones, heavy favorite Donna Weinbrecht completed a conservative but clean run and waited nervously at the bottom of the course for the final competitor, local favorite Raphaelle Monod. Monod began strong but lost control two-thirds of the way down and skidded home in last place.

NORDIC SKIING

MEN

10 Kilometers (Classical)
Combined Pursuit
30 Kilometers (Classical)
50 Kilometers (Freestyle)
4 × 10-Kilometer Relay
Ski Jump, Normal Hill, Individual

Ski Jump, Large Hill, Individual
Ski Jump, Large Hill, Team
Nordic Combined, Individual
Nordic Combined, Team
Discontinued Event

Cross-country, or *langlauf,* races are run against the clock with the skiers leaving the starting line at 30-second intervals. The only exceptions are the relays, in which the first racers for each team start together, and the second half of the combined pursuit events.

Two skiing techniques are used in nordic events. The "classical" requires a diagonal stride; the "freestyle" has no restrictions and employs the faster "skating" style. The choice of skis and ski wax is extremely important and based on the course profile and daily weather conditions. The leading nordic nations employ computers to help decide the ideal skis and wax for each race. Skis may not be switched once a race has begun except in a relay, where one broken or damaged ski may be changed. Skiers are allowed to be handed new wax or other accessories on the course, but they must apply them without aid. If a skier is about to be passed, he or she must give way as soon as the passing skier calls out "Track!"

MEN

Since the Winter Olympics began in 1924, 55 of the 56 gold medals awarded in men's cross-country skiing have been won by only four nations: Sweden (18), Norway (16, including all five in 1992), the U.S.S.R. (11), and Finland (10). The Scandinavians and Soviets have also won 154 of 168 total medals. Of the 14 remaining medals, seven have been won by Italy.

10 KILOMETERS (CLASSICAL)

1924-1988 not held

1992 Albertville-Les Saisies C: 110, N: 39, D: 2.13.

1.	Vegard Ulvang	NOR	27:36.0
2.	Marco Albarello	ITA	27:55.2
3.	Christer Majbäck	SWE	27:56.4
4.	Björn Dahlie	NOR	28:01.6
5.	Niklas Jonsson	SWE	28:03.1
6.	Harri Kirvesniemi	FIN	28:23.3
7.	Giorgio Vanzetta	ITA	28:26.9
8.	Alois Stadlober	AUT	28:27.5

Ulvang won the second of his three gold medals, but not without difficulty. Heavy snow began falling shortly before the race and continued throughout. Ulvang picked out his skis literally at the last minute and, for the first time in his career, he chose to ski without wax. In doing so he followed the advice not of his coaches, but of a Danish competitor, Ebbe Hartz. Shortly after the five-kilometer mark, Ulvang fell and broke the handle of his ski pole. Five hundred meters later, a nonracing teammate handed him a slightly shorter replacement. Fourth midway in the race, Ulvang finished strongly and posted a clear victory.

Silver medalist Albarello also had problems. Unable to avoid a fallen Austrian skier, he too fell and lost his goggles four kilometers from the finish. Last-place finisher Faissal Cherradi of Morocco completed the course in 1:11:07.4. Seventy-three of the other 109 competitors finished the race in less time than it took Cherradi to reach the halfway point.

COMBINED PURSUIT

On the first day of the combined pursuit event, skiers race 10 kilometers, using the classical technique. On the second day, setting out from a staggered start based on the results of the previous day, they race another 15 kilometers freestyle.

1924-1988 not held

1992 Albertville-Les Saisies C: 102, N: 39, D: 2.15.

			10KM CLASSICAL		15KM FREESTYLE		TOTAL
1.	Björn Dahlie	NOR	28:01	(4)	37:36.9	(1)	1:05:37.9
2.	Vegard Ulvang	NOR	27:36	(1)	38:55.3	(13)	1:06:31.3
3.	Giorgio Vanzetta	ITA	28:26	(7)	38:06.2	(3)	1:06:32.2
4.	Marco Albarello	ITA	27:55	(2)	38:38.3	(8)	1:06:33.3
5.	N. Torgny Mogren	SWE	28:37	(9)	38:00.4	(2)	1:06:37.4
6.	Christer Majbäck	SWE	27:56	(3)	39:21.0	(23)	1:07:17.0
7.	Silvio Fauner	ITA	28:53	(10)	38:41.9	(9)	1:07:34.9
8.	Vladimir Smirnov	SOV	29:13	(13)	38:22.8	(5)	1:07:35.8

Dahlie, the defending world champion of the 15-kilometer freestyle, spotted Ulvang 25 seconds at the start of the second day's race, passed him after four kilometers, and pulled away to an easy victory. Ulvang was also passed by Albarello at the eight-kilometer mark, but regained second place two kilometers later and fought off the two Italians in an exciting finish. The pursuit format proved a success with the spectators, but was less popular with the skiers themselves. The three medalists took advantage of the postrace press conference to criticize the concept and the rules. Their main complaint concerned the requirement that the leaders ski first. In normal cross-country races, the leading skiers get to choose if they ski early or late. Because the freestyle was held during a snowfall, Dahlie, Ulvang, and others felt they should have been given the option of starting later, after the course had been packed down, rather than early, according to the order of their finish in the classical race. Odd Martinsen, president of the Nordic Skiing commission of the International Ski Federation, and himself an Olympic gold medalist from Norway, rose to point out that the rules did not permit such a change and that rules are rules. In fact, race officials did bend the rules in one instance. According to the rule book, each skier's starting time in the 15-kilometer freestyle is determined by how far behind the leader he was in the 10-kilometer classical. This meant that Faissal Cherradi of Morocco should have started 43 minutes and 31 seconds after Vegard Ulvang. Because a women's race was scheduled immediately after the men's race, Cherradi was allowed to take off only 20 minutes after Ulvang. As it was, he crossed the finish line 52 minutes after the next-to-last competitor, his teammate Mohamed Oubahim.

30 KILOMETERS (CLASSICAL)

1924–1952 not held

1956 Cortina C: 54, N: 18, D: 1.27.

1.	Veikko Hakulinen	FIN	1:44:06.0
2.	Sixten Jernberg	SWE	1:44:30.0
3.	Pavel Kolchin	SOV	1:45:45.0
4.	Anatoly Shelyukin	SOV	1:45:46.0
5.	Vladimir Kuzin	SOV	1:46:09.0
6.	Fedor Terentyev	SOV	1:46:43.0
7.	Per-Erik Larsson	SWE	1:46:51.0
8.	Lennart Larsson	SWE	1:46:56.0

1960 Squaw Valley C: 48, N: 17, D: 2:19.

1.	Sixten Jernberg	SWE	1:51:03.9
2.	Rolf Rämgård	SWE	1:51:16.9
3.	Nikolai Anikin	SOV	1:52:28.2
4.	Gennady Vaganov	SOV	1:52:49.2
5.	Lennart Larsson	SWE	1:53:53.2
6.	Veikko Hakulinen	FIN	1:54:02.0
7.	Toimo Alatalo	FIN	1:54:06.5
8.	Aleksei Kuznyetsov	SOV	1:54:23.9

1964 Innsbruck-Seefeld C: 69, N: 22, D: 1.30.

1.	Eero Mäntyranta	FIN	1:30:50.7
2.	Harald Grönningen	NOR	1:32:02.3
3.	Igor Voronchikin	SOV	1:32:15.8
4.	Janne Stefansson	SWE	1:32:34.8
5.	Sixten Jernberg	SOV	1:32:39.6
6.	Kalevi Laurila	FIN	1:32:41.4
7.	Assar Rönnlund	SWE	1:32:43.6
8.	Einar Östby	NOR	1:32:54.6

1968 Grenoble-Autrans C: 66, N: 22, D: 2.6.

1.	Franco Nones	ITA	1:35:39.2
2.	Odd Martinsen	NOR	1:36:28.9
3.	Eero Mäntyranta	FIN	1:36:55.3
4.	Vladimir Voronkov	SOV	1:37:10.8
5.	Giulio De Florian	ITA	1:37:12.9
6.	Kalevi Laurila	FIN	1:37:29.8
7.	Kalevi Oikarainen	FIN	1:37:34.4
8.	Gunnar Larsson	SWE	1:37:48.1

Of the 56 men's cross-country events that have been held in the Olympics, 55 of them have been won by Sweden, Norway, the U.S.S.R., and Finland. The only gold medalist from a non-nordic nation has been Franco Nones, a 27-year-old customs officer from the village of Ziano di Fiemme in the Dolomite Mountains. It is true that Nones was trained in northern Sweden by a Swedish coach, but his victory was nonetheless a major surprise, particularly coming as it did in the first event of the 1968 Winter Games.

1972 Sapporo-Makomanal C: 59, N: 19, D: 2.4.

1.	Vyacheslav Vedenine	SOV	1:36:31.15
2.	Pål Tyldum	NOR	1:37:25.30
3.	Johs Harviken	NOR	1:37:32.44
4.	Gunnar Larsson	SWE	1:37:33.72
5.	Walter Demel	GER	1:37:45.33
6.	Fedor Simashev	SOV	1:38:22.50
7.	Alois Kälin	SWI	1:38:40.72
8.	Gert-Dietmar Klause	GDR	1:39:15.54

The 5-foot 4¼-inch Vedenine was the first Soviet skier to win an individual Olympic gold medal.

1976 Innsbruck-Seefeld C: 69, N: 21, D: 2.5.

1.	Sergei Saveliev	SOV	1:30:29.38
2.	William Koch	USA	1:30:57.84
3.	Ivan Garanin	SOV	1:31:09.29
4.	Juha Mieto	FIN	1:31:20.39
5.	Nikolai Bazhukov	SOV	1:31:33.14
6.	Gert-Dietmar Klause	GDR	1:32:00.91
7.	Albert Giger	SWI	1:32:17.71
8.	Arto Koivisto	FIN	1:32:23.11

Not a single American reporter was present to see Bill Koch of Guilford, Vermont, become the only American ever to have won an Olympic nordic skiing medal. When they finally caught up with him, Koch responded to his sudden celebrity in a typically Vermont manner. When a reporter asked, "Have you lived in Vermont all your life?" Koch replied, "Not yet." In 1982 Koch revolutionized cross-country skiing by introducing the skating technique to Olympic distances. The technique had previously been used only in marathon races. Skating was banned in 1983. Four years later, however, separate skating or "freestyle" events were included in the world championships and then at the 1988 Olympics. In 1982, Koch also pioneered the technique of "going hairies," in which the ski bottom is scuffed rather than waxed.

1980 Lake Placid C: 57, N: 20, D: 2.14.

1.	Nikolai Zimyatov	SOV	1:27:02.80
2.	Vassily Rochev	SOV	1:27:34.22
3.	Ivan Lebanov	BUL	1:28:03.87
4.	Thomas Wassberg	SWE	1:28:40.35
5.	Jósef Luszczek	POL	1:29:03.64
6.	Matti Pitkänen	FIN	1:29:35.03
7.	Juha Mieto	FIN	1:29:45.08
8.	Ove Aunli	NOR	1:29:54.02

Zimyatov won the first of his three gold medals at Lake Placid. Lebanov is the only Bulgarian to win a medal in the Winter Olympics.

1984 Sarajevo C: 72, N: 26, D: 2.10.

1.	Nikolai Zimyatov	SOV	1:28:56.3
2.	Aleksandr Zavialov	SOV	1:29:23.3
3.	Gunde Svan	SWE	1:29:35.7
4.	Vladimir Sakhnov	SOV	1:30:30.4
5.	Aki Karvonen	FIN	1:30:59.7
6.	Lars-Erik Eriksen	NOR	1:31:24.8
7.	Harri Kirvesniemi	FIN	1:31:37.4
8.	Juha Mieto	FIN	1:31:48.3

Soviet army captain Nikolai Zimyatov struggled through blizzard conditions to win his fourth Olympic gold medal.

1988 Calgary-Canmore C: 90, N: 32, D: 2.15.

1.	Aleksei Prokurorov	SOV	1:24:26.3
2.	Vladimir Smirnov	SOV	1:24:35.1
3.	Vegard Ulvang	NOR	1:25:11.6
4.	Mikhail Devyatyarov	SOV	1:25:31.3
5.	Giorgio Vanzetta	ITA	1:25:37.2
6.	Pål Gunnar Mikkelsplass	NOR	1:25:44.6
7.	Gianfranco Polvara	ITA	1:26:02.7
8.	Marco Albarello	ITA	1:26:09.1

1992 Albertville-Les Saisies C: 87, N: 34, D: 2.10.

1.	Vegard Ulvang	NOR	1:22:27.8
2.	Björn Dahlie	NOR	1:23:14.0
3.	Terje Langli	NOR	1:23:42.5
4.	Marco Albarello	ITA	1:23:55.7
5.	Erling Jevne	NOR	1:24:07.7
6.	Christer Majbäck	SWE	1:24:12.1
7.	Niklas Jonsson	SWE	1:25:17.6
8.	Jyrki Ponsiluoma	SWE	1:25:24.4

Ulvang earned the first of his three gold medals. He was the first Norwegian man to win an Olympic cross-country race in 16 years. The Norwegians broke their losing streak in a big way, winning all five events at the 1992 Olympics. In the 30-kilometer race, the first of the Albertville Games, the Norwegian skiers achieved the first sweep of a men's cross-country race since 1948. Ulvang came from Kirkenes, and iron-mining town 300 miles north of the Arctic Circle, near the Russian border. In addition to his competitive exploits, Ulvang was something of an adventurer. In the year preceding the Olympics, he climbed Mt. Denali (McKinley) in Alaska and spent 15 days skiing across Greenland in the footsteps of explorer Fridtjof Nansen.

50 KILOMETERS (FREESTYLE)

1924 Chamonix C: 33, N: 11, D: 1.30.

1.	Thorleif Haug	NOR	3:44:32.0
2.	Thoralf Strömstad	NOR	3:46:23.0
3.	Johan Gröttumsbråten	NOR	3:47:46.0
4.	Jon Maardalen	NOR	3:49:48.0
5.	Torkel Persson	SWE	4:05:59.0
6.	Ernst Alm	SWE	4:06:31.0
7.	Matti Raivio	FIN	4:06:50.0
8.	Oscar Lindberg	SWE	4:07:44.0

1928 St. Moritz C: 41, N: 11, D: 2.14.

1. Per Erik Hedlund	SWE	4:52:03.0
2. Gustaf Jonsson	SWE	5:05:30.0
3. Volger Andersson	SWE	5:05:46.0
4. Olav Kjelbotn	NOR	5:14:22.0
5. Ole Hegge	NOR	5:17:58.0
6. Tauno Lappalainen	FIN	5:18:33.0
7. Anders Ström	SWE	5:21:54.0
8. Johan Stöa	NOR	5:25:30.0

This race was accompanied by freakish weather. At the beginning of the race the temperature was near zero; however, by the end it had risen to 77° Fahrenheit (25° Centigrade). Hedlund's phenomenal margin of victory is unequaled in Olympic history.

1932 Lake Placid C: 32, N: 9, D: 2.13.

1. Veli Saarinen	FIN	4:28:00.0
2. Väinö Likkanen	FIN	4:28:20.0
3. Arne Rustadstuen	NOR	4:31:53.0
4. Ole Hegge	NOR	4:32:04.0
5. Sigurd Vestad	NOR	4:32:40.0
6. Sven Utterström	SWE	4:33:25.0
7. Tauno Lappalainen	FIN	4:45:02.0
8. Kari Lindberg	SWE	4:47:22.0

The 1932 race was held in a raging blizzard. The start was delayed three hours while contestants and officials argued about the course.

1936 Garmisch-Partenkirchen C: 36, N: 11, D: 2.15.

1. Elis Wiklund	SWE	3:30:11.0
2. Axel Wikström	SWE	3:33:20.0
3. Nils-Joel Englund	SWE	3:34:10.0
4. Hjalmar Bergström	SWE	3:35:50.0
5. Klaes Karppinen	FIN	3:39:33.0
6. Arne Tuft	NOR	3:41:18.0
7. Frans Heikkinen	FIN	3:42:44.0
8. Pekka Niemi	FIN	3:44:14.0

1948 St. Moritz C: 28, N: 9, D: 2.6.

1. Nils Karlsson	SWE	3:47:48.0
2. Harald Eriksson	SWE	3:52:20.0
3. Benjamin Vanninen	FIN	3:57:28.0
4. Pekka Vanninen	FIN	3:57:58.0
5. Anders Törnkvist	SWE	3:58:20.0
6. Edi Schild	SWI	4:05:37.0
7. Pekka Kuvaja	FIN	4:10:02.0
8. Jaroslav Cardal	CZE	4:14:34.0

1952 Oslo C: 36, N: 13, D: 2.20.

1. Veikko Hakulinen	FIN	3:33:33.0
2. Eero Kolehmainen	FIN	3:38:11.0
3. Magnar Estenstad	NOR	3:38:28.0
4. Olav Ökern	NOR	3:38:45.0
5. Kalevi Mononen	FIN	3:39:21.0
6. Nils Karlsson	SWE	3:39:30.0
7. Edvin Landsem	NOR	3:40:43.0
8. Harald Maartmann	NOR	3:43:43.0

This was the first of woodchopper Veikko Hakulinen's seven Olympic medals.

1956 Cortina C: 33, N: 13, D: 2.2.

1.	Sixten Jernberg	SWE	2:50:27.0
2.	Veikko Hakulinen	FIN	2:51:45.0
3.	Fedor Terentyev	SOV	2:53:32.0
4.	Eero Kolehmainen	FIN	2:56:17.0
5.	Anatoly Shelyukin	SOV	2:56:40.0
6.	Pavel Kolchin	SOV	2:58:00.0
7.	Victor Baranov	SOV	3:03:55.0
8.	Antti Sivonen	FIN	3:04:16.0

1960 Squaw Valley C: 31, N: 10, D: 2.27.

1.	Kalevi Hämäläinen	FIN	2:59:06.3
2.	Veikko Hakulinen	FIN	2:59:26.7
3.	Rolf Rämgård	SWE	3:02:46.7
4.	Lennart Larsson	SWE	3:03:27.9
5.	Sixten Jernberg	SWE	3:05:18.0
6.	Pentti Pelkonen	FIN	3:05:24.5
7.	Gennady Vaganov	SOV	3:05:27.6
8.	Veikko Rasanen	FIN	3:06:04.4

Finland, Norway, Sweden, and the U.S.S.R. took the first 15 places.

1964 Innsbruck-Seefeld C: 41, N: 14, D: 2.5.

1.	Sixten Jernberg	SWE	2:43:52.6
2.	Assar Rönnlund	SWE	2:44:58.2
3.	Arto Tiainen	FIN	2:45:30.4
4.	Janne Stefansson	SWE	2:45:36.6
5.	Sverre Steinsheim	NOR	2:45:47.2
6.	Harald Grönningen	NOR	2:47:03.6
7.	Einar Östby	NOR	2:47:20.6
8.	Ole Ellefsaeter	NOR	2:47:45.8

In 1956 Sixten Jernberg had predicted that whoever started the course last in the 50-kilometer race would win. Instead Jernberg, who started next to last, was the winner. At Innsbruck in 1964 he was the next to last starter again, and again he finished in first place. Three days later he earned another gold medal by skiing the second leg on Sweden's relay team. He closed out his Olympic career two days after his 35th birthday, having won nine medals: four gold, three silver, and two bronze.

1968 Grenoble-Autrans C: 51, N: 17, D: 2.15.

1.	Ole Ellefsaeter	NOR	2:28:45.8
2.	Vyacheslav Vedenine	SOV	2:29:02.5
3.	Josef Haas	SWI	2:29:14.8
4.	Pål Tyldum	NOR	2:29:26.7
5.	Melcher Risberg	SWE	2:29:37.0
6.	Gunnar Larsson	SWE	2:29:37.2
7.	Jan Halvarsson	SWE	2:30:05.9
8.	Reidar Hjermstad	NOR	2:31:01.8

Ole Ellefsaeter, a forestry technician and pop singer, celebrated his 29th birthday by winning the 50-kilometer gold medal.

1972 Sapporo-Makomanai C: 40, N: 13, D: 2.10.

1.	Pål Tyldum	NOR	2:43:14.75
2.	Magne Myrmo	NOR	2:43:29.45
3.	Vyacheslav Vedenine	SOV	2:44:00.19
4.	Reidar Hjermstad	NOR	2:44:14.51
5.	Walter Demel	GER	2:44:32.67
6.	Werner Geeser	SWI	2:44:34.13
7.	Lars-Arne Bölling	SWE	2:45:06.80
8.	Fedor Simachev	SOV	2:45:08.93

Tyldum, the next to last starter, was placed only 18th after 15 kilometers, 78½ seconds behind the leader, Werner Geeser. By the 25-kilometer mark he had moved up to tenth place, but he was now 103½ seconds slower than Geeser. At 40 kilometers Geeser was still in first, but fading, while Tyldum had moved up to third, less than 26 seconds off Geeser's pace. While Geeser and Simachev tired dramatically in the last 10 kilometers, Tyldum plowed on to victory.

1976 Innsbruck-Seefeld C: 59, N: 15, D: 2.14.

1.	Ivar Formo	NOR	2:37:30.05
2.	Gert-Dietmar Klause	GDR	2:38:13.21
3.	Benny Södergren	SWE	2:39:39.21
4.	Ivan Garanin	SOV	2:40:38.94
5.	Gerhard Grimmer	GDR	2:41:15.46
6.	Per Knut Aaland	NOR	2:41:18.06
7.	Pål Tyldum	NOR	2:42:21.86
8.	Tommy Limby	SWE	2:42:43.58

1980 Lake Placid C: 51, N: 14, D: 2.23.

1.	Nikolai Zimyatov	SOV	2:27:24.60
2.	Juha Mieto	FIN	2:30:20.52
3.	Alexandr Zavyalov	SOV	2:30:51.52
4.	Lars Erik Eriksen	NOR	2:30:53.00
5.	Sergei Saveliev	SOV	2:31:15.82
6.	Yevgeny Beliaev	SOV	2:31:21.19
7.	Oddvar Brå	NOR	2:31:46.83
8.	Sven-Åke Lundbäck	SWE	2:31:59.65

Zimyatov won this third gold medal in ten days, having skied a total of 105 kilometers.

1984 Sarajevo C: 54, N: 21, D: 2.19.

1.	Thomas Wassberg	SWE	2:15:55.8
2.	Gunde Svan	SWE	2:16:00.7
3.	Aki Karvonen	FIN	2:17:04.7
4.	Harri Kirvesniemi	FIN	2:18:34.1
5.	Jan Lindvall	NOR	2:19:27.1
6.	Andreas Grünfelder	SWI	2:19:46.2
7.	Aleksandr Zavyalov	SOV	2:20:27.6
8.	Vladimir Sakhnov	SOV	2:20:53.7

1988 Calgary-Canmore C: 70, N: 23, D: 2.27.

1.	Gunde Svan	SWE	2:04:30.9
2.	Maurilio De Zolt	ITA	2:05:36.4
3.	Andreas Grünenfelder	SWI	2:06:01.9
4.	Vegard Ulvang	NOR	2:06:32.3

5.	Holger Bauroth	GDR	2:07:02.4
6.	Jan Ottosson	SWE	2:07:34.8
7.	Kari Ristanen	FIN	2:08:08.1
8.	Uwe Bellmann	GDR	2:08:18.6

The 69th of 70 starters, Gunde Svan earned his second gold medal of the Calgary Games to match the two he won in Sarajevo in 1984.

Roberto Alvarez of Mexico, who had never skied more than 20 kilometers, was the last of the 61 finishers in a time of 3:22:25.1—almost 52 minutes slower than the man in sixtieth place, Battulga Dambajamtsyn of Mongolia. Alvarez was so far behind that race officials became worried that he had gotten lost and sent out a delegation to find him. In 1992, Alvarez was again the last of the finishers, this time in 3:09:04.7, only 31½ minutes behind the rest of the field.

1992 Albertville-Les Saisies C: 73, N: 29, D: 2.22.

1.	Björn Dahlie	NOR	2:03:41.5
2.	Maurilio De Zolt	ITA	2:04:39.1
3.	Giorgio Vanzetta	ITA	2:06:42.1
4.	Aleksei Prokurorov	SOV	2:07:06.1
5.	Hervé Balland	FRA	2:07:17.7
6.	Radim Nyc	CZE	2:07:41.5
7.	Johann Mühlegg	GER	2:07:45.2
8.	Pavel Benc	CZE	2:08:13.6

Dahlie led from the start and closed out the Albertville Olympics with three gold medals and one silver. De Zolt, at age 41, won his second straight silver medal.

4 × 10-KILOMETER RELAY

In 1988 this was a freestyle event; however, since 1992 two skiers on each team use the classical technique and two use the skating technique.

1924–1932 not held

1936 Garmisch-Partenkirchen T: 16, N: 16, D: 2.10.

1.	FIN	(Sulo Nurmela, Klaes Karppinen, Matti Lähde, Kalle Jalkanen)	2:41:33.0
2.	NOR	(Oddbjörn Hagen, Olaf Hoffsbakken, Sverre Brodahl, Bjarne Iversen)	2:41:39.0
3.	SWE	(John Berger, Erik Larsson, Arthur Häggblad, Martin Matsbo)	2:43:03.0
4.	ITA	(Giulio Gerardi, Severino Menardi, Vincenzo Demetz, Giovanni Kasebacher)	2:50:05.0
5.	CZE	(Cyril Musil, Gustav Berauer, Lukas Mihalak, František Simunek)	2:51:56.0
6.	GER	(Friedel Däuber, Willi Bogner, Herbert Leupold, Anton Zeller)	2:54:54.0
7.	POL	(Michal Górski, Marian Woyna-Orlewicz, Stanislaw Karpiel, Bronislaw Czech)	2:58:50.0
8.	AUT	(Alfred Robner, Harald Bosio, Erich Gallwitz, Hans Baumann)	3:02:48.0

Kalle Jalkanen, the last Finnish skier, staged a spectacular come-from-behind victory. Trailing Bjarne Iversen of Norway by 82 seconds when he took over the baton, he caught him as they entered the ski stadium and won by only 20 yards.

1948 St. Moritz T: 11, N: 11, D: 2.3.

1.	SWE	(Nils Östensson, Nils Täpp, Gunnar Eriksson, Martin Lundström)	2:32:08.0
2.	FIN	(Lauri Silvennoinen, Teuvo Laukkanen, Sauli Rytky, August Kiuru)	2:41:06.0
3.	NOR	(Erling Evensen, Olav Ökern, Reidar Nyborg, Olav Hagen)	2:44:33.0

4. AUT	(Josl Gstrein, Josef Deutschmann, Engelbert Hundertpfund, Karl Rafreider)	2:47:18.0
5. SWI	(Niklaus Stump, Robert Zurbriggen, Max Müller, Edi Schild)	2:48:07.0
6. ITA	(Vincenzo Perruchon, Silvio Confortola, Rizzieri Rodighiero, Severino Compagnoni)	2:51:00.0
7. FRA	(René Jeandel, Gerard Perrier, Marius Mora, Benoit Carrara)	2:51:53.0
8. CZE	(Stefan Kovalcik, František Balvin, Jaroslav Zejicek, Jaroslav Cardal)	2:54:56.0

1952 Oslo T: 13, N: 13, D: 2.23.

1. FIN	(Heikki Hasu, Paavo Lonkila, Urpo Korhonen, Tapio Mäkelä)	2:20:16.0
2. NOR	(Magnar Estenstad, Mikal Kirkholt, Martin Stokken, Hallgeir Brenden)	2.23:13.0
3. SWE	(Nils Täpp, Sigurd Andersson, Enar Josefsson, Martin Lundström)	2:24:13.0
4. FRA	(Gerard Perrier, Benoit Carrara, Jean Mermet, René Mandrillon)	2:31:11.0
5. AUT	(Hans Eder, Friedrich Krischan, Karl Rafreider, Josef Schneeberger)	2:34:36.0
6. ITA	(Arrigo Delladio, Nino Anderlini, Frederico de Florian, Vincenzo Perruchon)	2:35:33.0
7. GER	(Hubert Egger, Albert Mohr, Heinz Hauser, Rudi Kopp)	2:36:37.0
8. CZE	(Vladimir Simunek, Stefan Kovalcik, Vlastimil Melich, Jaroslav Cardal)	2:37:12.0

1956 Cortina T: 14, N: 14, D: 2.4.

1. SOV	(Fedor Terentyev, Pavel Kolchin, Nikolai Anikin, Vladimir Kuzin)	2:15:30.0
2. FIN	(August Kiuru, Jormo Kortalainen, Arvo Viitanen, Veikko Hakulinen)	2:16:31.0
3. SWE	(Lennart Larsson, Gunnar Samuelsson, Per-Erik Larsson, Sixten Jernberg)	2:17:42.0
4. NOR	(Håkon Brusveen, Per Olsen, Marten Stokken, Hallgeir Brenden)	2:21:16.0
5. ITA	(Pompeo Fattor, Ottavio Compagnoni, Innocenzo Chatrian, Frederico De Florian)	2:23:28.0
6. FRA	(Victor Arbez, René Mandrillon, Benoit Carrara, Jean Mermet)	2:24:06.0
7. SWI	(Werner Zwingli, Victor Kronig, Fritz Kocher, Marcel Huguenin)	2:24:30.0
8. CZE	(Emil Okuliar, Vlastimil Melich, Josef Prokes, Ilja Matous)	2:24:54.0

The first two Soviet skiers, Terentyev and Kolchin, built up an insurmountable lead of two and three-quarter minutes.

1960 Squaw Valley T: 11, N: 11, D: 2.25.

1. FIN	(Toimi Alatalo, Eero Mäntyranta, Väinö Huhtala, Veikko Hakulinen)	2:18:45.6
2. NOR	(Harald Grönningen, Hallgeir Brenden, Einar Östby, Håkon Brusveen)	2:18:46.4
3. SOV	(Anatoly Shelyukin, Gennady Vaganov, Aleksei Kuznetsov, Nikolai Anikin)	2:21:21.6
4. SWE	(Lars Olsson, Janne Stefansson, Lennart Larsson, Sixten Jernberg)	2:21:31.8
5. ITA	(Giulio De Florian, Giuseppe Steiner, Pompeo Fattor, Marcello De Dorigo)	2:22:32.5
6. POL	(Andrzej Mateja, Józef Rysula, Józef Gut-Misiaga, Kazimierz Zelek)	2:26:25.3
7. FRA	(Victor Arbez, René Mandrillon, Benoit Carrara, Jean Mermet)	2:26:30.8
8. SWI	(Fritz Kocher, Marcel Huguenin, Lorenz Possa, Alphonse Baume)	2:29:36.8

Until the introduction of the pursuit race in 1992, the relay was the only skiing event in which the participants actually raced against each other. It was also the only event that had the potential for a truly exciting finish. Such a finish occurred in 1960. Lars Olsson gave Sweden a seven-second lead at the end of the first leg, but the second Swedish skier, Janne Stefansson, was quickly overtaken by Brenden and Mäntyranta. At the halfway mark, Norway and Finland were tied. Then Norway's Einar Östby pulled away to a 20-second lead. Håkon Brusveen, winner of the 15-kilometer race two days earlier, took over the last leg for Norway, followed by six-time Olympic medalist, 35-year-old Veikko Hakulinen. After eight kilometers

Hakulinen overhauled Brusveen, but the Norwegian pulled back into the lead. With 100 meters to go, Hakulinen began to pass Brusveen again. Edging ahead in the final strides, the great Finnish veteran managed to win by three feet. It was a fitting ending to Hakulinen's marvelous Olympic career, during which he earned three gold medals, each in a different event and each in a different Olympics, as well as three silver medals and one bronze.

1964 Innsbruck-Seefeld T: 15, N: 15, D: 2.8.

1.	SWE	(Karl Åke Asph, Sixten Jernberg, Janne Stefansson, Assar Rönnlund)	2:18:34.6
2.	FIN	(Väinö Huhtala, Arto Tiainen, Kalevi Laurila, Eero Mäntyranta)	2:18:42.4
3.	SOV	(Ivan Utrobin, Gennady Vaganov, Igor Voronchikin, Pavel Kolchin)	2:18:46.9
4.	NOR	(Magnar Lundemo, Erling Steineidet, Einar Östby, Harald Grönningen)	2:19:11.9
5.	ITA	(Giuseppe Steiner, Marcello De Dorigo, Giulio De Florian, Franco Nones)	2:21:16.8
6.	FRA	(Victor Arbez, Felix Mathieu, Roger Pires, Paul Romand)	2:26:31.4
7.	GDR/ GER	(Heinz Seidel, Helmut Weidlich, Enno Röder, Walter Demel)	2:26:34.4
8.	POL	(Józef Gut-Misiaga, Tadeusz Jankowski, Edward Budny, Józef Rysula)	2:27:27.0

Another thrilling finish, in which Väinö Huhtala gave Finland a 5.9-second lead after the first lap with the U.S.S.R. in second, Norway third, and Sweden fourth. By the halfway mark, Vaganov of the Soviet Union had moved into an 11.6-second lead over second-place Norway, with Italy in third, followed by Sweden and Finland. Pavel Kolchin took over the last leg for the Soviet Union, followed 13.4 seconds later by Grönningen of Norway, 31.5 seconds later by Assar Rönnlund of Sweden, and 32.3 seconds later by Eero Mäntyranta. Grönningen passed Kolchin to take the lead, but he exhausted himself by his effort and was passed shortly afterward by Mäntyranta, Rönnlund, and Kolchin. A few hundred meters short of the finish line Rönnlund summoned an extra reserve of energy, pushed ahead of Mäntyranta, and won by 7.8 seconds.

1968 Grenoble-Autrans T: 15, N: 15, D: 2.14.

1.	NOR	(Odd Martinsen, Pål Tyldum, Harald Grönningen, Ole Ellefsaeter)	2:08:33.5
2.	SWE	(Jan Halvarsson, Bjarne Andersson, Gunnar Larsson, Assar Rönnlund)	2:10:13.2
3.	FIN	(Kalevi Oikarainen, Hannu Taipale, Kalevi Laurila, Eero Mäntyranta)	2:10:56.7
4.	SOV	(Vladimir Voronkov, Anatoly Akentiev, Valery Tarakanov, Vyacheslav Vedenine)	2:10:57.2
5.	SWI	(Konrad Hischier, Josef Haas, Florian Koch, Alois Kälin)	2:15:32.4
6.	ITA	(Giulio De Florian, Franco Nones, Palmiro Serafini, Aldo Stella)	2:16:32.2
7.	GDR	(Gerhard Grimmer, Axel Lesser, Peter Thiel, Gert-Dietmar Klause)	2:19:22.8
8.	GER	(Helmut Gerlach, Walter Demel, Herbert Steinbeisser, Karl Buhl)	2:19:37.6

Eero Mäntyranta made up over 26 seconds on the final leg to nip Vedenine at the finish line for the bronze medal. This gave Mäntyranta an Olympic medal total of three gold, two silver, and two bronze.

1972 Sapporo-Makomanai T: 14, N: 14, D: 2.13.

1.	SOV	(Vladimir Voronkov, Yuri Skobov, Fedor Simachev, Vyacheslav Vedenine)	2:04:47.94
2.	NOR	(Oddvar Brå, Pål Tyldum, Ivar Formo, Johs Harviken)	2:04:57.06
3.	SWI	(Alfred Kälin, Albert Giger, Alois Kälin, Eduard Hauser)	2:07:00.06
4.	SWE	(Thomas Magnusson, Lars-Göran Åslund, Gunnar Larsson, Sven-Åke Lundbäck)	2:07:03.60
5.	FIN	(Hannu Taipale, Juha Mieto, Juhani Repo, Osmo Karjalainen)	2:07:50.19
6.	GDR	(Gerd Hessler, Axel Lesser, Gerhard Grimmer, Gert-Dietmar Klause)	2:10:03.73

7.	GER	(Franz Betz, Urban Hettich, Hartmut Dopp, Walter Demel)	2:10:42.85
8.	CZE	(Stanislav Henych, Jan Fajstavr, Jan Michalko, Jan Ilavsky)	2:11:27.55

Vedenine began the final leg 61½ seconds behind Johs Harviken, but he overtook the Norwegian one kilometer from the finish and won by over nine seconds.

1976 Innsbruck-Seefeld T: 16, N: 16, D: 2.12.

1.	FIN	(Matti Pitkänen, Juha Mieto, Pertti Teurajärvi, Arto Koivisto)	2:07:59.72
2.	NOR	(Pål Tyldum, Einar Sagstuen, Ivar Formo, Odd Martinsen)	2:09:58.36
3.	SOV	(Yevgeny Beliaev, Nikolai Bazhukov, Sergei Saveliev, Ivan Garanin)	2:10:51.46
4.	SWE	(Benny Södergren, Christer Johansson, Thomas Wassberg, Sven-Åke Lundbäck)	2:11:16.88
5.	SWI	(Franz Renggli, Edi Hauser, Heinz Gähler, Alfred Kälin)	2:11:28.53
6.	USA	(Douglas Peterson, Timothy Caldwell, William Koch, Ronny Yaeger)	2:11:41.35
7.	ITA	(Renzo Chiocchetti, Tonio Biondini, Ulrico Kostner, Giulio Capitanio)	2:12:07.12
8.	AUT	(Rudolf Horn, Reinhold Feichter, Werner Vogel, Herbert Wachter)	2:12:22.80

East Germany was in second place when their second skier, Axel Lesser, ran into a spectator, injured his knee, and had to abandon the race.

1980 Lake Placid T: 10, N: 10, D: 2.20.

1.	SOV	(Vassily Rochev, Nikolai Bazhukov, Yevgeny Beliaev, Nikolai Zimyatov)	1:57:03.46
2.	NOR	(Lars Erik Eriksen, Per Knut Aaland, Ove Aunli, Oddvar Brå)	1:58:45.77
3.	FIN	(Harri Kirvesniemi, Pertti Teurajärvi, Matti Pitkänen, Juha Mieto)	2:00:00.18
4.	GER	(Peter Zipfel, Wolfgang Müller, Dieter Notz, Jochen Behle)	2:00:27.74
5.	SWE	(Sven-Åke Lundbäck, Thomas Eriksson, Benny Kohlberg, Thomas Wassberg)	2:00:42.71
6.	ITA	(Maurilio De Zolt, Benedetto Carrara, Giulio Capitanio, Giorgio Vanzetta)	2:01:09.93
7.	SWI	(Hansüli Kreuzer, Konrad Hallenbarter, Edi Hauser, Gaudenz Ambühl)	2:03:36.57
8.	USA	(William Koch, Timothy Caldwell, James Galanes, Stanley Dunklee)	2:04:12.17

1984 Sarajevo T: 17, N: 17, D: 2.16.

1.	SWE	(Thomas Wassberg, Benny Kohlberg, Jan Ottosson, Gunde Svan)	1:55:06.3
2.	SOV	(Aleksandr Batiuk, Aleksandr Zavyalov, Vladimir Nikitin, Nikolai Zimyatov)	1:55:16.5
3.	FIN	(Kari Ristanen, Juha Mieto, Harri Kirvesniemi, Aki Karvonen)	1:56:31.4
4.	NOR	(Lars-Erik Eriksen, Jan Lindvall, Ove Aunli, Tor Håkon Holte)	1:57:27.6
5.	SWI	(Giachem Guidon, Konrad Hallenbarter, Joos Ambühl, Andreas Grünenfelder)	1:58:06.0
6.	GER	(Jochen Behle, Stefan Dotzler, Franz Schöbel, Peter Zipfel)	1:59:30.2
7.	ITA	(Maurilio De Zolt, Alfred Runggaldier, Giulio Capitanio, Giorgio Vanzetta)	1:59:30.3
8.	USA	(Dan Simoneau, Timothy Caldwell, James Galanes, William Koch)	1:59:52.3

The anchor leg matched 15-kilometer gold medalist Gunde Svan against 30-kilometer gold medalist Nikolai Zimyatov. Zimyatov took off with a lead of a fraction of a second. Svan tracked him the whole way and then, as planned, launched his successful attack one kilometer from the finish.

1988 Calgary-Canmore T: 16, N: 16, D: 2.22.

1.	SWE	(Jan Ottosson, Thomas Wassberg, Gunde Svan, N. Torgny Mogren)	1:43:58.6
2.	SOV	(Vladimir Smirnov, Vladimir Sakhnov, Mikhail Devyatyarov, Aleksei Prokurorov)	1:44:11.3
3.	CZE	(Radim Nyc, Vaclav Korunka, Pavel Benc, Ladislav Švanda)	1:45:22.7

4.	SWI	(Andreas Grünenfelder, Jürg Capol, Giachem Guidon, Jeremias Wigger)	1:46:16.3
5.	ITA	(Silvano Barco, Albert Walder, Giorgio Vanzetta, Maurilio De Zolt)	1:46:16.7
6.	NOR	(Pål Gunnar Mikkelsplass, Oddvar Brå, Vegard Ulvang, Terje Langli)	1:46:48.7
7.	GER	(Walter Kuss, Georg Fischer, Jochen Behle, Herbert Fritzenwenger)	1:48:05.0
8.	FIN	(Jari Laukkanen, Harri Kirvesniemi, Jari Räsänen, Kari Ristanen)	1:48:24.0

The U.S.S.R. and Sweden were virtually even at the halfway point. Midway through the third leg, Gunde Svan pulled away from Mikhail Devyatyarov, who then fell, trying to maintain contact. By the time he passed off to Torgny Mogren, Svan had given Sweden a 27-second lead. Aleksei Prokurorov cut the deficit to 7 seconds with 5 kilometers to go. But he, too, fell, and he was never able to pick up the challenge again.

1992 Albertville-Les Saisies T: 16, N: 16, D: 2.18.

1.	NOR	(Terje Langli, Vegard Ulvang, Kristen Skjeldal, Björn Dahlie)	1:39:26.0
2.	ITA	(Giuseppe Pulié, Marco Albarello, Giorgio Vanzetta, Silvio Fauner)	1:40:52.7
3.	FIN	(Mika Kuusisto, Harri Kirvesniemi, Jari Räsänen, Jari Isometsä)	1:41:22.9
4.	SWE	(Jan Ottosson, Christer Majbäck, Henrik Forsberg, N. Torgny Mogren)	1:41:23.1
5.	SOV	(Andrei Kirillov, Vladimir Smirnov, Mikhail Botvinov, Aleksei Prokurorov)	1:43:03.6
6.	GER	(Holger Bauroth, Jochen Behle, Torald Rein, Johann Mühlegg)	1:43:41.7
7.	CZE	(Radim Nyc, Lubomir Buchta, Pavel Benc, Vaclav Korunka)	1:44:20.0
8.	FRA	(Patrick Remy, Philippe Sanchez, Stéphane Azambre, Hervé Balland)	1:44:51.1

Ottosson gave Sweden the early lead, but Ulvang pulled away during the second leg and Norway won easily. Anchorman Björn Dahlie celebrated by turning around and crossing the finish line backward. Sweden's anchor, Torgny Mogren, skied the second-fastest leg of the day, but Isometsä caught him in the final strides to give Finland the bronze.

SKI JUMP, NORMAL HILL, INDIVIDUAL

The first ski-jumping contest was held in Trysil, Norway, in 1862. Jumps are scored according to two criteria: distance and style. Style points are determined by five judges. The highest and lowest scores are dropped and the points awarded by the remaining three judges are added together. Each contestant takes two jumps. In 1964 the ski jump was split into two events: the small hill, or 70-meter jump, and the big hill, or 90-meter jump. The hills vary in size from Olympics to Olympics and the events are now known as normal hill and large hill.

In 1985, Swedish jumper Jan Boklöv began spreading the tips of his skis into a V shape. Initially he was laughed at and penalized. But when wind tunnel tests proved that the V provided 28 percent more lift than the traditional, parallel style, and when Boklöv won the 1989 World Cup, ski jumpers started changing their style en masse. In 1992, all the individual medal winners used the V style.

1924–1960 not held

1964 Innsbruck-Seefeld C: 53, N: 15, D: 1.31.

			FIRST JUMP (M)	SECOND JUMP (M)	TOTAL PTS.
1.	Veikko Kankkonen	FIN	80.0	79.0	229.9
2.	Toralf Engan	NOR	79.0	79.0	226.3
3.	Targeir Brandtzäg	NOR	79.0	78.0	222.9
4.	Josef Matous	CZE	80.5	77.0	218.2
5.	Dieter Neuendorf	GDR	78.5	77.0	214.7
6.	Helmut Recknagel	GDR	77.0	75.5	210.4
7.	Kurt Elima	SWE	76.0	75.0	208.9
8.	Hans Olav Sörensen	NOR	76.0	74.5	208.6

In 1964 the competitors were allowed to use the best two of three jumps. This rule saved Kankkonen, whose mediocre first jump landed him in 29th place. However his second and third leaps were masterpieces.

1968 Grenoble-Autrans C: 58, N: 18, D: 2.11.

			FIRST JUMP (M)	SECOND JUMP (M)	TOTAL PTS.
1.	Jiři Raška	CZE	79.0	72.5	216.5
2.	Reinhold Bachler	AUT	77.5	76.0	214.2
3.	Baldur Preiml	AUT	80.0	72.5	212.6
4.	Björn Wirkola	NOR	76.5	72.5	212.0
5.	Topi Mattila	FIN	78.0	72.5	211.9
6.	Anatoly Zheglanov	SOV	79.5	74.5	211.5
7.	Dieter Neuendorf	GDR	76.5	73.0	211.3
8.	Vladimir Beloussov	SOV	73.5	73.0	207.5

1972 Sapporo-Miyanomori C: 56, N: 16, D: 2.6.

			FIRST JUMP (M)	SECOND JUMP (M)	TOTAL PTS.
1.	Yukio Kasaya	JPN	84.0	79.0	244.2
2.	Akitsugu Konno	JPN	82.5	79.0	234.8
3.	Seiji Aochi	JPN	83.5	77.5	229.5
4.	Ingolf Mork	NOR	78.0	78.0	225.5
5.	Jiři Raška	CZE	78.5	78.0	224.8
6.	Wojciech Fortuna	POL	82.0	76.5	222.0
7.	Karel Kodejska	CZE	80.0	75.5	220.2
7.	Gari Napalkov	SOV	79.5	76.0	220.2

Before 1972 Japan had won a total of one medal in the Winter Olympics. Consequently, when 28-year-old Yukio Kasaya won three straight meets in Europe one month before the Sapporo Games, Japan's hopes for a gold medal in the first Winter Olympics to be held in Asia were concentrated on Kasaya. The excitement was particularly great because Kasaya was a hometown boy from Japan's northernmost island of Hokkaido, where the games were being held. Kasaya's teammates, Akitsugu Konno and Seiji Aochi, were also from Hokkaido. Scattered among the 100,000 people at the bottom of the jumping hill were old schoolmates of Kasaya's waving the flag of Yoichimachi High School, Kasaya's alma mater. Despite the enormous pressure, Kasaya produced the best jump of each round. While the nation rejoiced over the stunning Japanese sweep, Kasaya, who had made 10,000 jumps since he was 11 years old, reminded the press of his personal motto, "Challenge not your rivals, but yourself."

1976 Innsbruck-Seefeld C: 55, N: 15, D: 2.7.

		FIRST JUMP (M)	SECOND JUMP (M)	TOTAL PTS.
1. Hans-Georg Aschenbach	GDR	84.5	82.0	252.0
2. Jochen Danneberg	GDR	83.5	82.5	246.2
3. Karl Schnabl	AUT	82.5	81.5	242.0
4. Jaroslav Balcar	CZE	81.0	81.5	239.6
5. Ernst von Grüningen	SWI	80.5	80.5	238.7
6. Reinhold Bachler	AUT	80.5	80.5	237.2
7. Anton Innauer	AUT	80.5	81.5	233.5
7. Rudolf Wanner	AUT	79.5	79.5	233.5

Aschenbach later admitted to having taken anabolic steroids for eight years. He described his victory in 1976 as his greatest moment in sports, but also his most anxious. "Those were the worst hours of my life. I had won at the Olympic Winter Games on the small tower. Then the doping control. My God, what I went through. Will they catch you? Or was the timing correct once again? Was everything for nothing? Will you be the one they place the blame on, the idiot that is the butt of laughter for everybody? Nobody can imagine what you go through. You even forget that you have won."

1980 Lake Placid C: 48, N: 16, D: 2.17.

		FIRST JUMP (M)	SECOND JUMP (M)	TOTAL PTS.
1. Anton Innauer	AUT	89.0	90.0	266.3
2. Manfred Deckert	GDR	85.0	88.0	249.2
2. Hirokazu Yagi	JPN	87.0	83.5	249.2
4. Masahiro Akimoto	JPN	83.5	87.5	248.5
5. Pentti Kokkonen	FIN	86.0	83.5	247.6
6. Hubert Neuper	AUT	82.5	88.5	245.5
7. Alfred Groyer	AUT	85.5	83.5	245.3
8. Jouko Törmänen	FIN	83.0	85.5	243.5

Toni Innauer, a 21-year-old vegetarian, used his superb form to win by a huge margin.

1984 Sarajevo C: 58, N: 17, D: 2.12.

		FIRST JUMP (M)	SECOND JUMP (M)	TOTAL PTS.
1. Jens Weissflog	GDR	90.0	87.0	215.2
2. Matti Nykänen	FIN	91.0	84.0	214.0
3. Jari Puikkonen	FIN	81.5	91.5	212.8
4. Stefan Stannarius	GDR	84.0	89.5	211.1
5. Rolf Åge Berg	NOR	86.0	86.5	208.5
6. Andreas Felder	AUT	84.0	87.0	205.6
7. Piotr Fijas	POL	87.0	88.0	204.5
8. Vegard Opaas	NOR	86.0	87.0	203.8

Nineteen-year-old World Cup leader Jens Weissflog overcame his rival Matti Nykänen with a solid, though unspectacular, second jump.

1988 Calgary C: 58, N: 19, D: 2.14.

		FIRST JUMP (M)	SECOND JUMP (M)	TOTAL PTS.
1. Matti Nykänen	FIN	89.5	89.5	229.1
2. Pavel Ploc	CZE	84.5	87.0	212.1
3. Jiří Malec	CZE	88.0	85.5	211.8
4. Miran Tepeš	YUG	84.0	83.5	211.2
5. Jiří Parma	CZE	83.5	82.5	203.8
6. Heinz Kuttin	AUT	87.0	80.5	199.7
7. Jari Puikkonen	FIN	84.0	80.0	199.1
8. Staffan Tällberg	SWE	83.0	81.0	198.1

Matti Nykänen outclassed the opposition to win the first of his three Calgary gold medals. In last place was the popular English plasterer, Michael "Eddie the Eagle" Edwards, who scored less than half the points of any other jumper. Edwards once summed up the mental challenge of ski jumping with this description of his first encounter with the sport: "When I looked from the top of the jump, I was so frightened that my bum shriveled up like a prune."

1992 Albertville-Courcheval C: 58, N: 16, D: 2.9.

		FIRST JUMP (M)	SECOND JUMP (M)	TOTAL PTS.
1. Ernst Vettori	AUT	88.0	87.5	222.8
2. Martin Höllwarth	AUT	90.5	83.0	218.1
3. Toni Nieminen	FIN	88.0	84.5	217.0
4. Heinz Kuttin	AUT	85.5	86.0	214.4
5. Mika Laitinen	FIN	85.5	85.5	213.6
6. Andreas Felder	AUT	87.0	83.0	213.5
7. Heiko Hunger	GER	87.0	84.0	211.6
8. Didier Mollard	FRA	84.5	85.0	209.7

Twenty-seven-year-old Ernst Vettori, in third place after the first round, proved more consistent than the two teenagers ahead of him, Höllwarth (17) and Nieminen (16). Competing in his third Olympics, Vettori had been on the verge of retirement when the new V style revived his interest and his jumping career. Jan Boklöv, the inventor of the V, finished only 47th.

SKI JUMP, LARGE HILL, INDIVIDUAL

1924 Chamonix C: 27, N: 9, D: 2.4.

		FIRST JUMP (M)	SECOND JUMP (M)	TOTAL PTS.
1. Jacob Tullin Thams	NOR	49.0	49.0	18.960
2. Narve Bonna	NOR	47.5	49.0	18.689
3. Anders Haugen	USA	49.0	50.0	17.916
4. Thorleif Haug	NOR	44.0	44.5	17.821
5. Einar Landvik	NOR	42.0	44.5	17.521
6. Axel Nilsson	SWE	42.5	44.0	17.146
7. Menotti Jacobsen	SWE	43.0	42.0	17.083
8. Alexander Girardbille	SWI	40.5	41.5	16.794

The final results of this event were not decided until 50 years after it took place. In 1924 it appeared that the great Thorleif Haug had finished third, thus winning two medals at one time: a bronze in the ski jump and a gold in the nordic combined, to go with the two gold medals he had already won in the 50-kilometer and 15-kilometer races. However, in 1974 Toralf Strömstad, who had earned a silver medal in the 1924 nordic combined, discovered an error in the computation of the scores. Haug, who had been dead for 40 years, was demoted to fourth place, while Norwegian-born Anders Haugen, who had paid his own way to the Olympics, was moved up to third. Haugen, the only American ever to win a medal in ski-jumping, was awarded his medal in a special ceremony in Oslo. He was 83 years old.

1928 St. Moritz C: 38, N: 13, D: 2:18.

			FIRST JUMP (M)	SECOND JUMP (M)	TOTAL PTS.
1.	Alf Andersen	NOR	60.0	64.0	19.208
2.	Sigmund Ruud	NOR	57.5	62.5	18.542
3.	Rudolf Burkert	CZE	57.0	59.5	17.937
4.	Axel Nilsson	SWE	53.5	60.0	16.937
5.	Sven Lundgren	SWE	48.0	59.0	16.708
6.	Rolf Monsen	USA	53.0	59.5	16.687
7.	Sepp Muhlbauer	SWI	52.0	58.0	16.541
8.	Ernst Feuz	SWI	52.5	58.5	16.458

The longest jump of the day was recorded by defending champion Jacob Tullin Thams, who stretched out to 73 meters but fell badly when he reached the ground. The consequent loss in style points dropped him to 28th place.

1932 Lake Placid C: 34, N: 10, D: 2.12.

			FIRST JUMP (M)	SECOND JUMP (M)	TOTAL PTS.
1.	Birger Ruud	NOR	66.5	69.0	228.1
2.	Hans Beck	NOR	71.5	63.5	227.0
3.	Kaare Wahlberg	NOR	62.5	64.0	219.5
4.	Sven Eriksson	SWE	65.5	64.0	218.9
5.	Caspar Oimen	USA	63.0	67.5	216.7
6.	Fritz Kaufmann	SWI	63.5	65.5	215.8
7.	Sigmund Ruud	NOR	63.0	62.5	215.1
8.	Goro Adachi	JPN	60.0	66.0	210.7

Hans Beck and the Ruud brothers were brought up together in the mining town of Kongsberg. Confusion concerning the scoring computations caused a four-hour delay in the announcement of the placings, and even then it was orginally stated that Beck had won.

1936 Garmisch-Partenkirchen C: 48, N: 14, D: 2.16.

			FIRST JUMP (M)	SECOND JUMP (M)	TOTAL PTS.
1.	Birger Ruud	NOR	75.0	74.5	232.0
2.	Sven Eriksson	SWE	76.0	76.0	230.5
3.	Reidar Andersen	NOR	74.0	75.0	228.9
4.	Kaare Wahlberg	NOR	73.5	72.0	227.0
5.	Stanislaw Marusarz	POL	73.0	75.5	221.6
6.	Lauri Valonen	FIN	73.5	67.0	219.4
7.	Masaji Iguro	JPN	74.5	72.5	218.2
8.	Arnold Kongsgaard	NOR	74.5	72.5	217.7

1948 St. Moritz C: 49, N: 14, D: 2.7.

		FIRST JUMP (M)	SECOND JUMP (M)	TOTAL PTS.
1. Petter Hugsted	NOR	65.0	70.0	228.1
2. Birger Ruud	NOR	64.0	67.0	226.6
3. Thorleif Schjelderup	NOR	64.0	67.0	225.1
4. Matti Pietikainen	FIN	69.5	69.0	224.6
5. Gordon Wren	USA	68.0	68.5	222.8
6. Leo Laakso	FIN	66.0	69.5	221.7
7. Asbjörn Ruud	NOR	58.0	67.5	220.2
8. Aatto Pietikainen	FIN	69.0	68.0	215.4

Two-time gold medalist Birger Ruud, now 36 years old, went to St. Moritz as a coach. But when he saw the poor weather the night before the competition, he decided to compete in place of the less experienced George Thrane. Ruud's confidence in himself paid off with a silver medal.

1952 Oslo C: 44, N: 13, D: 2.24.

		FIRST JUMP (M)	SECOND JUMP (M)	TOTAL PTS.
1. Arnfinn Bergmann	NOR	67.5	68.0	226.0
2. Torbjörn Falkanger	NOR	68.0	64.0	221.5
3. Karl Holmström	SWE	67.0	65.5	219.5
4. Toni Brutscher	GER	66.5	62.5	216.5
4. Halvor Naes	NOR	63.5	64.5	216.5
6. Arne Hoel	NOR	66.5	63.5	215.5
7. Antti Hyvärinen	FIN	66.5	61.5	213.5
8. Sepp Weiler	GER	67.0	63.0	213.0

Between 1924 and 1952 Norway won 14 of the 18 medals awarded in the ski jumps. Since 1952, the Norwegians have earned only 6 of a possible 54 medals in individual events.

1956 Cortina C: 51, N: 16, D: 2.5.

		FIRST JUMP (M)	SECOND JUMP (M)	TOTAL PTS.
1. Antti Hyvärinen	FIN	81.0	84.0	227.0
2. Aulis Kallakorpi	FIN	83.5	80.5	225.0
3. Harry Glass	GDR	83.5	80.5	224.5
4. Max Bolkart	GER	80.0	81.5	222.5
5. Sven Pettersson	SWE	81.0	81.5	220.0
6. Andreas Däscher	SWI	82.0	82.0	219.5
7. Eino Kirjonen	FIN	78.0	81.0	219.0
8. Werner Lesser	GDR	77.5	77.5	210.0

1960 Squaw Valley C: 45, N: 15, D: 2.28.

		FIRST JUMP (M)	SECOND JUMP (M)	TOTAL PTS.
1. Helmut Recknagel	GDR	93.5	84.5	227.2
2. Niilo Halonen	FIN	92.5	83.5	222.6
3. Otto Leodolter	AUT	88.5	83.5	219.4

4. Nikolai Kamensky	SOV	90.5	79.0	216.9
5. Thorbjörn Yggeseth	NOR	88.5	82.5	216.1
6. Max Bolkart	GER	87.5	81.0	212.6
7. Ansten Samuelstuen	USA	90.0	79.0	211.5
8. Juhani Karkinen	FIN	87.5	82.0	211.4

1964 Innsbruck C: 52, N: 15, D: 2.9.

		FIRST JUMP (M)	SECOND JUMP (M)	TOTAL PTS.
1. Toralf Engan	NOR	93.5	90.5	230.7
2. Veikko Kankkonen	FIN	95.5	90.5	228.9
3. Torgeir Brandtzäg	NOR	92.0	90.0	227.2
4. Dieter Bokeloh	GDR	92.0	83.5	214.6
5. Kjell Sjöberg	SWE	90.0	85.0	214.4
6. Aleksandr Ivannikov	SOV	90.0	83.5	213.3
7. Helmut Recknagel	GDR	89.0	86.5	212.8
8. Dieter Neuendorf	GDR	92.5	84.5	212.6

A second ski jump event was added in 1964 in order to give more competitors a chance to win medals in a sport where a sudden gust of wind or a split-second mistake can send the best jumper down to defeat. As it turned out, however, the same three men took the medals in both events. The 1964 competition was the only one in which the contestants were allowed to use the two best of three jumps.

1968 Grenoble-St. Nizler C: 58, N: 17, D: 2:18.

		FIRST JUMP (M)	SECOND JUMP (M)	TOTAL PTS.
1. Vladimir Beloussov	SOV	101.5	98.5	231.3
2. Jiři Raška	CZE	101.0	98.0	229.4
3. Lars Grini	NOR	99.0	93.5	214.3
4. Manfred Queck	GDR	96.5	98.5	212.8
5. Bent Tomtum	NOR	98.5	95.0	212.2
6. Reinhold Bachler	AUT	98.5	95.0	210.7
7. Wolfgang Stöhr	GDR	96.5	92.5	205.9
8. Anatoly Zheglanov	SOV	99.0	92.0	205.7

1972 Sapporo-Okurayama C: 52, N: 15, D: 2.11.

		FIRST JUMP (M)	SECOND JUMP (M)	TOTAL PTS.
1. Wojciech Fortuna	POL	111.0	87.5	219.9
2. Walter Steiner	SWI	94.0	103.0	219.8
3. Rainer Schmidt	GDR	98.5	101.0	219.3
4. Tauno Käyhkö	FIN	95.0	100.5	219.2
5. Manfred Wolf	GDR	107.0	89.5	215.1
6. Gari Napalkov	SOV	99.5	92.0	210.1
7. Yukio Kasaya	JPN	106.0	85.0	209.4
8. Danilo Pudgar	YUG	92.5	97.5	206.0

Fortuna's first jump was so spectacular that he was able to win the gold medal even though his second jump was only the 22nd best of the round.

1976 Innsbruck C: 54, N: 15, D: 2.15.

			FIRST JUMP (M)	SECOND JUMP (M)	TOTAL PTS.
1.	Karl Schnabl	AUT	97.5	97.0	234.8
2.	Anton Innauer	AUT	102.5	91.0	232.9
3.	Henry Glass	GDR	91.0	97.0	221.7
4.	Jochen Danneberg	GDR	102.0	89.5	221.6
5.	Reinhold Bachler	AUT	95.0	91.0	217.4
6.	Hans Wallner	AUT	93.5	92.5	216.9
7.	Bernd Eckstein	GDR	94.0	91.5	216.2
8.	Hans-Georg Aschenbach	GDR	92.5	89.0	212.1

1980 Lake Placid C: 50, N: 16, D: 2.23.

			FIRST JUMP (M)	SECOND JUMP (M)	TOTAL PTS.
1.	Jouko Törmänen	FIN	114.5	117.0	271.0
2.	Hubert Neuper	AUT	113.0	114.5	262.4
3.	Jari Puikkonen	FIN	110.5	109.5	248.5
4.	Anton Innauer	AUT	110.0	107.0	245.7
5.	Armin Kogler	AUT	110.0	108.0	245.6
6.	Roger Ruud	NOR	110.0	109.0	243.0
7.	Hansjörg Sumi	SWI	117.0	110.0	242.7
8.	James Denney	USA	109.0	104.0	239.1

1984 Sarajevo C: 53, N: 17, D: 2.18.

			FIRST JUMP (M)	SECOND JUMP (M)	TOTAL PTS.
1.	Matti Nykänen	FIN	116.0	111.0	231.2
2.	Jens Weissflog	GDR	107.0	107.5	213.7
3.	Pavel Ploc	CZE	103.5	109.0	202.9
4.	Jeffrey Hastings	USA	102.5	107.0	201.2
5.	Jari Puikkonen	FIN	103.5	102.0	196.6
6.	Armin Kogler	AUT	106.0	99.5	195.6
7.	Andreas Bauer	GER	105.0	100.5	194.6
8.	Vladimir Podzimek	CZE	98.5	108.0	194.5

Notoriously ill-tempered Matti Nykänen of Jyväsklä put together two near-perfect jumps to achieve the largest winning margin in Olympic jumping history.

1988 Calgary C: 55, N: 18, D: 2.23.

			FIRST JUMP (M)	SECOND JUMP (M)	TOTAL PTS.
1.	Matti Nykänen	FIN	118.5	107.0	224.0
2.	Erik Johnsen	NOR	114.5	102.0	207.9
3.	Matjaž Debelak	YUG	113.0	108.0	207.7
4.	Thomas Klauser	GER	114.5	102.5	205.1
5.	Pavel Ploc	CZE	114.5	102.5	204.1
6.	Andreas Felder	AUT	113.5	103.0	203.9
7.	Horst Bulau	CAN	112.5	99.5	197.6
8.	Staffan Tällberg	SWE	110.0	102.0	196.6

In a competition that was postponed four times because of dangerous winds, Nykänen, mellowed somewhat by fatherhood, became the first ski jumper to win two gold medals in one Olympics.

1992 Albertville-Courcheval C: 59, N: 17, D: 2.16.

			FIRST JUMP (M)	SECOND JIMP (M)	TOTAL PTS.
1.	Toni Nieminen	FIN	122.0	123.0	239.5
2.	Martin Höllwarth	AUT	120.5	116.5	227.3
3.	Heinz Kuttin	AUT	117.5	112.0	214.8
4.	Masahiko Harada	JPN	113.5	116.0	211.3
5.	Jiří Parma	CZE	111.5	108.5	198.0
6.	Steeve Delaup	FRA	106.0	105.5	185.6
7.	Ivan Lunardi	ITA	110.5	102.5	185.2
8.	Franci Petek	SLO	107.0	99.5	177.1

Nieminen earned the two highest scores of the competition. At age 16, he became the youngest male to win a Winter Olympics gold in an individual event. The previous record holder was figure skater Dick Button, who was 18 when he won his first gold medal in 1948. At the other end of the standings was Germany's Heiko Hunger, who fell in his first jump and then withdrew. When asked for a comment, Hunger replied, "My horoscope said I shouldn't take any risks."

SKI JUMP, LARGE HILL, TEAM

Each team member takes two jumps. The lowest score of each round is dropped and the remaining six scores are added to determine the final team total.

1924–1984 not held

1988 Calgary T: 11, N: 11, D: 2.24.

			TOTAL PTS.
1.	FIN	(Matti Nykänen 228.8, Ari-Pekka Nikkola 207.9, Jari Puikkonen 193.6, Tuomo Ylipulli 192.3)	634.4
2.	YUG	(Matjaž Zupan 211.5, Matjaž Debelak 207.5, Primož Ulaga 207.1, Miran Tepeš 192.8)	625.5
3.	NOR	(Erik Johnsen 218.7, Ole Gunnar Fidjestol 193.9, Ole Christian Eidhammer 177.2, Jon Inge Kjorum 128.4)	596.1
4.	CZE	(Pavel Ploc 204.1, Jiří Malec 193.4, Jiří Parma 189.3, Ladislav Dluhoš 165.4)	586.8
5.	AUT	(Günter Stranner 197.5, Heinz Kuttin 193.3, Ernst Vettori 186.0, Andreas Felder 176.3)	577.6
6.	GER	(Thomas Klauser 197.6, Josef Heumann 180.9, Andreas Bauer 175.1, Peter Rohwein 174.3)	559.0
7.	SWE	(Jan Boklöv 180.1, Staffan Tällberg 178.7, Anders Daun 174.2, Per-Inge Tällberg 161.5)	539.7
8.	SWI	(Gérard Balanche 175.0, Christian Hauswirth 175.0, Fabrice Piazzini 166.2, Christoph Lehmann 156.7)	516.1

Matti Nykänen won his third gold medal of the Calgary Games to give him a two-Olympics total of four golds and one silver. Tuomo Ylipulli was the younger brother of Jukka Ylipulli, who won a bronze medal in the 1984 nordic combined.

1992 Albertville-Courcheval T: 14, N: 14, D: 2.14.

			TOTAL PTS.
1.	FIN	(Toni Nieminen 245.0, Ari-Pekka Nikkola 225.0, Risto Laakkonen 221.0, Mika Laitinen 216.0)	644.4
2.	AUT	(Martin Höllwarth 241.0, Heinz Kuttin 227.0, Andreas Felder 224.5, Ernst Vettori 224.0)	642.9
3.	CZE	(Jiří Parma 234.0, Tomas Goder 227.0, Frantisek Jez 218.0, Jaroslav Sakala 215.0)	620.1
4.	JPN	(Masahiko Harada 227.0, Jiro Kamiharako 215.0, Kenji Suda 206.5, Noriaki Kasai 203.5)	571.0
5.	GER	(Dieter Thoma 213.5, Heiko Hunger 212.0, Jens Weissflog 211.0, Christof Duffner 194.5)	544.6
6.	SLO	(Samo Gostisa 218.5, Franci Petek 212.5, Matjaž Zupan 207.5, Primoz Kipac 195.0)	543.3
7.	NOR	(Espen Bredesen 223.5, Magne Johansen 206.5, Rune Olijnyk 205.0, Lasse Ottesen 199.0)	538.0
8.	SWI	(Markus Gähler 214.5, Stefan Zünd 214.5, Sylvain Freiholz 209.5, Martin Trunz 198.5)	537.9

In ski-jumping contests the jury reserves the right to restart the competition if it believes the jumpers are going too far and endangering themselves. In such cases the scores for all completed jumps are erased and the starting point is moved. This is exactly what happened after Austria's second jumper, Ernst Vettori, uncorked a dazzling leap of 125.5 meters (411 feet). Martin Höllwarth then recorded the longest official jump in Olympic history—123.5 meters—to lead Austria to a one-point lead over Finland after the first round. In the second round, with only Toni Nieminen and Andreas Felder left to jump, the Austrians led by 30 points. But Nieminen came through with a magnificent 122-meter leap that earned 119.8 points. Felder could respond with only a 109.5-meter jump that ended up being dropped from the final tally. At the age of 16 years and 259 days, Nieminen became the youngest male winter gold medalist ever, breaking bobsledder Billy Fiske's record by one day.

NORDIC COMBINED, INDIVIDUAL

Nordic combined contests were held in Norway as early as the mid-19th century. On the first day of competition, the competitors take three jumps on a normal hill with only the two best jumps counting. The second day they ski 15 kilometers. Since 1988 the start order of the cross-country race has been based on the result of the ski jumping. The leader of the ski jumping starts first. The others follow. For each 1.5 points behind the leader, they must wait 10 seconds, 9 points being equal to one minute. Whoever crosses the finish line first is the winner.

1924 Chamonix C: 30, N: 9, D: 2.4.

			18 KM		SKI JUMP		TOTAL PTS.
1.	Thorleif Haug	NOR	1:14:31.0	(1)	17.821	(1)	18.906
2.	Thoralf Strömstad	NOR	1:17:03.0	(3)	17.687	(2)	18.219
3.	Johan Gröttumsbråten	NOR	1:15:51.0	(2)	16.333	(8)	17.854
4.	Harald Ökern	NOR	1:20:30.0	(4)	17.395	(3)	17.260
5.	Axel Nilsson	SWE	1:25:29.0	(6)	16.500	(7)	14.063
6.	Josef Adolf	CZE	1:31:17.0	(5)	12.833	(18)	13.729
7.	Vincenz Buchberger	CZE	1:32:32.0	(7)	16.250	(9)	13.625
8.	Menotti Jacobsson	SWE	1:37:10.0	(15)	16.896	(4)	12.823

1928 St. Moritz C: 35, N: 14, D: 2.18.

			18 KM		SKI JUMP		TOTAL PTS.
1.	Johan Gröttumsbråten	NOR	1:37:01.0	(1)	15.667	(8)	17.833
2.	Hans Vinjarengen	NOR	1:41:44.0	(2)	12.856	(19)	15.303
3.	John Snersrud	NOR	1:50:51.0	(9)	16.917	(3)	15.021
4.	Paavo Nuotio	FIN	1:48:46.0	(4)	15.729	(7)	14.927
5.	Esko Järvinen	FIN	1:46:33.0	(3)	14.286	(16)	14.810
6.	Sven Eriksson	SWE	1:52:20.0	(11)	16.312	(5)	14.593
7.	Ludwig Böck	GER	1:48:56.0	(5)	11.812	(21)	13.260
8.	Ole Kolterrud	NOR	1:50:17.0	(7)	13.500	(18)	13.146

1932 Lake Placid C: 33, N: 10, D: 2.11.

			18 KM		SKI JUMP		TOTAL PTS.
1.	Johan Gröttumsbråten	NOR	1:27:15.0	(1)	206.0	(6)	446.00
2.	Ole Stenen	NOR	1:28:05.0	(2)	200.3	(12)	436.05
3.	Hans Vinjarengen	NOR	1:32:40.0	(4)	221.6	(2)	434.60
4.	Sverre Kolterud	NOR	1:34:36.0	(7)	214.7	(5)	418.70
5.	Sven Eriksson	SWE	1:39:32.0	(12)	220.8	(3)	402.30
6.	Antonin Barton	CZE	1:33:39.0	(6)	188.6	(19)	397.10
7.	Bronislaw Czech	POL	1:36:37.0	(8)	197.0	(14)	392.00
8.	František Simunek	CZE	1:39:58.0	(14)	196.8	(15)	375.30

Gröttumsbråten closed out his Olympic career with three gold medals, one silver, and one bronze.

1936 Garmisch-Partenkirchen C: 51, N: 16, D: 2.13.

			18 KM		SKI JUMP		TOTAL PTS.
1.	Oddbjörn Hagen	NOR	1:15:33.0	(1)	190.3	(16)	430.3
2.	Olaf Hoffsbakken	NOR	1:17:37.0	(2)	192.0	(13)	419.8
3.	Sverre Brodahl	NOR	1:18:01.0	(3)	182.6	(28)	408.1
4.	Lauri Valonen	FIN	1:26:34.0	(26)	222.6	(1)	401.2
5.	František Simunek	CZE	1:19:09.0	(4)	175.3	(33)	394.3
6.	Bernt Osterklöft	NOR	1:21:37.0	(6)	188.7	(21)	393.8
7.	Stanislaw Marusarz	POL	1:25:27.0	(18)	208.9	(3)	393.3
7.	Timo Murama	FIN	1:24:52.0	(13)	205.8	(5)	393.3

1948 St. Moritz C: 39, N: 13, D: 2.1.

			18 KM		SKI JUMP		TOTAL PTS.
1.	Heikki Hasu	FIN	1:16:43.0	(1)	208.8	(8)	448.80
2.	Martti Huhtala	FIN	1:19:28.0	(2)	209.5	(6)	433.65
3.	Sven Israelsson	SWE	1:21:35.0	(4)	221.9	(1)	433.40
4.	Niklaus Stump	SWI	1:21:44.0	(7)	213.0	(5)	421.50
5.	Olavi Sihvonen	FIN	1:21:50.0	(8)	209.2	(7)	416.20
6.	Eilert Dahl	NOR	1:22:12.0	(10)	208.8	(8)	414.30
7.	Pauli Salonen	FIN	1:22:15.0	(9)	206.3	(10)	413.30
8.	Olav Dufseth	NOR	1:22:26.0	(5)	201.1	(16)	412.60

1952 Oslo C: 25, N: 11, D: 2.18.

		SKI JUMP		18 KM		TOTAL PTS.
1. Simon Slåttvik	NOR	223.5	(1)	1:05:40.0	(3)	451.621
2. Heikki Hasu	FIN	207.5	(5)	1:02:24.0	(1)	447.500
3. Sverre Stenersen	NOR	223.0	(2)	1:09:44.0	(9)	436.335
4. Paavo Korhonen	FIN	206.0	(6)	1:05:30.0	(2)	434.727
5. Per Gjelten	NOR	212.0	(3)	1:07:40.0	(6)	432.848
6. Ottar Gjermundshaug	NOR	206.0	(6)	1:06:13.0	(5)	432.121
7. Aulis Sipponen	FIN	198.5	(12)	1:06:03.0	(4)	425.227
8. Eeti Nieminen	FIN	206.0	(6)	1:08:24.0	(7)	424.181

February 18, 1952, was a great day in the history of Norwegian sports. Hjallis Andersen won the 1500-meter skating event, Hallgeir Brenden won the 18-kilometer cross-country race, and Simon Slåttvik won the nordic combined. People all over Oslo left their jobs and spilled into the streets to celebrate. The *New York Times* reported, with some annoyance, that at the Hotel Viking, where the press was staying, half of the waiters walked out, and "It took more than an hour to order food and another two hours to get it." The year 1952 was the first time that the jumping half of the nordic combined was held before the skiing.

1956 Cortina C: 36, N: 12, D: 1.31.

		SKI JUMP		15 KM		TOTAL PTS.
1. Sverre Stenersen	NOR	215.0	(2)	56:18.0	(1)	455.000
2. Bengt Eriksson	SWE	214.0	(3)	1:00:36.0	(15)	437.400
3. Franciszek Gasienica-Groń	POL	203.0	(10)	57:55.0	(7)	436.800
4. Paavo Korhonen	FIN	196.5	(17)	56:32.0	(2)	435.597
5. Arne Barhaugen	NOR	199.0	(15)	57:11.0	(3)	435.581
6. Tormod Knutsen	NOR	203.0	(11)	58:22.0	(9)	435.000
7. Nikolai Gusakov	SOV	200.0	(14)	58:17.0	(8)	432.300
8. Alfredo Prucker	ITA	201.0	(12)	58:52.0	(10)	431.100

1960 Squaw Valley C: 33, N: 13, D: 2.22.

		SKI JUMP		15 KM		TOTAL PTS.
1. Georg Thoma	GER	221.5	(1)	59:23.8	(4)	457.952
2. Tormod Knutsen	NOR	217.0	(4)	59:31.0	(5)	453.000
3. Nikolai Gusakov	SOV	212.0	(10)	58:29.4	(1)	452.000
4. Pekka Ristola	FIN	214.0	(6)	59:32.8	(6)	449.871
5. Dmitri Kochkin	SOV	219.5	(2)	1:01:32.1	(11)	444.694
6. Arne Larsen	NOR	215.0	(5)	1:01:10.1	(10)	444.613
7. Sverre Stenersen	NOR	205.5	(14)	1:00:24.0	(8)	438.081
8. Lars Dahlqvist	SWE	201.5	(19)	59:46.0	(7)	436.532

1964 Innsbruck-Seefeld C: 32, N: 11, D: 2.3.

		SKI JUMP		15 KM		TOTAL PTS.
1. Tormod Knutsen	NOR	238.9	(2)	50:58.6	(4)	469.28
2. Nikolai Kiselev	SOV	233.0	(3)	51:49.1	(8)	453.04
3. Georg Thoma	GER	241.1	(1)	52:31.2	(10)	452.88
4. Nikolai Gusakov	SOV	223.4	(7)	51:19.8	(5)	449.36
5. Arne Larsen	NOR	198.3	(17)	50:49.6	(3)	430.63

6.	Arne Barhaugen	NOR	191.3	(20)	50:40.4	(2)	425.63
7.	Vyacheslav Driagin	SOV	216.2	(10)	52:58.3	(12)	422.75
8.	Ezio Damolin	ITA	198.1	(18)	51:42.3	(7)	419.54

1968 Grenoble-Autrans C: 41, N: 13, D: 2.11.

			SKI JUMP		15 KM		TOTAL PTS.
1.	Franz Keller	GER	240.1	(1)	50:45.2	(13)	449.04
2.	Alois Kälin	SWI	193.2	(24)	47:21.5	(1)	447.99
3.	Andreas Kunz	GDR	216.9	(10)	49:19.8	(3)	444.10
4.	Tomáš Kučera	CZE	217.4	(9)	50:07.7	(6)	434.14
5.	Ezio Damolin	ITA	206.0	(13)	49:36.2	(4)	429.54
6.	Jósef Gąsienica	POL	217.7	(8)	50:34.5	(11)	428.78
7.	Robert Makara	SOV	222.8	(5)	51:09.3	(17)	426.92
8.	Vyacheslav Driagin	SOV	222.8	(5)	51:22.0	(19)	424.38

Had Kälin been able to finish the cross-country race 2.3 seconds sooner, he would have won the gold medal.

1972 Sapporo-Miyanomori/Makomanai C: 39, N: 14, D: 2.5.

			SKI JUMP		15 KM		TOTAL PTS.
1.	Ulrich Wehling	GDR	200.9	(4)	49:15.3	(3)	413.340
2.	Rauno Miettinen	FIN	210.0	(2)	51:08.2	(15)	405.505
3.	Karl-Heinz Luck	GDR	178.8	(17)	48:24.9	(1)	398.800
4.	Erkki Kilpinen	FIN	185.0	(9)	49:52.6	(4)	391.845
5.	Yuji Katsuro	JPN	195.1	(6)	51:10.9	(18)	390.200
6.	Tomáš Kučera	CZE	191.8	(7)	51:04.0	(14)	387.935
7.	Aleksandr Nossov	SOV	201.3	(3)	52:08.7	(27)	387.730
8.	Kåre Olav Berg	NOR	180.4	(16)	50:08.9	(7)	384.800

Hideki Nakano of Japan had the unusual distinction of finishing first among the competitors in the nordic combined in the ski jump, but last in the 15-kilometer race. This left him in 13th place overall.

1976 Innsbruck-Seefeld C: 34, N: 14, D: 2.8.

			SKI JUMP		15 KM		TOTAL PTS.
1.	Ulrich Wehling	GDR	225.5	(1)	50:28.95	(13)	423.39
2.	Urban Hettich	GER	198.9	(11)	48:01.55	(1)	418.90
3.	Konrad Winkler	GDR	213.9	(4)	49:51.11	(7)	417.47
4.	Rauno Miettinen	FIN	219.9	(2)	51:12.21	(19)	411.30
5.	Claus Tuchscherer	GDR	218.7	(3)	51:16.12	(20)	409.51
6.	Nikolai Nagovitzin	SOV	196.1	(16)	49:05.97	(3)	406.44
7.	Valery Kapayev	SOV	202.9	(9)	49:53.26	(8)	406.14
8.	Tom Sandberg	NOR	195.7	(17)	49:09.34	(4)	405.53

1980 Lake Placid C: 31, N: 9, D: 2.18.

			SKI JUMP		15 KM		TOTAL PTS.
1.	Ulrich Wehling	GDR	227.2	(1)	49:24.5	(9)	432.200
2.	Jouko Karjalainen	FIN	209.5	(7)	47:44.5	(1)	429.500
3.	Konrad Winkler	GDR	214.5	(5)	48:45.7	(8)	425.320

			SKI JUMP		15 KM		TOTAL PTS.
4.	Tom Sandberg	NOR	203.7	(9)	48:19.4	(5)	418.465
5.	Uwe Dotzauer	GDR	217.6	(4)	49:52.4	(13)	418.415
6.	Karl Lustenberger	SWI	212.7	(6)	50:01.1	(14)	412.210
7.	Aleksandr Maiorov	SOV	194.4	(13)	48:19.6	(6)	409.135
8.	Gunter Schmieder	GDR	201.7	(11)	49:42.0	(11)	404.075

The 27-year-old Wehling became the first non–figure skater to win three consecutive gold medals in the same individual Winter event.

1984 Sarajevo C: 28, N: 11, D: 2.12.

			SKI JUMP		15 KM		TOTAL PTS.
1.	Tom Sandberg	NOR	214.7	(1)	47:52.7	(2)	422.595
2.	Jouko Karjalainen	FIN	196.9	(15)	46:32.0	(1)	416.900
3.	Jukka Ylipulli	FIN	208.3	(5)	48:28.5	(5)	410.825
4.	Rauno Miettinen	FIN	205.5	(6)	49:02.2	(9)	402.970
5.	Thomas Müller	GER	209.1	(3)	49:32.7	(12)	401.995
6.	Aleksandr Prosvirnin	SOV	199.4	(13)	48:40.1	(6)	400.185
7.	Uwe Dotzauer	GDR	199.5	(12)	48:56.8	(7)	397.780
8.	Hermann Weinbuch	GER	201.6	(10)	49:13.4	(10)	397.390

1988 Calgary-Canmore C: 42, N: 13, D: 2.28.

			SKI JUMP		15 KM		TIME BEHIND
1.	Hippolyt Kempf	SWI	217.9	(3)	38:16.8	(2)	0
2.	Klaus Sulzenbacher	AUT	228.5	(1)	39:46.5	(17)	19.0
3.	Allar Levandi	SOV	216.6	(4)	39:12.4	(12)	1:04.3
4.	Uwe Prenzel	GDR	207.6	(13)	38:18.8	(4)	1:10.7
5.	Andreas Schaad	SWI	207.2	(14)	38:18.0	(3)	1:12.5
6.	Torbjörn Lökken	NOR	199.4	(19)	37:39.0	(1)	1:15.5
7.	Miroslav Kopal	CZE	208.7	(12)	38:48.0	(8)	1:32.5
8.	Marko Frank	GDR	209.4	(10)	39:08.2	(11)	1:48.1

Nineteen eighty-eight marked the first time that nordic combined used the Gundersen Method, in which the starting order and intervals in the cross-country race are based on the results of the ski jump. World Cup leader Klaus Sulzenbacher earned the right to start first, with Hippolyt Kempf in third place 1:10.7 behind. Kempf caught Sulzenbacher 2.3 kilometers from the finish and pulled away to win by 19 seconds.

Because of delays caused by poor weather, the ski jump and cross-country race were held on the same day.

1992 Albertville-Courcheval C: 45, N: 12, D: 2.12.

			SKI JUMP		15 KM		TIME BEHIND
1.	Fabrice Guy	FRA	222.1	(3)	43:45.4	(6)	0
2.	Sylvain Guillaume	FRA	208.1	(13)	43:00.5	(3)	48.4
3.	Klaus Sulzenbacher	AUT	221.6	(4)	44:48.4	(13)	1:06.3
4.	Fred Börre Lundberg	NOR	211.9	(9)	44:04.1	(9)	1:26.7
5.	Klaus Ofner	AUT	228.5	(1)	45:57.9	(21)	1:29.8
6.	Allar Levandi	EST	206.4	(14)	43:34.8	(6)	1:34.1
7.	Kenji Ogiwara	JPN	215.3	(6)	44:57.5	(16)	1:57.4
8.	Stanislaw Ustupski	POL	202.6	(18)	44:03.5	(8)	2:28.1

Two months before the Olympics, 23-year-old Fabrice Guy was an obscure athlete in a sport with almost no following in his home country of France. But when he won four of five pre-Olympic World Cup events, he suddenly found himself a superstar in a host nation short on gold-medal prospects. Amazingly, he was able to live up to his compatriots' huge expectations. Guy knew that he had to keep close to Sulzenbacher in the jumping portion of the competition in order to take advantage of his superior skiing ability. In fact, he jumped so well that he outscored his Austrian rival. The next day, with almost half of the inhabitants of his hometown of Mouthe (population: 920) in attendance, he pulled away from Sulzenbacher after 5 kilometers and won easily. The French joy was multiplied by the surprise success of Sylvain Guillaume, who came from 13th place to grab the silver medal. Guy's fans were so deliriously happy that they gathered outside the doping control room and sang "La Marseillaise" while he tried to produce a urine sample. It took him an hour.

NORDIC COMBINED, TEAM

In this event each team member takes three jumps, although only the two best count in the scoring. The next day, a 3 × 10-kilometer relay is held; the starting order is based on the results of the ski jump. Each 12 points behind the leading team in the ski jump is equal to a 1-minute handicap at the start of the relay.

1924–1984 not held

1988 Calgary-Canmore T: 11, N: 11, D: 2.23.

			SKI JUMP		10 KM		TIME BEHIND
1.	GER	Hans-Peter Pohl	204.7		27:26.7		0
		Hubert Schwarz	227.2		27:45.7		
		Thomas Müller	197.9	(1)	25:33.6	(8)	
2.	SWI	Andreas Schaad	195.4		25:34.7		3.4
		Hippolyt Kempf	199.8		25:12.9		
		Fredy Glanzmann	176.2	(6)	25:09.8	(1)	
3.	AUT	Günther Csar	193.7		26:39.7		30.9
		Hansjörg Aschenwald	204.5		28:33.7		
		Klaus Sulzenbacher	228.4	(2)	25:47.5	(9)	
4.	NOR	Hallstein Bögseth	195.0		26:18.6		48.6
		Trond Arne Bredesen	201.1		27:04.0		
		Torbjörn Lökken	200.5	(3)	25:25.8	(3)	
5.	GDR	Thomas Prenzel	183.9		26:23.9		2:18.5
		Marko Frank	195.9		26:12.1		
		Uwe Prenzel	191.8	(5)	25:37.5	(2)	
6.	CZE	Ladislav Patraš	192.0		26:49.7		2:57.1
		Ján Klimko	184.7		26:30.4		
		Miroslav Kopal	196.8	(4)	25:42.0	(4)	
7.	FIN	Pasi Saapunki	165.0		26:29.7		4:52.3
		Jouko Parviainen	201.9		26:42.3		
		Jukka Ylipulli	194.4	(7)	26:44.3	(7)	
8.	FRA	Jean Bohard	178.0		27:04.9		6:23.4
		Xavier Girard	187.2		26:43.2		
		Fabrice Guy	175.8	(8)	25:57.3	(5)	

The West Germans led after the ski jump, with Austria second and Switzerland back in sixth place. Günther Csar, starting 16 seconds after Hans-Peter Pohl, gave Austria a 31-second lead after the first leg of the relay, but Hubert Schwarz put West Germany back in the lead to stay. The Swiss, starting with a handicap of 4 minutes 52 seconds, staged a dramatic come-from-behind effort, but fell 3.4 seconds short of victory. "It's a very thrilling, frustrating feeling," said Swiss anchorman Fredy Glanzmann, who recorded the fastest leg of the day, "to be so near to the leader where you can almost touch him, but you can't touch him because your legs won't let you."

1992 Albertville-Courcheval T: 11, N: 11, D: 2.18.

			SKI JUMP		10 KM		TIME BEHIND
1.	JPN	Reiichi Mikata	218.6		28:22.5		0
		Takanori Kono	199.0		28:40.2		
		Kenji Ogiwara	227.5	(1)	26:33.8	(6)	
2.	NOR	Knut Apeland	185.3		26:22.8		1:26.4
		Fred Börje Lundberg	185.7		26:19.7		
		Trond Einar Elden	198.9	(6)	26:04.4	(1)	
3.	AUT	Klaus Ofner	195.5		27:56.6		1:40.1
		Stefan Kreiner	212.6		28:34.2		
		Klaus Sulzenbacher	207.5	(2)	26:18.8	(3)	
4.	FRA	Francis Repellin	177.2		27:27.0		2:15.5
		Sylvain Guillaume	191.1		26:28.8		
		Fabrice Guy	210.1	(5)	26:23.2	(2)	
5.	GER	Hans-Peter Pohl	180.1		28:01.2		4:45.4
		Jens Deimel	207.4		29:53.5		
		Thomas Dufter	222.2	(3)	27:30.2	(8)	
6.	CZE	Josef Kovarik	166.0		27:47.8		9:04.7
		Milan Kucera	184.5		29:37.8		
		František Maka	196.2	(8)	27:03.6	(7)	
7.	FIN	Pasi Saapunki	195.2		27:15.5		9:06.8
		Jari Mantila	166.4		30:23.1		
		Teemu Summanen	199.6	(7)	28:05.7	(9)	
8.	USA	Joseph Holland	184.3		29:44.9		9:08.3
		Timothy Tetreault	198.1		28:48.6		
		Ryan Heckman	208.9	(4)	29:42.3	(10)	

The Japanese jumped so well that they put the gold medal out of reach after the first day. They began the relay 2 minutes and 27 seconds before second-place Austria and, more important, 6 minutes and 16 seconds before sixth-place Norway.

Discontinued Event

15 KILOMETERS (CLASSICAL)

The 18- and 15-kilometer cross-country race was thoroughly dominated by four nations: Norway, Sweden, Finland, and the U.S.S.R. These four nations won all 45 medals, and only five other countries ever managed to finish in the top eight.

1924 Chamonix C: 41, N: 12, D: 2.2.
18 Kilometers

1.	Thorleif Haug	NOR	1:14.31.0
2.	Johan Gröttumsbråten	NOR	1:15.51.0
3.	Tapani Niku	FIN	1:16.26.0
4.	Jon Maardalen	NOR	1:16.56.0
5.	Einar Landvik	NOR	1:17.27.0
6.	Per Erik Hedlund	SWE	1:17.49.0
7.	Matti Raivio	FIN	1:19.10.0
8.	Elis Sandin	SWE	1:19.24.0

Thorleif Haug won the second of his three gold medals, having won the 50-kilometer race three days earlier. The Scandinavians took the first 11 places.

1928 St. Moritz C: 49, N: 15, D: 2.17.
18 Kilometers

1.	Johan Gröttumsbråten	NOR	1:37.01.0
2.	Ole Hegge	NOR	1:39.01.0
3.	Reidar Ödegaard	NOR	1:40.11.0
4.	Veli Saarinen	FIN	1:40:57.0
5.	Hagbart Haakonsen	NOR	1:41:29.0
6.	Per Erik Hedlund	SWE	1:41:51.0
7.	Lars Theodor Johnsson	SWE	1:41:59.0
7.	Martti Lappalainen	FIN	1:41:59.0

1932 Lake Placid C: 42, N: 11, D: 2.10.
18 Kilometers

1.	Sven Utterström	SWE	1:23.07.0
2.	Axel Wikström	SWE	1:25:07.0
3.	Veli Saarinen	FIN	1:25:24.0
4.	Martti Lappalainen	FIN	1:26:31.0
5.	Arne Rustadstuen	NOR	1:27:06.0
6.	Johan Gröttumsbråten	NOR	1:27:15.0
7.	Valmari Toikka	FIN	1:27:51.0
8.	Ole Stenen	NOR	1:28:05.0

Once again, Scandinavians took the first 11 places.

1936 Garmish-Partenkirchen C: 75, N: 22, D: 2.12.
18 Kilometers

1.	Erik-August Larsson	SWE	1:14:38.0
2.	Oddbjörn Hagen	NOR	1:15:33.0
3.	Pekka Niemi	FIN	1:16:59.0
4.	Martin Matsbo	SWE	1:17:02.0
5.	Olaf Hoffsbakken	NOR	1:17:37.0
6.	Arne Rustadstuen	NOR	1:18:13.0
7.	Sulo Nurmela	FIN	1:18:20.0
8.	Artur Häggblad	SWE	1:18:55.0

1948 St. Moritz C: 84, N: 15, D: 1.31.
18 Kilometers

1.	Martin Lundström	SWE	1:13:50.0
2.	Nils Östensson	SWE	1:14:22.0
3.	Gunnar Eriksson	SWE	1:16:06.0
4.	Heikki Hasu	FIN	1:16:43.0
5.	Nils Karlsson	SWE	1:16:54.0
6.	Sauli Rytky	FIN	1:18:10.0
7.	August Kiuru	FIN	1:18:25.0
8.	Teuvo Laukkanen	FIN	1:18:51.0

1952 Oslo C: 80, N: 18, D: 2.18.
18 Kilometers

1.	Hallgeir Brenden	NOR	1:01:34.0
2.	Tapio Mäkelä	FIN	1:02:09.0
3.	Paavo Lonkila	FIN	1:02:20.0
4.	Heikki Hasu	FIN	1:02:24.0
5.	Nils Karlsson	SWE	1:02:56.0
6.	Martin Stokken	NOR	1:03:00.0
7.	Nils Täpp	SWE	1:03:35.0
8.	Tauno Sipila	FIN	1:03:40.0

In an amazing display of regional dominance, Finland, Norway, and Sweden claimed the first 17 places. Hallgeir Brenden, a 23-year-old lumberjack and farmer from the small town of Trysil, was also Norway's national steeplechase champion.

1956 Cortina C: 62, N: 20, D: 1.30.

1.	Hallgeir Brenden	NOR	49:39.0
2.	Sixten Jernberg	SWE	50:14.0
3.	Pavel Kolchin	SOV	50:17.0
4.	Veikko Hakulinen	FIN	50:31.0
5.	Håkon Brusveen	NOR	50:36.0
6.	Martin Stokken	NOR	50:45.0
7.	Nikolai Anikin	SOV	50:58.0
8.	Lennart Larsson	SWE	51:03.0

Kolchin and Anikin were the first non-Scandinavians to crack the top eight in this event. This was also the first time that the race was conducted at 15 kilometers rather than 18.

1960 Squaw Valley C: 54, N: 19, D: 2.23.

1.	Håkon Brusveen	NOR	51:55.5
2.	Sixten Jernberg	SWE	51:58.6
3.	Veikko Hakulinen	FIN	52:03.0
4.	Einar Östby	NOR	52:18.0
4.	Gennady Vaganov	SOV	52:18.0
6.	Eero Mäntyranta	FIN	52:40.6
7.	Janne Stefansson	SWE	52:41.0
8.	Rolf Rämgård	SWE	52:47.3

Brusveen was considered past his prime and was originally not selected to go to the Olympics. However, public pressure forced Norwegian ski officials to change their minds.

1964 Innsbruck-Seefeld C: 71, N: 24, D: 2.2.

1. Eero Mäntyranta   FIN   50:54.1
2. Harald Grönningen   NOR   51:34.8
3. Sixten Jernberg   SWE   51:42.2
4. Väinö Huhtala   FIN   51:45.4
5. Janne Stefansson   SWE   51:46.4
6. Pavel Kolchin   SOV   51:52.0
7. Igor Voronchikin   SOV   51:53.9
8. Magnar Lundemo   NOR   51:55.2

Mäntyranta and Grönningen took the same places they had taken in the 30-kilometer race three days earlier. Mäntyranta made his living on skis as a border patrol officer, a common vocation for state-supported skiers.

1968 Grenoble-Autrans C: 75, N: 24, D: 2:10.

1. Harald Grönningen   NOR   47:54.2
2. Eero Mäntyranta   FIN   47:56.1
3. Gunnar Larsson   SWE   48:33.7
4. Kalevi Laurila   FIN   48:37.6
5. Jan Halvarsson   SWE   48:39.1
6. Bjarne Andersson   SWE   48:41.1
7. Pål Tyldum   NOR   48:42.0
8. Odd Martinsen   NOR   48:59.3

A three-time silver medalist, Grönningen finally beat his friend and rival Mäntyranta.

1972 Sapporo-Makomanai C: 62, N: 19, D: 2.7.

1. Sven-Ake Lundbäck   SWE   45:28.24
2. Fedor Simashev   SOV   46:00.84
3. Ivar Formo   NOR   46:02.68
4. Juha Mieto   FIN   46:02.74
5. Yuri Skobov   SOV   46:04.59
6. Axel Lesser   GDR   46:17.01
7. Walter Demel   GER   46:17.36
8. Gunnar Larsson   SWE   46:23.29

1976 Innsbruck-Seefeld C: 80, N: 25, D: 2.8.

1. Nikolai Bazhukov   SOV   43:58.47
2. Yevgeny Beliaev   SOV   44:01.10
3. Arto Koivisto   FIN   44:19.25
4. Ivan Garanin   SOV   44:41.98
5. Ivar Formo   NOR   45:29.11
6. William Koch   USA   45:32.22
7. Georg Zipfel   GER   45:38.10
8. Odd Martinsen   NOR   45:41.33

1980 Lake Placid C: 63, N: 22, D: 2.17.

1. Thomas Wassberg   SWE   41:57.63
2. Juha Mieto   FIN   41:57.64
3. Ove Aunli   NOR   42:28.62
4. Nikolai Zimyatov   SOV   42:33.96
5. Yevgeny Beliaev   SOV   42:46.02
6. Józef Luszczek   POL   42:59.03
7. Aleksandr Zavyalov   SOV   43:00.81
8. Harri Kirvesniemi   FIN   43:02.01

Six-foot 5-inch Juha Mieto could be forgiven if he cursed the invention of electronic timing. In 1972 he missed winning a bronze medal because a clock registered his time as six one-hundredths of a second slower than that of Ivar Formo. Eight years later in Lake Placid, Mieto was the 54th skier to start and he finished 36 seconds faster than any of the other 53. But then he watched anxiously as Thomas Wassberg strained toward the finish line and crossed in 41 minutes and 57.63 seconds—one one-hundredth of a second faster than Juha Mieto. This incident led the rulemakers to decree that henceforth all times in cross-country races would be rounded to the nearest tenth of a second.

1984 Sarajevo C: 91, N: 34, D: 2.13.

1.	Gunde Svan	SWE	41:25.6
2.	Aki Karvonen	FIN	41:34.9
3.	Harri Kirvesniemi	FIN	41:45.6
4.	Juha Mieto	FIN	42:05.8
5.	Vladimir Nikitin	SOV	42:31.6
6.	Nikolai Zimyatov	SOV	42:34.5
7.	Uwe Bellmann	GDR	42:35.8
8.	Tor Håkon Holte	NOR	42:37.4

DISQ: Ove Aunli (NOR) 42:31.6

At age 22, Gunde Svan became the youngest person ever to win an Olympic cross-country title. Ove Aunli, who finished in a tie for fifth place, was disqualified for using a skating step during the last 200 meters.

1988 Calgary-Canmore C: 90, N: 32, D: 2.19.

1.	Mikhail Devyatyarov	SOV	41:18.9
2.	Pål Gunnar Mikkelsplass	NOR	41:33.4
3.	Vladimir Smirnov	SOV	41:48.5
4.	Oddvar Brå	NOR	42:17.3
5.	Uwe Bellmann	GDR	42:17.8
6.	Maurilio De Zolt	ITA	42:31.2
7.	Vegard Ulvang	NOR	42:31.5
8.	Harri Kirvesniemi	FIN	42:42.8

Devyatyarov attributed the success of the Soviet Nordic skiers at the Calgary Games to the fact that they trained on a course with the same profile as the one at Canmore and at the same altitude.

This race saw the unusual inclusion of an entrant from Fiji. Rusiate Rogoyawa learned to ski while studying electrical engineering in Oslo, Norway. He finished 83d.

NORDIC SKIING

WOMEN
5 Kilometers (Classical)
Combined Pursuit
15 Kilometers (Classical)
30 Kilometers (Freestyle)
4 × 5-Kilometer Relay
Discontinued Events

Except for the combined pursuit, participants in the individual events start at 30-second intervals and race against the clock. In the relay all teams start at the same time.

WOMEN

5 KILOMETERS (CLASSICAL)

1924–1960 not held

1964 Innsbruck-Seefeld C: 32, N: 14, D: 2.5.

1.	Claudia Boyarskikh	SOV	17:50.5
2.	Mirja Lehtonen	FIN	17:52.9
3.	Alevtina Kolchina	SOV	18:08.4
4.	Eudokia Mekshilo	SOV	18:16.7
5.	Toini Pöysti	FIN	18:25.5
6.	Toini Gustaffson	SWE	18:25.7
7.	Barbro Martinsson	SWE	18:26.4
8.	Eeva Ruoppa	FIN	18:29.8

In 1964 Claudia Boyarskikh, a 24-year-old teacher from Siberia, swept all three women's nordic events.

1968 Grenoble-Autrans C: 34, N: 12, D: 2.13.

1.	Toini Gustafsson	SWE	16:45.2
2.	Galina Kulakova	SOV	16:48.4
3.	Alevtina Kolchina	SOV	16:51.6
4.	Barbro Martinsson	SWE	16:52.9
5.	Marjatta Kajosmaa	FIN	16:54.6
6.	Rita Achkina	SOV	16:55.1
7.	Inger Aufles	NOR	16:58.1
8.	Senja Pusula	FIN	17:00.3

Toini Gustafsson was the last skier to leave the starting line. Kept informed of Kulakova's time at each kilometer, she knew exactly what time she had to beat.

Four seconds off Kulakova's pace with only one kilometer to go, Gustafsson poured it on to win with three seconds to spare. A 30-year-old physical education teacher, Gustafsson also won the 10-kilometer contest and gained a silver medal in the relay after recording the fastest leg of the race.

1972 Sapporo-Makomanai C: 43, N: 12, D: 2.9.

1.	Galina Kulakova	SOV	17:00.50
2.	Marjatta Kajosmaa	FIN	17:05.50
3.	Helena Šikolová	CZE	17:07.32
4.	Alevtina Olunina	SOV	17:07.40
5.	Hilkka Kuntola	FIN	17:11.67
6.	Lyubov Moukhatcheva	SOV	17:12.08
7.	Berit Mördre-Lammedal	NOR	17:16.79
8.	Aslaug Dahl	NOR	17:17.49

Kulakova, a 29-year-old physical education teacher from Izhevsk, matched Claudia Boyarskikh's feat of capturing all three women's nordic gold medals.

1976 Innsbruck-Seefeld C: 44, N: 14, D: 2.9.

1.	Helena Takalo	FIN	15:48.69
2.	Raisa Smetanina	SOV	15:49.73
3.	Nina Baldycheva	SOV	16:12.82
4.	Hilkka Kuntola	FIN	16:17.74
5.	Eva Olsson	SWE	16:27.15
6.	Zinaida Amosova	SOV	16:33.78
7.	Monika Debertshäuser	GDR	16:34.94
8.	Grete Kummen	NOR	16:35.43
	DISQ (Drugs): Galina Kulakova (SOV)		16:07.36

Defending champion Kulakova finished third, but was disqualified for having used a nasal spray that contained the banned drug ephedrine. She was, however, allowed to compete in the 10-kilometer race and the relay.

1980 Lake Placid C: 38, N: 12, D: 2.15.

1.	Raisa Smetanina	SOV	15:06.92
2.	Hilkka Riihivuori [Kuntola]	FIN	15:11.96
3.	Květoslava Jeriová	CZE	15:23.44
4.	Barbara Petzold	GDR	15:23.62
5.	Nina Baldycheva	SOV	15:29.03
6.	Galina Kulakova	SOV	15:29.58
7.	Veronika Hesse	GDR	15:31.83
8.	Helena Takalo	FIN	15:32.12

1984 Sarajevo C: 52, N: 14, D: 2.12.

1.	Marja-Liisa Hämäläinen	FIN	17:04.0
2.	Berit Aunli [Kvello]	NOR	17:14.1
3.	Květoslava Jeriová	CZE	17:18.3
4.	Lillemor Marie Risby [Johansson]	SWE	17:26.3
5.	Inger Helene Nybråten	NOR	17:28.2
6.	Brit Pettersen	NOR	17:33.6
7.	Anne Jahren	NOR	17:38.3
8.	Ute Noack	GDR	17:46.0

Hämäläinen won the second of her three gold medals.

1988 Calgary-Canmore C: 55, N: 17, D: 2.17.

1.	Marjo Matikainen	FIN	15:04.0
2.	Tamara Tikhonova	SOV	15:05.3
3.	Vida Venciené	SOV	15:11.1
4.	Anne Jahren	NOR	15:12.6
5.	Marja-Liisa Kirvesniemi [Hämäläinen]	FIN	15:16.7
6.	Inger Helene Nybråten	NOR	15:17.7
7.	Marie-Helene Westin	SWE	15:28.9
8.	Svetlana Nageikina	SOV	15:29.9

Matikainen moved ahead after four kilometers, then used every last ounce of energy to push herself across the finish line 1.3 seconds faster than Tikhonova's time, before collapsing. The following year, Matikainen retired at the age of 23 in order to study engineering.

1992 Albertville-Les Saisies C: 62, N: 21, D: 2.13.

1.	Marjut Lukkarinen	FIN	14:13.8
2.	Lyubov Yegorova	SOV	14:14.7
3.	Yelena Vialbe	SOV	14:22.7
4.	Stefania Belmondo	ITA	14:26.2
5.	Inger Helene Nybråten	NOR	14:33.3
6.	Olga Danilova	SOV	14:37.2
7.	Larissa Lazutina	SOV	14:41.7
8.	Solveig Pedersen	NOR	14:42.1

Whereas Marjo Matikainen retired early to pursue a career, Marjut Lukkarinen waited until she had completed her nursing studies before taking her racing seriously. She joined the World Cup circuit at age 24, two years before the Olympics, but continued to work twenty hours a week in an after-care ward in her hometown of Lohja. Skiing in a wet snowstorm, she won the fastest and closest women's nordic race in Olympic history. She did have to engage in unusual tactics to gain her victory. At one point she found herself behind Katerina Neumannová of Czechoslovakia. She yelled, "Track," to get Neumannová to move over, as is the custom in cross-country skiing, but Neumannová did not respond. She tried again, but still Neumannová remained in her way. Finally Lukkarinen began hitting her on the legs with her ski pole. Neumannová moved over.

COMBINED PURSUIT

1928-1988 not held

1992 Albertville-Les Saisies C: 58, N: 21, D: 2.15.

		5 KM CLASSI-CAL		10 KM FREESTYLE		TOTAL
1. Lyubov Yegorova	SOV	14:14	(2)	25:53.7	(1)	40:07.7
2. Stefania Belmondo	ITA	14:26	(4)	26:05.8	(2)	40:31.8
3. Yelena Vialbe	SOV	14:22	(3)	26:29.7	(3)	40:51.7
4. Marjut Lukkarinen	FIN	14:13	(1)	26:52.1	(7)	41:05.1
5. Elin Nilsen	NOR	14:50	(10)	26:36.9	(4)	41:26.9
6. Marie-Helene Westin	SWE	14:42	(8)	27:46.2	(6)	41:28.2
7. Inger Helene Nybråten	NOR	14:33	(5)	27:02.1	(8)	41:35.1
8. Larissa Lazutina	SOV	14:41	(7)	27:07.8	(10)	41:48.8

On the second day of the competition, Yegorova let Belmondo take the lead. She tracked her for 6.5 kilometers, then took off and ran away with the race.

15 KILOMETERS (CLASSICAL)

1928-1988 not held

1992 Albertville-Les Saisies C: 53, N: 21, D: 2.9.

1.	Lyubov Yegorova	SOV	42:20.8
2.	Marjut Lukkarinen	FIN	43:29.9
3.	Yelena Vialbe	SOV	43:42.3
4.	Raisa Smetanina	SOV	44:01.5
5.	Stefania Belmondo	ITA	44:02.4
6.	Marja-Liisa Kirvesniemi [Hämäläinen]	FIN	44:02.7
7.	Inger Helene Nybråten	NOR	44:18.6
8.	Trude Dybendahl	NOR	44:31.5

Although she thought the course defeated her, Yegorova's intermediate times showed that she led from start to finish to win the first of her three gold medals.

30 KILOMETERS (FREESTYLE)

1928-1988 not held

1992 Albertville-Les Saisies C: 57, N: 19, D: 2.21.

1.	Stefania Belmondo	ITA	1:22:30.1
2.	Lyubov Yegorova	SOV	1:22:52.0
3.	Yelena Vialbe	SOV	1:24:13.9
4.	Elin Nilsen	NOR	1:26:25.1
5.	Larissa Lazutina	SOV	1:26:31.8
6.	Manuela Di Centa	ITA	1:27:04.4
7.	Marie-Helene Westin	SWE	1:27:16.2
8.	Simone Opitz	GER	1:27:17.4

Belmondo, only 5-foot 1-inch and 104 pounds, had placed fifth, fourth, second, and third before striking gold in the final women's cross-country event. Over half of her home village of Pontebernardo (population 160) traveled to Les Saisies to cheer her on to victory. Yegorova and Vialbe both won medals in all five nordic events. Yegorova's final haul was three gold and two silver, while Vialbe became the first female winter athlete to win four bronze medals.

4 × 5-KILOMETER RELAY

Through 1988 this was a freestyle event, but since 1992 two skiers on each team use the classical technique and two use the skating technique.

1924–1952 not held

1956 Cortina T: 10, N: 10, D: 2.1.
3 × 5-Kilometer

1.	FIN	(Sirkka Polkunen, Mirja Hietamies, Siiri Rantanen)	1:09.01.0
2.	SOV	(Lyubov Kozyreva, Alevtina Kolchina, Radya Eroshina)	1:09.28.0
3.	SWE	(Irma Johansson, Anna-Lisa Eriksson, Sonja Edström)	1:09.48.0

4.	NOR	(Kjellfrid Brusveen, Gina Regland, Rakel Wahl)	1:10.50.0
5.	POL	(Maria Gąsienica-Bukowa, Józefa Pęksa, Zofia Krzeptowska)	1:13.20.0
6.	CZE	(Eva Benešová, Libuse Patocková, Eva Lauermanová)	1:14.19.0
7.	GDR/ GER	(Elfriede Uhlig, Else Ammann, Sonnhilde Hausschild)	1:15:33.0
8.	ITA	(Fides Romanin, Rita Bottero, Ildegarda Taffra)	1:16.11.0

Rantanen of Finland took off six seconds behind Eroshina, passed her, lost the lead, then passed her again to win by 100 yards.

1960 Squaw Valley T: 5, N: 5, D: 2.26.
3 × 5-Kilometer

1.	SWE	(Irma Johansson, Britt Strandberg, Sonja Ruthström [Edström])	1:04.21.4
2.	SOV	(Radya Eroshina, Maria Gusakova, Lyubov Baranova [Kozyreva])	1:05:02.6
3.	FIN	(Siiri Rantanen, Eeva Ruoppa, Toini Pöysti)	1:06:27.5
4.	POL	(Stefania Biegun, Helena Gaşienica-Daniel, Józefa Pęksa-Czerniawska)	1:07:24.6
5.	GDR/ GER	(Rita Czech-Blasl, Renate Borges, Sonnhilde Kallus [Hausschild])	1:09:25.7

On the first leg, Radya Eroshina fell and broke one of her skis. She picked up a replacement, but lost over a minute, a delay which cost the U.S.S.R. the gold medal. The Soviets lodged a protest, claiming that Irma Johansson of Sweden had cut in front of Eroshina and caused her to fall. After viewing films of the race, the U.S.S.R. withdrew their protest.

1964 Innsbruck-Seefeld T: 8, N: 8, D: 2.7.
3 × 5-Kilometer

1.	SOV	(Alevtina Kolchina, Eudokia Mekshilo, Claudia Boyarskikh)	59:20.2
2.	SWE	(Barbro Martinsson, Brit Strandberg, Toini Gustafsson)	1:01:27.0
3.	FIN	(Senja Pusula, Toini Pöysti, Mirja Lehtonen)	1:02:45.1
4.	GER/ GDR	(Christine Nestler, Rita Czech-Blasl, Renate Dannhauser)	1:04:29.9
5.	BUL	(Rosa Dimova, Nadezhda Vasileva, Krastana Stoeva)	1:06:40.4
6.	CZE	(Jarmila Skodová, Eva Brizová, Eva Paulusová)	1:08:42.8
7.	POL	(Teresa Trzebunia, Czeslawa Stopka, Stefania Biegun)	1:08:55.4
8.	HUN	(Éva Blazs, Mária Tarnai, Ference Hemrik)	1:10:16.3

1968 Grenoble-Autrans T: 8, N: 8, D: 2.16.
3 × 5-Kilometer

1.	NOR	(Inger Aufles, Babben Damon-Enger, Berit Mördre)	57:30.0
2.	SWE	(Britt Strandberg, Toini Gustafsson, Barbro Martinsson)	57:51.0
3.	SOV	(Alevtina Kolchina, Rita Achkina, Galina Kulakova)	58:13.6
4.	FIN	(Senja Pusula, Marjatta Olkkonen, Marjatta Kajosmaa)	58:45.1
5.	POL	(Weronika Budny, Józefa Pęksa-Czerniawska, Stefania Biegun)	59:04.7
6.	GDR	(Renate Köhler, Gudrun Schmidt, Christine Nestler)	59:33.9
7.	GER	(Michaela Endler, Barbara Barthel, Monika Mrklas)	1:01:49.3
8.	BUL	(Pandeva Velitska, Nadezhda Vasileva, Szvetana Sotirova)	1:05:35.7

1972 Sapporo-Makomanai T: 11, N: 11, D: 2.12.
3 × 5-Kilometer

1.	SOV	(Lyubov Moukhatcheva, Alevtina Olunina, Galina Kulakova)	48:46.15
2.	FIN	(Helena Takalo, Hilkka Kuntola, Marjatta Kajosmaa)	49:19.37
3.	NOR	(Inger Aufles, Aslaug Dahl, Berit Mördre-Lammedal)	49:51.49
4.	GER	(Monika Mrklas, Ingrid Rothfuss, Michaela Endler)	50:25.61

5.	GDR	(Gabriele Haupt, Renate Fischer, Anni Unger)	50:28.45
6.	CZE	(Alena Bartušová, Helena Šikolová, Milena Cillerová)	51:16.16
7.	POL	(Anna Duraj, Józefa Chromik, Weronika Budny)	51:49.13
8.	SWE	(Meeri Bodelid, Eva Olsson, Birgitta Lindqvist)	51:51.84

1976 Innsbruck-Seefeld T: 9, N: 9, D: 2.12.

1.	SOV	(Nina Baldycheva, Zinaida Amosova, Raisa Smetanina, Galina Kulakova)	1:07:49.75
2.	FIN	(Liisa Suihkonen, Marjatta Kajosmaa, Hilkka Kuntola, Helena Takalo)	1:08:36.57
3.	GDR	(Monika Debertshäuser, Sigrun Krause, Barbara Petzold, Veronika Schmidt)	1:09:57.95
4.	SWE	(Lena Carlzon, Görel Partapuoli, Marie Johansson, Eva Olsson)	1:10:14.68
5.	NOR	(Berit Kvello, Marit Myrmael, Berit Johannessen, Grete Kummen)	1:11:09.08
6.	CZE	(Hana Pasiárová, Gabriela Sekajová, Alena Bartošová, Blanka Paulů)	1:11:27.83
7.	CAN	(Shirley Firth, Joan Groothuysen, Susan Holloway, Sharon Firth)	1:14:02.72
8.	POL	(Anna Pawlusiak, Anna Gębala-Duraj, Maria Trebunia, Wladyslawa Majerczyk)	1:14:13.40

1980 Lake Placid T: 8, N: 8, D: 2.21.

1.	GDR	(Marlies Rostock, Carola Anding, Veronika Hesse [Schmidt], Barbara Petzold)	1:02:11.10
2.	SOV	(Nina Baldycheva, Nina Rocheva, Galina Kulakova, Raisa Smetanina)	1:03:18.30
3.	NOR	(Brit Pettersen, Anette Böe, Marit Myrmael, Berit Aunli [Kvello])	1:04:13.50
4.	CZE	(Dagmar Palecková, Gabriela Svobodová, Blanka Paulů, Květoslava Jeriová)	1:04:31.39
5.	FIN	(Marja Auroma, Marja-Liisa Hämäläinen, Helena Takalo, Hilkka Riihivuori [Kuntola])	1:04:41.28
6.	SWE	(Lillemor Marie Johansson, Karin Lamberg, Eva Olsson, Lena Carlzon-Lundbäck)	1:05:16.32
7.	USA	(Alison Owen-Spencer, Beth Paxson, Leslie Bancroft, Margaret Spencer)	1:06:55.41
8.	CAN	(Angela Schmidt, Shirley Firth, Esther Miller, Joan Groothuysen)	1:07:45.75

The U.S.S.R.'s second-place finish gave Kulakova her eighth Olympic medal—four gold, two silver, and two bronze.

1984 Sarajevo T: 12, N: 12, D: 2.15.

1.	NOR	(Inger Helene Nybråten, Anne Jahren, Brit Pettersen, Berit Aunli [Kvello])	1:06:49.7
2.	CZE	(Dagmar Švubová, Blanka Paulů, Gabriela Svobodová, Kvetoslava Jeriová)	1:07:34.7
3.	FIN	(Pirkko Määttä, Eija Hyytiäinen, Marjo Matikainen, Marja-Liisa Hämäläinen)	1:07:36.7
4.	SOV	(Julia Stepanova, Lyubov Liadova, Nadezhda Bourlakova, Raisa Smetanina)	1:07:55.0
5.	SWE	(Karin Lamberg, Doris Hugosson, Lillemor Marie Risby [Johansson], Ann Rosendahl)	1:09:30.0
6.	SWI	(Karin Thomas, Monika Germann, Christine Brügger, Evi Kratzer)	1:09:40.3
7.	USA	(Susan Long, Judy Rabinowitz, Lynn Spencer-Galanes, Patricia Ross)	1:10:48.4
8.	GDR	(Petra Voge, Petra Rohrmann, Carola Anding, Ute Noack)	1:11:10.7

The fastest time of the race, 16:12.6, was recorded by Květa Jeriová who actually overcame triple gold-medalist Marja-Liisa Hämäläinen on the anchor leg to win the silver medal for Czechoslovakia.

1988 Calgary-Canmore T: 12, N: 12, D: 2.21.

1.	SOV	(Svetlana Nageikina, Nina Gavrylyuk, Tamara Tikhonova, Anfisa Reztsova)	59:51.1
2.	NOR	(Trude Dybendahl, Marit Wold, Anne Jahren, Marianne Dahlmo)	1:01:33.0
3.	FIN	(Pirkko Määttä, Marja-Liisa Kirvesniemi [Hämäläinen], Marjo Matikainen, Jaana Savolainen)	1:01:53.8
4.	SWI	(Karin Thomas, Sandra Parpan, Evi Kratzer, Christina Gilli-Brügger)	1:01:59.4
5.	GDR	(Kerstin Moring, Simone Opitz, Silke Braun, Simone Greiner-Petter)	1:02:19.9
6.	SWE	(Lis Frost, Anna-Lena Fritzon, Karin Lamberg-Skog, Marie-Helene Westin)	1:02:24.9
7.	CZE	(Lubomira Balazová, Viera Klimková, Ivana Radlova, Alžběta Havrančiková)	1:03:37.1
8.	USA	(Dorcas Denhartog, Leslie Thompson, Nancy Fiddler, Leslie Krichko)	1:04:08.8

In a move almost without precedent, the Sunday night television news in the U.S.S.R. was delayed two minutes to allow the broadcast of the end of this race.

1992 Albertville-Les Saisies T: 13, N: 13, D: 2.17.

1.	SOV	(Yelena Vialbe, Raisa Smetanina, Larissa Lazutina, Lyubov Yegorova)	59:34.8
2.	NOR	(Solveig Pedersen, Inger Helene Nybråten, Trude Dybendahl, Elin Nilsen)	59:56.4
3.	ITA	(Bice Vanzetta, Manuela Di Centa, Gabriella Paruzzi, Stefania Belmondo)	1:00:25.9
4.	FIN	(Marja-Liisa Kirvesniemi [Hämäläinen], Pirkko Määttä, Jaana Savolainen, Marjut Lukkarinen)	1:00:52.9
5.	FRA	(Carole Stanisiere, Sylvie Giry Rousset, Sophie Villeneuve, Isabelle Mancini)	1:01:30.7
6.	CZE	(Lubomira Balazová, Katerina Neumannová, Alžběta Havrančiková, Iveta Zelingerová)	1:01:37.4
7.	SWE	(Carina Görlin, Magdalena Wallin, Karin Säterkvist, Marie-Helene Westin)	1:01:54.5
8.	GER	(Heike Wezel, Gabriele Hess, Simone Opitz, Ina Kummel)	1:02:22.6

With this race Raisa Smetanina became the first winter athlete to earn ten Olympic medals. Eight days earlier she had almost set the record when she placed fourth in the 15-kilometer race. She also became the only athlete to win medals in five Winter Olympics and, 12 days shy of her fortieth birthday, the oldest female medalist in Winter Olympics history.

Discontinued Events

10 KILOMETERS (CLASSICAL)

1952 Oslo C: 20, N: 8, D: 2.23.

1.	Lydia Wideman	FIN	41:40.0
2.	Mirja Hietamies	FIN	42:39.0
3.	Siiri Rantanen	FIN	42:50.0
4.	Märta Norberg	SWE	42:53.0
5.	Sirkka Polkunen	FIN	43:07.0
6.	Rakel Wahl	NOR	44:54.0
7.	Marit Oiseth	NOR	45:04.0
8.	Margit Albrechtsson	SWE	45:05.0

1956 Cortina C: 40, N: 11, D: 1:28.

1.	Lyubov Kosyreva	SOV	38:11.0
2.	Radya Eroshina	SOV	38:16.0
3.	Sonja Edström	SWE	38:23.0
4.	Alevtina Kolchina	SOV	38:46.0
5.	Siiri Rantanen	FIN	39:40.0
6.	Mirja Hietamies	FIN	40:18.0
7.	Irma Johansson	SWE	40:20.0
8.	Sirkka Polkunen	FIN	40:25.0

1960 Squaw Valley C: 24, N: 7, D: 2.20.

1.	Maria Gusakova	SOV	39:46.6
2.	Lyubov Baranova [Kosyreva]	SOV	40:04.2
3.	Radya Eroshina	SOV	40:06.0
4.	Alevtina Kolchina	SOV	40:12.6
5.	Sonja Ruthström [Edström]	SWE	40:35.5
6.	Toini Pöysti	FIN	40:41.9
7.	Barbro Martinsson	SWE	41:06.2
8.	Irma Johansson	SWE	41:08.3

1964 Innsbruck-Seefeld C: 35, N: 13, D: 2.1.

1.	Claudia Boyarskikh	SOV	40:24.3
2.	Eudokia Mekshilo	SOV	40:26.6
3.	Maria Gusakova	SOV	40:46.6
4.	Britt Strandberg	SWE	40:54.0
5.	Toini Pöysti	FIN	41:17.4
6.	Senja Pusula	FIN	41:17.8
7.	Alevtina Kolchina	SOV	41:26.2
8.	Toini Gustafsson	SWE	41:41.1

1968 Grenoble-Autrans C: 34, N: 11, D: 2.9.

1.	Toini Gustafsson	SWE	36:46.5
2.	Berit Mördre	NOR	37:54.6
3.	Inger Aufles	NOR	37:59.9
4.	Barbro Martinsson	SWE	38:07.1
5.	Marjatta Kajosmaa	FIN	38:09.0
6.	Galina Kulakova	SOV	38:26.7
7.	Alevtina Kolchina	SOV	38:52.9
8.	Babben Damon-Enger	NOR	38:54.4

1972 Sapporo-Makomanai C: 42, N: 11, D: 2.6.

1.	Galina Kulakova	SOV	34:17.82
2.	Alevtina Olunina	SOV	34:54.11
3.	Marjatta Kajosmaa	FIN	34:56.45
4.	Lyubov Moukhatcheva	SOV	34:58.56
5.	Helena Takalo	FIN	35:06.34
6.	Aslaug Dahl	NOR	35:18.84
7.	Helena Šikolová	CZE	35:29.33
8.	Hilkka Kuntola	FIN	35:36.71

1976 Innsbruck-Seefeld C: 44, N: 15, D: 2.10.

1.	Raisa Smetanina	SOV	30:13.41
2.	Helena Takalo	FIN	30:14.28
3.	Galina Kulakova	SOV	30:38.61

4.	Nina Baldycheva	SOV	30:52.58
5.	Eva Olsson	SWE	31:08.72
6.	Zinaida Amosova	SOV	31:11.23
7.	Barbara Petzold	GDR	31:12.20
8.	Veronika Schmidt	GDR	31:12.33

1980 Lake Placid C: 38, N: 12, D: 2.18.

1.	Barbara Petzold	GDR	30:31.54
2.	Hilkka Riihivuori [Kuntola]	FIN	30:35.05
3.	Helena Takalo	FIN	30:45.25
4.	Raisa Smetanina	SOV	30:54.48
5.	Galina Kulakova	SOV	30:58.46
6.	Nina Balycheva	SOV	31:22.93
7.	Marlies Rostock	GDR	31:28.79
8.	Veronika Hesse [Schmidt]	GDR	31:29.14

The East German propaganda apparatus broke down somewhat in the case of Barbara Petzold, who was described in half the press releases as a medical student and in the other half as a law student. Either way, she told the press that training and competing left her little time for her studies.

1984 Sarajevo C: 52, N: 15, D: 2.9.

1.	Marja-Liisa Hämäläinen	FIN	31:44.2
2.	Raisa Smetanina	SOV	32:02.9
3.	Brit Pettersen	NOR	32:12.7
4.	Berit Aunli [Kvello]	NOR	32:17.7
5.	Anne Jahren	NOR	32:26.2
6.	Lillemor Marie Risby [Johansson]	SWE	32:34.6
7.	Marit Myrmael	NOR	32:35.3
8.	Julia Stepanova	SOV	32:45.7

Hämäläinen, a 28-year-old physiotherapist from Simpele, near the Soviet border, gained revenge over Finnish journalists. "A hundred times they've written that I would never become anybody," she would say, "and I wanted to show people that I am somebody and that if I didn't do well, there was always a reason."

1988 Calgary-Canmore C: 52, N: 17, D: 2.14.

1.	Vida Vencienė	SOV	30:08.3
2.	Raisa Smetanina	SOV	30:17.0
3.	Marjo Matikainen	FIN	30:20.5
4.	Svetlana Nageikina	SOV	30:26.5
5.	Tamara Tikhonova	SOV	30:38.9
6.	Inger Helene Nybråten	NOR	30:51.7
7.	Pirkko Määttä	FIN	30:52.4
8.	Marie-Helene Westin	SWE	30:53.5

20 KILOMETERS (FREESTYLE)

1984 Sarajevo C: 40, N: 13, D: 2.18.

1.	Marja-Liisa Hämäläinen	FIN	1:01:45.0
2.	Raisa Smetanina	SOV	1:02:26.7
3.	Anne Jahren	NOR	1:03:13.6
4.	Blanka Paulů	CZE	1:03:16.9
5.	Lillemor Marie Risby [Johansson]	SWE	1:03:31.8

6. Brit Pettersen	NOR	1:03:49.0
7. Lyubov Liadova	SOV	1:03:53.3
8. Evi Kratzer	SWI	1:03:56.4

After winning her third gold medal, Marja-Liisa Hämäläinen tried to avoid Finnish reporters by jumping over a fence and running away. Finally headed off and trapped, the farmer's daughter submitted to photographs and interviews. In addition to her three individual golds, she earned a bronze medal in the relay. Her fiancé, Harri Kirvesniemi, won two nordic bronze medals.

1988 Calgary-Canmore C: 55, N: 18, D: 2.25.

1. Tamara Tikhonova	SOV	55:53.6
2. Anfisa Reztsova	SOV	56:12.8
3. Raisa Smetanina	SOV	57:22.1
4. Christina Gilli-Brügger	SWI	57:37.4
5. Simone Opitz	GDR	57:54.3
6. Manuela Di Centa	ITA	57:55.2
7. Kerstin Moring	GDR	58:17.2
8. Marianne Dahlmo	NOR	58:31.1
DISQ: Nina Gavrylyuk	SOV	58:26.9

Nina Gavrylyuk placed eighth but was disqualified for wearing the logo of a shoe manufacturer on the front of her headband.

WINTER OLYMPIC RECORDS

GENERAL

Most Medals
10 Raisa Smetanina (SOV, Nordic Skiing, 1976–1992)

Most Medals, Men
9 Sixten Jernberg (SWE, Nordic Skiing, 1956–1964)

Most Gold Medals
6 Lydia Skoblikova (SOV, Speed Skating, 1960–1964)

Most Gold Medals, Men
5 A. Clas Thunberg (FIN, Speed Skating, 1924–1928)
5 Eric Heiden (USA, Speed Skating, 1980)

Most Silver Medals
5 Andrea Ehrig (Mitscherlich, Schöne) (GDR, Speed Skating, 1976, 1984–1988)
5 Raisa Smetanina (SOV, Nordic Skiing, 1976–1988)

Most Silver Medals, Men
3 several athletes

Most Bronze Medals
4 Roald Larsen (NOR, Speed Skating, 1924–1928)
4 Yelena Vialbe (SOV, Nordic Skiing, 1992)

Most Family Names Used While Winning Medals
3 Andrea Mitscherlich-Schöne-Ehrig (GDR, Speed Skating, 1976, 1984–1988)

Most Years Between Medals
20 John Heaton (USA, Luge, 1928–1948)
20 Richard Torriani (SWI, Ice Hockey, 1928–1948)

Most Years Between Medals, Women
16 Raisa Smetanina (SOV, Nordic Skiing, 1976–1992)

Most Medals in Individual Events
8 Karin Kania (Enke) (GDR, Speed Skating, 1980–1988)

Most Medals in Individual Events, Men
7 A. Clas Thunberg (FIN, Speed Skating, 1924–1928)
7 Ivar Ballangrud (NOR, Speed Skating, 1928–1936)

Most Consecutive Victories in the Same Event
3 Gillis Grafström (SWE, Men's Figure Skating, 1920–1928)
3 Sonja Henie (NOR, Women's Figure Skating, 1928–1936)
3 Ulrich Wehling (GDR, Nordic Combined, 1972–1980)

Youngest Medalist
14 years 363 days Scott Allan (USA, Men's Figure Skating, 1964)

Youngest Medalist, Women
15 years 7 days Manuela Gross (GDR, Pairs Figure Skating, 1972)

Youngest Medalist in an Individual Event
14 years 363 days Scott Allan (USA, Men's Figure Skating, 1964)

Youngest Medalist in an Individual Event, Women
15 years 68 days Andrea Mitscherlich (GDR, 3000-Meter Speed Skating, 1976)

Youngest Gold Medalist
15 years 127 days Maxi Herber (GER, Pairs Figure Skating, 1936)

Youngest Gold Medalist, Men
16 years 259 days Toni Nieminen (FIN, Team Ski Jumping, 1992)

Youngest Gold Medalist in an Individual Event
15 years 315 days Sonja Henie (NOR, Women's Figure Skating, 1928)

Youngest Gold Medalist in an Individual Event, Men
16 years 261 days Toni Nieminen (FIN, Large Hill Ski Jumping, 1992)

Oldest Medalist
49 years 278 days Max Houben (BEL, Four-Man Bobsled, 1948)

Oldest Medalist, Women
39 years 354 days Raisa Smetanina (SOV, 4 × 5-Kilometer Relay, 1992)

Oldest Medalist in an Individual Event
44 years 77 days Martin Stixrud (NOR, Men's Figure Skating, 1920)

Oldest Medalist in an Individual Event, Women
37 years 184 days Eevi Huttunen (FIN, 3000-Meter Speed Skating, 1960)

Oldest Gold Medalist
48 years 357 days Jay O'Brien (USA, Four-Man Bobsled, 1932)

Oldest Gold Medalist, Women
39 years 354 days Raisa Smetanina (SOV, 4 × 5-Kilometer Relay, 1992)

Oldest Gold Medalist in an Individual Event
35 years 4 days Magnar Solberg (NOR, 20-Kilometer Biathlon, 1972)

Oldest Gold Medalist in an Individual Event, Women
33 years 268 days Christina Baas-Kaiser (HOL, 3000-Meter Speed Skating, 1972)

Most Olympics Competed in
6 Carl-Erik Eriksson (SWE, Bobsled, 1964–1984) Eriksson's best finish was a sixth in the 1972 two-man bob.
6 Colin Coates (AUS, Speed Skating, 1968–1988) Coates' best finish was a sixth in the 1976 10,000 meters.

Youngest Competitor
11 years 74 days Cecilia Colledge (GBR, Women's Figure Skating, 1932) Colledge finished in eighth place.

Youngest Competitor, Men
12 years 113 days Jan Hoffman (GDR, Men's Figure Skating, 1988) Hoffman placed 26th out of 28.

Oldest Competitor
53 years 328 days James Coates (GBR, Skeleton Luge, 1948) Coates finished in seventh place.

Oldest Competitor, Women
45 years 318 days Edwina Chamier (CAN, Alpine Combined Skiing, 1936) Chamier withdrew before the final slalom run.

Most Competitors in a Single Event
131 Men's Giant Slalom, 1992

Most Nations Represented in a Single Event
46 Men's Giant Slalom, 1992

Longest National Win Streak in a Single Event
8 Soviet Union, Pairs Figure Skating, 1964–1992 The Soviet Union has also won 8 straight gold medals in Ice Hockey (1956–1992) in Olympics held *outside* the United States.

Longest Streak in an Event With a Different Nation Winning Each Year
7 Women's Slalom, 1968–1992

Least Universal Event
Pairs figure skating has been held eighteen times, but has never attracted entrants from more than twelve nations at a time.

Best Performance by an Athlete From a Snowless Country
In 1988 Seba Johnson of the U.S. Virgin Islands placed 28th in the women's giant slalom. It is true that only one other competitor had a slower time than Johnson, but because 35 of the 64 starters failed to complete both runs and because Olympic protocol places all finishers ahead of all non-finishers, Johnson remains the only athlete from a snowless nation to place in the top half of the field in a winter event.

BIATHLON

Largest Margin of Victory
3 minutes 49.94 seconds Soviet Union, Men's 4 × 7.5-Kilometer Relay, 1976

Slowest Performance
The only biathlete ever to record an adjusted time twice that of the winner was Herman Carazo of Costa Rica in the 1984 20-kilometer race. Carazo's time of 2:24:59.9 included eleven penalty minutes. He finished 35 minutes and 5 seconds behind the skier in next-to-last place. The race was won by Peter Angerer in 1:11:52.7. Three days later Carazo attempted the 10-kilometer race, but failed to finish.

Worst Shooters
In the 1960 20-kilometer race, two French biathletes, Victor Arbez and Paul Romand, both missed 18 of 20 shots. Tomislav Lopatič of Yugoslavia matched their percentage in the 1984 10-kilometer when he missed 9 of 10 shots, as did Fabiana Lovece of Argentina in the 1992 women's 7.5-kilometer sprint.

BOBSLED

Largest Margin of Victory
3.29 seconds Swiss four-man team driven by Edward Scherrer, 1924

Largest Margin of Victory, Single Run
5.65 seconds Reto Capadrutt and Oscar Geier (SWI), first run of the 1932 two-man bob.

Fastest Speed, Single Run
59.05 miles per hour Swiss four-man team driven by Ekkehard Fasser, third run, 1988

ICE HOCKEY

Longest Winning Streaks
16 Canada, 1920–1932
15 Soviet Union, 1980–1988

Longest Unbeaten Streak
20 Canada, 1920–1936

Most Lopsided Match
Canada 33 Switzerland 0 in 1924

LUGE

Largest Margin of Victory
2.75 seconds Ortrun Enderlein (GDR), 1964 women's single. In 1968 Enderlein placed first again, but was disqualified for heating her runners.

Largest Margin of Victory, Single Run
45 hundredths of a second Josef Feistmantl and Manfred Stengl (AUT), first run of the 1964 two-seater

Fastest Speed, Single Run
61.85 miles per hour Georg Hackl (GER), first run, 1992

Fastest Speed, Single Run, Women
54.87 miles per hour Angelika Neuner (AUT), third run, 1992

Slowest Performance
It's not easy to record a really slow time in a four-run luge competition. Most mediocre lugists crash and fail to finish or fall once and do reasonably well on the other three runs. In 1976, however, Huang Liu-chong of Taiwan lost control on the second and third runs, but managed to finish both times. His combined time for the two runs was 3:32.341. That would have been good enough for tenth place except that the times for the other competitors were for *four* runs. Huang's final time of 5:22.646 was over 50 seconds slower than anyone else's in the history of the event.

FIGURE SKATING

Highest Score
107.4 out of a possible 108 points, Jayne Torvill and Christopher Dean (GBR), 1984 Ice Dance, Free dance. Their score included three 6.0s for technical merit and a complete set of nine 6.0s for artistic impression.

Highest Score, Individual
105.9 out of a possible 108 points, Janet Lynn (USA), 1972 free skating
105.9 out of a possible 108 points, John Curry (GBR), 1976 free skating

Lowest Score
In 1928 Anita de St.-Quentin of France scored only 1114.25 points, compared to 1648.75 for the skater in next-to-last place and 2452.25 for the winner, Sonja Henie. De St.-Quentin is the only figure

skater in Olympic history to earn less than half as many points as the winner. Since current rules have been in effect, the lowest score has been the 53.6 out of 108 awarded to Kim Hai-sung of South Korea for her short program in 1984.

Greatest Ranges of Scores

In 1964 Inge Paul of West Germany, competing in a field of thirty, was ranked eleventh by three judges and twenty-seventh by another judge. Her remaining rankings were thirteenth, fourteenth, sixteenth, seventeenth, and nineteenth.

Greatest Judging Aberration

In 1984 Soviet skater Yelena Vodorezova's admirably traced compulsory figures earned her high marks from eight of the nine judges: four firsts, three seconds, and one third. Belgian judge Claude Carlens was not so impressed. He ranked her twelfth.

SPEED SKATING

Largest Margin of Victory

24.8 seconds Hjalmar Andersen (NOR), 1952 10,000 meters

Largest Margin of Victory, Women

6.53 seconds Christina Baas-Kaiser (HOL), 1972 3000 meters

Slowest Performance

In 1948, Richard "Buddy" Solem of the United States required 26 minutes 22.4 seconds to complete the 10,000-meter race. He was 8:56.1 behind the winner and 4:47.6 slower than the next-to-last skater. However, there were extenuating circumstances. By the time Solem, the last skater in the program, took the ice, the sun had turned the course into slush and eight other skaters, including 5000-meter gold medalist Reidar Liaklev, had withdrawn out of frustration. Solem was applauded loudly for his perseverance.

A more consistently slow skater was Charles de Ligne of Belgium. De Ligne began his 1936 Olympic experience by falling in the 500 meters. Rather than give up, de Ligne cruised to the finish line, eventually stopping the clock in 1:44.6—over 23 seconds slower than anyone else in the history of the event. The next day he attempted the 5000 meters, but gave up after 2600 meters by which time he had already fallen 1 minute 45 seconds off the pace set by Ivar Ballangrud. The day after that, de Ligne finished last in the 1500 meters, once again recording the slowest time in the history of the event. De Ligne closed out his Olympic career in the 10,000 meters. Race officials didn't bother to record his split times, but his final time of 23:32.9 was over four minutes behind the other skaters. Only Solem's 1948 time was slower.

ALPINE SKIING

Largest Margin of Victory

6.2 seconds Anton Sailer (AUT), 1956 Giant Slalom

Largest Margin of Victory, Women

4.7 seconds Madeleine Berthod (SWI), 1956 Downhill

Fastest Average Speed

64.95 miles per hour William Johnson (USA), 1984 Downhill

Fastest Average Speed, Women
61.89 miles per hour Annemarie Moser-Pröll (AUT), 1980 Downhill

Slowest Downhill Skiers
In 1952, Alexandre Vouxinos of Greece eased his way down the 2600-meter downhill course in 6 minutes 10.8 seconds—averaging 15.70 miles per hour. Four years later, his compatriot, Christos Papageorgiou, managed to break 17 miles per hour on a longer course, but achieved a larger margin of defeat. His time of 8:03.2 was over five minutes slower than that of the winner, Toni Sailer.

Slowest Slalom Skiers
The slowest speed ever achieved in an Olympic slalom race is 6.33 miles per hour by Antoin Miliordos of Greece in 1952. He picked his way down the 422.5-meter qualifying course in 2 minutes 26.9 seconds. The largest margin of defeat belongs to Alejandro Preinfalk Lavagni of Costa Rica, whose 1992 combined time of 4:29.13 was over two and a half times slower than that of gold medalist Finn Christian Jagge.

The All-Time Slowest Alpine Skier
In 1936 the alpine combined event began with a 3300-meter downhill run. Four skiers broke five minutes, but the four-man team from Turkey had a harder time. Nagim Aslanbigo completed the course in 13 minutes 56.8 seconds, only 34.4 seconds slower than the slowest non-Turk. Ulker Pamir and Mahmut Sevket both beat 14½ minutes, but Resat Erceş didn't. Meandering down the two-mile course at a rate of 5.41 miles per hour, Erceş finished in a time of 22 minutes 44.4 seconds. He and Sevket withdrew from the competition, but Aslanbigo and Pamir moved on to the slalom half of the contest. Neither of them completed the first run. Sevket also finished last in the 18-kilometer cross-country race. Erceş recorded the slowest relay leg in Olympic history in the 4 × 10-kilometer cross-country contest, which Turkey failed to finish when Sevket, their anchorman, became injured and withdrew.

Slowest Alpine Skier, Women
In the 1936 alpine combined downhill, E. Baenza de Herreros of Spain needed 18 minutes 51.4 seconds to cover the 2900-meter course. Her average speed was almost 5.73 miles per hour. Baenza de Herreros did not attempt the slalom runs.

NORDIC SKIING

Largest Margin of Victory
7 minutes 27 seconds Per Erik Hedlund (SWE), 1928 50 Kilometers

Largest Margin of Victory, Women
2 minutes 7 seconds Soviet Union, 1964 3 × 5-Kilometer Relay

Slowest Nordic Skier
In the 1924 50-kilometer race, the final time recorded by Yugoslavia's Dusan Zinaja was exactly 4 hours. This would have been good enough for fifth place behind Thorleif Haug's time of 3:44:32.0—except that Zinaja made it only halfway through the course before giving up. Zinaja's performance was only the beginning of a long history of nordic futility for Yugoslavian skiers. Between 1924 and 1984 nineteen Yugoslavians entered the 50-kilometer race. Four failed to finish, two finished last, two only beat other Yugoslavians, and none placed in the top half of the field. Then, in 1988, came the big Yugoslavian breakthrough: Jani Krsinar placed 30th out of 61. However, following the Calgary Olympics, Slovenia declared its independence from Yugoslavia, taking with it all the nation's best skiers. In 1992 what was left of Yugoslavia entered two skiers in the 50-kilometer race. One placed 65th out of 67; the other failed to finish.

SKI JUMPING

Longest Jump
123.5 meters Martin Höllwarth (AUT), first jump in the 1992 team event

Shortest Jump
32 meters Mario Cavalla (ITA), Gilbert Ravanel (FRA), and Andrezn Krzeptowski (POL), 1924

Shortest Jump in a Nordic Combined Event
20 meters A. Harbel (HUN), second jump, 1924

Most Style Points for a Single Jump
58.0 Birger Ruud (NOR), second jump on 1936 large hill

Least Style Points for a Single Jump
4.0 Josef Zehner (CZE), second jump on 1964 normal hill
4.0 Jan Holmlund (SWE), first jump on 1980 large hill

Least Style Points for a Single Jump in a Nordic Combined Event
3.0 Modesto De Silvestro (ITA), third jump, 1976 The lowest score possible is 3.0.

OFFICIAL ABBREVIATIONS

Some of the national designations used in this book differ from those approved by the International Olympic Committee. Here is a complete list of nations that are currently recognized by the I.O.C.

AFG	Afghanistan	CRC	Costa Rica
AHO	Netherlands Antilles	CRO	Croatia
ALB	Albania	CUB	Cuba
ALG	Algeria	CYP	Cyprus
AND	Andorra	DEN	Denmark
ANG	Angola	DJI	Djibouti
ANT	Antigua	DOM	Dominican Republic
ARG	Argentina	ECU	Ecuador
ARM	Armenia	EGY	Arab Republic of Egypt
ARU	Aruba	ESA	El Salvador
ASA	American Samoa	ESP	Spain
AUS	Australia	EST	Estonia
AUT	Austria	ETH	Ethiopia
AZE	Azerbaijan	FIJ	Fiji
BAH	Bahamas	FIN	Finland
BAN	Bangladesh	FRA	France
BAR	Barbados	GAB	Gabon
BEL	Belgium	GAM	The Gambia
BEN	Benin	GBR	Great Britain
BER	Bermuda	GEO	Géorgie (Georgia)
BHU	Bhutan	GER	Germany
BIZ	Belize	GEQ	Equatorial Guinea
BLR	Belarus	GHA	Ghana
BOL	Bolivia	GRE	Greece
BOT	Botswana	GRN	Grenada
BRA	Brazil	GUA	Guatemala
BRN	Bahrain	GUI	Guinea
BRU	Brunei	GUM	Guam
BSH	Bosnia-Herzegovina	GUY	Guyana
BUL	Bulgaria	HAI	Haiti
BUR	Burkina Faso	HKG	Hong Kong
CAF	Central African Republic	HON	Honduras
CAN	Canada	HUN	Hungary
CAY	Cayman Islands	INA	Indonesia
CGO	Congo	IND	India
CHA	Chad	IRI	Islamic Republic of Iran
CHI	Chile	IRL	Ireland
CHN	People's Republic of China	IRQ	Iraq
CIV	Côte-d'Ivoire (Ivory Coast)	ISL	Iceland
CMR	Cameroon	ISR	Israel
COK	Cook Islands	ISV	Virgin Islands
COL	Colombia	ITA	Italy

IVB	British Virgin Islands	PRK	Democratic People's Republic of Korea
JAM	Jamaica		
JOR	Jordan	PUR	Puerto Rico
JPN	Japan	QAT	Qatar
KEN	Kenya	ROM	Romania
KGZ	Kyrgyzstan	RSA	South Africa
KOR	Korea	RUS	Russia
KSA	Kingdom of Saudi Arabia	RWA	Rwanda
KUW	Kuwait	SAM	Western Samoa
KZK	Kazakhstan	SEN	Senegal
LAO	Laos	SEY	Seychelles
LAT	Latvia	SIN	Singapore
LBA	Jamahiriya Libya	SLE	Sierra Leone
LBR	Liberia	SLO	Slovenia
LES	Lesotho	SMR	San Marino
LIB	Lebanon	SOL	Solomon Islands
LIE	Liechtenstein	SOM	Somalia
LTU	Lithuania	SRI	Sri Lanka
LUX	Luxembourg	SUD	Sudan
MAD	Madagascar	SUI	Switzerland
MAR	Morocco	SUR	Surinam
MAS	Malaysia	SVK	Slovakia
MAW	Malawi	SWE	Sweden
MDV	Maldives	SWZ	Swaziland
MEX	Mexico	SYR	Syria
MGL	Mongolia	TAN	Tanzania
MKD	Macedonia	TCH	Czech Republic
MLD	Moldova	TGA	Tonga
MLI	Mali	THA	Thailand
MLT	Malta	TJK	Tajikistan
MON	Monaco	TKM	Turkmenistan
MOZ	Mozambique	TOG	Togo
MRI	Mauritius	TPE	Chinese Taipei
MTN	Mauritania	TRI	Trinidad and Tobago
MYA	Myanmar	TUN	Tunisia
NAM	Namibia	TUR	Turkey
NCA	Nicaragua	UAE	United Arab Emirates
NED	Netherlands	UGA	Uganda
NEP	Nepal	UKR	Ukraine
NGR	Nigeria	URU	Uruguay
NIG	Niger	USA	United States of America
NOR	Norway	UZB	Uzbekistan
NZL	New Zealand	VAN	Vanuatu
OMA	Oman	VEN	Venezuela
PAK	Pakistan	VIE	Vietnam
PAN	Panama	VIN	St. Vincent and the Grenadines
PAR	Paraguay	YEM	Yemen
PER	Peru	YUG	Yugoslavia
PHI	Philippines	ZAI	Zaïre
PNG	Papua-New Guinea	ZAM	Zambia
POL	Poland	ZIM	Zimbabwe
POR	Portugal